Mike Meyers' CompTIA

A+™ Core 2

CERTIFICATION
PASSPORT

(Exam 220-1102)

About the Series Editor

Michael Meyers is the industry's leading authority on CompTIA A+ and CompTIA Network+ certifications. He is the president and co-founder of Total Seminars, LLC, a major provider of computer and network repair curriculum and seminars for thousands of organizations throughout the world, and a member of CompTIA.

Mike has written numerous popular textbooks, including the best-selling *Mike Meyers' CompTIA A+ Guide to Managing and Troubleshooting PCs, Mike Meyers' CompTIA Network+ Guide to Managing and Troubleshooting Networks*, and *Mike Meyers' CompTIA Security+ Certification Guide*.

About the Author

Ron Gilster is a well-known best-selling author with over 40 published books on IT career certification, technology, business, and finance. Ron's career has spanned over multiple decades, ranging from punched-card equipment to senior executive and author. His books have covered CompTIA's A+, Network+, Server+, Security+, and Cloud+ as well as Cisco CCNA, CCDA, and several others. He has also been an educator, teaching IT, IS, networking, and cybersecurity at the high school, baccalaureate, and graduate levels. Ron has always admired Mike and his books and videos and is honored to be working directly with Mike on this project.

About the Technical Editor

Chris Crayton is a technical consultant, trainer, author, and industry-leading technical editor. He has worked as a computer technology and networking instructor, information security director, network administrator, network engineer, and PC specialist. Chris has authored several print and online books on PC repair, CompTIA A+, CompTIA Security+, and Microsoft Windows. He has also served as technical editor and content contributor on numerous technical titles for several of the leading publishing companies. He holds numerous industry certifications, has been recognized with many professional and teaching awards, and has served as a state-level SkillsUSA final competition judge.

Mike Meyers' CompTIA

A+™ Core 2

CERTIFICATION PASSPORT

(Exam 220-1102)

Mike Meyers, Series Editor

Ron Gilster

New York   Chicago   San Francisco   Athens
London   Madrid   Mexico City   Milan
New Delhi   Singapore   Sydney   Toronto

Mike Meyers' CompTIA A+™ Core 2 Certification Passport (Exam 220-1102)

1 2 3 4 5 6 7 8 9   LCR   28 27 26 25 24 23

Library of Congress Control Number: 2022950089

ISBN   978-1-264-61214-7
MHID   1-264-61214-1

Sponsoring Editor Tim Green	**Acquisitions Coordinator** Caitlin Cromley-Linn	**Proofreader** Lisa McCoy	**Composition** KnowledgeWorks Global Ltd.
Editorial Supervisor Janet Walden	**Technical Editor** Chris Crayton	**Indexer** Claire Splan	**Illustration** KnowledgeWorks Global Ltd.
Project Manager Tasneem Kauser, KnowledgeWorks Global Ltd.	**Copy Editor** Bart Reed	**Production Supervisor** Thomas Somers	**Art Director, Cover** Jeff Weeks

Contents at a Glance

Contents

Acknowledgments

As with every book, a lot of work from a lot of people went into making it happen.

Our acquisitions editor, Tim Green, kept us on track with kind words and pointy sticks. Always a pleasure working with you, Tim!

Our acquisitions coordinator, Caitlin Cromley-Linn, did an outstanding job acquiring and coordinating, with gentle yet insistent reminders for us to get stuff to her on a timely basis. Likewise, our project manager, Tasneem Kauser at KnowledgeWorks Global Ltd. This was a fun project, and we look forward to the next one!

Bart Reed did great work as our copy editor. He transformed every awkward stumble of language into a grammatical gem.

Our technical editor, Chris Crayton, took what some would describe as gleeful delight in pointing out every technical error he found. But since he helped us fix every error too, we won't hold it against him. Thanks, once again, for your technical expertise.

The layout team at KnowledgeWorks Global Ltd. did a remarkable job, putting the prose and pictures into printable form, which you now get to enjoy!

Finally, thanks to our proofreader, Lisa McCoy, for catching every last error. There's no error too big or small—she'll find them all. Thank you.

Introduction

Your Passport to Certification

Hello! I'm Mike Meyers, series editor, co-founder of Total Seminars, and author of many best-selling certification books. On any given day, you'll find me replacing a hard drive, setting up a website, or writing code. The book you hold in your hands is part of a powerful book series called the *Mike Meyers' Certification Passports*. Every book in this series combines easy readability with a condensed format—in other words, it's the kind of book I always wanted when I went for my certifications. Putting a huge amount of information in an accessible format is an enormous challenge, but I think we have achieved our goal and I am confident you'll agree.

I designed this series to do one thing and only one thing—to get you the information you need to achieve your certification. You won't find any fluff in here. We packed every page with nothing but the real nitty-gritty of the CompTIA A+ Core 2 certification exam.

Your Destination: CompTIA A+ Certification

This book is your passport to CompTIA A+ Core 2 certification, the vendor-neutral industry standard certification for PC hardware technicians, the folks who build and fix PCs. To get fully CompTIA A+ certified, you need to pass two exams: 220-1101 (Core 1) and 220-1102 (Core 2). To help you prepare for the Core 1 exam, please see our companion book, *Mike Meyers' CompTIA A+ Core 1 Certification Passport (Exam 220-1101)*.

The CompTIA A+ Exams

The 220-1101 Core 1 exam concentrates on five areas: Mobile Devices, Networking, Hardware, Virtualization and Cloud Computing, and Hardware and Network Troubleshooting. This exam focuses on your understanding of the terminology and hardware technology used in each of the five subject areas.

The 220-1102 Core 2 exam works the same way, covering Operating Systems, Security, Software Troubleshooting, and Operational Procedures. The 1102 exam is focused mainly on Windows, including installing, updating, maintaining, troubleshooting, and more. The other operating systems covered—macOS, Linux, iOS, and Android—get more of a big picture view. Security and troubleshooting, in both Windows and applications, make up half the exam questions.

Speaking of questions, each exam consists of up to 90 questions. Each exam takes 90 minutes. You must score at least 675 on a scale of 100–900 to pass exam 220-1101 (Core 1) and at least 700 on a scale of 100–900 to pass exam 220-1102 (Core 2). Remember, you must pass *both* exams to achieve your CompTIA A+ certification.

Question Types and Examples

Both of the exams are extremely practical, with little or no interest in theory. When you take the exams, you will see three types of questions: multiple choice, drag-and-drop matching, and performance based (simulation).

The following is an example of the type of multiple-choice question you will see on the exams:

> A company is planning to upgrade its Fast Ethernet network to Gigabit Ethernet.
> The existing network uses a mixture of Cat 5, Cat 5e, and Cat 6 cables. Which of the
> following needs to be performed during the upgrade process?
>
> **A.** Replace all cables with Cat 6.
>
> **B.** Keep the same cables.
>
> **C.** Replace Cat 5 with Cat 5e or Cat 6.
>
> **D.** Replace all cables with Cat 5e.

The best answer is C, "Replace Cat 5 with Cat 5e or 6." The cable standards mentioned in Answers A and D support Gigabit Ethernet, but since some parts of the network already use these cable types, it is not necessary to replace them. You might also see multiple-response questions, essentially multiple choice with more than one correct answer.

Drag-and-drop questions involve dragging and dropping a picture onto the relevant text. For example, you might see the words "HDMI" and "DisplayPort" and then two video port illustrations next to them. You would need to drag the HDMI illustration onto the word "HDMI" and then drag the other illustration onto the word "DisplayPort."

Performance-based (simulation) questions ask you to re-create a real process used by techs when working on PCs. You might be asked to copy a file or change a setting in Control Panel, but instead of you picking a multiple-choice answer, your screen will look like a Windows desktop and you will follow the provided instructions, just like you were using the real thing.

Always read the questions very carefully, especially when dealing with performance-based and multiple-choice questions with two or more correct responses. Remember to look for the *best* answer, not just the right answer. Check the CompTIA website for the most up-to-date exam information, as CompTIA does make changes.

Signing Up for Your CompTIA A+ Certification Exams

So, how do you sign up to take the CompTIA A+ certification exams? As this book went to press, the procedure looks like this: Go to https://home.pearsonvue.com/CompTIA. Click the Sign In button or, if you don't already have a Pearson VUE account, click Create Account and create one. Then, click View Exams, select the 1101 or 1102 exam (you must pass both to get fully certified), select your preferred language, review the details, and click Schedule This Exam. Enter your user name and password; choose an exam center, date, and time; and provide payment or an exam voucher when required. Repeat this process to schedule the other exam. Be sure to see the Pearson VUE website for the latest details.

You can also now take your tests over the Internet. To schedule an Internet-based exam through OnVUE, go to www.onvue.com. You'll need a solid Internet connection and a webcam, such as one built into most portable computers. Pearson VUE will accommodate any special needs, although this may limit your selection of testing locations.

A single exam voucher purchased directly from the CompTIA website is $239. However, there are many sources, including Total Seminars, that offer discounts. Some vendors offer bundles that include a free retest voucher. This book comes with a coupon code you can use to purchase a discounted exam voucher from the CompTIA Store. See the ad in the front of the book for more information on the code and the discount. Take it from me, you might like the opportunity to have a "mulligan" if you get test jitters!

CompTIA A+ certification can be your ticket to a career in IT or simply an excellent step in your certification pathway. This book is your passport to success on the CompTIA A+ Core 2 certification exam.

Your Guides: Mike Meyers and Ron Gilster

You get a pair of tour guides for this book—both me and Ron Gilster. I've written numerous computer certification books—including the best-selling *CompTIA A+ Certification All-in-One Exam Guide* and the *CompTIA Network+ Certification All-in-One Exam Guide*. More to the point, I've been working on PCs and teaching others how to make and fix them for a very long time, and I love it! When I'm not lecturing or writing about PCs, I'm working on PCs! My personal e-mail address is michaelm@totalsem.com. Please feel free to contact me directly if you have any questions, complaints, or compliments.

Ron has written or co-authored many books on career certification and books on hardware and software principles and troubleshooting, networking, and security. As an educator, he has developed and taught courses in computer technology, information systems, cybersecurity, and networking. He sees himself as a trainer, teacher, and guide and works to exhibit these qualities in his writing. Ron can be contacted at rgilster@pm.me.

About the Book

This *Passport* is divided into "Domains" that follow the exam domains. Each Domain is further divided into "Objective" modules covering each of the top-level certification objectives for the Core 2 exam. The goal is to facilitate accelerated review of the exam objectives in a quick-review format that will allow you to quickly gauge what you can expect to be tested on. Whether you want a last-minute review or you have enough experience that you don't need full coverage of every topic, this format is designed for you. This isn't meant to be a course in a book, but we hope you will find the *Passport* helpful as you prepare for your exam. If you find you need more in-depth coverage of the exam topics, we suggest using Mike's *CompTIA A+ Certification All-in-One Exam Guide, Eleventh Edition* to supplement your studies.

We've created a set of learning elements that call your attention to important items, reinforce key points, and provide helpful exam-taking hints. Take a look at what you'll find:

- Each Domain begins with a **Domain Objectives** list of the official CompTIA A+ Core 2 exam objectives, which correspond to the titles of the individual Objective modules in that Domain. The structure of each Objective module is based on the subobjectives listed under the corresponding exam objective.
- The following elements highlight key information throughout the modules:

 EXAM TIP   The Exam Tip element focuses on information that pertains directly to the exam. These helpful hints are written by authors who have taken the exam and received their certification—who better to tell you what to worry about? They know what you're about to go through!

Cross-Reference

This element points to related topics covered in other Objective modules or Domains.

 ADDITIONAL RESOURCES   This element points to books, websites, and other media for further assistance.

 CAUTION   These cautionary notes address common pitfalls or real-world issues.

 NOTE   This element calls out any ancillary but pertinent information.

- **Tables** allow for a quick reference to help quickly navigate quantitative data or lists of technical information.

Video Cable Type	Standard Name	Reduced-Size Version	Signal Types Supported	Notes
VGA	Video Graphics Array	N/A	Analog video	VGA displays can be connected to HDMI, DVI-I, and DisplayPort ports with suitable adapters.
HDMI	High Definition Multimedia Interface	Mini-HDMI	HD video and HD audio	Video signal is compatible with DVI.

- Each Objective module ends with a brief **Review**. The review begins by repeating the official exam objective number and text, followed by a succinct and useful summary, geared toward quick review and retention.
- **Review Questions and Answers** are intended to be similar to those found on the exam. Explanations of the correct answer are provided.

Online Content

For more information on the practice exams and other bonus materials included with the book, please see the "About the Online Content" appendix at the back of this book.

After you've read the book, complete the free online registration and take advantage of the free practice questions! Use the full practice exam to hone your skills, and keep the book handy to check answers.

When you're acing the practice questions, you're ready to take the exam.

Go get certified!

What's Next?

The IT industry changes and grows constantly, and so should you. Finishing one certification is just a step in an ongoing process of gaining more and more certifications to match your constantly changing and growing skills. Remember, in the IT business, if you're not moving forward, you are way behind!

Good luck on your certification! Stay in touch.

Mike Meyers, Series Editor
Mike Meyers' Certification Passport

Operating Systems

Domain Objectives

- **1.1** Identify basic features of Microsoft Windows editions.
- **1.2** Given a scenario, use the appropriate Microsoft command-line tool.
- **1.3** Given a scenario, use features and tools of the Microsoft Windows 10 operating system (OS).
- **1.4** Given a scenario, use the appropriate Microsoft Windows 10 Control Panel utility.
- **1.5** Given a scenario, use the appropriate Windows settings.
- **1.6** Given a scenario, configure Microsoft Windows networking features on a client/desktop.
- **1.7** Given a scenario, apply application installation and configuration concepts.
- **1.8** Explain common OS types and their purposes.
- **1.9** Given a scenario, perform OS installations and upgrades in a diverse OS environment.
- **1.10** Identify common features and tools of the macOS/desktop OS.
- **1.11** Identify common features and tools of the Linux client/desktop OS.

Objective 1.1 Identify basic features of Microsoft Windows editions

The Windows operating system (OS) has evolved from the "operating environment" of Windows 1.0 that didn't include any networking capabilities of 1985 to the fully featured desktop, mobile, and server OSs of Windows 10/11 and Server 2022. In this objective, we look at the basic features of the Windows OS and how they're used.

64-Bit vs. 32-Bit

A 32-bit operating system (OS) can be used with either a 32-bit or 64-bit processor. The once-common 32-bit processors are now used primarily by very low-performance tablets. Consequently, most computers and mobile devices use 64-bit operating systems. Software, whether system software (such as an OS) or application software (such as a word processor or game), runs best on the architecture for which it was developed. A 64-bit OS version cannot run on a 32-bit CPU. However, a 64-bit OS runs on either a 64-bit or 32-bit CPU, although it runs much better on the 64-bit CPU, with some vendor-related exceptions.

 EXAM TIP A 32-bit CPU can only address 4 gigabytes (GB) of RAM.

All of the 64-bit versions of Windows 10 support only 64-bit device drivers that have been "signed" (which means authenticated and authorized) by Microsoft. Without a signed device driver, Windows won't support an installed or attached device. A 32-bit architecture limits 32-bit versions of Windows to 4 GB of system memory (RAM), but a 64-bit architecture allows the 64-bit Windows versions to support much larger amounts of RAM, depending on the edition (see Table 1.1-2, later in this objective).

 EXAM TIP For the CompTIA A+ Core 2 (220-1102) exam, be sure you know the RAM limits for the Home, Pro, Pro for Workstations, and Enterprise editions of Windows 10.

Windows 10 Editions

Windows 10 is the ninth released graphical user interface (GUI) version of the Windows NT operating system. Windows 10 is the most installed version of all the Windows versions.

NOTE   Why is Windows 10 the ninth version? Some upgrade versions have overlapped, and there was no Windows 9 version.

Version, editions, and releases all mean something different when associated with Windows 10 (and other Microsoft products). Officially, editions have names, such as Enterprise and Pro. Versions are associated with builds, which have identification codes (build numbers). Another identifier that can be added to this mix is release, which is an update to a version or edition that is released on a periodic basis (annual mostly).

Figure 1.1-1 shows the Control Panel System About page detailing the installed version information on a PC. To display this information, access the Settings option on the Start menu and select the System icon. On the System page, select the About option in the left menu pane.

Windows 10 editions can be divided into three basic groups: home editions, work editions, and pro and enterprise editions. Each of these groups and the editions included are described in the following sections.

FIGURE 1.1-1   The System/About page of a Windows 10 Enterprise system

Home Edition

The Windows 10 Home edition is the original equipment manufacturer (OEM) and retail edition. Home is designed specifically for desktop, mobile, tablet, and all-in-one PCs in home or small office/home office (SOHO) use. The Home edition includes all core features, including Cortana and the Edge web browser.

The Windows 10 Home edition supports multicore processes (as many as 64), but it doesn't have support features for multiple CPUs. Its 64-bit version supports a maximum of 128 GB of RAM.

Work Edition

The edition of Windows 10 that is considered to be the work edition is Windows 10 Pro. Pro combines the core features of the Home edition with the services and applications used to support the centralized installation and management of remote network nodes. Pro adds professional and business features to the Home version, including Active Directory, BitLocker, the Hyper-V hypervisor, and Windows Defender Device protection. Windows 10 Pro has features specifically for supporting local area networks (LANs) and network users. Windows 10 Pro is typically sold under a volume license.

Windows 10 Pro for Workstations and Enterprise Editions

Windows 10 Pro edition is also available with volume licensing, which grants price discounts for larger numbers of licenses as Windows Pro for Workstations.

Windows 10 Pro for Workstations includes all the features of the base Pro edition, plus it allows more RAM and supports newer and more advanced software and hardware technologies, such as the Resilient File System (ReFS), Windows Storage Spaces, and persistent RAM (NVDIMM-N).

The Windows 10 Enterprise edition adds additional features to support the computing needs of large corporate and enterprise-level networks. These features include high-level protection for emerging security threats, customizable installation, update and maintenance procedures and processes, and robust device and application management and control features, among many others. Enterprise also includes several features not available in the Windows 10 Pro edition, such as Microsoft Direct Access virtual private network (VPN) technology, AppLocker software executive management tool, and the Microsoft Desktop Optimization Pack.

The Windows 10 Enterprise Long-Term Servicing Channel (LTSC) provides a long-term support and maintenance version of Windows 10 Enterprise. New releases of Windows Enterprise LTSC are issued approximately every two years, and each release is then supported with security and operational updates for five or ten years after its release.

EXAM TIP   The feature that distinguishes the Pro, Pro for Workstations, and Enterprise editions from other Windows editions is their capability to join a domain network. Windows 10 (or Windows 11) Home cannot join a domain.

Cross-Reference

Domain networks are discussed in the upcoming section of this objective as well as in Objective 1.6.

The Pro for Workstations and the Enterprise editions include several advanced features for medium-to-large network environments, such as the Group Policy Editor, BitLocker, and Remote Desktop Protocol (RDP). These three features are covered later in this objective.

Domains and Workgroups

The terms *domain* and *workgroup* are often used interchangeably but are actually quite different. Whereas a workgroup is a peer-to-peer or node-to-node network to which only users configured as members can log in and access its resources, such as a departmental office in a business or a home network, a domain can be either of two network configurations:

- An Internet top-level grouping, such as a country (.us), a business (.com), an island in the Pacific Ocean (.tv), and so on
- A logical grouping of network servers, nodes, and resources configured in a pool that can be accessed by user accounts configured as members

In the context of the CompTIA A+ Core 2 (220-1102) exam, it's the second definition that is important. Whereas a workgroup limits a user to logging in only at their designated work-station, a Windows domain permits remote (or roaming) access. Table 1.1-1 compares the characteristics of workgroups and domains.

TABLE 1.1-1   Comparison of Workgroups and Domains

Workgroup	Domain
Users can log in only on designated workstations.	Users can log in to local or remote workstations.
Each computer has a unique database.	Users share a domain database.
Intended for sharing non-sensitive information because of less security.	Users are able to share sensitive and important information because of higher security.
Used for smaller networks such as LANs and CANs.	Used for large or public networks, such as WANs and MANs.
Commonly used for a smaller number of nodes.	Supports higher numbers of nodes.

Joining a Computer to a Domain

Two basic methods can be used to join a computer running Windows 10 to a domain: using system properties and using Windows 10 settings. The process of each of these methods is described in the following sections.

Joining a Computer to a Domain Using System Properties

The steps used to join a computer to an existing domain are as follows:

1. Open the Control Panel using one of the following methods:
   a. Press WIN-R to display the Run command box, enter **control panel** in the Open box, and click OK.
   b. Click the Start button, type **control panel**, and press ENTER.
   c. Expand the Windows System option on the Start menu and click Control Panel.
2. On the Control Panel display, select System to display the System Configuration window.
3. Open the System Properties dialog box using one of the following two methods:
   a. Click the Remote Settings, System Protections, or Advanced System Settings option on the left-side of the page and select the Computer Name tab.
   b. Click the Change Settings link at the extreme lower-right side of the Computer Name, Domain, and Workgroup Settings section of the dialog box.
4. Depending on whether the computer is already a member of a domain, select the Network ID button or the Change button. Figure 1.1-2 illustrates the dialog box that displays when you click the Change button.

Joining a Windows 10 Computer to a Domain Using Settings

A Windows 10 computer can join a domain through the Windows 10 Settings. Here are the steps to use this method:

1. Open the Power User menu by right-clicking the Start button.
2. Select the Settings option to display the Windows Settings menu.
3. Select the Accounts option to display the user's Accounts page, shown in Figure 1.1-3.
4. Click the Access Work or School option in the left menu list.
5. Following the instructions on the Microsoft Account dialog box, shown in Figure 1.1-4, contact the domain authority for how to proceed.

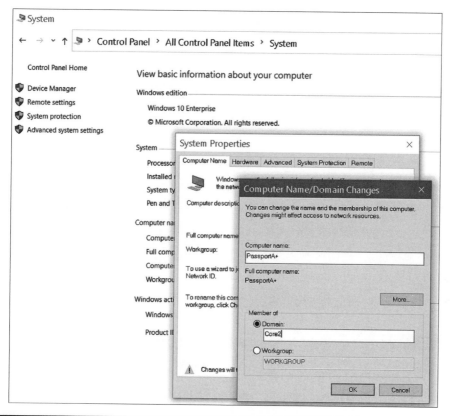

FIGURE 1.1-2   The Computer Name/Domain Changes dialog box

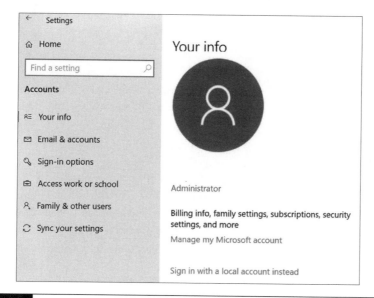

FIGURE 1.1-3   The Accounts page

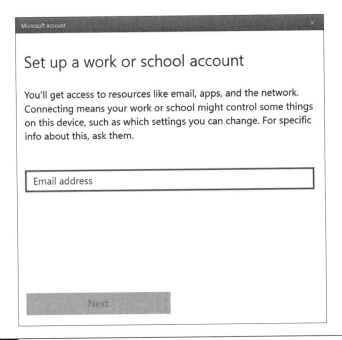

Desktop Styles/User Interface

The primary user interface of Windows 10 (and Windows 11 for that matter) is the graphical user interface (GUI) that constitutes the Desktop. The Desktop can be customized to a certain extent, but with limitations. After all, its purpose is to provide the user with a means of accessing resources easily.

Desktop Views

The Windows 10 Desktop can be viewed in two basic display styles: Desktop and Task View. Task View has two options for its display, plus the ability to create virtual desktops. Each of these options is described in the following sections.

Desktop GUI

The default display and user interface for Windows 10 is the Desktop, which can be a solid color, a provided graphic background (an example of which is shown in Figure 1.1-5), or an image or a slideshow of images provided by the user. The icons on the Desktop are optional and at the discretion of the user. The Desktop can be populated with icons linked to virtually any addressable object on the computer, such as files, programs, folders, shortcuts, and the like.

FIGURE 1.1-5   An example of a default Windows 10 Desktop background

The Desktop contains four major components: the GUI display, the Start menu, the taskbar, and the object icons. The Start menu contains links to system services as well as the applications and utilities available on the system.

Task View

Task View, shown in Figure 1.1-6, allows a user to switch between the program and applications actively running on Windows. The display may also include notes or reminders as well. The Task View can be displayed two ways: by clicking the Task View icon on the taskbar or by pressing ALT-TAB. However, there is a difference between the two displays. The view opened with the taskbar icon, like the one shown in Figure 1.1-6, shows only the programs running and the active view. The view displayed by the ALT-TAB key combination, shown in Figure 1.1-7, shows all the currently open pages, including web pages, on the computer.

If the Task View icon (see Figure 1.1-8) is not on the taskbar, you can add it by right-clicking the taskbar and choosing the Show the Task View button option.

You can change the display of the Task View by accessing the Settings option on the Start menu and choosing System and then Multitasking. On the Multitasking page, you can change the options of the Task View display, as shown in Figure 1.1-9.

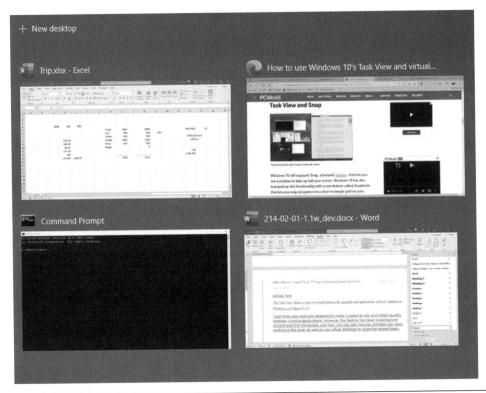

FIGURE 1.1-6 The Task View displayed by the Task View icon on the taskbar

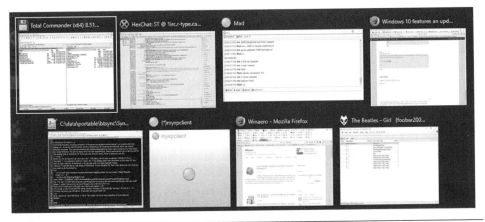

FIGURE 1.1-7 The Task View displayed by the ALT-TAB key combination

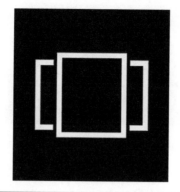

FIGURE 1.1-8   The Task View icon

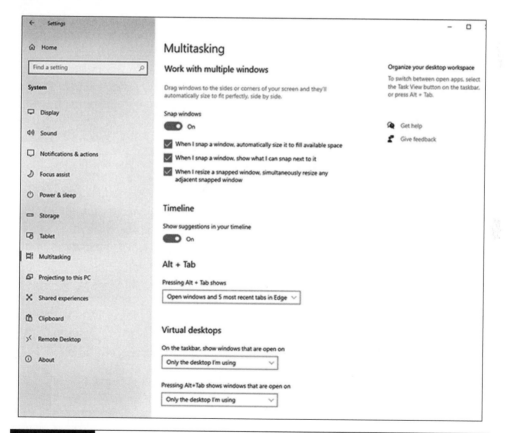

FIGURE 1.1-9   The Task View options on the Settings/System/Multitasking page

FIGURE 1.1-10   Desktop 1 is the main Windows Desktop, and Desktop 2 is a new virtual desktop.

Task View with Virtual Desktops

At the top of the Task View display is an option to add a new desktop (also referred to as a virtual desktop). Clicking the plus sign opens a new virtual desktop, as shown in Figure 1.1-10. The active window is displayed in Desktop 1, and the new virtual desktop is shown as Desktop 2.

With the virtual desktop feature, a user on a computer that has only a single monitor (regardless of it being a desktop, laptop, or any other Windows system) is able to work with two or more different environments, applications, or tasks on just the one computer. In effect, a virtual desktop is a means to virtualize a single computer into simulating multiple systems. One feature a virtual desktop provides is the ability to move a running application from one desktop to another using Drag and Drop or the Move To options.

Remote Desktop Protocol

The Remote Desktop Protocol (RDP) provides the capability for a user to log on to a remote system and effectively control that system as a local user. An administrator can use RDP for troubleshooting, diagnosing, or fixing a problem, and a user can access their own PC from a remote location. RDP has recently been in heavy use by users working from home accessing their workplace workstations.

The Windows Home edition is able to make RDP connections to other computers but cannot act as an RDP server. Only the Windows Pro and Enterprise editions are able to act as an RDP server.

EXAM TIP   RDP uses TCP/UDP port 3389, and this port must be open for RDP to function.

RDP does require some setup. The two PCs—the local PC of the administrator or user and the remote PC to be accessed—must have the Remote Desktop option enabled. This is typically the default setting, but it should certainly be checked before attempting to connect.

FIGURE 1.1-11   The Remote Desktop Connection dialog box

The connection is then made through the Remote Desktop Connection, shown in Figure 1.1-11, by entering the full name or the IP address of the remote PC. A login is required, but after access is granted, the PC and the user appear to be local.

RAM Support Limitations

The 32-bit editions of Windows 10, which Microsoft refers to as "x86," support up to 4 GB of RAM. The 64-bit editions of Windows 10 support much higher amounts of RAM, as shown in Table 1.1-2. The maximum RAM size in a given system is also affected by the chipset and motherboard design of the hardware.

EXAM TIP   Be sure to know differences between 32-bit (x86) and 64-bit Windows editions.

NOTE   Windows 11 is the first version of Windows that does not have 32-bit support.

TABLE 1.1-2   Maximum RAM Supported by Windows 10 Versions

Windows 10 Edition	Maximum RAM
Windows 10 Home 64 bit	128 GB
Windows 10 Pro 64 bit	2 TB
Windows 10 Pro for Workstations	6 TB
Windows 10 Enterprise 64-bit	6 TB

BitLocker

Like most everyone else, you probably store confidential or sensitive files on your PC. And, like most other people, you really need to secure them, just in case. If the operating system on your PC is Windows 10 or later, the best and easiest way to secure your files is with full volume encryption and BitLocker.

 EXAM TIP The purpose and application of BitLocker is something you need to understand for the CompTIA A+ Core 2 (220-1102) exam.

Encryption is a process that converts plain text (or readable data) into cipher text (or unreadable code). Encrypted data can only be unscrambled (decrypted) with an associated key value back into readable data. Once data is encrypted, it remains scrambled regardless of it being at rest or in transit. Only you, or anyone you share the decryption key with, can unscramble it for use. Therefore, encrypting an entire storage volume is a sure way to protect any sensitive or confidential data that's stored on it.

BitLocker is a Windows feature that can be used to encrypt the data on a hard drive or USB flash drives, including the installation drive, startup drive, and secondary storage. Data encrypted by BitLocker is protected from access by anyone other than users who use a certain user login account or the recovery (decryption) key.

 EXAM TIP The Windows feature BitLocker To Go can be used to encrypt removable media.

BitLocker Requirements

BitLocker is available on the Windows 10 Pro, Windows 10 Pro for Workstations, and Enterprise editions. However, there are a few hardware and software requirements a system must have for BitLocker to be enabled. The following are the most crucial of these requirements:

- A Trusted Platform Module (TPM) should be on or attached to the motherboard. A TPM is a dedicated microprocessor that stores security data, such as BitLocker and other encryption keys and user account biometric data. BitLocker can be used without TPM, but additional authentication steps are required for encryption and decryption. Many motherboards now include a TPM, but some require it to be added. Figure 1.1-12 shows the Windows Security page of Settings that details the TPM.

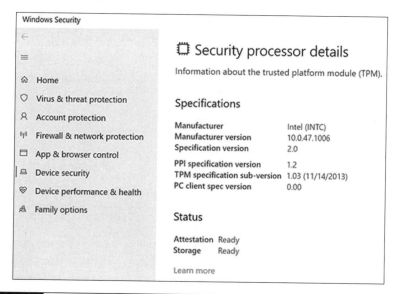

□ Security processor details

Information about the trusted platform module (TPM).

⌂ Home

○ Virus & threat protection

Specifications

R Account protection

Manufacturer	Intel (INTC)
Manufacturer version	10.0.47.1006
Specification version	2.0
PPI specification version	1.2
TPM specification sub-version	1.03 (11/14/2013)
PC client spec version	0.00

(ᵖ) Firewall & network protection

▢ App & browser control

⊟ Device security

♡ Device performance & health

⚐ Family options

Status

Attestation	Ready
Storage	Ready

Learn more

FIGURE 1.1-12   The Windows Security page for the security processor details

- Basic Input/Output System (BIOS) or Unified Extensible Firmware Interface (UEFI) support for the TPM device to be enabled for startup. If this is not available, the firmware may need to be updated.
- The hard drive must have two NTFS (New Technology File System) partitions: a system partition with startup files and a partition containing the Windows 10 files. BitLocker creates these partitions, if necessary.

EXAM TIP   Device Encryption on Windows is a security feature alternative to BitLocker for encrypting storage devices available on all Windows 10 editions.

Enabling BitLocker

BitLocker is enabled or disabled using the BitLocker Drive Encryption settings page (see Figure 1.1-13) of the System and Security option of the Windows Control Panel. On some Windows 10 versions, the Control Panel no longer lists the System and Security option, in which case you should search for "BitLocker Drive Encryption."

On the BitLocker Drive Encryption page, you can enable the BitLocker feature and configure where you wish to secure the recovery key, the amount of space you wish to encrypt, and the encryption mode you wish to use. You can also check to see if BitLocker encryption is compatible with the devices chosen.

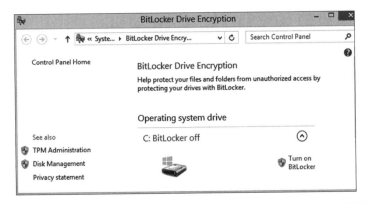

FIGURE 1.1-13 The BitLocker Drive Encryption page of the Windows Control Panel

After BitLocker is active on a drive, you can suspended BitLocker (typically used when you're upgrading Windows or the system firmware or when making hardware changes), recover the recovery key, change or remove the password, or disable BitLocker, which decrypts all the files on the encrypted drives.

The Group Policy Editor

In the Windows OS environment, a group policy is a way for an administrator to configure and apply configurations and settings to multiple computers or network nodes from a single source. The options that can be configured in a group policy include settings for Registry policies, security, software installs, OS scripts, startup and shutdowns, user account access, and more. An example would be settings that restrict access to particular folders or block the use of one or more Microsoft Management Console (MMC) utilities. A related set of group policy settings is called a Group Policy Object (GPO).

Accessing the Group Policy Editor

The Windows 10 Pro, Windows 10 for Workstations, and Enterprise editions have access to the Group Policy Editor, which means the Windows 10 Home edition does not. The Windows 10 Home edition must use the Local Group Policy Editor.

There are a number of ways to access the Group Policy Editor on the Windows 10 editions with access to it. In addition to creating a desktop or Start object for the editor, here are the most popular ways to open the Group Policy Editor:

- **Windows Search**   Open the Start menu and search for **gpedit.msc**.
- **Run Command box**   Press WIN-R, type **gpedit.msc** in the Run window, and select OK.

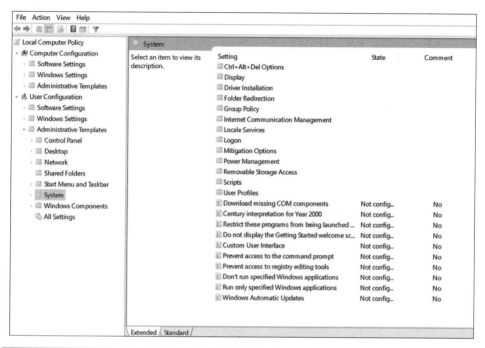

File Action View Help

Local Computer Policy	System			
Computer Configuration	Select an item to view its description.	Setting	State	Comment
Software Settings		Ctrl+Alt+Del Options		
Windows Settings		Display		
Administrative Templates		Driver Installation		
User Configuration		Folder Redirection		
Software Settings		Group Policy		
Windows Settings		Internet Communication Management		
Administrative Templates		Locale Services		
Control Panel		Logon		
Desktop		Mitigation Options		
Network		Power Management		
Shared Folders		Removable Storage Access		
Start Menu and Taskbar		Scripts		
System		User Profiles		
Windows Components		Download missing COM components	Not config...	No
All Settings		Century interpretation for Year 2000	Not config...	No
		Restrict these programs from being launched ...	Not config...	No
		Do not display the Getting Started welcome sc...	Not config...	No
		Custom User Interface	Not config...	No
		Prevent access to the command prompt	Not config...	No
		Prevent access to registry editing tools	Not config...	No
		Don't run specified Windows applications	Not config...	No
		Run only specified Windows applications	Not config...	No
		Windows Automatic Updates	Not config...	No

Extended / Standard /

FIGURE 1.1-14   The opening display of the Group Policy Editor

As shown in Figure 1.1-14, the Group Policy Editor window includes two primary administration groups in the left pane:

- **Computer Configuration**   These policies apply to every computer and its OS and remain the same for all computers in a group.
- **User Configuration**   These policies are used to create custom user/workgroup Desktop configurations and permissions. If these policies are applied to the Active Directory, they apply to individuals, groups, or all users, depending on the policy level designated.

You should review the Administrative Templates sections of both the Computer and User Configuration groups. Both of these sections contain a number of predefined templates that an administrator can use to create policies in a wide range of system areas. In addition, administrative templates can be added for specific functions or software. Many software publishers provide administrative templates for their products.

Upgrade Paths and In-Place Upgrades

When Microsoft releases new editions of its Windows OS, an upgrade path and process are provided for corporations and individuals to follow to install the new editions. Upgrade paths are also released for upgrading from one edition of Windows to another. In every case, upgrading from one edition of the Windows OS to a newer edition requires a volume license or a product key for each device affected.

Most upgrades made to a currently supported edition are performed with the *in-place upgrade*. This upgrade process requires an attendant. In other words, the user must be at the computer during the upgrade process. An in-place upgrade is used to add new features to an OS without downloading an upgrade media.

An in-place upgrade process uses the following steps:

1. After signing in as Administrator, idle, disable, or uninstall any non-Windows antivirus and security software.

2. If not already available, download the Windows 10 Installation Media Tool from the Windows 10 download page at https://www.microsoft.com/en-us/software-download/windows10/. After it downloads, run this program to begin the in-place update.

3. This tool will take some time while "getting a few things ready," which includes an Applicable Notices and License Terms agreement. Choose the Upgrade This PC Now option and then follow the instructions of the software to complete the update.

4. During the progress of the update, expect the PC to restart many times.

5. When the update process ends, the user login screen displays. Log in and reset any privacy, language, or other settings, as needed.

REVIEW

Objective 1.1: Identify basic features of Microsoft Windows editions

- A 32-bit (x86) OS only runs on a 32-bit CPU, and a 64-bit OS runs on either a 64-bit or 32-bit CPU, but it runs better on a 64-bit CPU.
- Windows won't support an installed or attached device without a signed device driver.
- The Windows 10 Home edition supports up to 128 GB of RAM. Windows 10 Pro supports up to 2 TB of RAM.
- Windows 10 Pro for Workstations and Windows 10 Enterprise editions support up to 6 TB of RAM.
- Operating systems are clients, network operating systems, or mobile device systems.
- Windows 10 editions are grouped as home editions, work editions, and pro and enterprise editions, which are designated for specific markets.
- The Windows Home edition is the OEM and retail edition, designed for desktop PCs, mobile devices, tablets, and all-in-one PCs in SOHO use.
- Windows 10 Pro adds professional and business features, including Active Directory, BitLocker, Hyper-V, and more.

- Windows 10 Pro for Workstations allows more RAM and supports newer and more advanced software and hardware technologies, such as the ReFS, Storage Spaces, and persistent RAM (NVDIMM-N).
- Windows 10 Enterprise supports enterprise-level networks and includes features such as Direct Access VPN, AppLocker, and Desktop Optimization Pack.
- A workgroup is a peer-to-peer or node-to-node network and a domain is a logical grouping of network servers, nodes and resources.
- The Windows 10 Desktop supports two basic display styles: Desktop and Task View.
- RDP allows users to log in to a remote system and control it as a local user.
- BitLocker encrypts the data on hard drives or USB drives and is available on Windows 10 Pro and Enterprise versions.
- The Group Policy Editor (gpedit.msc) is used to configure settings for multiple computers from a single source.
- Windows OS upgrade paths are used to install new Windows editions or apply updates to an existing edition.
- Upgrades to a supported Windows edition use an in-place upgrade, which requires the user's assistance.

1.1 QUESTIONS

1. When you're installing a new hardware device on a Windows 10 Pro system, what must be present before the OS will support the device?

   A. USB hub

   B. Signed device driver

   C. BIOS/UEFI support for the device

   D. PnP support

2. Which one of the 64-bit Windows 10 editions does not support up to 512 GB of primary memory?

   A. Enterprise

   B. Pro

   C. Home

   D. Pro for Workstations

3. In a Windows environment, what is a domain?

   A. A logical grouping of network servers, nodes, and resources.

   B. A peer-to-peer network

   C. A grouping of workstations from remote networks

   D. A workgroup

4. Which Windows 10 edition is limited to settings and configurations for a local computer only using the Group Policy Editor?

   A. Pro

   B. Enterprise

   C. Pro for Workstations

   D. Home

5. What is the type of upgrade process most commonly used to apply new features to a supported Windows edition?

   A. Feature update

   B. Cumulative update

   C. In-place upgrade

   D. Servicing stack update

1.1 ANSWERS

1. **B**　Windows requires a Microsoft signed device driver for all installed devices.

2. **C**　Windows Home 64-bit edition supports only 128 GB of RAM.

3. **A**　A domain is a logical grouping of network servers, nodes, and resources.

4. **D**　The Home edition cannot create settings for multiple computers through the Active Directory.

5. **C**　The in-place upgrade process is used to apply new features to a supported Windows edition.

Objective 1.2 ## Given a scenario, use the appropriate Microsoft command-line tool

Although most routine operations in Windows are performed through the graphical user interface (GUI), Windows retains a command prompt that is used for a variety of navigation commands and tools. In this objective, we'll cover all the information on the commands you should know for the CompTIA A+ 220-1102 exam.

Windows Navigation Commands

The Windows command prompt, an example of which is shown in Figure 1.2-1, is made up of three components: the active storage device (C:), the active folder or directory (\Windows\System32), and the command prompt termination symbol (>), which acts as the separator between the prompt and the command entered by the user. In this discussion on the Windows

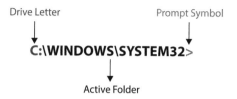

Drive Letter   Prompt Symbol

C:\WINDOWS\SYSTEM32>

Active Folder

FIGURE 1.2-1   The components of the Windows command prompt

navigation commands, the active folder is important because any command that affects sub-folders, files, or objects will immediately apply to the contents of that folder. In the example shown in Figure 1.2-1, the subfolders and files in the \Windows\System32 folder represent the content of the active folder.

 NOTE   The Windows OS uses the backslash character (\) to separate elements of the pathname, but the forward slash (/) is accepted in its place in file pathnames by the Windows File Explorer or at the command prompt. On a Linux command prompt, only the forward slash is used.

Table 1.2-1 provides a list of the Windows navigation commands.

 EXAM TIP   Given a scenario on the exam, be sure you are familiar with command-line navigation commands, including cd, dir, md, and rmdir.

TABLE 1.2-1   Windows Navigation Commands

Command	Name	Use	Example
cd	Change directory	Moves from the present active directory to an indicated pathname.	cd /Windows
dir	Display directory contents	Displays the contents of the active folder or directory or that of a supplied pathname.	dir *.jpg (Displays all files with a .jpg extension in the current folder.)
md or mkdir	Make directory	Creates a new directory within the present active directory.	md \newdir
rmdir	Remove directory	Removes an empty directory	rmdir newdir

Drive Navigation in Windows

The Windows OS designates disk drives, volumes, and disk partitions using alphabetic characters, such as C, D, E, X, and the like. When using a navigation command at the command prompt, you can include a drive designation to change to another drive or to a directory on that drive.

For example, the command **cd \newdir** changes the active directory to the newdir folder on the active disk drive. However, the command **cd E:\newdir** changes the active drive to the E: drive and then to \newdir on that drive.

NOTE   Drives A and B were legacy designations for floppy disk drives and have not been reused since the demise of those devices.

Changing folders can also make use of two special designations: a single dot and a double dot. A single dot (.) represents "this place" in the current active folder. This can be used to refer to an object in the current folder, including a subfolder. For example, **./newdir** refers to a subfolder of the active folder. The double dot refers to the folder above the active directory. An example is **cd ..** (which means change to the parent folder of the active folder, if there is one).

Command-Line Tools

Table 1.2-2 presents a variety of command-line tools you can use at the command prompt to administer a Windows system.

TABLE 1.2-2   Windows Command-Line Tools

Command	Usage	Examples (Notes)
ipconfig	Displays Internet configuration (IP address and such).	ipconfig /all (Displays all information for all installed network adapters.)
ping	Checks connectivity.	ping 8.8.8.8 (Checks connectivity to the specified IP address.) ping www.evansville.net (Checks connectivity to the specified website; some websites block pings for security reasons.)
hostname	Displays the host name of the computer.	hostname

TABLE 1.2-2 Windows Command-Line Tools *(continued)*

Command	Usage	Examples (Notes)
netstat	Displays network statistics.	Lists TCP connections.
nslookup	Displays the IP address of the specified domain or server or displays the domain or server associated with the specified IP address.	nslookup microsoft.com (Displays the IP address for Microsoft.com.)
chkdsk	Scans, detects, and (optionally) repairs file and directory structure issues on drives.	Requires an elevated command prompt.
net user	Manages and lists network users.	net user administrator /active:yes (Activates the local user account.)
net use	Manages connections to shared network resources.	net use \\myserver\myfolder (Connects to the listed resource.)
tracert	Traces the route to the specified IP address or server.	tracert www.evansville.net
format	Prepares a blank drive for use or clears the contents of a used drive.	format d: /FS:NTFS
xcopy	Creates a copy of the specified files and folders (directories) on the target drive.	xcopy *.docx U:\MyDOCS\ /S
copy	Creates a copy of the specified files on the target drive.	copy *.docx U:
robocopy	Copies or moves files and folders with options to log, retry failures, use multithreading, and more; GUIs are available to make this command easier to use.	robocopy H:\MyDOCS\ U:\YourDOCS\ /MIR
gpupdate	Immediately applies group policy updates.	gpupdate /Force
gpresult	Displays the current user or computer's group policy settings.	gpresult /X GPRfilename
shutdown	Shuts down, hibernates, or restarts a local or network system.	shutdown /r (Shuts down and restarts.)
sfc	The System File Checker verifies Windows system files, folders, and paths and replaces corrupt versions.	Requires administrator-level permissions.

TABLE 1.2-2 Windows Command-Line Tools *(continued)*

Command	Usage	Examples (Notes)
[command name] /?	Displays the syntax for the specified command.	format /?
diskpart	Advanced disk management tool; it opens the diskpart> prompt when started. Some commands can cause data loss if misused (such as clean all).	list disk (Displays connected drives.) select disk 3 (Selects third disk.) clean all (Overwrites contents of the selected disk, disk 3.)
pathping	Identifies the routers on the path to the domain provided and pings each of the routers on the path to compute latency.	pathping totalsem.com
winver	Displays the Windows edition, version, build number, and trademark information.	winver

 EXAM TIP Be prepared to use the appropriate command-line tools listed in Table 1.2-2 in response to a scenario on the exam.

REVIEW

Objective 1.2: Given a scenario, use the appropriate Microsoft command-line tool Windows command-line tools can be used for many purposes:

- Navigation (dir, cd, and ..)
- Network reporting and troubleshooting (ipconfig, ping, tracert, netstat, nslookup, net use, and net user)
- System management and repairs (shutdown, sfc, chkdsk, gpupdate, and gpresult)
- Disk and file management (format, diskpart, copy, xcopy, and robocopy)
- Help (available for almost any command-line tool by adding /? to the command)

Note that an elevated (administrative) command prompt is required for some commands.

1.2 QUESTIONS

1. What Windows command prompt command verifies system files, folders, and paths and replaces corrupt versions?

   A. chkdsk

   B. gpupdate

   C. sfc

   D. ipconfig

2. You are unable to remove all the contents of an existing hard disk using Disk Management. Which command should you use instead?

   A. format

   B. diskpart

   C. gpupdate

   D. gpresult

3. A user calls you to ask for help with her network connection. To find out what her network settings are, which of the following commands should you run?

   A. ping

   B. netstat

   C. net use

   D. ipconfig

4. You need to use ping to check the connectivity to network server 164.172.1.150, also known as MyServer.net. Which of the following is the correct syntax?

   A. ping //MyServer.net

   B. ping 164-172-1-150

   C. ping MyServer.net

   D. ping theserverforthisnetwork

5. You are providing telephone support to a user named Miranda who needs to access her personal folders at a command prompt. From her Users folder, which of the following commands would she need to use to get to her personal folders?

   A. cd \Miranda

   B. Miranda.exe

   C. ls Miranda

   D. cd Miranda

1.2 ANSWERS

1. **C**   The sfc command verifies system files, folders, and paths and replaces corrupt versions.

2. **B**   The diskpart command has an option (clean all) to remove all contents from a connected drive.

3. **D**   The ipconfig command can display various amounts of information about the user's network connection, depending on which options are used.

4. **C**   You can use either the IP address or the URL with ping. However, the syntax must be correct.

5. **D**   The command **cd *foldername*** drops the focus of the command prompt down one level, and Miranda is in the next level below the Users folder.

Objective 1.3 **Given a scenario, use features and tools of the Microsoft Windows 10 operating system (OS)**

Windows includes a variety of features and tools that help you manage systems, users, drives, devices, policies, and updates. The Task Manager, Microsoft Management Console (MMC), and other tools you should know for the CompTIA A+ Core 2 (220-1102) exam are discussed in this objective.

EXAM TIP   The current edition of the CompTIA A+ Core 2 (220-1102) exam focuses primarily on Windows 10 editions. However, since Windows 11 has been released, you should expect that over the life of this exam, Windows 11 and its features are likely to begin appearing in the exam to supplement or perhaps even to supplant the Windows 10 content. This objective, which as its title states is focused on Windows 10, contains Windows 11 content where appropriate. If you've registered for the exam and are reading this to prepare for it, be sure to review the CompTIA A+ exam objectives to determine the Windows version(s) in each area. The A+ exam objectives (and the exam itself) have been known to change over the life of an exam release. You should anticipate that there will very likely be a transitioning from Windows 10 to Windows 11 in the Core 2 exam, so prepare accordingly.

Task Manager

The Windows operating system (OS) relies on the *Task Manager* to manage its tasks, which are the applications, processes, and services running on the computer at any one time. Although the Task Manager is a very advanced utility, from the user's point of view it's a tool that's used for some simple functions, such as ending a service or program that's causing a problem.

Among its more advanced functions, the Task Manager provides a range of system environment management tools that can be used to display both an overview and the details of how hard a system is working. If a problem exists, the Task Manager can help you to find the cause and perhaps a way to resolve it.

The Task Manager can be opened using any one of the following methods:

- Press the CTRL-SHIFT-ESC keys in combination.
- Right-click the Start icon or the taskbar and select Task Manager from the Power User menu.
- Press the CTRL-ALT-DEL keys in combination to display the Windows Security menu and then select Task Manager.
- Open the Run dialog box and enter **taskmgr**.

 EXAM TIP   Some tasks that are done through the Task Manager can also be performed from a command prompt. For example, you can start and stop services with **net start <service>** and **net stop <service>**, list processes with **tasklist**, and kill them with **taskkill**, among others.

The Task Manager window, as shown in Figure 1.3-1, includes seven tabs, each of which displays specific information relating to the applications, services, and utilities running on the system; the users who are logged on to the system; the running performance of the system; and more. These tabs and their specific information and functions are discussed in the following sections.

General Display

When the Task Manager opens, the Processes tab is selected by default (more on the Processes tab in the next section). However, on the menu bar above the Task Manager tabs are three choices:

- **File**   The File menu presents two choices: Run New Task and Exit. The Run New Task option allows you to start a program or open a folder, document, or resource by providing its address, as shown in Figure 1.3-2. The Exit option closes the Task Manager.

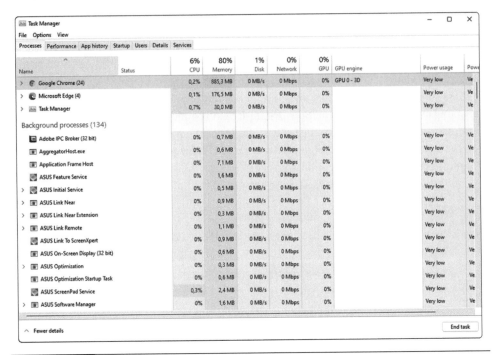

Name	Status	6% CPU	80% Memory	1% Disk	0% Network	0% GPU	GPU engine	Power usage	Powe
> ⦿ Google Chrome (24)		0,2%	885,3 MB	0 MB/s	0 Mbps	0%	GPU 0 - 3D	Very low	Ve
> ⦿ Microsoft Edge (4)		0,1%	176,5 MB	0 MB/s	0 Mbps	0%		Very low	Ve
> ⦿ Task Manager		0,7%	30,0 MB	0 MB/s	0 Mbps	0%		Very low	Ve
Background processes (134)									
⦿ Adobe IPC Broker (32 bit)		0%	0,7 MB	0 MB/s	0 Mbps	0%		Very low	Ve
⦿ AggregatorHost.exe		0%	0,6 MB	0 MB/s	0 Mbps	0%		Very low	Ve
⦿ Application Frame Host		0%	7,1 MB	0 MB/s	0 Mbps	0%		Very low	Ve
⦿ ASUS Feature Service		0%	1,6 MB	0 MB/s	0 Mbps	0%		Very low	Ve
> ⦿ ASUS Initial Service		0%	0,5 MB	0 MB/s	0 Mbps	0%		Very low	Ve
> ⦿ ASUS Link Near		0%	0,9 MB	0 MB/s	0 Mbps	0%		Very low	Ve
> ⦿ ASUS Link Near Extension		0%	0,3 MB	0 MB/s	0 Mbps	0%		Very low	Ve
> ⦿ ASUS Link Remote		0%	1,1 MB	0 MB/s	0 Mbps	0%		Very low	Ve
⦿ ASUS Link To ScreenXpert		0%	0,9 MB	0 MB/s	0 Mbps	0%		Very low	Ve
⦿ ASUS On-Screen Display (32 bit)		0%	0,6 MB	0 MB/s	0 Mbps	0%		Very low	Ve
> ⦿ ASUS Optimization		0%	0,3 MB	0 MB/s	0 Mbps	0%		Very low	Ve
⦿ ASUS Optimization Startup Task		0%	0,6 MB	0 MB/s	0 Mbps	0%		Very low	Ve
⦿ ASUS ScreenPad Service		0,3%	2,4 MB	0 MB/s	0 Mbps	0%		Very low	Ve
> ⦿ ASUS Software Manager		0%	1,6 MB	0 MB/s	0 Mbps	0%		Very low	Ve

FIGURE 1.3-1   The Task Manager on a Windows 11 system

- **Options**   The Options menu choices are toggles that turn on or off a display feature. Here are the ones you should know:
  - **Always on Top**   This option, when selected, displays the Task Manager as the foremost window.
  - **Minimize on Use**   This option, when selected, minimizes the Task Manager when a process is right-clicked and the Switch To option is chosen.
  - **Hide When Minimized**   The Task Manager will stay running in the notification area (system tray) when you click the minimize button if you enable this option.

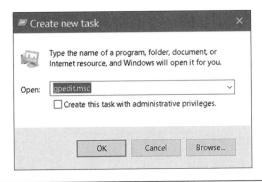

FIGURE 1.3-2   The Run New Task dialog box is opened from the Run New Task option on the File menu.

- **View** The View menu provides options to manage how the Task Manager displays its information. Here are the available options:
  - **Refresh Now** This option refreshes the Task Manager display. After clicking this option, you may or may not see a change in the information displayed in the Task Manager.
  - **Update Speed** This option sets the frequency for updating and refreshing the information displayed by the Task Manager: The speeds (frequencies) available are High, Medium, Low, and Paused. Paused freezes the display until a higher frequency is selected or the Refresh Now option is selected.
  - **Group By Type** This selection, which is the default, groups active processes into three categories: Apps, Background Processes, and Windows Processes. With this option not selected, the processes are displayed in alphabetical order by name. Another way to sequence the active processes is to click the column heading by which you wish to order the list.
  - **Expand All** This is a view option that displays (expands) the components, if any, of each process. For example, the Local Security Authority Process expands to list four subprocesses (see Figure 1.3-3). A process with an expansion arrow to the left of its name can also be expanded in the collapsed mode.
  - **Collapse All** Collapses all process groups listed. An individual process group can be collapsed by clicking the down arrow to the left of the group process item names.

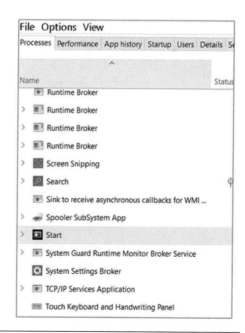

FIGURE 1.3-3 Examples of the Task Manager display showing the Expand All (left) and the Collapse All (right) options

Task Manager Tabs

The Task Manager separates and categorizes the elements of the current state of a Windows system using seven tabs (shown in Figure 1.3-4), each of which focuses on a particular activity, resource, or result.

The Task Manager tabs are as follows:

- **Processes** This tab (refer back to Figure 1.3-1) is selected by default unless another tab has been set using the Set Default Tab option. The Processes tab displays the status and resources consumption for each active process and provides you with the ability to kill it.

 NOTE Every program that runs on your system is composed of one or more processes.

- **Performance** This tab displays CPU usage, available physical memory, the size of the disk cache, commit charge (memory for programs), and kernel memory (memory used by Windows). Along the left side of the Performance tab display are several selectable report or view options. These options are typically CPU, Memory, Disk 0, Disk 1 to Disk *n*, Ethernet or Wi-Fi, and GPU. Each of these options presents a display that indicates the current activity, load, and configuration of the device or component selected. Figure 1.3-5 shows the display for the Memory option.

Cross-Reference

The Performance tab also provides a link for opening the Resource Monitor, which is covered later in this objective.

- **App History** This tab displays information on the resource and CPU utilization for each application or service executed by the active user account. The default list shows only Windows Store applications, but all applications can be displayed by selecting Show History for All Applications on the Options menu. The App History tab displays the application name and its accumulated CPU, network, metered network, and Tile (network usage for updates and notifications) time.
- **Startup** This tab lists the applications or programs that are to start automatically whenever Windows starts up as well as any programs previously enabled to start up that have been disabled. Each item in the startup list is indicated as enabled or disabled, who its publisher is, and the impact each may have on the startup process,

Processes Performance App history Startup Users Details Services

FIGURE 1.3-4 The Task Manager tabs

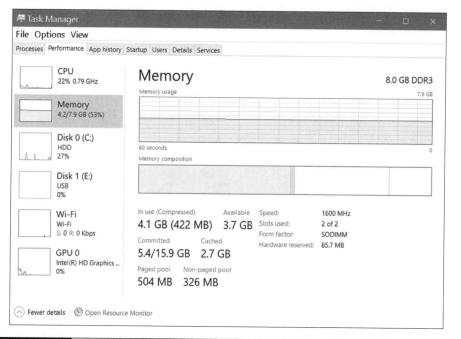

FIGURE 1.3-5 The Performance tab on the Task Manager showing the Memory display

if measurable. In the upper-right corner of the Startup tab display is the Last BIOS Time value, which indicates the length of time required for the last time Windows fully completed its startup (not including the user's sign-in).

> **NOTE** To get more detail for an application or program on the Startup tab, use the msconfig tool in the Run command (WIN-R).

- **Users** This tab displays the fluctuating percentage of a resource's capacity for the currently active user(s). The resource items include the CPU, memory, disk, network, and GPU.

- **Details** This tab provides the "details" for each of the processes (applications, programs, services, and so on) active on the system at the time this tab is opened, as shown in Figure 1.3-6. Right-click any process listed to see the administrative actions available for that process (see Figure 1.3-7).

- **Services** This tab provides basically the same information and functions of the services.msc utility (also accessible via the Administrative Tools app on the Control Panel). It can be used to manage the services (running or stopped) installed on the system.

Task Manager

File Options View

| Processes | Performance | App history | Startup | Users | **Details** | Services |

Name	PID	Status	User name	CPU	Memory (active private ...	UAC virtualization
System Idle Process	0	Running	SYSTEM	37	8 K	
System	4	Running	SYSTEM	07	20 K	
Registry	100	Running	SYSTEM	00	4,072 K	Not allowed
services.exe	420	Running	SYSTEM	00	3,272 K	Not allowed
lsass.exe	448	Running	SYSTEM	00	5,648 K	Not allowed
RdrCEF.exe	476	Running	ronpr	00	1,752 K	Disabled
smss.exe	524	Running	SYSTEM	00	152 K	Not allowed
esif_uf.exe	724	Running	SYSTEM	00	16 K	Not allowed
csrss.exe	752	Running	SYSTEM	00	692 K	Not allowed
svchost.exe	812	Running	SYSTEM	00	3,384 K	Not allowed
ApplicationFrameHo...	848	Running	ronpr	00	40 K	Disabled
svchost.exe	852	Running	SYSTEM	03	15,052 K	Not allowed
WUDFHost.exe	884	Running	LOCAL SER...	00	752 K	Not allowed
fontdrvhost.exe	936	Running	UMFD-0	00	276 K	Disabled
wininit.exe	940	Running	SYSTEM	00	0 K	Not allowed
AvastUI.exe	980	Running	ronpr	00	1,508 K	Disabled
BingWallpaperApp.e...	1052	Running	ronpr	00	4,896 K	Disabled
svchost.exe	1116	Running	NETWORK ...	02	9,660 K	Not allowed
svchost.exe	1132	Running	LOCAL SER...	03	24,932 K	Not allowed
svchost.exe	1176	Running	SYSTEM	00	1,548 K	Not allowed
svchost.exe	1316	Running	SYSTEM	00	344 K	Not allowed
svchost.exe	1344	Running	SYSTEM	00	536 K	Not allowed
svchost.exe	1352	Running	SYSTEM	00	604 K	Not allowed
ScreenClippingHost...	1384	Running	ronpr	00	8,916 K	Disabled
svchost.exe	1456	Running	LOCAL SER...	00	1,152 K	Not allowed
svchost.exe	1476	Running	SYSTEM	00	296 K	Not allowed
svchost.exe	1524	Running	SYSTEM	00	296 K	Not allowed
svchost.exe	1532	Running	SYSTEM	00	268 K	Not allowed
svchost.exe	1588	Running	LOCAL SER...	00	1,604 K	Not allowed
RdrCEF.exe	1604	Running	ronpr	00	2,404 K	Disabled
ibtsiva.exe	1672	Running	SYSTEM	00	16 K	Not allowed
svchost.exe	1680	Running	LOCAL SER...	00	960 K	Not allowed
svchost.exe	1688	Running	SYSTEM	00	3,376 K	Not allowed
svchost.exe	1712	Running	NETWORK ...	00	2,192 K	Not allowed
dllhost.exe	1748	Running	ronpr	00	116 K	Disabled

Fewer details

FIGURE 1.3-6 The display of processes shown on the Task Manager's Details tab

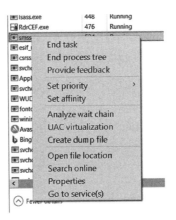

FIGURE 1.3-7 The administrative options for any process listed on the Task Manager's Details tab

EXAM TIP   Be sure you know how to start and stop services in Task Manager.

Microsoft Management Console Snap-In

The *Microsoft Management Console (MMC)* is a framework and repository of *snap-in tools* that can be used to administer and configure hardware, software, and network elements of a Windows OS. The MMC itself has no inherent system or network tools. Rather, it provides a user interface and framework that supports the functions of any snap-ins or consoles added to it.

The MMC is customizable, and the user/administrator is able to pick and choose the specific snap-ins needed, such as only those for local administration or only those for remote administration, or both. A snap-in tool is an OS object designed to communicate directly with a specific service or feature. For example, gpedit.msc is the snap-in for group and local policies (this snap-in can also be executed outside the MMC), and lusrmgr.msc is the snap-in for Local Users and Groups.

Opening the MMC

The MMC is opened using one of the following methods:

- Open a Run command dialog box, enter **MMC** in the Open box, and press ENTER.
- Open a Command Prompt window and enter **MMC** on a command line.
- Open a PowerShell window and enter **mmc.exe** at the command prompt.

The first time the MMC window opens on a system and until one or more snap-ins are added to it, the MMC display will be empty, as shown in Figure 1.3-8.

Adding/Removing a Snap-in with the MMC

To add/remove a snap-in with the MMC, use the following process:

1. Click the File menu and select the Add/Remove Snap-In option to open the Add or Remove Snap-Ins dialog box (see Figure 1.3-9).

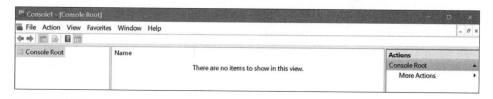

FIGURE 1.3-8   The MMC before snap-ins are added

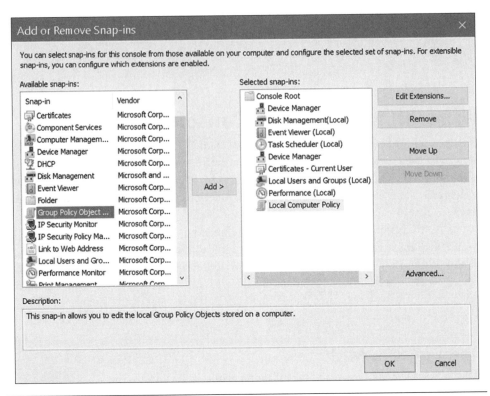

FIGURE 1.3-9 The Add or Remove Snap-Ins dialog box

2. Choose the snap-in to be added from the Available Snap-Ins list in the left-pane and click the Add arrow button in the center to add the snap-in to the Selected Snap-Ins list. Repeat this action to add other snap-ins.

3. To remove a snap-in, select it from the list in the right pane and click the Remove button on the right side of the box.

Snap-ins on the Core 2 Exam

The following sections describe the snap-ins you should know and understand for the CompTIA A+ Core 2 exam.

Event Viewer

The Event Viewer snap-in, which can also be executed in the Run command box or at a command prompt as eventvwr.msc, can be used to record an audit of virtually any event occurring on a system, which makes it useful as both a troubleshooting tool and a security tool. Figure 1.3-10 shows the default view of the Event Viewer display.

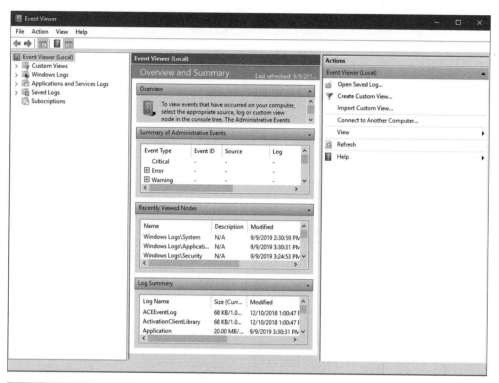

FIGURE 1.3-10   Windows 10 Event Viewer default screen

Note the four main bars in the center pane: Overview, Summary of Administrative Events, Recently Viewed Nodes, and Log Summary. The Summary of Administrative Events breaks down the events into different levels: Critical, Error, Warning, Information, Audit Success, and Audit Failure. You can click any event to see its description.

 EXAM TIP   Be sure to know the four sections (Overview, Summary of Administrative Events, Recently Viewed Nodes, and Log Summary) as well as Application, Security, and System logs in Event Viewer.

The Windows Event Viewer includes classic Application, Security, and System logs, but it leans heavily on filtering their contents through *views* that enable custom reports by beginning/end times, error levels, and more. You can use the built-in views or easily create your own. Administrators can configure log file location as well as maximum size and what to do when it's reached, as shown in Figure 1.3-11.

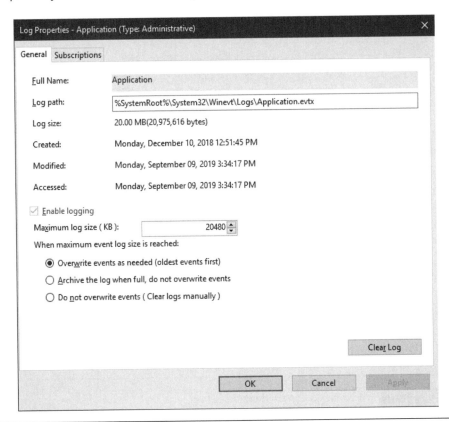

FIGURE 1.3-11 Log Properties dialog box in Windows 10

Disk Management

Disk Management is the snap-in for adding or modifying drives or arrays to and on a Windows system. To open the Disk Management tool, click it in the MMC snap-in navigation pane (left side), run diskmgmt.msc in the Run box or at a command prompt, or choose it from the Power User menu (right-click the Start icon). Figure 1.3-12 shows the display of the Disk Management snap-in.

The Disk Management snap-in can be used to manage hard disk drives and their volumes and partitions. This tool can create, remove, and format disk volumes or partitions with any of the Microsoft file systems, including the *File Allocation Table (FAT), FAT32,* and the *New Technology File System (NTFS)*. The actions supported include the capability of changing basic disks to dynamic disks and back again as well as to create and format fault-tolerant disk volumes. The effects applied from using the Disk Management tool are immediate and can be applied without the need for a system restart.

The specific actions available on the Disk Management snap-in are described in the following sections.

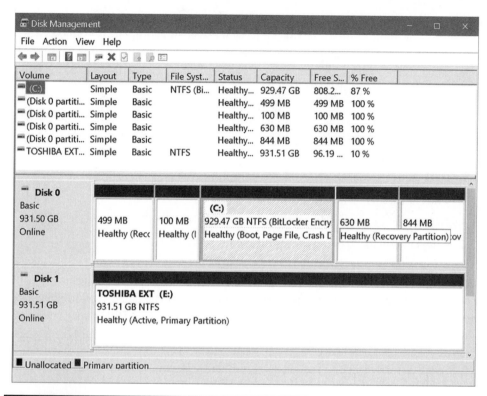

Volume	Layout	Type	File Syst...	Status	Capacity	Free S...	% Free
▬ (C:)	Simple	Basic	NTFS (Bi...	Healthy...	929.47 GB	808.2...	87 %
▬ (Disk 0 partiti...	Simple	Basic		Healthy...	499 MB	499 MB	100 %
▬ (Disk 0 partiti...	Simple	Basic		Healthy...	100 MB	100 MB	100 %
▬ (Disk 0 partiti...	Simple	Basic		Healthy...	630 MB	630 MB	100 %
▬ (Disk 0 partiti...	Simple	Basic		Healthy...	844 MB	844 MB	100 %
▬ TOSHIBA EXT...	Simple	Basic	NTFS	Healthy...	931.51 GB	96.19 ...	10 %

FIGURE 1.3-12   The Disk Management snap-in display

Drive Status   Disk Management shows the *drive status* of every initialized mass storage device in your system, making it handy for troubleshooting. Hopefully, you'll see each drive listed as "Healthy." The following is a list of the possible drive statuses.

- **Unallocated**   The disk has no file system or has a file system that is not recognized by Windows (such as a Linux- or macOS-specific file system).
- **Active**   The disk partition used to boot the system.
- **Foreign drive**   Shown when you move a dynamic disk to another system.
- **Formatting**   Shown while you're formatting a drive.
- **Failed**   The disk is damaged or corrupt; you've probably lost some data.
- **Online**   The disk is healthy and communicating properly with the computer.
- **Offline**   The disk is either corrupt or having communication problems.

A newly installed drive is set as a basic disk; there's nothing wrong with basic disks, though you'll miss out on some handy features.

Mounting   You can use Disk Management to mount a volume to an empty folder. This is helpful if you want to access an additional drive through an existing folder instead of as an additional drive letter. For example, a drive containing photos could be mounted into an empty folder called Photos that is a subfolder of your Pictures folder. A folder that is used to mount a volume is known as a *mount point*.

Follow these steps to create a mount point:

1. In Disk Management, right-click the volume you want to mount and select Change Drive Letter and Paths.
2. Click Add.
3. Click Browse.
4. Navigate to the empty folder you want to use or click New Folder to create a folder.
5. After clicking the folder to use for the mount point, click OK.

Initializing   A drive that has not been previously connected to Disk Management must be initialized before use in your system, even if it has been formatted and contains data. Don't worry; initialization in "Disk Management speak" simply means that Disk Management identifies the drive and what its role is, such as whether it is part of a software RAID array or a spanned volume. No data is harmed. A drive is listed as Unknown until it is initialized. To initialize the disk drive, right-click it and select Initialize Disk.

Extending, Shrinking, and Splitting Partitions   Disk Management can be used to increase or decrease the size of a volume without using dynamic disks. You can shrink a volume with available free space (though you can't shrink it by the whole amount, based on the location of unmovable sectors such as the MBR), and you can expand volumes by adding unallocated space on the same drive.

To reduce the size of a volume, right-click it and select Shrink Volume from the pop-up menu. Disk Management calculates how much the volume can "shrink" and then lets you choose the size reduction (up to that amount). Extending volumes is equally straightforward; right-click the volume, select Extend Volume, and indicate the amount you wish to add.

EXAM TIP   Should you encounter a question on the CompTIA A+ Core 2 (220-1102) exam that references "splitting" a disk partition, remember that there is no specific "splitting" option available on the Disk Management tool. What this is referring to is turning one partition into two. This requires the deletion of the partition to be divided and the creation of two new partitions in its place. So, if you see "splitting" on the exam, this is what CompTIA means.

Assigning/Changing Drive Letters Drive letters are assigned automatically by Windows when fixed or removable storage drives are connected. You can see the drive letters assigned to existing drives using Disk Management, and you can also change them. Use the New Simple Volume Wizard to assign a drive letter to a volume when you create it. To change the drive letter used by an existing volume, right-click it and choose Change Drive Letter and Paths.

 CAUTION When you change a drive letter, make sure that any apps using that drive letter for program or data storage are configured to use the new drive letter; otherwise, they will fail.

Adding Drives A drive that already has a file system recognized by Windows, such as an external USB hard disk or thumb drive or a flash memory card, is automatically recognized by Disk Management and assigned a drive letter.

However, a hard drive that has not been connected to the system before must first be initialized. Then it can be partitioned if it has no recognized file system.

Adding Arrays Dynamic disks can't be used as boot disks, but they support the following types of drive arrays (also known as dynamic disk volume types) you can create with Disk Management:

- **Spanned** The capacities of two or more disks are added together. Equivalent to just a bunch of disks (JBOD) hardware array.
- **Striped** Data is written across two drives to enhance speed. This is a software version of a RAID 0 hardware array.
- **Mirrored** Data is written to two drives at the same time, so if one drive fails, the array can be rebuilt from the copy on the other drive. This is a software version of a RAID 1 array.
- **RAID 5** Data and parity (recovery) information is written across three or more drives, so the array can be rebuilt if one disk fails. This is a software version of a RAID 5 hardware array.

To create any of these arrays, you start with empty or backed-up disks (existing contents will be wiped out during the creation process). Right-click the first drive to add to the array, select the type, and add additional drives to the array. After formatting the array, specify a drive letter or mount point and then convert the disks to dynamic disks when prompted. In Disk Management, each array is color-coded and identified as the type of array (mirror, spanned, or striped).

EXAM TIP Be sure to know the differences among spanned, striped, mirrored, and RAID 5 arrays in Disk Management.

Task Scheduler

Windows uses Task Scheduler to schedule its own automatic maintenance, and you can use its powerful options to create your own tasks or modify existing schedules. The Task Scheduler can be accessed on the MMC or by running taskschd.msc in the Run box or at a command prompt. Among other useful settings, each task has *triggers, actions,* and *conditions* (see Figure 1.3-13) that, respectively, define when it runs, what it does, and criteria that must be met before it runs. The Windows default overnight maintenance schedules are fine for most of us—but they might be no good for users on the night shift.

 EXAM TIP Task Scheduler illustrates why you need to know executable names and command-line options for common utilities. This is how a task action specifies the options a utility needs to run without user input.

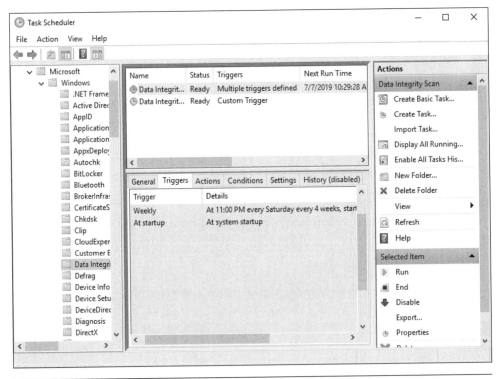

FIGURE 1.3-13 Viewing Task Scheduler's Triggers tab

Device Manager

The Device Manager, which can be accessed several different ways, is actually an extension of the MMC that provides consolidated access to the hardware components and devices installed on a Windows system. It provides a single point for configuring and managing hardware devices, including such tasks as setting options, installing and updating device drivers, and troubleshooting possible device and resource conflicts. An example of the Device Manager's display is shown in Figure 1.3-14.

The Device Manager can be accessed using a variety of methods, including from the Control Panel, on the Power User menu, using the Run command box, from the MMC or the Computer Management consoles, or on a command prompt with the command devmgmt.msc.

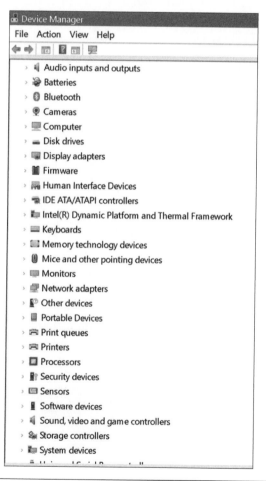

FIGURE 1.3-14   The Device Manager lists all installed hardware on a Windows system.

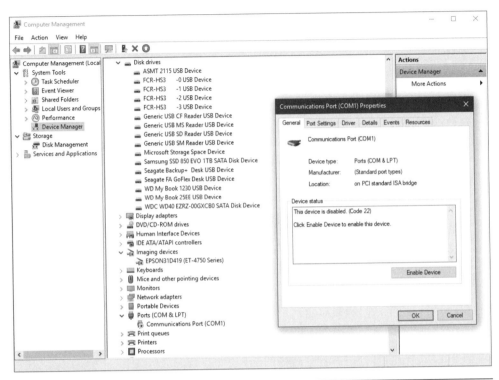

FIGURE 1.3-15   Device Manager window and device properties in Computer Management

 EXAM TIP   A downward-pointing arrow on (or next to) a device in the Device Manager means that the device has been disabled.

Use the Device Manager to view the status of system components and connected devices. You can use it to troubleshoot problem devices such as the disabled COM port in Figure 1.3-15. You can also update or roll back drivers, see power usage for USB devices, and view events for a particular device.

 EXAM TIP   Use Device Manager's Roll Back Driver feature (on the Driver tab of a device's Properties dialog box) to use a possible known-good driver if a driver update causes problems.

Certificate Manager

The Certificate Manager (certmgr.exe) is used to manage, import, export, or request digital certificates for a user, the system, or a service. Certificates are a key component in authentication processes and the exchange of data and information between network nodes.

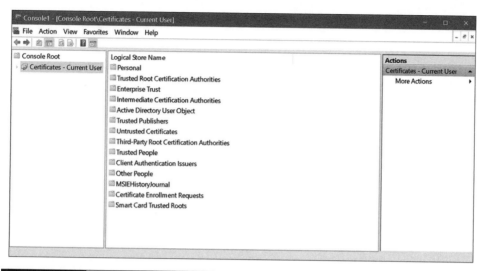

FIGURE 1.3-16   The Certificate Manager displayed in the MMC

As shown in Figure 1.3-16, the Certificate Manager can be accessed in the MMC. It can also be executed from the Run command box or at a command prompt with *certmgr.msc*. The Certificate Manager lists the certificate categories as folders for the level chosen, which in Figure 1.3-16 is Personal. Each of the folders, when selected, displays the certificate's listing information, which includes who the certificate is issued to, issued by, its expiration date, and its intended purpose.

Local Users and Groups

The Windows Pro, Pro for Workstations, and Enterprise editions of Windows 10 and Windows 11 include the Local Users and Groups tool (see Figure 1.3-17), a more powerful tool for working with user accounts.

To add a group, right-click a blank spot in the Groups folder, select New Group, and enter a group name and description in the New Group dialog box. Click Add below the member list to open a dialog box that you can use to add multiple *object* types, such as user accounts, computers, and even other groups (see Figure 1.3-18).

You can also add or remove group membership through the user's properties. Just open the user's folder, right-click the user, select Properties, click the Member Of tab, and click Add below the group list.

 EXAM TIP   Local Users and Groups is not available in the Home edition of Windows.

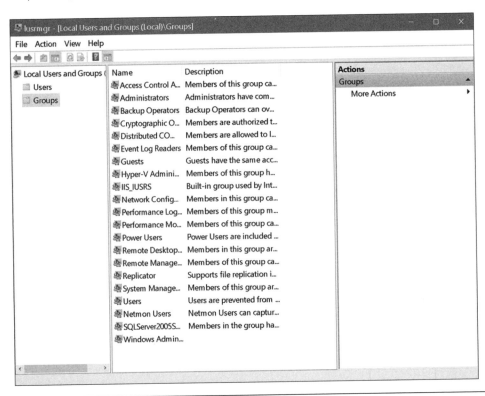

FIGURE 1.3-17   The Local Users and Groups tool of Windows 10/11

FIGURE 1.3-18   Creating a new local group and selecting users in Windows 10/11

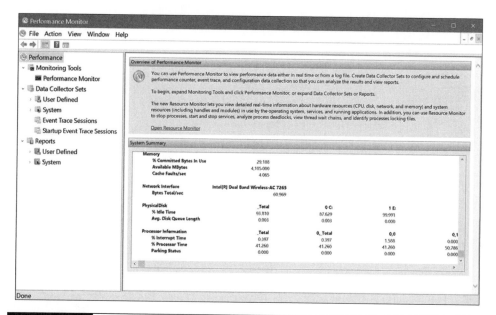

FIGURE 1.3-19   Initial Performance Monitor display

Performance Monitor

The Performance Monitor (perfmon.exe) monitors system performance and presents the data gathered in real time or as a log file. This is essentially a troubleshooting tool that can be accessed through the Computer Management console, as a part of the MMC, or from a command line or the Run command box using the command perfmon or perfmon.msc, respectively.

 NOTE   The Resource Monitor, which can be started from the Performance Monitor, is a different-yet-related tool. See the section "Resource Monitor" later in this objective.

When you open the Performance Monitor, it displays the Performance screen, which is a two-part main section that contains an overview of the tool and a system summary of the memory, network, disk, and processor information of the system (see Figure 1.3-19).

In what may seem redundant, within the Performance Monitor is the Monitoring Tools section, which typically includes only one item, Performance Monitor (see Figure 1.3-19 or Figure 1.3-20). This Performance Monitor is a graphing tool that plots real-time data of *objects*, which are system components such as memory, physical disk, processors, and networks. The initial display of the Performance Monitor is a graph of the data collected in a *counter* that tracks a specific object in real time. The default object is % Processor Time (see Figure 1.3-20).

Counters   By default, the Performance Monitor has only one counter selected, but additional counters can be added to the graph by clicking the green plus sign (+) in the toolbar at the top of the graph or pressing CTRL-I to display the Add Counters window (shown in Figure 1.3-21).

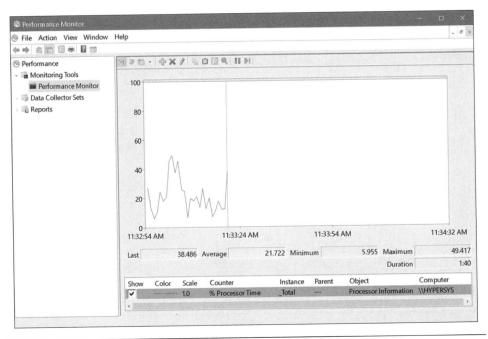

FIGURE 1.3-20   Performance Monitor displaying % Processor Time

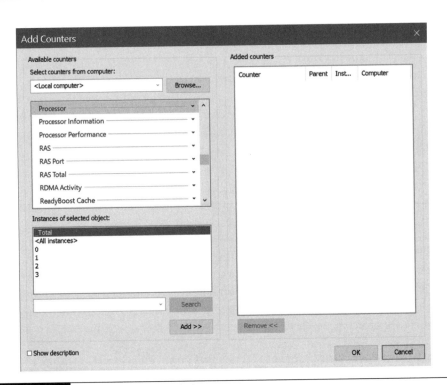

FIGURE 1.3-21   The Add Counters window

TABLE 1.3-1   Examples of Performance Monitor Counters

Counter	Type	Use
% Processor Time	Processor utilization	Percentage of elapsed time the processor is/was busy
% User Time	Processor utilization	Percentage of elapsed time the processor spent executing in user mode
% Idle Time	Physical disk	Percentage of time the disk was idle (no pending disk requests from the OS)
Avg. Disk sec/Read or Avg. Disk sec/Write	Physical disk	Measures the latency of a disk with the average time a disk transfer takes to complete
Available MBytes	Memory	The total amount of available memory on the system
Bytes Total/sec	Network interface	The number of bytes transferred through a network adapter

The Add Counters window provides an extensive list of counters that can be selected and added to the graph. After a counter is added to the graph, its properties (color, width, scales, and so on) can be changed by right-clicking the line. To highlight a particular line on the graph, use CTRL-H to toggle the emphasis on or off.

Table 1.3-1 describes a few examples from the extensive list of counters available in the Performance Monitor.

Data Collectors   In the navigation pane (left pane) of the Performance Monitor are other tools that can be used to define data collector sets and reports that you create and wish to use in the future. The *data collector sets* are groups of counters you can use for a report. A data collector set, once defined, continues to gather data for use in a report. The Reports option can then be used to display the results of a data collector set (see Figure 1.3-22). Data collector sets also allow you to schedule when a collector is to be active.

There are four types of data collector sets:

- **System (performance) counters**   Collects data by polling an event over a specific period of time.
- **Event traces**   Collects data on specific event occurrences.
- **Startup event trace sessions**   Captures information on events relating to system configuration that occur during system startup.
- **User-defined**   Collects data on performance and/or events as defined by the user.

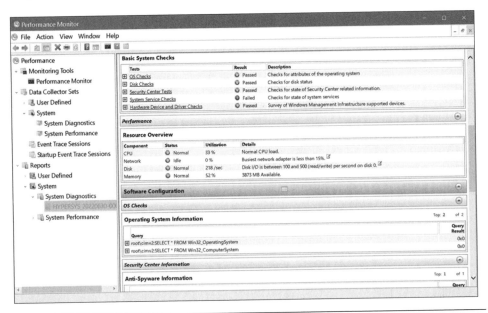

FIGURE 1.3-22   A sample Performance Monitor report of a data collector set

Group Policy Editor

The Group Policy Editor (aka the Local Group Policy Editor) is an MMC snap-in available on the Windows Pro, Pro for Workstations, and Enterprise editions that provides administrators with a tool for managing group policies within Group Policy Objects (GPOs). As shown in Figure 1.3-23, the features of this tool are divided into two primary configuration sections: Computer Configuration and User Configuration. The Computer Configuration contains the settings that are or can be applied to computer systems. The User Configuration section contains the settings that are or can be applied to one user account or a group of user accounts. Group policies are applied when the OS initializes or refreshes.

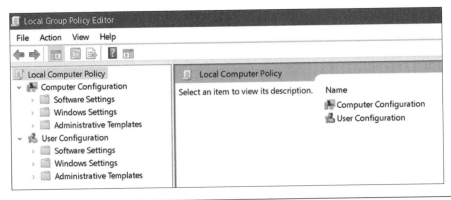

FIGURE 1.3-23   An example of the display on the Group Policy Editor

EXAM TIP   The policies and settings in the Computer Configuration section take precedence over those in the User Configuration section.

The settings and policies in the Computer Configuration section set general policies for how a computer and its operating system function. These policies apply to all parts of a computer and are the same regardless of the privileges or rights of the user account logged on to the computer.

The settings and policies in the User Configuration section control specific OS behaviors as well as settings for desktop, security, applications, user logon and logoff scripts, and more. These policies are applied when a user logs on to a computer and may be reapplied using a loopback process or a periodic refresh. Some user settings, such as those in the Software Settings folder, are applied to users wherever they log on.

EXAM TIP   The Group Policy Editor is only available on the Windows Pro, Pro for Workstations, and Enterprise editions, which means it is not available on the Windows Home edition.

The Group Policy Editor is used to create, manage, and remove group policies at both centralized and local levels. At a centralized level, which is typically in an Active Directory environment, group policies are defined on a domain controller, which provides a single point of definition for a variety of settings that may apply to some or all nodes on a network. On a single computer, group policies can be configured using the Local Group Policy Editor from the Control Panel.

Using the Group Policy Editor, an administrator can create and manage GPOs, enable or disable computer and user settings, and create and apply scripts for performing functions not otherwise available.

Opening the Group Policy Editor   There are several different ways to open the Group Policy Editor, which is actually named the Local Group Policy Editor on the Windows editions that support it. There are no default shortcuts for this tool, but you can access and open this tool using one of the following methods:

- **MMC**   To open the Local Group Policy Editor from the MMC, it must first be added to the console using the following steps:
  1. With the MMC open, click the File menu and choose Add/Remove Snap-In.
  2. Find Local Group Policy Editor, which may be listed as Local Computer Policy instead, in the Available Snap-Ins list. Select it and click the Add button between the two panes to move it to the Selected Snap-Ins list.
  3. Click the OK button to add it to the console.
  4. The console should now list this snap-in, as illustrated in Figure 1.3-24.

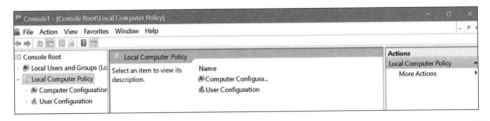

FIGURE 1.3-24   The MMC showing the Local Computer Policy snap-in added

- **Settings**   Use the following steps to open the Local Group Policy Editor from the Setting page:
  1. Press WIN-I to open the Settings page.
  2. Enter **edit group policy** in the Find a Setting search box at the top of the page.
  3. Click the Edit Group Policy tag that displays to open the Local Group Policy Editor.

 NOTE   The process outlined for opening the Local Computer Policy Editor from the Setting page can also be used to open it from the Control Panel.

- **Run command box**   Use the following steps to open the Local Group Policy Editor from the Run command box:
  1. Press WIN-R to open the Run command box.
  2. Enter **gpedit.msc** and click OK.

There are many other ways to open the Local Group Policy Editor, including using Windows Search, a command prompt, or a PowerShell prompt.

Administrative Templates   Within each of the two sections of the Group Policy Editor is a folder of administrative templates. An *administrative template* is a policy-setting XML document that can be enabled or applied to provide a control or feature to a service or an application. All Microsoft applications, such as the Office applications, have a set of application templates, generally added to the Group Policy Editor by default. Many other companies provide application templates for their applications as well. Figure 1.3-25 shows the detail of an administrative template that allows non-administrative users to add device drivers.

 ADDITIONAL RESOURCES   To learn more in-depth information on Windows policies, navigate to https://www.microsoft.com/en-us/download/details .aspx?id=25250 and download "Group Policy Settings Reference for Windows and Windows Server."

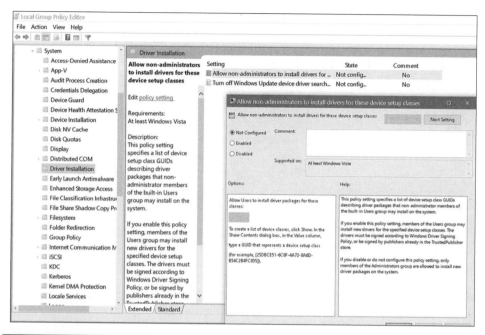

The details of an administrative template

Additional Windows Tools

The CompTIA A+ Core 2 exam objectives list some additional, perhaps less-often used tools that a system administrator, and a certified A+ technician, should know and have a basic understanding of when and how each is used. The following sections provide a description of each of these tools, its purpose, and an example of how it is used.

System Information

The *System Information* tool, aka the MSInfo utility, is technically the program msinfo32.exe (no, there isn't an msinfo64.exe). This utility displays information about a computer, which can then be used to diagnose a problem.

The easiest way to run this tool is to open the Run command box (WIN-R) and enter **msinfo32.exe**. The System Information program displays a great deal of information about the computer, an example of which is shown in Figure 1.3-26.

The msinfo32.exe program display includes the following data:

- Windows and BIOS/UEFI versions
- Hardware manufacturer, model, and type
- CPU version and manufacturer

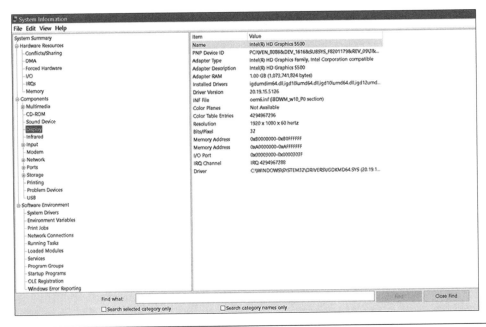

FIGURE 1.3-26   An example of the opening screen of the System Information tool

- Boot device
- Memory and system resources
- Page file location
- Location and time zone
- User name in a domain
- Hardware resources by category

The data displayed by the System Information tool can be saved as an .nfo file, which can be viewed in the System Information program, or as a text file. Comparing versions of the system information data can be handy for diagnosing a problem.

Resource Monitor

The Resource Monitor is a Windows utility application that can be used to view the presence and current usage and health of a computer's hardware resources, such as the CPU, disk drives, and memory. This tool can be used to see how the system resources are being used statistically or graphically. Figure 1.3-27 shows an example of the Resource Monitor's display.

The Resource Monitor can be opened from the Performance Monitor, as mentioned earlier, from the Task Manager, or from the Run command box or a command prompt using resmon.exe. When the Resource Monitor opens, it starts monitoring and recording

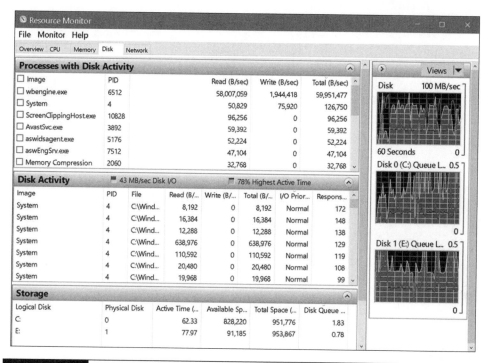

The Resource Monitor showing the Disk tab display

the system resources and their activities. The record of a monitoring session, which can be started and stopped on the Monitor menu item, can be later compared to another recorded session for diagnostic review.

System Configuration

The System Configuration utility (also known as msconfig.exe) is used to edit and trouble-shoot startup processes and services. The System Configuration tool is primarily used for managing the startup process for Windows, but it can also be used for troubleshooting system performance issues.

There are two ways to open the System Configuration tool:

- Enter **msconfig** at the Start menu and click the System Configuration App result.
- Use WIN-R to open the Run command box and enter **msconfig**.

The System Configuration utility (shown in Figure 1.3-28) offers a number of handy features, distributed across the following tabs:

- **General** For the next boot, select a normal startup with all programs and services, a diagnostic startup with only basic devices and services, or a custom boot called selective startup.

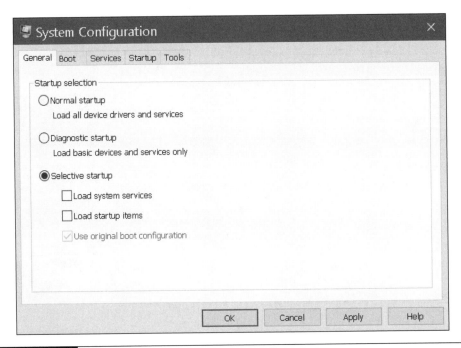

FIGURE 1.3-28   Windows 10 System Configuration utility

- **Boot**   See every copy of Windows you have installed, set a default OS, or delete an OS from the boot menu. You can set up a safe boot or adjust options like the number of cores or amount of memory to use. While selected, Safe Boot will always start the system in *Safe mode* with minimal, generic, trusted drivers for troubleshooting purposes.
- **Services**   Enable or disable services running on your system.
- **Startup**   In Windows 10 and 11, this feature is moved to the Task Manager. A link is provided.
- **Tools**   Lists many of the tools and utilities available elsewhere in Windows, including Event Viewer, Performance Monitor, Command Prompt, and so on.

Disk Cleanup

If you haven't already, at some point you may see a Windows system message to the effect that you've run out of disk storage space. This message, typically "Low Disk Space," essentially translates to something like "Get rid of the files you don't need on the hard disk." In other words, you've run out of disk space on one or more hard disk drives on your system.

Windows users have a tool they can use to resolve this condition: the Windows Disk Cleanup tool. Not only does this tool help you open up space on a disk drive by removing old or unneeded files, but it can possibly increase the speed of the drive and improve application processing.

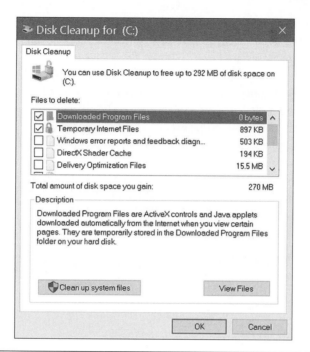

FIGURE 1.3-29   The Disk Cleanup dialog box

Like most of the tools in this section, you can run the cleanmgr.exe utility from a search or using the Run command box. Disk Cleanup first asks which disk drive you wish to "clean up." Then it scans the files on the drive chosen and presents a dialog box (see Figure 1.3-29) with the types or categories of files it's found for you to allow it to remove (or not remove; it's your choice). You also have the choice of compressing the files you wish to keep and reducing their impact on disk space.

 ADDITIONAL RESOURCES   To learn more about Disk Cleanup, go to https://support.microsoft.com and search for "Disk Cleanup."

Disk Defragment

A fragmented system drive can slow down many aspects of Windows, including boot, user profile loading, and application loading. Fragmentation takes place when a file cannot be stored in a single contiguous location on a drive but must be stored in sections at different locations on the drive. A drive that stores frequently changed files or temporary files, such as the system drive used by Windows, is more likely to be fragmented than a drive that has few changes to its contents. Optimizing the arrangement of files on a disk is done through a defragmentation process. However, Windows automatically defragments drives as needed, and defragmentation is not needed on solid-state drives, but you can run defragmentation manually if it becomes necessary.

To run defragmentation on a Windows system, search for "defrag" in the Start Search. Choose the result Defragment and Optimize Drives to display the Optimize Drives dialog box, shown in Figure 1.3-30. Disk Defragment can also be opened with the Command Prompt box (WIN-R) using the command dfrgui.exe.

The disk drives formatted with NTFS are listed in the Status box. Click the drive on which you wish to act and then choose either Analyze or Optimize to begin the action chosen. The Analyze function looks at the disk and reports on its status. The Optimize function performs the disk defragmentation if the system deems this action may be required. When the defrag action ends, the current status of the drive will reflect "OK (0% fragmented)."

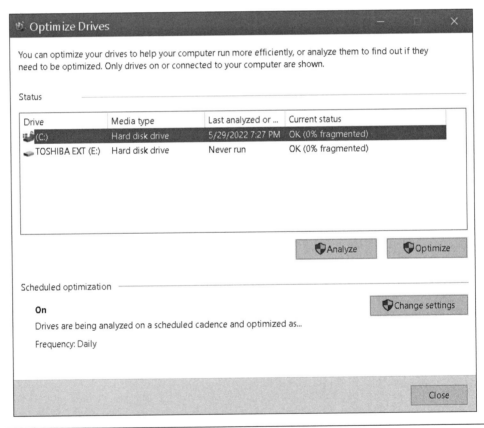

FIGURE 1.3-30   The Optimize Drives dialog box

Registry Editor

The Windows Registry (regedit.exe) is a database that stores the Windows hardware, software, and user configuration data in the form of keys and values. The Registry Editor, shown in Figure 1.3-31, is used to view, archive, and modify Windows Registry settings when necessary. The settings and values stored in the Registry database are typically created, changed, or removed through actions taken in the Control Panel, Settings, or by individual applications. The need to use the Registry Editor is typically necessary only when no other method is available to add or correct a setting.

 EXAM TIP   The Registry Editor doesn't have an Undo command, and modifications to the Registry database, once saved, are permanent. Therefore, it's a best practice to create a backup of the Registry before altering any of its data.

To open the Registry Editor, enter **regedit** into the Run command box (WIN-R) or use the Start Search and enter **registry editor**. The initial view of the Registry Editor is shown in Figure 1.3-31.

After you find the target Registry key in the Registry Editor window, you can double-click the name of the Registry key and then change its value data to make changes to the target Registry.

 EXAM TIP   You should know the five main keys of the Registry (as shown in Figure 1.3-31):
- HKEY_CLASSES_ROOT
- HKEY_CURRENT_USER
- HKEY_LOCAL_MACHINE
- HKEY_USERS
- HKEY_CURRENT_CONFIG

FIGURE 1.3-31   The Registry Editor window

REVIEW

Objective 1.3: Given a scenario, use features and tools of the Microsoft Windows 10 operating system (OS)

- The Windows 10 OS provides a variety of administrative, configuration, and diagnostic tools that can be used for managing a standalone PC or network nodes.
- The Task Manager (taskmgr) is used to manage applications, processes, and services running on the computer, including system environment tools and user information.
- The Microsoft Management Console (MMC; mmc.exe) supports snap-in tools used to administer and configure the hardware, software, and network elements of a Windows system.
- The Event Viewer (eventvwr.msc) snap-in has four sections: Overview, Summary of Administrative Events, Recently Viewed Nodes, and Log Summary.
- The Disk Management (diskmgmt.msc) snap-in is used to add or change drives or arrays. RAID 5 arrays can be spanned, striped, and mirrored.
- The Task Scheduler (taskschd.msc) snap-in is used to schedule tasks using triggers, actions, and conditions.
- The Device Manager (devmgmt.msc) provides a single point for configuring and managing hardware devices and should be the first tool used to diagnose hardware issues.
- The Certificate Manager (certmgr.exe) is used to manage, import, export, and request digital certificates for a user, the system, or a service.
- The Local Users and Groups (lusrmgr.msc), used to set or change policies, is available only on Windows Pro, Pro for Workstations, and Enterprise and is not available on Windows Home.
- The Performance Monitor (perfmon.exe) monitors system performance and presents the data gathered in a real-time graph or in a log file.
- The Group Policy Editor (gpedit.msc) is used to administer policies at both centralized and local levels. The Group Policy Editor is not available on the Windows Home edition.
- The System Information (msinfo32.exe) tool displays information about a computer, which can then be used to diagnose a problem.
- The Resource Monitor (resmon.exe) is used to view the presence and current usage and health of a computer's hardware resources.
- The System Configuration utility (msconfig.exe) is used to edit and troubleshoot startup processes and services.
- The Disk Cleanup (cleanmgr.exe) tool is used to remove old or unneeded files.
- The Disk Defragment (dfrgui.exe) can be used to defrag and optimize disk drives.
- The Registry Editor (regedit.exe) is used to view, archive, and modify Windows Registry settings. The Registry's five main keys are HKEY_CLASSES_ROOT, HKEY_CURRENT_USER, HKEY_LOCAL_MACHINE, HKEY_USERS, and HKEY_CURRENT_CONFIG.

1.3 QUESTIONS

1. Some Task Manager tasks or services can be executed from a command prompt. Which of the following commands can be used to execute or kill a task? (Choose two.)

   A. net start <service>

   B. net stop <service>

   C. net kill <service>

   D. net execute <service>

   E. taskstart <service>

2. Which of the following is not one of the four sections of the Event Viewer?

   A. Summary of Administrative Events

   B. Recently Viewed Nodes

   C. Log Summary

   D. Future Events

3. Two primary sections are available when the Local Group Policy Editor first opens: the Computer Configuration and which of the following?

   A. User Configuration

   B. Local Configuration

   C. Group Configuration

   D. Network Configuration

4. What system utility should be used to investigate a failed device that is causing problems for a Windows system?

   A. Device Manager

   B. Configuration Manager

   C. System Information

   D. Disk Management

5. Which of the following is not one of the five main keys of the Windows Registry?

   A. HKEY_CLASSES_ROOT

   B. HKEY_CURRENT_USERS

   C. HKEY_LOCAL_MACHINE

   D. HKEY_USERS

   E. HKEY_CURRENT_CONFIG

1.3 ANSWERS

1. **A B**   These two commands can be run from a command prompt to execute or kill a task.

2. **D**   The Event Viewer cannot anticipate events that may occur.

3. **A**   The User Configuration section over which the Computer Configuration section takes precedence.

4. **A**   The Device Manager should be used to investigate device issues.

5. **B**   The Registry key for the configuration and settings for the current user is HKEY_CURRENT_USER.

Objective 1.4 Given a scenario, use the appropriate Microsoft Windows 10 Control Panel utility

NOTE   It may seem that some of the apps and features move around in the discussion. From version to version an app may move from the Control Panel to the Settings app or appear on both. The focus in this objective is on the Control Panel, but you'll see an occasional reference to the Settings app. In this instance, most likely the icon for an app is on one or the other but selects the app from the other.

Although the Settings app in Windows 10 has replaced many of the traditional Control Panel utilities, the Control Panel is still used for much of the system management functions of Windows 10. This objective covers the Control Panel utilities you need to understand—what each is, when it's used, and how it works—for the CompTIA A+ Core 2 (220-1102) exam.

NOTE   These Control Panel functions can also be found using the Start Search function.

EXAM TIP   The CompTIA A+ 220-1102 exam assumes the Large icon view with large icons, so you should do what every tech does, which is switch from the Category view to the Large icon view, shown in Figure 1.4-1. The discussions in this objective assume you are using the Large icon view.

FIGURE 1.4-1 The Large icon view of the Windows Control Panel

Internet Options

CompTIA refers to *Internet Options,* which is in fact the name of an icon on the Control Panel, but the dialog box that it opens is named Internet Properties, as shown in Figure 1.4-2. Therefore, if you cannot make the configuration changes you need in your browser, make them in Internet Properties.

 NOTE You cannot configure non-Microsoft browsers with Internet Properties.

The Internet Properties dialog box includes the following tabs:

- **General** Set your home page, startup options, browsing history, and appearance settings.
- **Security** Set security levels for websites in different zones (Internet, Local intranet, and so on).
- **Privacy** Configure the pop-up blocker as well as set up InPrivate browsing, per-site settings, and cookie management.
- **Content** This tab contains features associated more with Internet Explorer than the Edge or other browsers. You won't see any questions on this tab on the exam.
- **Connections** Set up Internet, VPN, LAN, and proxy settings.
- **Programs** Select default programs for browsing, HTML editing, and file associations.
- **Advanced** Configure accessibility, graphics acceleration, multimedia, and other settings.

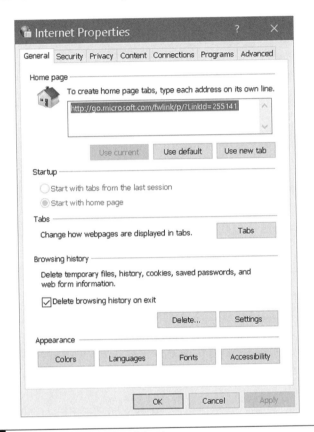

EXAM TIP   Know how to access Internet Options on the Control Panel and how to use it to configure the various Internet Properties settings for a given scenario.

Devices and Printers

The Devices and Printers applet provides centralized viewing and management of computers, monitors, printers, and peripherals (see Figure 1.4-3). This tool allows you to interact with external devices and some internal devices connected to a Windows system. However, the configuration and interaction options available through Devices and Printers are dependent on the drivers and support available for each connected device. The devices (and printers) that have full support for this tool can be completely managed, and those with little or limited support will have a matching level of manageability.

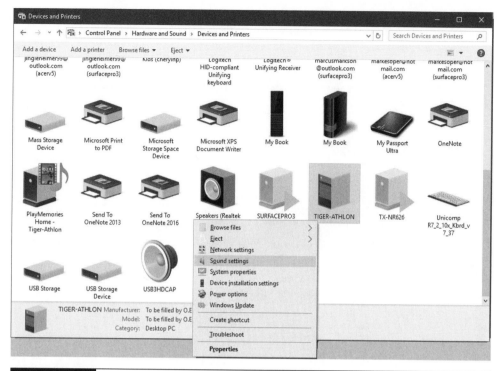

FIGURE 1.4-3   Using Devices and Printers to access computer settings

 NOTE   If Windows fails to automatically detect a newly connected device or printer, use the corresponding toolbar option in the Devices and Printers applet to add or enable the device.

 EXAM TIP   Know how to add and manage a printer or peripheral device using Devices and Printers in a given scenario.

Programs and Features

Programs and Features (see Figure 1.4-4) is used to view and manage installed programs, uninstall or repair programs, and turn Windows features on and off. On the Windows 10 Control Panel, this tool is accessed through the Programs and Features icon or by using the Apps option on the Settings window to open the Apps & Features dialog box. Figure 1.4-4 shows the initial display of the Programs and Features applet, and Figure 1.4-5 shows an example of the Settings | Apps & Features window.

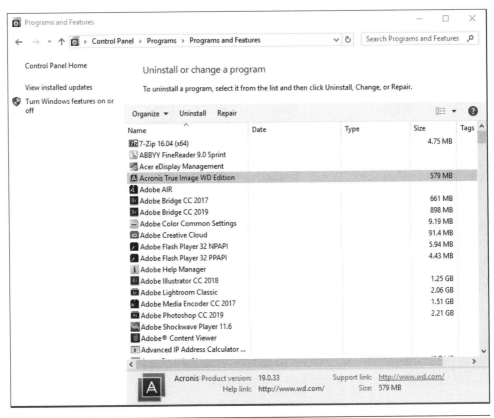

FIGURE 1.4-4   Using Programs and Features to uninstall or repair an app

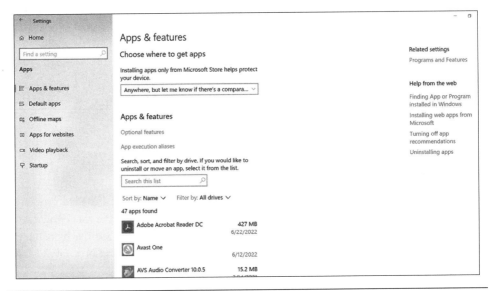

FIGURE 1.4-5   The Settings | Apps & Features window

The primary display of the Apps & Features window shows the installed applications and services on the computer. To remove or uninstall one of the items, right-click it and choose Uninstall.

There are two other links to functions on the Apps & Features page:

- View installed updates
- Turn Windows features on or off

The first option opens a register that contains a list of the updates that have been applied to the system. The second option is used to enable and disable specific Windows OS features as needed. Figure 1.4-6 shows an example of the Windows Features dialog box.

 NOTE Any installed program not listed on the Programs and Features dialog box may not have been specifically written for the installed version of Windows and must be uninstalled per its instructions.

FIGURE 1.4-6 The Windows Features dialog box accessed through the Turn Windows Features On or Off link on the Control Panel's Programs and Features app

Network and Sharing Center

The Network and Sharing Center applet, shown in Figure 1.4-7, allows you to perform the following actions:

- **Set up a new connection or network** This link displays four separate actions:
  - **Connect to the Internet** Configure a new connection to the Internet via a broadband or dial-up service.
  - **Set up a new network** Configure a new router or access point.
  - **Manually connect to a wireless network** Set up a hidden connection or create a new wireless profile.
  - **Connect to a workplace** Configure a VPN or dial-up connection to a workplace.
- **Change adapter settings** Displays an icon for each installed network adapter. Clicking an adapter opens its status dialog box.
- **Change advanced sharing settings** Windows generates a separate profile for each network in use. The settings of each profile can be modified on this option.
- **Media streaming options** Use this action to turn on or turn off media streaming from your computer to other computers and vice versa.
- **Troubleshoot problems** This action links to the Troubleshooting page in Settings.

 EXAM TIP To see the status of your network, choose Status from the left-side navigation bar on the Network and Internet page of the Settings app.

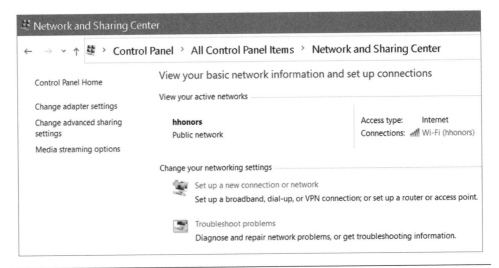

FIGURE 1.4-7 The Network and Sharing Center

System

The Windows 10 OS replaced the Control Panel System applet with a Control Panel System link that opens the About system page of the Settings app (see Figure 1.4-8). The About page displays configuration and specification information on the system, including details on the CPU, RAM, and Windows OS.

 NOTE When you open the Settings applet from the Start menu or from a command prompt, it opens with the Display settings and not the About page.

The About page displays information concerning the following system components:

- **Security status** A statement immediately beneath the "About" heading that indicates the security status of the system.
- **Device specifications** This block of information contains the following elements:
  - **Device name** The user-assigned identity for the computer.
  - **Processor** The technical specifications of the CPU.
  - **Installed RAM** The amount of RAM on the computer, typically in GB.
  - **Device ID** A string generated by the device bus driver.
  - **Product ID** A code generated by the computer that describes the installation. A device has only one device ID, but it may not be unique.
  - **System type** The OS and processor compatibilities (that is, 32- or 64-bit system).
  - **Pen and touch** Indicates support for pen (stylus) and touch (touch screen) systems installed.

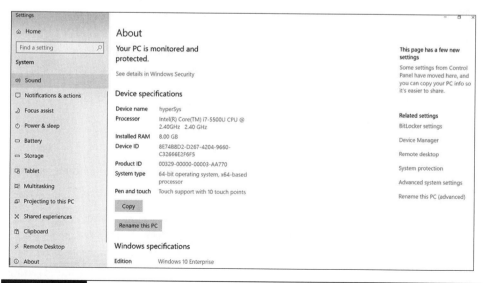

FIGURE 1.4-8 The About page of the Settings applet

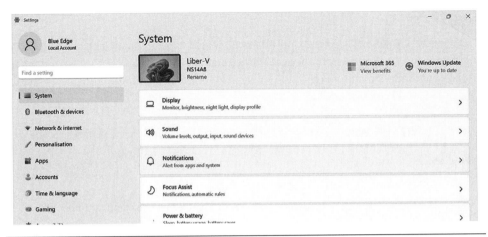

FIGURE 1.4-9   An example of the Windows 11 Settings applet page

- **Windows specifications:**
  - **Edition**   The Windows OS edition.
  - **Version**   The version to which the OS has been updated.
  - **Installed on**   The date the OS was installed on this computer originally.
  - **OS build**   This number represents a compilation of the OS at a given point in time.
  - **Experience**   The Windows Feature Experience Pack is a mysterious collection of Windows features that Microsoft doesn't wish to define specifically. However, this item identifies the version of the Experience Pack installed.

The Settings | System | About page also includes buttons for copying the content of each specification area and a button you can use to change the computer name.

 NOTE   Windows 11 has a significantly changed Settings applet, an example of which is shown in Figure 1.4-9. Most of the same functions, plus a couple more, are accessible through this page and its navigation pane.

Settings Options

As shown earlier in Figure 1.4-8, the navigation pane on the left side of the About page contains links to several Settings specifications and action features:

- **Display**   Manage the settings for brightness using a slide control and configure the Night Light settings, configure High Dynamic Range (HDR) color settings, set the resolution, range, scale, and orientation of the display, and set up multiple displays.
- **Sound**   Configure the settings for input and output as well as customize sound settings.

- **Notifications & actions**   Specify whether you wish to have notifications displayed on the Desktop, which notification you wish to see, and the applications that can send notifications.

- **Focus assist**   This feature is an extension of the Notifications & Actions settings where you can set the rules to allow or minimize interruptions from notifications.

- **Power & sleep**   You can use these settings to specify when the display and the PC are to reduce power consumption and be put into a sleep mode.

- **Battery**   This is obviously a mobile device feature that sets the battery power level at which the battery saver is activated, provided it's enabled at all. You can also track the system's activity while it's on battery power only.

- **Storage**   Enable and configure the Storage Sense and Storage Spaces tools to automatically remove unnecessary files from storage media. You can also view storage stats on peripheral and remote drives, designate where new content is stored, optimize disk drives, and review backup options.

- **Tablet**   Another mobile device tool that can be used to control when tablet mode is enabled.

- **Multitasking**   Enable Snap windows, specify motion gestures, and configure the use of the timeline and virtual desktops.

- **Projecting to this PC**   Control the capability for a smartphone or another PC to project onto a PC's display.

- **Shared experiences**   Set up peer-to-peer sharing with authorized nearby or remote devices.

- **Clipboard**   Configure the Clipboard to keep multiple accessible images, synchronize Clipboard content across multiple devices, and clear the Clipboard.

- **Remote Desktop**   Enable or disable Remote Desktop and authorize remote systems that can interface.

 EXAM TIP   You should know when and why each of these features is used for the Core 2 exam.

Windows Defender Firewall

The Windows Defender Firewall provides separate settings for private networks and guest or public networks. The Windows Defender Firewall is the Microsoft proprietary firewall software for protecting Windows operating systems. Like most firewall software, Windows Defender Firewall protects a Windows system by allowing or rejecting requests for access to applications.

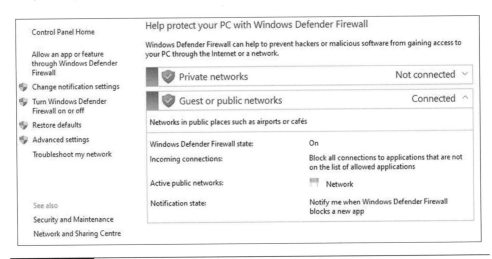

Control Panel Home

Allow an app or feature through Windows Defender Firewall

Change notification settings

Turn Windows Defender Firewall on or off

Restore defaults

Advanced settings

Troubleshoot my network

See also

Security and Maintenance

Network and Sharing Centre

Help protect your PC with Windows Defender Firewall

Windows Defender Firewall can help to prevent hackers or malicious software from gaining access to your PC through the Internet or a network.

Private networks — Not connected ⌄

Guest or public networks — Connected ⌃

Networks in public places such as airports or cafés

Windows Defender Firewall state:	On
Incoming connections:	Block all connections to applications that are not on the list of allowed applications
Active public networks:	Network
Notification state:	Notify me when Windows Defender Firewall blocks a new app

FIGURE 1.4-10 The Windows Defender Firewall's configuration page

NOTE The Windows Defender Firewall, although sounding very similar, should not be confused with the legacy Windows Defender antivirus program.

You can access the Windows Defender Firewall through the Control Panel by clicking its icon, which opens the Windows Defender Firewall with Advanced Security page (see Figure 1.4-10). The Windows Defender Firewall can also be opened from the Run command box or at a command prompt with the command **control firewall.cpl**.

Cross-Reference

Objective 2.5 provides more information on the Windows Defender Firewall.

Mail (Microsoft Outlook)

The Mail icon on the Windows 10 Control Panel doesn't link to an electronic mail application (as it once did). Rather, it displays an action box (see Figure 1.4-11) with buttons for setting up e-mail accounts and directories for the Microsoft Outlook application, changing the settings for an Outlook user's mail-related files and directories, and configuring Outlook user profiles.

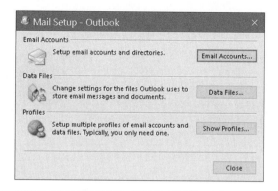

FIGURE 1.4-11 The action box displayed by the Mail (Microsoft Outlook) icon on the Windows 10 Control Panel

Sound

The Sound applet features a Playback tab for managing speakers and headset volume and balance (see Figure 1.4-12), a Recording tab for managing microphone volume and gain, a Sounds tab for selecting and modifying sound schemes (the sounds that play during events such as system startup or errors), and a Communications tab to specify what to do with sound volume during telephone calls. Click the Configure button to set up the selected device, the Set Default button to specify which device to use as the default, and the Properties button to tweak additional volume or other properties.

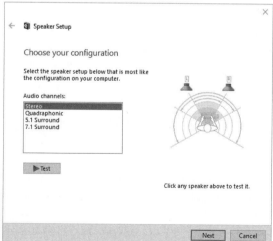

FIGURE 1.4-12 Selecting the speaker setup using the Configure button in the Sound applet

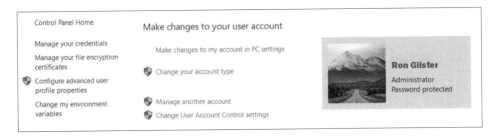

FIGURE 1.4-13   The User Accounts page in Control Panel

User Accounts

The User Accounts applet in the Control Panel (see Figure 1.4-13) enables you to manage your account and the accounts of others as well as to change User Account Control settings. You can also use the Accounts tool in Settings to manage only your account. As shown in Figure 1.4-13, you also have options to manage file encryption certificates, configure advanced user profile properties, and modify environmental variables related to your login account.

Device Manager

The Device Manager link in Control Panel displays the same Device Manager tool as discussed in Objective 1.3. The Device Manager provides specific information about the hardware of a computer system. Selecting a specific device from its device category provides you with the capability to enable or disable the device, verify its status, and manage its device drivers, if applicable.

Cross-Reference

To learn more about using Device Manager, see the "Device Manager" section in Objective 1.3.

Indexing Options

Indexing Options, accessed from the Control Panel, is all about the speed of searches for the most commonly accessed files and objects on your computer. By default, Indexing Options creates an index for the commonly accessed items and locations on your drives. These typically include files accessed offline, the elements of the Start menu, your user profile, and the browsing history of your web browser. Using the Indexing Options and the Advanced Options dialog boxes (see Figure 1.4-14), you can control what is indexed.

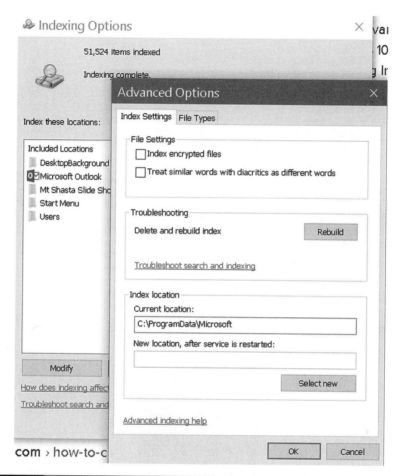

FIGURE 1.4-14   The Indexing Options and the Advanced Options dialog boxes

Administrative Tools

The Administrative Tools icon on the Control Panel opens the File Explorer Control Panel/Administrative Tools folder and the list of tools it includes (see Figure 1.4-15). This list is also available on the Start menu under the Windows Administrative Tools menu item (see Figure 1.4-16). Most of the tools listed are covered in context at some point in this book.

☐ Name	Date modified	Type	Size
Component Services	12/7/2019 1:09 AM	Shortcut	2 KB
Computer Management	12/7/2019 1:09 AM	Shortcut	2 KB
Defragment and Optimize D...	12/7/2019 1:09 AM	Shortcut	2 KB
DHCP	11/4/2020 12:31 AM	Shortcut	2 KB
Disk Cleanup	12/7/2019 1:09 AM	Shortcut	2 KB
Event Viewer	12/7/2019 1:09 AM	Shortcut	2 KB
iSCSI Initiator	12/7/2019 1:09 AM	Shortcut	2 KB
Local Security Policy	12/7/2019 1:10 AM	Shortcut	2 KB
ODBC Data Sources (32-bit)	12/7/2019 1:10 AM	Shortcut	2 KB
ODBC Data Sources (64-bit)	12/7/2019 1:09 AM	Shortcut	2 KB
Performance Monitor	12/7/2019 1:09 AM	Shortcut	2 KB
Print Management	12/6/2019 1:46 PM	Shortcut	2 KB
Recovery Drive	12/7/2019 1:09 AM	Shortcut	2 KB
Registry Editor	12/7/2019 1:09 AM	Shortcut	2 KB
Resource Monitor	12/7/2019 1:09 AM	Shortcut	2 KB
Services	12/7/2019 1:09 AM	Shortcut	2 KB
System Configuration	12/7/2019 1:09 AM	Shortcut	2 KB
System Information	12/7/2019 1:09 AM	Shortcut	2 KB
Task Scheduler	12/7/2019 1:09 AM	Shortcut	2 KB
Windows Defender Firewall ...	12/7/2019 1:08 AM	Shortcut	2 KB
Windows Memory Diagnostic	12/7/2019 1:09 AM	Shortcut	2 KB

FIGURE 1.4-15 The list of tools accessed via the Administrative Tools icon on the Control Panel

FIGURE 1.4-16 The list of tools under the Windows Administrative Tools menu item on the Start menu

File Explorer Options

File Explorer Options, also known as Folder Options, provides you with the ability to configure file and folder options for viewing, searching, and setting the default location for the initial display of File Explorer, among many other options. The following sections describe the tools and methods found in the File Explorer Options dialog box that are used for several scenarios.

Show Hidden Files

A file is hidden from view for a few reasons, but the most important reason is that being out of sight makes it just a little more difficult to accidently or even intentionally change or delete the file. However, there are occasions when you actually need to see, edit, or remove a hidden file. Changing a file from hidden to visible requires only changing a radio button. Here's how:

1. On the Control Panel with the view in Large Icons or Small Icons, click the icon for File Explorer Options.

   If the view is set to Category, click the Appearance and Personalization link and then click the Show Hidden Files and Folders link under the File Explorer Options heading and skip to step 3.

2. On the File Explorer Options dialog box that appears (see Figure 1.4-17), select the View tab.

3. As shown in Figure 1.4-17, you can choose to show or hide files and folders by choosing the appropriate radio button.

Hide Extensions

Filename extensions are character sets that are appended to the end of a filename, typically to identify the type of file or to associate it with a specific application or service. File Explorer hides filename extensions, but you have the choice to have them displayed.

To make the filename extensions visible, open File Explorer, select the View menu option, and in the Show/Hide Group, check (show) or uncheck (hide) the box for File Name Extensions, as shown in Figure 1.4-18.

General Options

On the General tab of the Folder Options dialog box (opened from the Options icon on the View menu of the File Explorer), you can set options to open a folder in a new browser window or in the existing one, indicate the number of mouse clicks to be used to open a file or launch

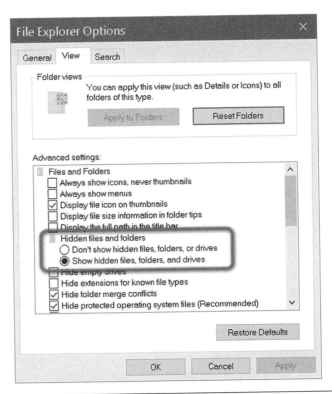

FIGURE 1.4-17 The View tab selected on the File Explorer Options dialog box

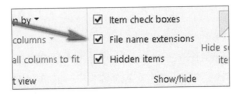

FIGURE 1.4-18 The File Name Extensions checkbox in the Show/Hide Group on the View menu of File Explorer

an application, control the level of privacy on your account, and set whether to display recent folders in a sidebar or to hide them when the File Explorer closes (see Figure 1.4-19).

View Options

The View tab on the Folder Options dialog box (refer back to Figure 1.4-17) contains settings that are more about what is displayed than how it's displayed. The settings on this tab allow you to elect whether to show or hide certain system files, which icons are displayed and how they are displayed, and whether certain file-related wizards are to be used.

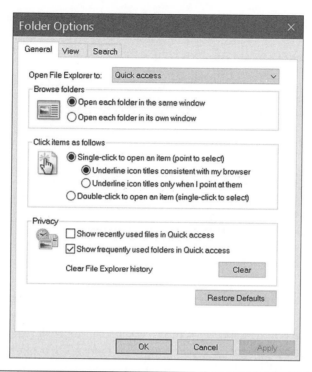

FIGURE 1.4-19   The General tab of the Folder Options dialog box.

Power Options

The Power Options icon on the Control Panel provides the power management tools on a Windows system (see Figure 1.4-20). *Power management* involves settings that provide the system with the capability to shut down unused devices, which involves the coordination

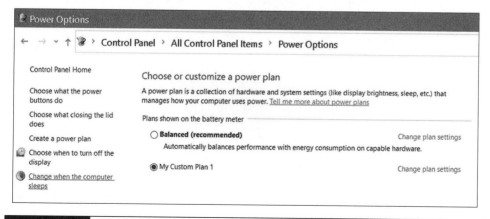

FIGURE 1.4-20   The Power Options page of the Control Panel

of hardware, BIOS/UEFI, and the OS. The objective of power management is to control a computer's actions and devices as they relate to its electrical power based on defined time triggers (in other words, what happens on the computer after it sits idle for a certain length of time).

Sleep (Suspend), Standby, and Hibernate

The default power options of Windows 10 are sleep/suspend/standby and hibernate. Each of these options are described next:

EXAM TIP Be sure to understand the differences between sleep/suspend/ standby and hibernate.

- **Sleep/Suspend/Standby** The Sleep power mode, also known as suspend or standby mode, reduces electrical power while the computer is not in use, and all actions are suspended and open applications and documents are stored in memory. This allows normal operations to be resumed in a few seconds. Sleep mode is handy to use if you need to leave your computer for a relatively short time but will return to continue where you left off. To put a computer into Sleep mode, click the Power option on the Start menu and choose Sleep from the pop-up menu, shown in Figure 1.4-21.

NOTE The Sleep mode is what most users think of as Standby. There is a Windows Standby mode that can be configured via a PowerShell command prompt using the powercfg command.

Hibernate The Hibernate mode takes everything in active memory, stores it on the hard drive, and then powers down the system. When the system is powered up, the stored memory image is reloaded into RAM and processing continues. The Hibernate mode is designed for laptops and other mobile computers to facilitate lid closures and other, perhaps longer, interruptions than are appropriate for the Sleep mode.

FIGURE 1.4-21   The Power menu choices

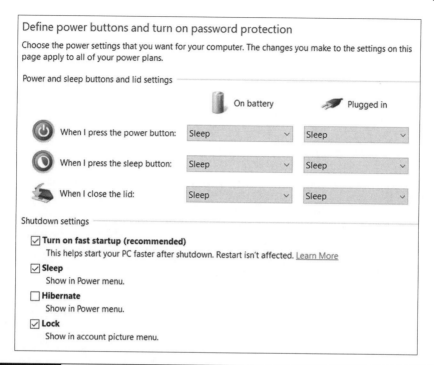

Define power buttons and turn on password protection

Choose the power settings that you want for your computer. The changes you make to the settings on this page apply to all of your power plans.

Power and sleep buttons and lid settings

	On battery	Plugged in
When I press the power button:	Sleep	Sleep
When I press the sleep button:	Sleep	Sleep
When I close the lid:	Sleep	Sleep

Shutdown settings

☑ **Turn on fast startup (recommended)**
This helps start your PC faster after shutdown. Restart isn't affected. <u>Learn More</u>
☑ **Sleep**
Show in Power menu.
☐ **Hibernate**
Show in Power menu.
☑ **Lock**
Show in account picture menu.

FIGURE 1.4-22   The Define Power Buttons and Turn On Password Protection page

NOTE   The Hibernate option is not a default power option on the Windows 11 OS.

To enable these modes, open Power Options and click the link for Choose What the Power Buttons Do. On the page that displays, the checked items in Shutdown settings are enabled. To change any of these settings, click the Change Settings That Are Currently Unavailable link to display the Define Power Buttons and Turn On Password Protection page (see Figure 1.4-22).

Power Plans

In Windows, the power plan settings are accessed through the Power Options icon on the Control Panel. Windows offers three default power plans: Balanced, Power Saver, and High Performance. Depending on the use of a computer and its environment, one of these plans may provide better control of the system's power. Should none of the three default plans fit a given situation, a custom plan can be defined (see Figure 1.4-23).

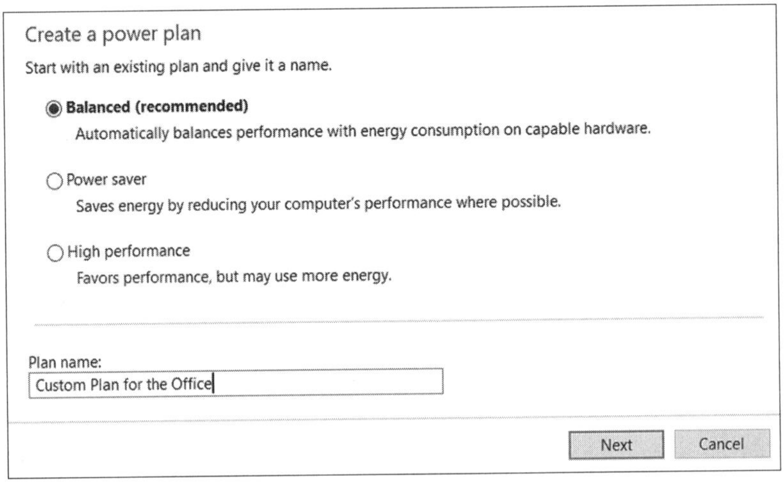

Create a power plan

Start with an existing plan and give it a name.

◉ **Balanced (recommended)**
 Automatically balances performance with energy consumption on capable hardware.

○ Power saver
 Saves energy by reducing your computer's performance where possible.

○ High performance
 Favors performance, but may use more energy.

Plan name:
Custom Plan for the Office

Next   Cancel

FIGURE 1.4-23 The Create a Power Plan dialog box

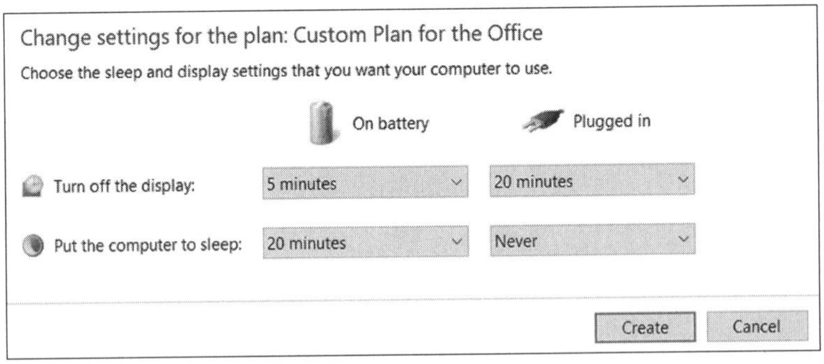

Change settings for the plan: Custom Plan for the Office

Choose the sleep and display settings that you want your computer to use.

	On battery	Plugged in
Turn off the display:	5 minutes	20 minutes
Put the computer to sleep:	20 minutes	Never

Create   Cancel

FIGURE 1.4-24 The Change Settings for the Plan dialog box

You can customize a power plan for a computer that turns off the display or puts the computer in Sleep or Hibernation mode at different time intervals. Mobile computers can have a power plan geared specifically to when they are operating on battery power (see Figure 1.4-24). You can create a custom plan based on one of the three default plans.

Default Power Plans

The default power plans—Balanced, Power Saver, and High Performance—have varied settings and are, as the names imply, designed for different environments, situations, and uses. The configuration of these plans and the capability to change between them provides tradeoffs of power consumption and computer performance:

- The *Balanced* plan is the default power plan that's suitable for most users. This plan defines a "balance" between the High Performance and the Power Saver plans.

- The *Power Saver* plan is designed to lower power consumption and extend battery life for mobile devices. However, performance is also lowered as well.

- The *High Performance* plan provides higher performance by disabling dynamic performance matching. However, this comes at the cost of higher power consumption. This plan is appropriate for situations where high performance is needed and power consumption isn't an issue.

Custom Power Plans

You have the ability to create a custom power plan. To do so, use the following steps:

1. Click the Change Plan Settings link associated with an existing or new My Custom Plan option on the Power Options page (refer back to Figure 1.4-20).

2. On the Change Setting for the Plan <Plan Name> page, set the configuration box as you wish.

Other Power Plan Options

On the Power Options page titled Choose or Customize a Power Plan, there are five special-purpose links on the left side:

- **Choose what the power buttons do**   This option allows you to set the resulting action when you press the power button or close the lid on a mobile computer.

- **Choose what closing the lid does**   This option takes you to the same group of settings as the option Choose What the Power Buttons Do.

- **Create a power plan**   This option displays the opening screen of Power Options (refer to Figure 1.4-23, earlier).

- **Choose when to turn off the display and Change when the computer sleeps**   These options open the settings page for the active power plan, an example of which is shown in Figure 1.4-24, earlier.

Fast Startup

The Windows 10 Fast Startup feature boots up a computer a bit faster than it would normally. Fast Startup, which is enabled by default, uses the hibernation file of the Hibernate mode to restore an image of the Windows OS kernel that was saved by the preceding shutdown. The hibernation file contains the kernel image and the device drivers for the installed devices. With Fast Startup enabled, the Shut Down function closes all running applications and services and logs off all user sessions and then captures the system image to a hibernation file. The captured image is the same as it would be immediately after a normal startup.

To disable or enable the Fast Startup feature, go to Control Panel | Hardware and Sound | Power Options, click the Choose What the Power Buttons Do link, and check or uncheck the Turn on Fast Startup checkbox (refer to Figure 1.4-22). You can override the Fast Startup function and do a full shutdown by holding down the SHIFT key when you choose Shut Down from the Power User menu. This action doesn't create a hibernation file and forces the system to do a full startup, also known as a cold startup, when it restarts.

 NOTE   To access the faded gray options on the Power Options settings, click the Change Settings That Are Currently Unavailable link.

USB Selective Suspend

USB devices draw their electrical power from their connections to a host device, commonly a mobile computer. When the computer is running on battery power, you may want to suspend this power draw from devices that aren't in use, such as one or more USB devices. Windows 10 provides this capability and applies it automatically. For example, a laptop computer has a biometric fingerprint reader and an external hard drive connected to it by two separate USB connections. The hard drive is in constant use, and the fingerprint reader is used only for multifactor authentication (MFA) at log-in. If either of these devices is idle for an extended period of time, such as an hour, Windows will suspend the USB port by placing it in a low power state, which lessens the power draw of the fingerprint reader on the computer's battery power.

Ease of Access

Ease of Access (also known as accessibility and assistive technology) refers to the tools and features that can be used by individuals with disabilities to perform tasks on a computer. The Windows 10 Ease of Access features aid in several areas. For example, Windows 10 provides features to assist users with various eyesight disabilities, including weak eyesight, color blindness, and total blindness. These features and their settings are accessed from the Control Panel by clicking the Ease of Access Center icon, which opens the Make Your Computer Easier to Use page, as shown in Figure 1.4-25.

The tools and features available in the Ease of Access Center are loosely arranged in three areas: Sight, Hearing, and Interaction. The Sight features include capabilities to change the brightness of the display and change visual effects, such as animations, scrolling, backgrounds, mouse settings, user interface (UI) settings, display magnification and colors, and the narration voice of the reader. The Hearing features include audio settings and how captions are read. The Interaction tools include the use of voice dictation, on-screen touch keyboard, and keypad or external sensor (eye or control stick) control of the mouse.

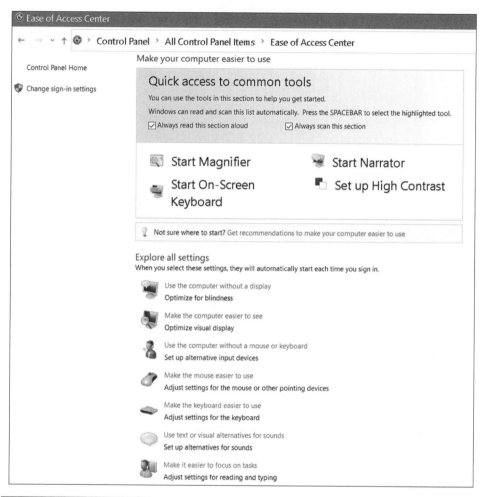

FIGURE 1.4-25 The opening page of the Ease of Access Center

REVIEW

Objective 1.4: Given a scenario, use the appropriate Microsoft Windows 10 Control Panel utility The Control Panel and system utilities you need to be familiar with include the following:

- Internet Options
- Devices and Printers
- Programs and Features
- Network and Sharing Center

- System
- Windows Defender Firewall
- Mail (Microsoft Outlook)
- Sound
- User Accounts
- Device Manager
- Indexing Options
- Administrative Tools
- File Explorer Options: show hidden files, hide extensions, general and view options
- Power Options: sleep/suspend, standby, hibernate, power plans, fast startup, and USB selective suspend
- Ease of Access

1.4 QUESTIONS

1. What Control Panel option is used to configure the Internet security zone for a given scenario?
   A. System
   B. File Explorer Options
   C. Security Options
   D. Internet Options

2. Which Control Panel option do you select to access the media streaming settings?
   A. Internet Options
   B. AutoPlay
   C. Network and Sharing Center
   D. Sync Center

3. What Control Panel option provides for centralized viewing and management of monitors, printers, and peripheral devices?
   A. Devices and Printers
   B. Printers and Devices
   C. Device Manager
   D. Programs and Features

4. What Windows 10 applet allows a user to modify a computer's tools, features, and settings?
   A. Utility Manager
   B. Control Panel
   C. System Information
   D. MMC

5. Windows 10 Power Settings are configured from which category of the Control Panel?
   A. Appearance and Personalization
   B. Clock, Language, and Region
   C. User Accounts
   D. System and Security

1.4 ANSWERS

1. **D**   Internet Options is used to configure the Internet security zone.

2. **C**   The Network and Sharing Center is used to access the media streaming settings.

3. **A**   The Devices and Printers option is used for centralized viewing and management of monitors, printers, and peripheral devices.

4. **B**   The Control Panel provides tools and services to access and control the system settings and features.

5. **D**   From the Category view of the Control Panel, power settings are accessed through the System and Security category.

Objective 1.5 # Given a scenario, use the appropriate Windows settings

Over the latest versions of the Windows operating system (OS), the Settings applet has changed to include additional configuration functions, many of which have been moved from other Windows applets, largely from the Control Panel. For the most part, the Windows Settings applet, shown in Figure 1.5-1, provides access to the configuration or specification settings for the majority of the OSs' most basic user interface and operational features. This objective discusses and describes the individual settings and configurations accessed through the Settings applet that you should expect to encounter on the CompTIA A+ Core 2 (220-1102) exam.

Time & Language

During installation, Windows prompts the user to select or confirm the local time, the current date, the region in which the computer is located (such as United States, Japan, India, and so on), and language settings (such as U.S. English, U.K. English, Japanese, and so on). A user in the United States only needs to set the time zone to designate nearly all of these settings, with the language setting sometimes needing a non-default designation. The default is typically either the Eastern or Pacific Standard or Daylight Saving time zone, which includes defaults for most of the other settings. A user in another country would need to make these settings individually in most cases.

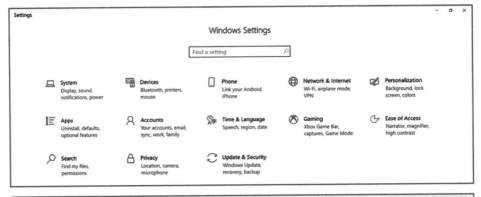

FIGURE 1.5-1 The System page of the Windows 10 (top) and Windows 11 (bottom) Settings applet

EXAM TIP You should know the Windows OS settings associated with your location and language.

Update & Security

Although its primary use is to identify, download, and install updates to your Windows OS, the Update & Security option on the Settings app does include several other options related to efficiency, security, and problem diagnostics. The settings options on the Update & Security page of the Windows 10 Settings app are described in the following sections.

Windows Update

The page displayed by default for the Update & Security option on the Windows 10 Settings app is the Windows Update page, shown in Figure 1.5-2. The options in the body of this page allow you to control if, when, and what updates are applied to the Windows OS and its components. The navigation pane on the left side of the page contains other functions and features related to updating the OS and its security. Windows Update is used to check for available updates either by command or automatically. Windows 10/11 will download and install updates automatically without letting you pick and choose, if so configured.

 NOTE   On Windows 11 systems, the Settings app opens directly to the System option. The settings options are listed in the left-side navigation pane. Each of these options opens a page similar to Windows 10. However, as shown in Figure 1.5-1, the Windows Update option and a few others are moved around in the list.

 EXAM TIP   For the 220-1102 exam, you should know how to access Windows Update, check for updates, and download and install updates.

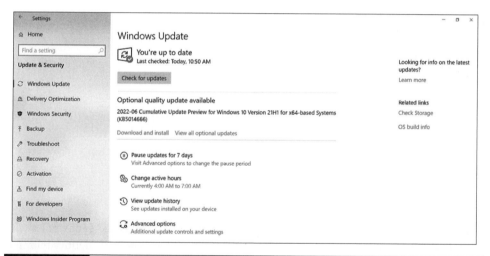

FIGURE 1.5-2   The Windows Update page of the Windows 10 Settings app

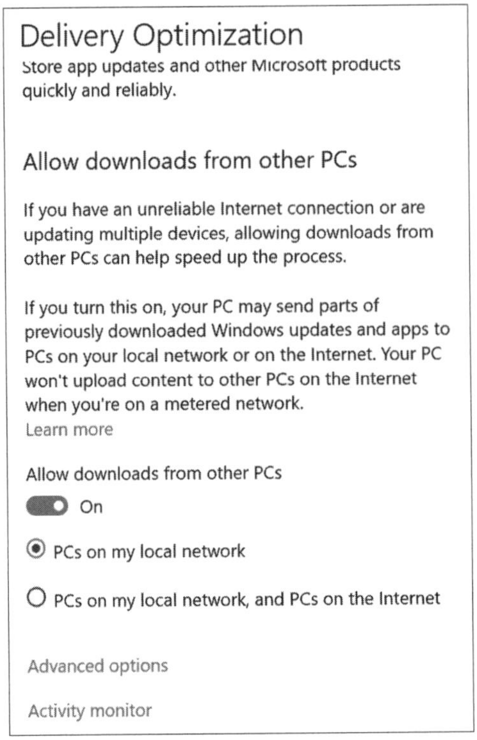

Delivery Optimization

Store app updates and other Microsoft products quickly and reliably.

Allow downloads from other PCs

If you have an unreliable Internet connection or are updating multiple devices, allowing downloads from other PCs can help speed up the process.

If you turn this on, your PC may send parts of previously downloaded Windows updates and apps to PCs on your local network or on the Internet. Your PC won't upload content to other PCs on the Internet when you're on a metered network.

Learn more

Allow downloads from other PCs

On

⊙ PCs on my local network

○ PCs on my local network, and PCs on the Internet

Advanced options

Activity monitor

FIGURE 1.5-3   The Delivery Optimization settings page

Delivery Optimization

This feature allows computers in a network, including directly connected peer-to-peer devices, to upload or download files, updates, or applications to or from one another. Delivery Optimization, shown in Figure 1.5-3, is an on/off setting. In Advanced Options, bandwidth, download, and upload limits can be set, and Activity Monitor can be used to show download statistics.

Windows Security

The Windows Security option opens what is essentially a status page (see Figure 1.5-4) that displays the status of the Windows Security settings. The Open Windows Security button at the top of the page opens the Security at a Glance page (see Figure 1.5-5) of the Windows Security app (virtually the same in Windows 10 and 11). This is where the Windows OS security can be configured. It includes the following options: Virus & Threat Protection, Account Protection, Firewall & Network Protection, App & Browser Control, Device Security, Device Performance & Health, and Family Options.

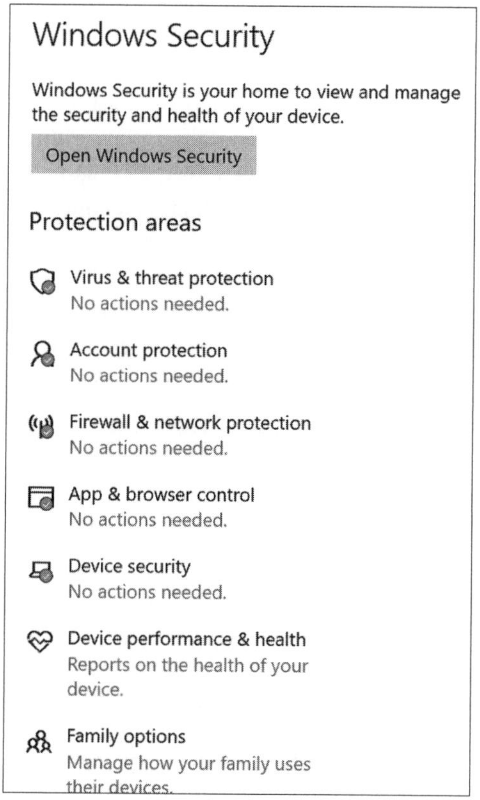

Windows Security
Windows Security is your home to view and manage the security and health of your device.
Open Windows Security
Protection areas
Virus & threat protection
No actions needed.
Account protection
No actions needed.
Firewall & network protection
No actions needed.
App & browser control
No actions needed.
Device security
No actions needed.
Device performance & health
Reports on the health of your device.
Family options
Manage how your family uses their devices.

FIGURE 1.5-4 The Windows Security page

Windows Security
Home
Virus & threat protection
Account protection
Firewall & network protection
App & browser control
Device security
Device performance & health
Family options
Security at a glance
See what's happening with the security and health of your device and take any actions needed.
Virus & threat protection
No action needed.
Account protection
No action needed.
Firewall & network protection
No action needed.
App & browser control
No action needed.
Device security
View status and manage hardware security features
Device performance & health
No action needed.
Family options
Manage how your family uses their devices.

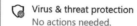

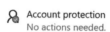

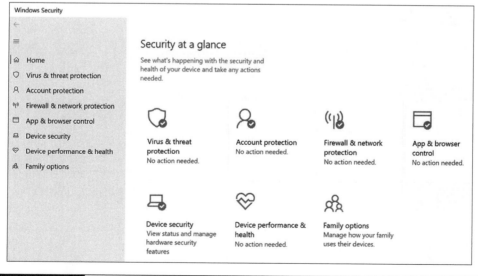

FIGURE 1.5-5 The Security at a Glance page

Personalization

The Personalization settings in Windows 10/11 provide the tools and features that allow you to "paint" the system's displays to your liking. These tools and features include settings and adjustments for the background and colors of the Desktop as well as the background for the Lock Screen. Also, you can choose and apply a theme to the Desktop, manage the fonts installed and available to applications, and configure the display and contents of the Start menu and the taskbar. Figure 1.5-6 shows the Personalization page of the Settings app.

On the right edge of the Personalization page, under the heading Related Settings, you will find a link for Sync Your Settings. Click this link to open the Sync Your Settings page, shown in Figure 1.5-7. When the Sync Settings slider is in the On position, the Windows OS

FIGURE 1.5-6 The Windows 10 Personalization page

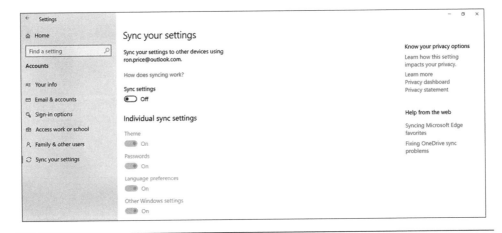

FIGURE 1.5-7 The Sync Your Settings page

synchronizes the settings chosen in the Individual Sync Settings section to all the Windows devices you've signed into with your Microsoft account.

 NOTE   You can also sync your settings for a work or school account if it's allowed by your organization.

Apps

In Windows 10, the Apps icon in the Settings app opens the Apps & Features page (shown in Figure 1.5-8). On this page, you have the ability to move an app from one folder or system to another, install or uninstall an application, and assign the default apps by function, file type, or protocol. You can also manage map applications for use offline, where a map app is stored on the system, and turn on or off automatic map updates.

Another feature set available in Windows 10/11 Apps & Features is the Video Playback page, shown in Figure 1.5-9. The settings on this page are used to configure the Windows 10/11 video playback platform. The video playback settings on this page are the HDR (high dynamic range) color settings for video streaming, turning on or off video stream enhancement, and the handling of video streams when the computer is operating on battery power.

The last of the settings on the Apps & Features page is Startup. This option lists the installed applications on the computer, each with a slider you can use to set whether the app is to be started when the Windows system starts up (on) or not (off).

FIGURE 1.5-8   The Windows 10 Apps & Features settings page

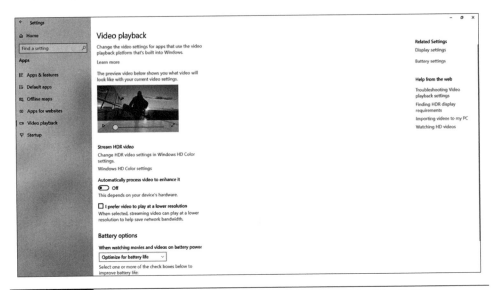

FIGURE 1.5-9   The Video Playback page of the Apps & Features area of the Settings app

Privacy

The Windows 10 and 11 Privacy settings page allows you to set permissions for Windows and most of its features as well as a wide range of access and resource permissions for applications. The default page provides for setting general permissions, as shown in Figure 1.5-10.

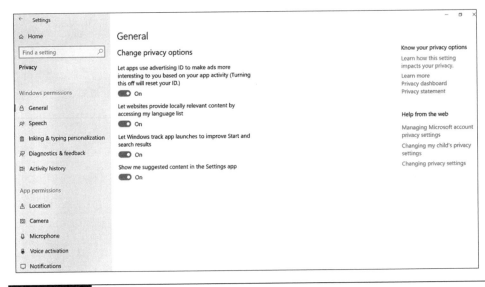

FIGURE 1.5-10   The General page of the Privacy settings

The different areas for which you can set privacy and permission settings are separated into two groups in the left-side navigation pane: Windows Permissions and App Permissions. The elements of each group are described next.

Windows Permissions

The Windows permissions you can set are accessed by the following links: General, Speech, Inking & Typing Personalization, Diagnostics & Feedback, and Activity History.

General   Here are the general settings you can turn on or off:

- **Let apps use my advertising ID for experiences across apps**   User accounts are assigned *advertising IDs,* which are used to track your preferences. Turning this setting off closes the assigned advertising ID.
- **Let websites provide locally relevant content by accessing my language list**   Windows 10/11 maintains a *Language Code Identifier (LCID)* that lists all the language packs installed on the system. Turning on this permission allows apps to access the LCID to present outputs in the languages installed.
- **Let Windows track app launches to improve Start and search results**   Turning this setting on allows Windows to keep track of which applications you use the most so it can personalize the Start menu and optimize searches.
- **Show me suggested content in the Settings app**   Turning this setting on enables Windows 10/11 to provide you with suggestions and hints about your settings.

Speech   This setting enables Windows to "use your voice for dictation and other apps."

Inking & Typing Personalization   This setting enables Windows to use how and what you type and enter via handwriting (inking) to make suggestions as you work.

Diagnostics & Feedback   The privacy settings in this area are as follows:

- **Diagnostic data**   This is data provided to Microsoft regarding issues or problems with a system. The two types of diagnostic data are Required and Optional:
    - **Required (basic)**   This is data about the device, its settings and configuration, and how the device is performing.
    - **Optional (full)**   This data includes the Required data but also includes your browsing habits, which apps and Windows features you use, as well as data on device health, device use, and any problems or issues that have occurred.
- **Improve inking and typing**   This setting is dependent on the Inking & Typing Personalization setting. If that setting is enabled, additional diagnostics and usage data is provided to Microsoft.

- **Tailored experiences**   This setting allows Microsoft to collect and use diagnostic data to provide personalization hints, recommendations, and advertising to improve your Windows experiences. Web browsing is not included in this data.
- **View diagnostic data**   With this setting turned on, you can use the Diagnostic Data Viewer to view captured diagnostic data. Turning this setting on reserves as much as 1 GB of disk space to support the viewer.
- **Delete diagnostic data**   Removes any saved diagnostic data from your system.
- **Feedback frequency**   How often you wish to provide Microsoft with your diagnostic data, if ever.

Activity History   This setting, if enabled with a check in the checkbox, sets up tracking for what apps, services, files, and websites you use, open, or visit. This information is used to generate suggestions on future activity.

Application Permissions

Windows 10/11 apps accessed from the Microsoft Store, known as Universal Windows Platform (UWP) apps, can be limited as to the resources they can access, such as location, video and audio devices, and stored images. The settings in this group are used to allow/disallow apps access to these resources. Essentially, the permissions settings in this group permit or deny access to data, devices, or interactions with applications and users.

 NOTE   Legacy apps or apps not acquired from the Microsoft Store are not limited by these settings.

System

In the context of Windows 10/11 Settings, *system* refers to the settings used to personalize or customize the display, sound, battery, and other actions, features, or elements with which the user interfaces. Each of the options in the left-side pane of the System page generally represents a grouping of related settings or indicators, with a few exceptions. The settings options on the various pages of the System app (see Figure 1.5-11) are discussed in the following sections.

Display   The settings on the Display page control the characteristics of what is shown on your video display:

- **Brightness**   Lighten or darken the background of the display. The Night Light on/off toggle is used to display warmer (less blue) colors to help some users sleep better.
- **Windows HD Color**   This setting area enables high dynamic range (HDR) and wide color gamut (WCG) color encoding for photos, videos, games, and other images.

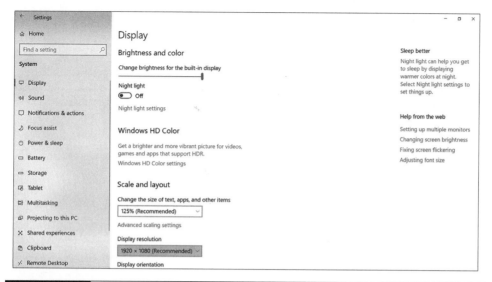

FIGURE 1.5-11   The Display page of the System app

- **Scale and layout**   You can change the display size of text and graphics relative to the display's size and resolution. The settings accessed via the Advanced Scaling Settings link are used to reduce blurriness and setting customer scale and layout features.
- **Display resolution**   The pull-down box contains a variety of pixel width and height sizing that can be applied to your video display. The larger the numbers, the higher the resolution of the display. Figure 1.5-12 illustrates the difference between a 1920×1080 resolution and an 800×600 resolution of the same page. The Display orientation can be set to either portrait (taller) or landscape (wider).
- **Multiple displays**   This settings option is used to detect and configure a system using two or more video displays.

 EXAM TIP   Display resolution is an area you can expect to encounter on the CompTIA A+ Core 2 exam.

Sound   This settings group provides you with the ability to set the default capture and playback devices for sound on your system and set the standard volumes for apps and Windows sounds.

Notifications & Actions   In addition to configuring if and from whom you receive notifications, you can set the *Quick Actions,* which displays frequently used apps in a grid.

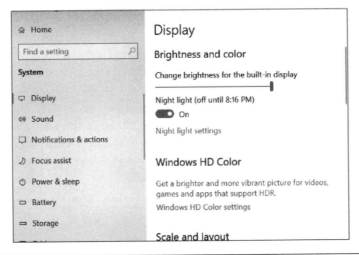

FIGURE 1.5-12 A 1920×1080 resolution setting (top) and an 800×600 resolution setting (bottom)

Focus Assist These settings allow you to configure if and when you receive notification alerts or alarms from apps or other sources. The idea here is that you may wish to limit these alerts to retain your focus while working on the system.

Power & Sleep The settings in this group are used to indicate at which point, measured in minutes, the display and the PC go into Sleep mode when idle.

Battery This setting group controls at which point the OS is placed in Battery Saver mode to conserve power.

Storage   This setting enables/disables the Windows app *Storage Sense,* which can be configured to remove junk or unneeded files from the system to free up storage space.

Tablet   These settings control whether or not the system moves into Tablet mode upon login and what action it takes when it does.

Multitasking   The settings in this group deal with how multiple windows, the timeline, and the taskbar are displayed. The Snap feature is also configured in this settings group.

Projecting to This PC   These settings are used to enable/disable the PC to allow other devices to project onto it and use its resources.

Shared Experiences   These settings enable/disable the PC to share a file (documents or images) with other devices using either Bluetooth (nearby) or Wi-Fi (distance).

Clipboard   The settings in this option allow you to create a Clipboard history or to clear its content.

Remote Desktop   These settings allow remote PCs to connect to and operate the system.

About   This is an information display that includes the status of the security and the configuration specifications for the hardware and software.

EXAM TIP   In a given scenario regarding the System settings, know which setting is used and why.

On Windows 11, the System app is similar to that of Windows 10, with a few exceptions. The options in the navigation pane for Windows 11 now include Nearby Sharing, Activation, Troubleshoot, and Recovery. The Tablet and Shared Experiences settings in the Windows 10 System app exist in Windows 11 but have been moved to the Action Center and the Apps settings, respectively.

Devices

The Devices area of the Settings app (see Figure 1.5-13) allows you to manage the components of your PC. Here are the specific devices that can be configured:

- **Bluetooth & other devices**   When the Bluetooth On/Off slider is set to On, the system begins scanning for any Bluetooth devices within its range.
- **Printers & scanners**   This option allows you to add a new imaging device to your system. The printers and scanners already configured to the system are listed.
- **Mouse**   The operating configuration of a mouse is set on this page.

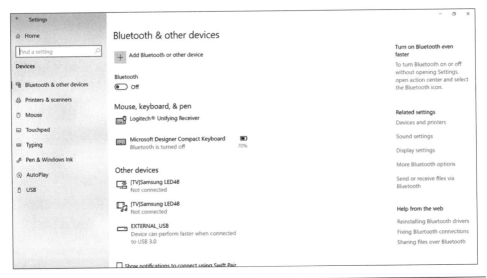

FIGURE 1.5-13 The Devices section of the Settings app opens to the Bluetooth and Other Devices page by default.

- **Touchpad**   This page is used to set the cursor delay of pointing devices and to set the touch sensitivity of the touchpad device.
- **Typing**   You can enable/disable the autocorrect and spelling functions along with several other hardware and virtual keyboard settings.
- **Pen & Windows ink**   If you wish to write using your fingertip or a stylus, the font that your writing uses is designated on this page.
- **AutoPlay**   On this page, you can enable or disable the automatic playing of removable media.
- **USB**   Enable/disable notifications regarding actions and issues relating to USB devices.

EXAM TIP   For the exam, remember that you can turn Bluetooth on or off in the Bluetooth & Other Devices area of the Devices app. You should also remember that AutoPlay can be turned on or off in the AutoPlay area. Disabling AutoPlay for security is mentioned again later in the book when we cover Objective 2.6. Remember where these settings are located!

Network & Internet

The Network & Internet settings are used to configure and modify the networking features on a Windows 10/11 system. In this settings group, shown in Figure 1.5-14, you can configure a computer's wireless (Wi-Fi) and wired (Ethernet) network adapters, enable or disable Airplane

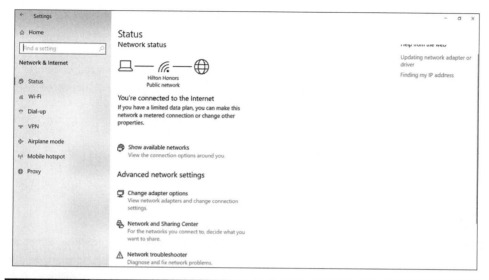

FIGURE 1.5-14   The Network & Internet settings opens with the Status page.

mode, and set up a virtual private network (VPN) link, among other network-related settings. However, this settings area is mostly used for checking the status of network connections and for turning on (or off) certain features. For the time being, network adapter settings are still done primarily through the Control Panel.

The Windows 10 Network & Internet settings group includes the following options:

- **Status**   This settings group is shown in Figure 1.5-14. The Show Available Networks option, available on devices with wireless network adapters, opens a list of the wireless networks detected within range. The Change Adapter Options and the Network and Sharing Center options in the Advanced Network Settings section link to Control Panel apps. The Network Troubleshooter opens the Windows Troubleshooter for the active network adapter.

- **Wi-Fi**   This settings group allows you to configure the network adapter to use a randomized hardware address when connecting to other wireless networks and enable the Hotspot 2.0 Network feature that provides enhanced security and safety for connecting to public hotspots.

- **Dial-up**   This option allows you to establish a new dial-up network connection.

- **VPN**   This settings option is used to set up a new VPN connection and then enable/ disable operating characteristics, such as operating on a metered network and using a VPN while roaming.

- **Airplane mode**   When enabled, airplane mode ends all wireless communication. Toggle switches apply or remove airplane mode on Wi-Fi and Bluetooth devices.

- **Mobile hotspot**   This option allows you to create a mobile hotspot that you can share with other devices. The connection to the hotspot is controlled by a generated network name and password.
- **Proxy**   Using the settings in this group, you can configure a proxy server to be automatically discovered or enter the proxy configuration data manually.

 NOTE   The Windows 11 Network & Internet options removed the Status settings but added Ethernet and Advanced network settings options.

Gaming

The Windows 10 Gaming settings configure the audio and video, broadcasting, keyboard controls, and Xbox game bar. The settings options in the left-side navigation pane are used to configure the Xbox game bar, screen captures, and broadcasting and recording as well as to optimize a PC for game play and check the status of the connection to an Xbox network.

 NOTE   The Windows 11 Gaming settings include only the settings for the game bar, captures, and game mode.

Accounts

The Windows 10 Accounts settings provide you with the tools and options needed to manage your Microsoft user account, including inserting a picture, setting your login options, managing your password or personal identification number (PIN), using a picture as a password, adding family members to your account, setting up a connection to a school or work account, and enabling synchronization with a mobile device.

 NOTE   The Windows 11 Accounts settings include the following options: Your Info, Email & Accounts, Sign-in Options, Family & Other Users, Windows Backup, and Access Work or School.

REVIEW

Objective 1.5: Given a scenario, use the appropriate Windows settings   The Settings applet includes the tools and settings that configure and control the system from a user's point of view. For the CompTIA A+ Core 2 exam, you should be familiar with the following areas covered in this objective:

- **Time & Language**   Used to select or confirm the local time, the current date, the region where the device is located, and the language to be used.
- **Update & Security**   Includes options for efficiency, security, and problem diagnostics, including the following settings groups:
  - **Windows Update**   Used to control updates applied to the Windows OS and its components.
  - **Delivery Optimization**   Allows computers in a network to upload/download files, updates, or applications to/from one another.
  - **Windows Security**   Displays the Windows security status with the Windows Security at a Glance page used to configure Virus & Threat Protection, Account Protection, Firewall & Network Protection, App & Browser Control, Device Security, Device Performance & Health, and Family Options.
- **Personalization**   Provides the tools and features for customizing the display.
- **Apps**   Provides the ability to move apps, install applications, and assign default apps by function, file type, or protocol. The Video Playback settings can be used to configure the HDR color settings for video streaming.
- **Privacy**   Used to set permissions for Windows and its features as well as to set access and resource permissions for applications. The permissions are grouped as Windows permissions and application permissions:
  - Windows permissions are General, Speech, Inking & Typing Personalization, Diagnostics & Feedback, Activity History, and Application Permissions.
  - Application permissions apply to UWP apps and limit access to resources.
- **System**   Includes settings to personalize the display, sound, battery, and other actions, features, or elements. These settings are Display, Sound, Notifications & Actions, Focus Assist, Power & Sleep, Battery, Storage, Tablet, Multitasking, Projecting to This PC, Shared Experiences, Clipboard, Remote Desktop, and About.
- **Devices**   Used to manage PC components. The devices configured with these settings are Bluetooth and other devices, printers and scanners, mice, touchpads, typing, pen and Windows Ink, AutoPlay, and USB.
- **Network & Internet**   Used to configure networking features of network adapters, enable or disable Airplane mode, set up a VPN, and other network settings.
- **Gaming**   Used to configure audio and video, broadcasting, the keyboard controls, and the Xbox game bar.
- **Accounts**   Provides the tools and settings to manage user accounts. Settings groups are for inserting a picture, setting login options, managing password or PIN, using a picture as a password, adding family members, setting up a school or work account, and enabling sync.

1.5 QUESTIONS

1. A customer is having trouble reading the text on their computer screen because it is too small. What setting in the Settings Display app can you use to adjust the size of the text, apps, and other items?

   A. Scale and layout

   B. Display resolution

   C. Display orientation

   D. HDR color

2. Which of the following is not a setting that can be configured on the System settings Display option?

   A. Brightness

   B. Background tint

   C. Scaling

   D. Resolution

   E. HDR color

3. You are setting up a new mobile PC for an in-house client and need to configure the settings that personalize the PC's display, sound, and battery. What section of the Settings app should you use for these settings?

   A. Display

   B. Personalization

   C. System

   D. Devices

4. The Diagnostics & Feedback settings are found in which section of the Settings app?

   A. Privacy

   B. Accounts

   C. Devices

   D. Optimization

5. On what Windows 10/11 app are the settings for the image or color of the Lock Screen found?

   A. System

   B. Apps

   C. Control Panel

   D. Settings

1.5 ANSWERS

1. **D** Windows will make suggestions or provide hints, but it doesn't make judgments.
2. **B** The background tint is not a setting of the Display settings.
3. **C** The settings for these devices are on the System section of the Settings app.
4. **A** The Diagnostics & Feedback settings are in the Privacy section of the Settings app.
5. **D** The settings for the Windows Lock screen are found on the Personalization section of the Settings app.

Objective 1.6 Given a scenario, configure Microsoft Windows networking features on a client/desktop

Microsoft Windows is ready to connect to a network as soon as it is installed. However, a number of configuration settings are needed that depend on the network type. This objective covers the Windows network settings you need to understand.

Workgroup vs. Domain Setup

The standard network type for Windows is a *workgroup,* which allows the computers on the network to share files, folders, and printers with each other. However, each computer on the network must have its local and remote users manually configured. The default name for a workgroup in Windows is WORKGROUP, but you can change it in the System applet.

A *domain* uses a domain controller (typically running some version of Windows Server and Active Directory) to provide centralized administration of all users on the network. With a domain server, a user logs in to an account stored on the domain controller (DC) rather than an account set up on an individual computer. Each user on a domain can be placed into a group of users, each of which can have different levels of access to network resources such as apps, folders, printers, and other network hardware.

Workgroups and domains are differentiated through accounts. A workgroup account is the default account type of Windows 10/11 systems. In a workgroup, all workgroup accounts are equal and will remain as-is unless they're joined into a domain. A domain account, on the other hand, is designed to be used in most larger networks and enterprise environments.

EXAM TIP   Make sure you can explain the differences between workgroups and domains.

Shared Resources

A *shared resource* is any object to which permission to access or use has been granted to one or more users. The resource could be directly attached to a specific workstation or be a network node on its own. Shared resources can be printers, network-attached storage (NAS), a fax machine, other types of hardware devices, or a folder or file made accessible to other local or remote computers and users. Sharing resources eliminates duplication and redundancy, especially with hardware devices, and potential errors in data files.

The term *network share* is a specific type of shared resource. Network shares are folders or files to which one or more users have been granted access. To create a network share in Windows 10/11, use the following steps:

 EXAM TIP For the CompTIA A+ Core 2 (220-1102) exam, you should understand the makeup and purpose of shared resources.

1. Verify that the File and Printer Sharing setting (via the Control Panel or the Settings app) is enabled on each of the devices that will share the resource, including the host device.

2. Find and right-click the folder in the File Explorer and choose one of the following ways to create the share:

   • Choose Properties and click the Sharing tab on the Properties dialog box. Then click Advanced Sharing to open the Advanced Sharing dialog box (see Figure 1.6-1). You can specify up to 20 simultaneous users and click Permissions to set up unique permissions for each separate user or user group (the rightmost dialog box in Figure 1.6-1).

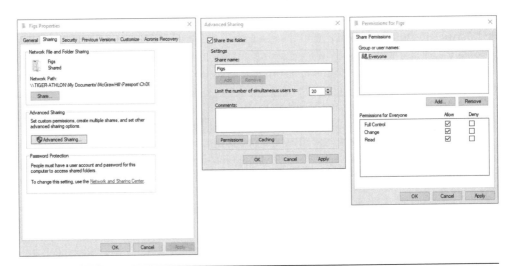

FIGURE 1.6-1   Windows 10 Advanced Sharing dialog boxes

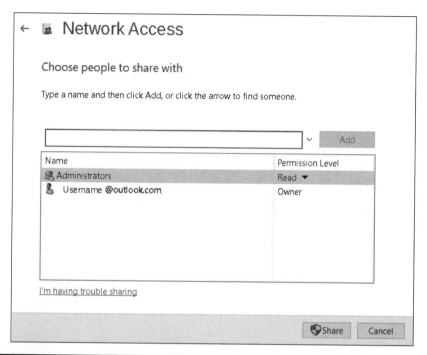

FIGURE 1.6-2 The Choose People to Share With dialog box

- Alternatively, choose Share. Then, in the Choose People to Share With dialog box (see Figure 1.6-2), add the individual users to share the file with.

 NOTE By default, new Windows shares only have Read permission; click the Permission Level drop-down to set your share to Full Control.

Printers

A *workgroup* consists of computers, all on the same network, connected to a primary service. This variation of a client/server arrangement allows the workgroup members to share files, printers, and other resources. Let's focus on the printers here.

A *workgroup printer* is usually physically connected to the workgroup server, or in an Active Directory environment, to the computer serving as a DC. Centralizing the printer this way allows the workgroup or domain users access to the device, which could also be a fax, scanner, or another peripheral device. A workgroup printer to be shared can be found using the printer's IP address, physical address, or host name using the Find a Printer by Name or TCP/IP Address option in the Add Printer dialog box (see Figure 1.6-3).

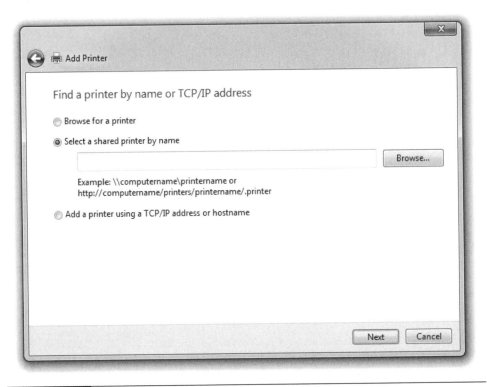

FIGURE 1.6-3   Options for setting up network printers

 EXAM TIP   Before a printer can be accessed from a workgroup or domain, it must be configured for sharing.

Like network shares, printer sharing requires that File and Printer Sharing be enabled on each computer that will share a printer with others. To share a printer, open Devices and Printers from the Control Panel. Choose the printer to be shared to add a printer as a network printer. The process then displays the available shared printers (see Figure 1.6-4). Choose a printer, and the drivers are installed for you.

Configuring a share on a printer manually is simple when there are only a few workstations on a network, but you will want to automate the process with a group policy setting (which works with either workgroup or domain networks) or a login script if you have a domain.

 EXAM TIP   Expect a question or two on the CompTIA A+ 220-1102 exam giving you a scenario in which you set up printer sharing.

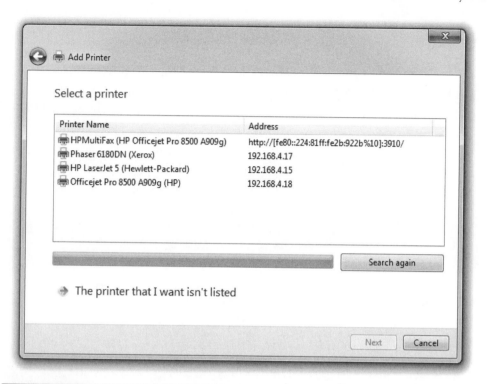

FIGURE 1.6-4   List of available shared printers on a network

File Servers

A *file server* stores files shared by computers and other devices on a network. On small office/home office (SOHO) or small-to-medium business (SMB) networks, the function of a file server is enabled simply by sharing files with accounts and devices on the same network. Larger and enterprise networks most typically centralize shared files onto a dedicated file server computer with larger and faster storage devices and high-performance network adapters.

Mapped Devices

A printer, storage device, or another type of peripheral device can be either local or mapped. The difference is that a *local device* is actually (physically) connected (attached) to your computer. However, a *mapped device* is not physically attached to your computer but yet appears to be local. A good way to visualize this difference is to compare pathnames.

A data file stored on a local hard drive looks something like this:

```
D:\Local_Device_Files\local file.txt
```

On the other hand, a data file stored on a mapped hard drive needs a bit more addressing:

```
\\Mapped_Disk_Drive\Shared_Files\remote file.doc
```

However, you can *map* a single folder or file, which assigns a drive letter to it and lists it in File Explorer. To map a file or folder in Windows 10, use the following steps:

1. In File Explorer, right-click the This PC item in the navigation pane to display its pop-up menu (see Figure 1.6-5).

2. Click the Map Network Drive option to display the What Network Folder Would You Like to Map? dialog box.

3. Using the Drive pull-down list, choose the drive letter you wish to assign to the mapped drive. Avoid duplicating an existing local drive letter.

4. Enter the name of the file to be mapped or use the Browse button to find the file.

 NOTE If you are unable to map a remote folder, you may need to enable the remote location in the Network and Sharing function on the Control Panel.

The mapped folder will now appear in the Navigation pane in File Explorer.

 NOTE On Windows 11, the mapping process is the same up to when you right-click This PC. Windows 11 opens a This PC page, and the Map Network Drive option is displayed by clicking the ellipses icon (...) at the right end of the menu bar. The remainder of the process is then the same.

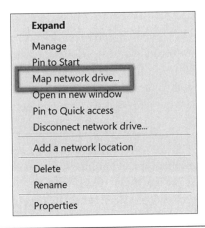

FIGURE 1.6-5 The pop-up menu displayed from right-clicking This PC in File Explorer

Local OS Firewall Settings

Windows Defender Firewall with Advanced Security (not to be confused with the older Windows Firewall) is a host-based application that prevents unauthorized or unwanted application and network traffic from flowing in or out of a local host.

 NOTE Microsoft recommends that you keep the default settings when first enabling Windows Defender Firewall. These settings can be viewed on the Overview panel.

To open Windows Defender Firewall to its Overview page, shown in Figure 1.6-6, you have two primary choices:

- Open Windows Defender Firewall by clicking its icon in the Control Panel and clicking Advanced Settings in the left-side navigation pane.
- Enter **WF.msc** in the Run command box and click OK.

Application Restrictions and Exceptions

Windows Defender Firewall with Advanced Security operates by comparing the traffic passing through it with rules that specify which traffic is allowed to pass and which will be denied.

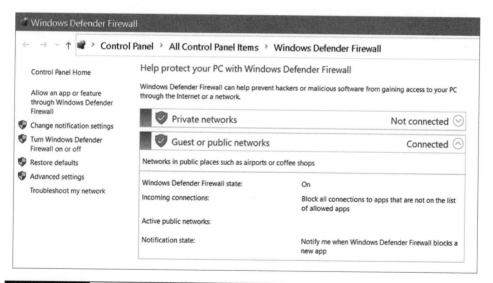

FIGURE 1.6-6 The Overview page of Windows Defender Firewall with Advanced Security

Windows Defender Firewall supports three types of rules:

- **Inbound rules**   These rules apply to network traffic coming into the firewall from the external network.
- **Outbound rules**   These rules apply to network traffic coming into the firewall from the internal network.
- **Connection security rules**   These rules specify how the Internet Protocol Security (IPSec) protocol is to be applied to network traffic passing from one computer to other computers on the same network.

Firewall Rules

Inbound and outbound rules can be one of three different types:

- **Allow or deny rules**   An *allow rule* sets the conditions that network traffic must meet to be passed through the firewall. A *deny rule* sets the conditions that block network traffic from passing through.
- **If secure rules**   Even if network traffic is allowed, if it's not secure, as defined by IPSec rules, it's denied.
- **Bypass if authenticated rules**   If network traffic is denied initially, if it can be authenticated, it's allowed to pass.

Default Rules

Windows Defender Firewall includes an extensive set of default (predefined) inbound rules and outbound rules. The predefined rules cannot be altered, but those applying to third-party (non-Microsoft) applications or rules that you define can be tailored as needed. Figure 1.6-7 shows an example of a predefined inbound rule. In the Inbound Rules list (visible behind the open rule dialog box), the rules with green checkmarks are enabled.

Rules can also be restrictions or exceptions. A *restriction* sets up a filtering rule based on one or more characteristics of an inbound or outbound message. A message type from a certain application or to or from a specific network address may normally be permitted to pass. However, there may be some conditions, such as message length, protocol, and perhaps even time or day, that may cause the message to be denied passage.

An *exception* rule is essentially the opposite of a restriction. A message that may normally be denied could be allowed to pass due to some condition it meets, such as an authentication overriding any other denial.

Create an Exception

Many applications will create their own rules when installed on a Windows 10/11 system with Windows Defender Firewall. Applications create rules to prevent the firewall from blocking

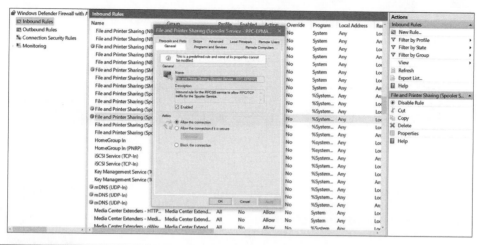

FIGURE 1.6-7   An example of predefined rules in Windows Defender Firewall

their traffic, which means a Windows 10/11 user doesn't typically need to configure rules for applications.

However, this may not always be true. Windows Defender Firewall may have a predefined rule that restricts a specific application, the application may not be able to create a rule, or the firewall's rules and those of the application may conflict and have to guess which wins. In any of these cases, it may be necessary to define an exception rule or, more rarely, a restriction.

 NOTE   You must have administrator rights to work with Windows Defender Firewall settings.

An exception rule is a custom rule that is added to enable an application or program to pass or receive traffic through the firewall. What an exception does, in effect, is to let the firewall know about the application. An exception can be created from scratch using the Inbound Rules option (in the left-side navigation pane) and its New Rule option (in the right-side pane) or by modifying an existing rule for that application if one exists.

Modify an Existing Rule

You can also add an application rule using the Allow an App or Feature Through Windows Defender Firewall option from the Windows Defender Firewall landing page. This option opens a dialog box on which you can modify the details of a rule for an existing application or add a rule for a new application, as shown in Figure 1.6-8.

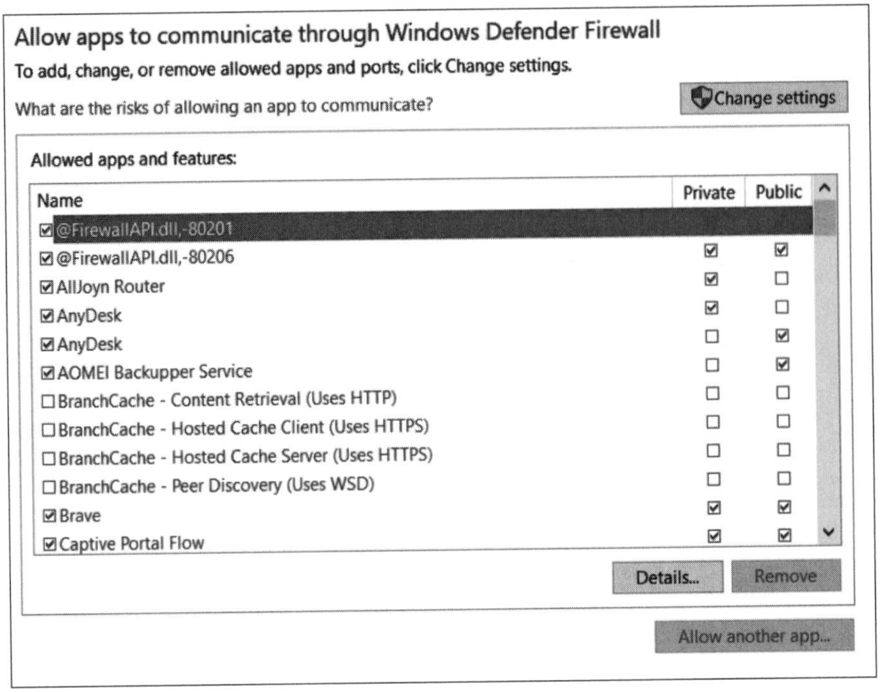

Allow apps to communicate through Windows Defender Firewall

To add, change, or remove allowed apps and ports, click Change settings.

What are the risks of allowing an app to communicate?   🛡Change settings

Allowed apps and features:

Name	Private	Public
☑ @FirewallAPI.dll,-80201		
☑ @FirewallAPI.dll,-80206	☑	☑
☑ AllJoyn Router	☑	☐
☑ AnyDesk	☑	☐
☑ AnyDesk	☐	☑
☑ AOMEI Backupper Service	☐	☑
☐ BranchCache - Content Retrieval (Uses HTTP)	☐	☐
☐ BranchCache - Hosted Cache Client (Uses HTTPS)	☐	☐
☐ BranchCache - Hosted Cache Server (Uses HTTPS)	☐	☐
☐ BranchCache - Peer Discovery (Uses WSD)	☐	☐
☑ Brave	☑	☑
☑ Captive Portal Flow	☑	☑

Details...   Remove

Allow another app...

FIGURE 1.6-8   Adding a rule for a newly added application

Restriction Rules

A *restriction rule,* as its name implies, blocks or limits traffic from passing through the firewall. Windows Defender Firewall supports two levels of restriction rules, in addition to its predefined rules:

- **Program**   This type of restriction blocks all or some type of traffic from a program.
- **Port**   This type of restriction blocks all or some traffic from a single TCP/UDP port, a range of ports, or a specific protocol.

A restriction rule differs from application or program inbound rules because it defines only what it doesn't permit. A *program restriction rule* specifies the source, destination, protocol, and more that aren't allowed, which by exception defines the messages to be allowed. A program restriction rule is specific to a program and is created as an inbound or outbound rule, or both, with the *New Rule* option.

For example, you may need to create a rule that prevents an application from communicating through the firewall with a site on the Web. You can create a new outbound rule that blocks all of the application's outbound traffic, or you can modify an existing outbound rule to do the same by setting the rule to Block the Connection.

EXAM TIP   Be familiar with the process for configuring the OS firewall settings. For the CompTIA A+ Core 2 exam, focus on the application restrictions and exceptions. Remember that public connections to LAN devices are blocked for security purposes.

Client Network Configuration

The CompTIA A+ Core 2 (220-1102) exam focuses on the client side of networking, which means its focus is on the computer workstation and its configuration. Therefore, a CompTIA A+ certified technician works from the client side, as opposed to the network side, to ensure that the workstation (client) is configured properly for communication over the network.

Most network clients get their Internet addressing and associated configuration, by default, from a *Dynamic Host Configuration Protocol (DHCP)* server, but there are several situations where a client must be configured manually, such as when the DHCP server is down, when the client is to operate with a static address, and so on.

Fortunately, Windows 10/11 provide a number of tools that can be used to configure a network client. The following sections provide an overview of the Internet Protocol (IP) versions 4 and 6 addressing schemes and then provide a description for each of the tools you can use to configure a network client.

EXAM TIP   On most SOHO networks, the DHCP server that provides automatic IP addresses is a function built into the router.

Internet Protocol Addressing Schemes

Two versions of Internet Protocol (IP) are in use on local and wide area networks: IP version 4 (IPv4) and IP version 6 (IPv6). When it became apparent that the world was consuming IPv4 addresses at a rate that would soon deplete their availability, the IPv6 standard was developed and has been in the process of being implemented for some time now.

IPv4 Addressing

IPv4 addresses are expressed in a *dot/decimal* format, which is likely the one with which you are most familiar. For example, in the IPv4 network address 34.200.194.131, the values actually represent two separate parts of the address. The first value (34) is the network ID, which is 34.0.0.0, and the last three values (200.194.131) are the host address, which may be a network client or perhaps even a network router.

Some IPv4 addresses are reserved for special purposes. Table 1.6-1 lists the most common of these addresses and their use. These addresses represent the IPv4 addresses most commonly assigned to network clients. The 10.x.x.x, 172.16.x.x, and 192.168.x.x ranges are each reserved

TABLE 1.6-1	Reserved Private IPv4 Addresses

Reserved IPv4 Address	Purpose
10.0.0.0–10.255.255.255	Class A private addressing on a private LAN
127.0.0.0–127.255.255.255	Loopback addresses on the localhost (client)
169.254.0.0–168.254.255.255	APIPA addresses, used when no IP address is provided by DHCP
172.16.0.0–172.31.255.255	Class B private addressing on a private LAN
192.168.0.0–192.168.255.255	Class C private addressing on a private LAN

for use within a single LAN and cannot be routed over the Internet. These addresses are the reserved private addresses for address classes A, B, and C, respectively.

The 127.x.x.x addresses are essentially the addresses of a client's network adapter and network interface card (NIC). The 169.254.x.x addresses are known as Automatic Private IP Addresses (APIPA) and are assigned to a client automatically when it cannot receive its configuration from a DHCP server. Clients with APIPA addresses can communicate on a LAN only.

 EXAM TIP Be sure you know the differences between an alternate IP address, an APIPA IP address, and a DHCP-assigned IP address.

Another address type a client may receive is an *alternate IP address*. This is an IP address you assign to the client. To put an alternate address in perspective, there are two addresses the client can receive automatically: an address from a DHCP server and a Windows-assigned APIPA address. In Windows parlance, an address manually assigned by an administrator is an alternate address.

An alternate address is assigned using the following steps:

1. Open the Network and Sharing Center on the Control Panel.
2. Click the Change Adapter Settings link to open the Network Connections window.
3. Click the connection used by the client.
4. On the General tab of the adapter's dialog box, click Properties.
5. Find Internet Protocol Version 4 (TCP/IPv4) in the list of protocols and make sure its checkbox is checked. Then, with this protocol selected, click Properties.
6. On the Properties dialog box that displays, choose the Alternate Configuration tab.
7. Select the radio button for User Configured and fill in the alternate address, subnet mask, and default gateway fields, as shown in Figure 1.6-9.
8. Click OK to complete the assignment of the alternate address.

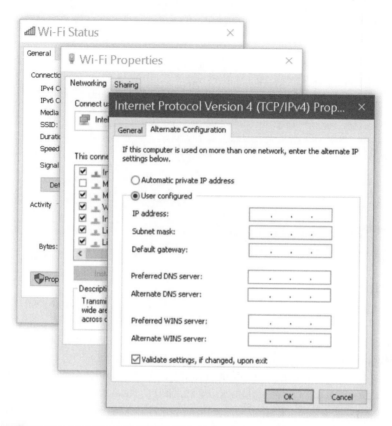

FIGURE 1.6-9   The data fields for the user-configured entries to assign an alternate address to a network adapter

Subnet Mask   The *subnet mask* distinguishes which part of the IP address identifies the network ID and which part of the address identifies the host. Network devices used the subnet mask to extract the network ID from an IP address. The same subnet mask is used for all computers that will connect to each other. For example, a subnet mask of 255.255.255.0 is used for all of the network nodes on a Class C network. Figure 1.6-10 shows the output of an **ipconfig /all** command prompt entry that shows the subnet mask for a PC.

Gateway   The default gateway is the IP address for your network's router. On private networks in a home or small office, a common value is 192.168.0.1. Figure 1.6-10 shows the default gateway in the ipconfig results. Check your network configuration for details.

 EXAM TIP   Objective 1.6 lists subnet mask and gateway under client network configuration. Understand what they are used for and where to configure them.

```
Wireless LAN adapter Wi-Fi:

   Connection-specific DNS Suffix  . :
   Description . . . . . . . . . . . : Intel(R) Dual Band Wireless-AC 7265
   Physical Address. . . . . . . . . : 5C-E0-C5-B6-B3-9A
   DHCP Enabled. . . . . . . . . . . : Yes
   Autoconfiguration Enabled . . . . : Yes
   Link-local IPv6 Address . . . . . : fe80::41aa:2a97:bc6c:4765%4(Preferred)
   IPv4 Address. . . . . . . . . . . : 192.168.23.147(Preferred)
   Subnet Mask . . . . . . . . . . . : 255.255.252.0
   Lease Obtained. . . . . . . . . . : Monday, July 25, 2022 7:08:43 PM
   Lease Expires . . . . . . . . . . : Thursday, August 11, 2022 8:08:54 AM
   Default Gateway . . . . . . . . . : 192.168.20.1
   DHCP Server . . . . . . . . . . . : 192.168.20.1
   DHCPv6 IAID . . . . . . . . . . . : 56418501
   DHCPv6 Client DUID. . . . . . . . : 00-01-00-01-27-DE-C7-94-5C-E0-C5-B6-B3-9A
   DNS Servers . . . . . . . . . . . : 192.168.20.1
   NetBIOS over Tcpip. . . . . . . . : Enabled
```

FIGURE 1.6-10   The results of an ipconfig command showing the subnet mask and the default gateway

IPv6 Addressing

An IPv6 address is made up of 128 bits, compared to the 32 bits of the IPv4 address, and uses a colon/hexadecimal format, which means its format is x:x:x:x:x:x:x:x, where the eight x's represent 16-bit hexadecimal numbers separated by colons. An example of an IPv6 address is 2001:0000:3238:DFE1:0063:0000:0000:FEFB.

Because there is essentially an unlimited number of IPv6 addresses available, there is no need to assign unrouteable private blocks of addresses, and virtually all IPv6 addresses are routable. However, static IPv6 address can be assigned to a network client. To do so, use the following steps:

1. Open the Network and Sharing Center in the Control Panel.
2. Click the Change Adapter Settings link to open the Network Connections window.
3. Click the connection used by the client.
4. On the General tab of the adapter's dialog box, click Properties.
5. Find Internet Protocol Version 6 (TCP/IPv6) in the list of protocols and make sure its checkbox is checked. Then, with this protocol selected, click Properties.
6. Select the radio button for Use the Following IPv6 Address and fill in the alternate address, subnet prefix length, and default gateway fields, as shown in Figure 1.6-11.
7. Click OK to complete the assignment of the alternate address.

Notice that in step 6, one of the values to be entered is the *subnet prefix length*. This value identifies the number of bits of the IPv6 address (left to right) that are being used to represent the network ID portion of the address. For example, for an IPv6 address of 2001:0000:3238:DFE 1:0063:0000:0000:FEFB and a subnet prefix length of 64 (the default), 2001:0000:3238:dfe1:: is the network ID.

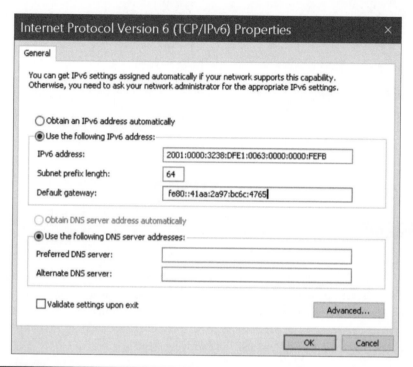

Domain Name System

When you enter a *fully qualified domain name (FQDN)* or a *Uniform Resource Locator (URL)* "address" (such as www.microsoft.com) in a browser's address bar, the text characters you've entered mean absolutely nothing to the Internet. The Internet's internal addressing is either an IPv4 or IPv6 address for each location. The Domain Name System (DNS) translates the human-readable (and memorable) text string into the IP address that corresponds directly to it.

 NOTE   Google and other vendors offer freely available DNS servers you can use. Google's DNS servers are 8.8.8.8 and 8.8.4.4.

To make the translation needed between the text and the numerical addressing, a browser sends a request message to the DNS server configured to the client asking for the IP address it needs. After it receives the address from the DNS server, the browser can issue a request to the server at the IP address provided.

Edit IP settings

| Manual ∨ |

IPv4
⬤ Off

IPv6
⬤ Off

| Save | Cancel |

FIGURE 1.6-12   The Edit IP Settings pop-up window

The DNS translation process typically requires only a few milliseconds, and most users don't realize it has happened at all. However, there are situations where this process can slow down the responses of the browser and the Internet. In many commercial and office situations, specific settings can be made to Windows 10/11 to speed the process along. To change the DNS settings on a Windows 10/11 system, use the following steps:

1. Open the Settings app and click the Network & Internet option.

2. Click the network type (Ethernet or Wi-Fi) and select the network connection you wish to change.

3. Scroll down the page to the IP settings section and click the Edit button.

4. On the Edit IP Settings pop-up, shown in Figure 1.6-12, select the IP version you wish to edit.

5. For the preferred DNS server, verify the address of the primary DNS server or enter the address of the DNS server you wish to use.

6. For the alternate DNS server, verify the address of the secondary DNS server or enter the address of the alternate DNS server you wish to use.

7. Click Save and restart the client to complete the changes, if any.

Static vs. Dynamic

You will often see the two terms *static* and *dynamic* used in the context of computer networking. Their meanings are actually very simple, as they are essentially opposites. *Static* means that something doesn't change. For example, an alternate IP address entry, entered manually, remains constant, which makes it static. *Dynamic,* on the other hand, means that something can change and usually does. For example, a client's IP configuration settings provided by a DHCP server can be completely different each time the client is started up, which makes them dynamic.

When the DHCP configuration is set to Obtain an IP Address Automatically, it means the DHCP server is to provide the IP configuration, which includes a dynamic IP address. However, when an IP address, like the one in Figure 1.6-11, is entered manually, a static IP configuration is created. Dynamic and static have really nothing to do with whether the IP address is IPv4 or IPv6, and either address version can be either dynamic or static. Instead, this has to do with how the IP address is configured. Automatic configuration is dynamic, and manual configuration is static.

 NOTE   Remember that a manually assigned IP address is a static address, and an automatically configured address is dynamic.

Establish Network Connections

There's no doubt that the most important part of interacting on a computer network is to establish a network connection. Without that, a client has no means of communicating on the network at all. In this section, we look at the means of establishing a network connection that are included on the CompTIA A+ Core 2 exam.

VPN

To set up a virtual private network (VPN) connection in Windows 10/11, use the following steps:

1. Open the Settings app and choose the Network & Internet option.

2. Choose VPN from the left-side navigation pane to open the VPN page (see Figure 1.6-13).

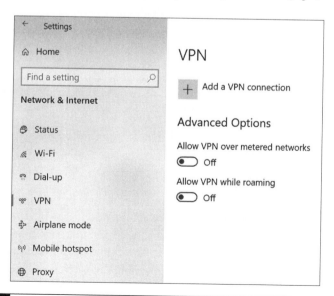

FIGURE 1.6-13   The VPN page

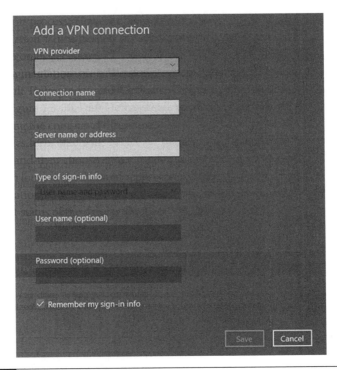

FIGURE 1.6-14   The Add a VPN connection page

3. To add a VPN connection, click Add a VPN Connection to open the Add a VPN Connection page shown in Figure 1.6-14.

4. After adding the information for the new VPN connection, click Save to return to the VPN page. If necessary, set the Allow VPN Over Metered Networks and the Allow VPN While Roaming sliders.

 NOTE   The process to add a VPN connection on a Windows 11 system is only slightly different, primarily in the layout of the Settings pages.

Wireless

Configuring a Wi-Fi adapter after it has been installed is done by opening the Settings app, choosing the Network & Internet option, and selecting Wi-Fi from the left-side navigation pane. This opens the Wi-Fi page shown in Figure 1.6-15. On this page, you can display a list of the wireless networks that Windows has detected within range and connect to one of your choice. You can also connect to a Wi-Fi network using the wireless network icon included in the right-hand navigation area of the taskbar (see Figure 1.6-16). If it's hidden, click the up-arrow icon first.

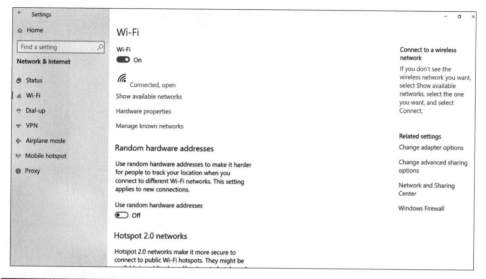

The Wi-Fi page

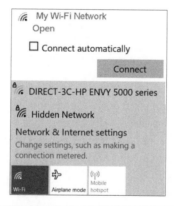

The Wi-Fi connections pop-up menu is opened from the taskbar.

To connect, click the wireless network desired. To reuse the network connection the next time the system starts up, click the Connect Automatically checkbox (see Figure 1.6-16). If the network is secured, enter the encryption key when prompted.

Wired

Windows automatically connects to a wired network when an Ethernet (wired) network adapter or NIC is embedded in the chipset or motherboard or inserted as an expansion card in the computer and connected to a router, switch, or hub. A computer may also have two or more network adapters. Virtually all wired network adapters are Plug and Play

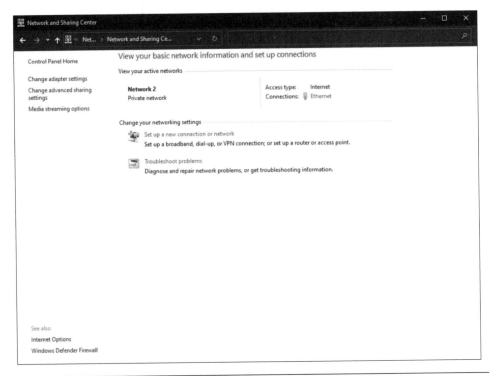

FIGURE 1.6-17   The Network and Sharing Center on the Windows Control Panel

(PnP), so the configuration of the network connection is essentially automatic. To view the configuration and status of a wired network connection, open the Network and Sharing Center from the Control Panel (see Figure 1.6-17). On this page, you can access these pages: Change Adapter Settings, Change Advanced Sharing Settings, and Media Streaming Options, among other actions.

However, it may be necessary to configure a proxy server (see the upcoming "Proxy Settings" section) or the IP address settings to establish a working connection. More on these topics can be found later in this objective.

Wireless Wide Area Network

To create a wireless wide area network (WWAN, or cellular) connection in Windows, click the Network icon on the taskbar and then click the name of the network. If prompted, enter the user name, password, and APN (access point name). Provide any other information requested or needed.

EXAM TIP   Make sure you can explain the differences between the Windows configuration of VPN, wireless, wired, and WWAN (cellular) connections.

Proxy Settings

A *proxy server* is an intermediary between its users and the resources they request. Applications send requests to the proxy server instead of trying to access the Internet directly, and the proxy server fetches the resources on behalf of the users. This enables the proxy server to monitor usage; restrict access to or modify insecure or objectionable content; cache, compress, or strip out resources to improve performance; and more.

To set up manual proxy server settings, use the following steps:

1. On the Settings app, click the Network & Internet option.

2. Click the Proxy option in the left-side navigation pane to open the Proxy page, the body of which is shown in Figure 1.6-18.

3. If you are using a proxy server, you can choose to have it configured automatically using the settings in the Automatic Proxy Setup section at the top of the Proxy page. You have two choices for the automatic settings: either let the OS detect its settings or use a script file to guide the configuration. If you are using a script, enter the full pathname of the script and click Save.

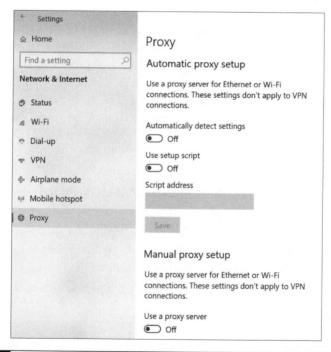

FIGURE 1.6-18 The Proxy page

4. To manually configure a proxy server, move the slide switch in the Manual Proxy Setup area to On and enter the IP address and port number of the proxy in the appropriate boxes. If you wish to exempt certain addresses or address ranges from using the proxy, enter them in the exceptions box, following its instructions. Click Save to complete the proxy settings.

Public Network vs. Private Network

When you first connect to a network, regardless of the medium in use, the Windows OS wants to know whether the network is public or private so that the proper security configuration applies. The security settings for a private (home) network connection are typically much different from a public (work or hotspot) network connection.

A *private network* exists in an environment where the control for all of the clients, servers (if any), and devices are under the control of one person or a small group or family. A private network most commonly exists in a home or SOHO. The security applied by Windows to a private network assumes that all the software and devices are trustworthy, and the security applied should allow them to interact.

A *public network* setting tells Windows that the system administration doesn't control the network and not necessarily all of the network devices. Windows then assumes that a higher level of security is required for this network. Examples of public networks are coffee shop Wi-Fi, hotel wired and wireless networks, and hotspots in public libraries and public spaces. On a public network, Windows believes its primary duty is to protect its client from the other devices on the network. This effectively isolates the client so that none of the other devices on the public network can see or access what the client does on the network.

To set or change the network type on a Windows 10 system, use the following steps:

1. Open the Network & Internet option on the Settings app.
2. From the left-side pane, choose the medium you wish to modify.
3. If your choice is Ethernet, click the Properties link and select the network type you wish to assign.
4. Otherwise, if your choice is Wi-Fi, click the Show Available Networks link to display the wireless networks within range. In the blue pop-up list of available Wi-Fi networks, click the Properties link of the active connection.
5. On the page that opens for the connection selected, set the network to either Public or Private.

 EXAM TIP Given a scenario, know the differences between a public network and a private network.

File Explorer Navigation

The File Explorer, previously known as the Windows Explorer, provides a variety of ways to find, select, and work with files, folders, and mapped elements on a local system or on a network. Navigation within the File Explorer is primarily accomplished through the navigation pane on the left side of the display. An example is shown in Figure 1.6-19.

File Explorer Navigation

The navigation pane in Windows 10 and 11 displays links to the files, folders, and drives that are accessed the most frequently. These items are organized under the following group headings:

- **Quick Access**   These are the items the system has noticed that the user accesses most frequently or items that the user has added so that they are available immediately.
- **OneDrive**   If the OneDrive app is installed on the system, Windows adds its content structure to the File Explorer display.
- **Desktop (aka "This PC")**   This group includes the drives, folders, and files on the local PC. It commonly shows Documents, Downloads, Music, Pictures, Videos, and more.

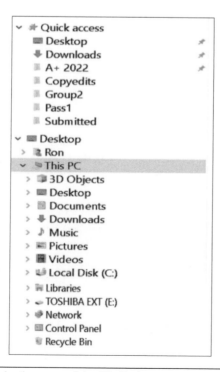

FIGURE 1.6-19   The Navigation pane of the File Explorer

File Explorer—Network Paths

Windows 10/11 File Explorer provides a means to share folders and files with other users on the same network. Files can be shared individually between single users, but this can become burdensome as the shares multiply.

When you click a folder or file in the File Explorer, the address bar will show only its name, by default, which may not always be enough information. In many cases, a full pathname is what's needed.

To display a full pathname for a selected folder or file in the File Explorer address bar, do the following:

1. Select the folder or file for which you wish to see the full pathname.

2. On the File Explorer display, select the View menu option.

3. Click the Options icon to display the Change Folder and Search Options choice to display the Folder Options dialog box (see Figure 1.6-20).

4. In the Folder Options dialog box, select the View tab.

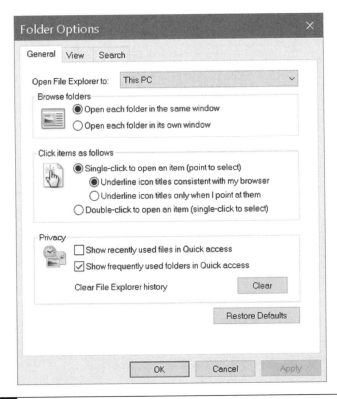

FIGURE 1.6-20   The Folder Options dialog box

FIGURE 1.6-21   The Display the Full Path in the Title Bar selection in the Advanced Settings list in the Folder Options dialog box

5. In the Advanced Settings list, check the box next to Display the Full Path in the Title Bar (see Figure 1.6-21) and then click Apply.

6. If you wish to apply this change to all folders, click the Apply to Folders button.

7. Click OK to complete the change.

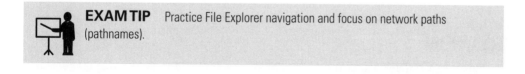

EXAM TIP   Practice File Explorer navigation and focus on network paths (pathnames).

Metered Connections and Limitations

A *metered connection* (aka a metered network) provides a network connection, but with a preset limit of usage, typically measured in megabytes (MB) or gigabytes (GB). This data limit, which is a measurement of the amount of data transferred over the connection, can be daily, but most typically it's monthly. Should the user exceed the limit, an additional charge is made.

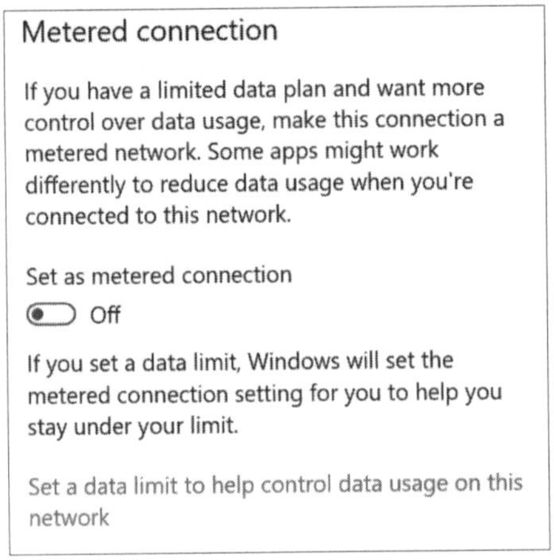

Metered connection

If you have a limited data plan and want more
control over data usage, make this connection a
metered network. Some apps might work
differently to reduce data usage when you're
connected to this network.

Set as metered connection

 Off

If you set a data limit, Windows will set the
metered connection setting for you to help you
stay under your limit.

Set a data limit to help control data usage on this
network

FIGURE 1.6-22   The Metered Connection section on a Wi-Fi connection's Properties page

A common metered connection is a smartphone's data plan, which is generally set in GBs of data transferred. A metered connection can be throttled, which slows down the data transfer as a way to avoid exceeding the limits. Metered connections are rare for subscribed Internet services, but they still exist for Wi-Fi connections in some areas.

To set up a metered connection, use the following steps:

1. Open the Settings app and select the Network & Internet icon.
2. Choose the Wi-Fi option from the left-side navigation pane.
3. On the Wi-Fi page, choose the Manage Known Networks option to display a list of the networks detected within range of your PC.
4. Select the Wi-Fi connection that you want to make a metered connection and then click the Properties button that appears to open the Properties page for that connection.
5. Scroll down to the Metered Connection section (see Figure 1.6-22).
6. Use the toggle switch to enable the Set as Metered Connection option.

REVIEW

Objective 1.6: Given a scenario, configure Microsoft Windows networking features on a client/desktop   Here are the Windows 10 (and some Windows 11) networking concepts and features in this objective:

- The standard network type for Windows is a workgroup, but each computer must have its local and remote users manually configured.
- A Microsoft Active Directory domain uses a domain controller (DC) to provide centralized administration of all users on the network.

- A workgroup account is the default account type of Windows 10/11 systems.
- A shared resource is accessible to authorized remote computers and users over a network.
- A network share is a folder or file that local and remote users have access to.
- A workgroup printer is physically connected to a workgroup server or to the DC.
- A file server stores and shares files on a network.
- A mapped device is physically remote but appears to be local.
- Windows Defender Firewall with Advanced Security is a host-based application that prevents unauthorized or unwanted application and network traffic from flowing in or out of a local host.
- Windows Defender Firewall supports three rule types: inbound, outbound, and connection security.
- Client-side networking concerns computer workstations and their configuration.
- IPv4 addresses are 32 bits in dot/decimal format, and IPv6 addresses are 128 bits in a colon/hexadecimal format.
- DNS provides a translation between a URL and its corresponding IP address.
- A static IP address is fixed and changes manually. A dynamic IP address can be easily changed automatically.
- A VPN is a dedicated secured private network.
- A proxy server is an intermediary device between its users and the network resources they request.
- A private network is controlled by one person or a small group.
- In a public network setting, Windows applies a higher level of security to protect its client.
- The Windows File Explorer provides ways to find, select, and work with files, folders, and mapped elements on a local system or network.
- Windows 10/11 File Explorer shares folders and files on a network with a full pathname.
- A metered connection provides a network connection to a preset limit of usage, typically measured in megabytes (MB) or gigabytes (GB).

1.6 QUESTIONS

1. A user needs to access a network printer but only knows the network printer's IP address. What should you tell the user?

    A. Find the printer brand and model.

    B. Use a wireless connection to the printer.

    C. The IP address is the only information needed to use the printer.

    D. Find out the host name.

2. A Windows user has just returned from a trip during which she connected to the Internet via Wi-Fi networks in coffee shops and airport lounges. The user wants to connect to the new wireless LAN to print a report to a network printer she has used before, but she can't connect to the printer. Which of the following is the most likely cause?

 A. Windows Firewall is set for a private network.

 B. Windows Firewall is set for a public network.

 C. The user must reinstall the printer driver.

 D. A printer app can't work on a wireless LAN.

3. You are performing telephone support with a user who has lost his Internet connection on a SOHO network. After running ipconfig, the user reports his IP address as 169.254.0.23. Which of the following should you check first?

 A. Broadband modem

 B. Network switch

 C. Network hub

 D. Network router

4. A client says she needs to access an important document that was sent to her over the Internet by one of her clients, but no matter how many times the document has been sent, it never arrives on her computer. What should you check first when resolving this problem?

 A. Network adapter

 B. Network router

 C. Network firewall rules

 D. Proxy server

5. A company salesperson is telecommuting from home three days a week. She is setting up a home office but cannot connect to any IP address beyond her home network's router. She ran an ipconfig command and learned that the IP address assigned to her computer is 169.254.0.1. What do you believe to be the source of her problem?

 A. No connection to the DHCP server or DHCP server is faulty.

 B. The network adapter is faulty.

 C. The default gateway is configured incorrectly.

 D. The proxy server settings are incorrect.

1.6 ANSWERS

1. **C** With the IP address of the printer, the user can find and set up the printer using Devices and Printers.

2. **B** When Windows Firewall is set to Public, connections to LAN devices are blocked for security.

3. **D**   On most SOHO networks, the DHCP server that provides automatic IP addresses is a function built into the router. Thus, the router is the first device to check.

4. **C**   The network firewall rules may be denying the source IP address, the document type, or some other characteristic of the missing document.

5. **A**   It appears that an APIPA address was assigned automatically when a DHCP request failed.

Objective 1.7 Given a scenario, apply application installation and configuration concepts

After you have installed and updated an operating system, the next step in preparing a computer for use is installing applications. The exact procedure for installing an app depends on whether you are installing it on a Windows system (and which version), Linux system, or macOS system and whether the app is located in an app store or a repository. However, there are fundamental procedures that should be followed with any of the operating systems covered on the CompTIA A+ 220-1102 exam.

System Requirements for Applications

Before installing an application, compare its hardware requirements to the computer system where it will be installed (often called the *target computer*). In most cases, these requirements will include the following:

- 32-bit vs. 64-bit dependent application requirements
- Dedicated vs. integrated graphics card
- Video random access memory (VRAM) requirements
- RAM requirements
- Central processing unit (CPU) requirements
- External hardware tokens
- Storage requirements

For example, the system requirements for a Microsoft Office 365 installation on a Windows desktop computer are as follows:

- **CPU/Processor**   1.6 GHz or faster 64-bit processor. If the Skype for Business app is to be installed, the processor requirement is a 2.0 GHz dual-core processor.
- **Memory**   4 GB of RAM on a 64-bit system. On a 32-bit system, the RAM requirement is 2 GB.

- **Hard disk space**   4 GB of available disk space. However, future updates could expand the disk space required.
- **Display**   1280×768 screen resolution on a 64-bit system. A 32-bit system needs to have 4K hardware acceleration or higher.
- **Graphics**   Graphic hardware acceleration with a minimum of DirectX 9 and WDDM 2.0.
- **OS version**   Windows 10, Windows 8.1, Windows Server 2019, or Windows Server 2016.
- **Compatible browser**   The preferred browsers are the current versions of Microsoft Edge, Internet Explorer, Safari, and Chrome. Office 365 apps are compatible with Firefox.
- **.NET requirement**   NET 3.5 or 4.6 or higher.

Here are the system requirements to run Office 365 on a macOS computer:

- **CPU/Processor**   An Apple computer with an Intel processor.
- **Memory**   4 GB of RAM.
- **Hard disk space**   Disk formatted to HFS+ or APFS with 10 GB of available disk space.
- **Display**   1280×800 resolution.
- **Graphics**   Default Apple PC graphics.
- **OS version**   Any of the three latest Apple macOS releases, with the latest release preferred.
- **Compatible browser**   Microsoft Edge, Safari, or Chrome.
- **.NET requirement**   This requirement is not applicable to macOS systems.

32-bit vs. 64-bit Dependent Application Requirements

Perhaps the most important system characteristic when installing an application is the architecture of the CPU, bus structure, and memory, all of which directly impact the compatibility and performance of the OS and any applications you install.

 EXAM TIP   CompTIA refers to 32-bit systems as "X86" and 64-bit systems as "X64." This is important for the CompTIA A+ Core 1 exam, but you should be aware of this for both exams.

For example, a 32-bit system supports (meaning addresses) up to 4 GB of RAM. A 64-bit system supports much more, which is largely dependent on the OS installed. On a Windows 10/11 Pro for Workstations system, the maximum RAM supported is 6 TB (terabytes). Many Linux distros support up to 48 TB, and the Apple M1 Max can be configured to support up to 128 GB.

More importantly, a 64-bit application won't run on a 32-bit system in native mode but will run in an emulator or virtual machine. However, a 32-bit application will run on a 64-bit system in any case.

Dedicated vs. Integrated Graphics Card

There are two basic types of graphics cards: *dedicated* (or discrete) and *integrated*. Other than producing displayed graphics, they have different functions.

A *dedicated graphics card* is a separate and independent device with its own graphics processing unit (GPU), cooling system, and onboard memory. However, a dedicated graphics card does require a compatible CPU. A dedicated graphics card is a better choice when playing AAA games, editing video, and rendering 3D models. Figure 1.7-1 shows an example of a dedicated graphics card.

An *integrated graphics card* is built into the CPU, and power is shared between the CPU and GPU. An integrated graphics card provides adequate support for web browsing, social media, e-mail, and personal productivity applications.

Video Random Access Memory Requirements

Much like RAM stores some low-level graphics and data, video random access memory (VRAM) stores higher-level graphic data. VRAM is present on dedicated graphics cards, close to the GPU, to speed up the display of the visual images you see. VRAM supports the GPU's functions for texture mapping, image rendering, and other graphics-producing functions.

Graphics applications typically have VRAM requirements, which are dependent on the graphics resolution and the use of features such as anti-aliasing. Here are a couple examples of application VRAM requirements:

- **Gaming**   The amount of VRAM needed for gaming is directly related to the resolution of a game's display. At a resolution of 1920×1080, known as 1080P (the *P* stands for *progressive*) or Full HD, an application may require 2 to 3 GB of VRAM. However, at 1440P, which is the more common resolution in gaming, at least 6 GB of VRAM may be required. High-end graphics that produce 4K (4096×2160) resolutions can require at least 8 GB of VRAM.
- **Video editing**   Like gaming, the amount of VRAM for video editing is a function of the video resolution. The more common video formats are 1080P, 1440P, and 4K, with some 8K now emerging. To edit a 1080P video, at least 8 GB of VRAM is needed. 1440P and 4K can require 16 GB of VRAM, with 32 GB of VRAM given as the most commonly recommended size.

RAM Requirements

The amount of RAM needed for an application can be an issue on non-upgradeable systems, such as many of the latest laptops, tablets, and 2-in-1 convertible devices. Although operating systems can use hard disk space as virtual memory, application performance depends on a system having adequate RAM. In fact, some applications won't install if there isn't sufficient RAM to support them.

Virtually all applications specify the minimum amount of RAM required to run them. If possible, you should increase the amount of RAM on the system if the application demands it. Alternatively, you can simply choose not to use the application. However, if you really want or need to use the application and you cannot expand the amount of RAM on the system, you have another option: you can increase the size of the virtual memory.

Windows automatically configures virtual memory, but the default may not be enough to satisfy your needs. To increase virtual memory, use the following steps:

1. Search for "performance" in the Start menu or the Power User Search.
2. Click Adjust the Appearance and Performance of Windows to open the Performance Options dialog box.
3. Select the Advanced tab and click the Change button in the Virtual Memory section to display the Virtual Memory dialog box (see Figure 1.7-2).
4. Adjust the virtual memory settings as needed. The most common change is to check the box for Automatically Manage Paging File Size for All Drives.
5. Click OK to save your changes.

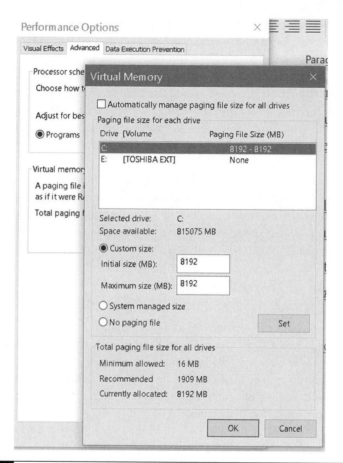

FIGURE 1.7-2   The Virtual Memory dialog box

   NOTE   A commonly used rule of thumb for calculating the size of a paging file is that it should be 1.5 times the amount of RAM on the system.

Central Processing Unit Requirements

A dilemma can arise each time newer versions of operating systems (OSs) or apps are announced. For example, the system requirements of Windows 11 essentially eliminates its installation on a significant number of mobile PC devices (laptops and notebooks). So, the user has the decision to upgrade the PC, which is not always easy or even possible, or remain on Windows 10 or an older version. This same dilemma can occur with an app the user wishes to use. The app may require a CPU upgrade and the user decides to make the upgrade or use another app or earlier version.

Applications like Office 365 and other personal productivity apps typically don't have system requirements that are outside of what is required by the operating system. However, this may not be true in all cases. As shown in the examples given earlier in this objective, the system requirements for an application can be unique. However, applications such as gaming, graphics, and video production can have specific requirements that may exceed the capabilities of an existing computer.

One area of general confusion is cores versus clock speed. Most modern PCs have multiple processor cores that give the CPU the capability to execute several programs simultaneously. Some applications require multiple-core CPUs. On the other hand, clock speed affects how fast the CPU is able to fetch and execute instructions. Some, although fewer, applications specify a minimum clock speed.

External Hardware Tokens

An *external hardware token* is a security tool that can be a key element in the identification or authentication process of a network or even a single computer. A hardware token, like the one shown in Figure 1.7-3, is a small (about the size of key fob), commonly handheld, physical device that can be easily incorporated into a multifactor authentication system.

Hardware tokens take many forms, including USB tokens, key fobs (like the one shown in Figure 1.7-3), and wireless Bluetooth or RFID tokens. Regardless of their form, hardware tokens are categorized as one of three types:

- **Connected**   This type of token must contact a reader, scanner, or the like, typically by being inserted into the reading device.
- **Contactless**   As the name of this group implies, this type of hardware token makes a connection with its reader wirelessly, using Bluetooth or RFID.
- **Disconnected**   Perhaps the most common type of disconnected token is an app on a smartphone using a one-time access code. This type of token is independent of the reader but communicates a code or signal to validate.

FIGURE 1.7-3   A hardware token (image courtesy of RSA Security LLC)

Storage Requirements

The amount of storage space available on the system drive (C: in Windows) can be a big concern, especially on systems with limited space, such as systems running solid-state drives (SSDs). To find out how much space an application needs, check its installation requirements first.

With Windows 10/11, you have the option of installing an application on a non-system drive, but if that's not an option and space is limited, you might need to remove seldom-used applications to make room. Run Disk Cleanup to remove unnecessary temp files, old installations, and unused system files and other files no longer needed.

 ADDITIONAL RESOURCES   To learn more about Disk Cleanup, go to https://support.microsoft.com/en-us/windows and search for "Disk Cleanup."

OS Requirements for Applications

Most applications made for Windows, macOS, or Linux are designed to run on a range of operating system versions. However, issues such as the following can prevent an application from working on a particular OS:

- The application runs in 64-bit mode only (you can't run it on a 32-bit system).
- The application is made for a newer version of the OS than what is in use.
- The application requires a newer version of DirectX 3D support than what the OS provides. Windows 10 supports DirectX 3D versions 11.3 and 12, and Windows 11 supports version 12.
- The application is not compatible with the version of OS in use. Some proprietary applications cannot run on Windows 10, for example.

Application-to-OS Compatibility

Windows includes the following tools to enable apps made for older versions of Windows to run on the installed version of Windows:

- The Compatibility Wizard in Control Panel of Windows 7/8/8.1
- The Program Compatibility Troubleshooter in Windows 10/11 (see Figure 1.7-4)
- The Compatibility tab in a program's Properties dialog box (see Figure 1.7-5)

The types of compatibility settings that can be used include the following:

- Changing the version of Windows the app detects
- Adjusting how the app uses the screen
- Running the app in administrator mode

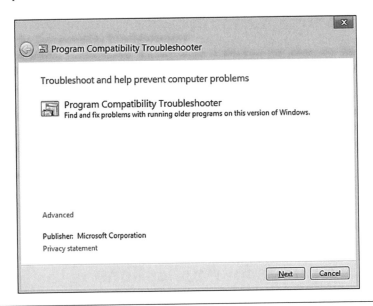

FIGURE 1.7-4   The Windows 10 Program Compatibility Troubleshooter

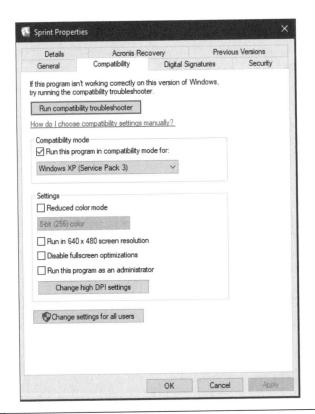

FIGURE 1.7-5   Using the Compatibility tab for an older app

The Compatibility Wizard and Program Compatibility Troubleshooter can be used to determine the specific compatibility fixes needed for an app and apply them. The Compatibility tab, shown in Figure 1.7-5, enables you to apply desired settings to the app before running it.

 EXAM TIP   Compatibility tools can help newer versions of Windows to run apps made for older versions.

32-bit vs. 64-bit OS

As stated earlier in this objective, a 64-bit application will not run on a 32-bit OS, but a 32-bit application will run on a 64-bit OS, although not as well as a 64-bit application will. The best solution is to run legacy (32-bit) applications in a virtual machine (VM) or another form of emulator.

Distribution Methods

Applications can be installed either locally (via DVD/USB) or from the network. The rise of high-speed networking, Internet access, and frequent software updates has transformed application installation so that most packaged software sold at retail now contains a key card with a code number that validates the purchase and releases the application to be downloaded and installed.

Network-based application installations in Windows may come from vendor websites or, with Windows 8 and later, from the Microsoft Store. In macOS, almost all apps are provided by the App Store.

 EXAM TIP   Understand the differences between local (DVD/USB) and network-based application installations.

In Linux, apps are provided primarily by the software repository associated with the publisher and distro in use. Typical distro disk image files (ISO) also include a large software repository, and new applications and updates to existing ones can be found in a online repository. Linux uses a hybrid of local and network-based application installation processes.

Android and iOS apps can be installed through the app store or, in corporate environments, via mobile device management (MDM) and mobile applications management (MAM) software.

 EXAM TIP   The distribution methods specifically mentioned in this objective are physical media, downloadable files, and .ISO mountable content.

Other Considerations for New Applications

Applications can have impacts on other components of a system—some good and some not so much. The Microsoft Store, Apple App Store, or Google Play can provide information about the permissions an app requires for installation and functionality. You should review the following information before you install an app:

- **Impact to device**   Most apps require access to other parts of the device's hardware or software subsystems to work.
- **Impact to network**   Many apps require access to a network to work and may need more of the network resources than anticipated.
- **Impact to operation**   An app can have both positive and negative impact on IT and general operations. An app can speed up communications and the processing of routine tasks. However, an app can require staff training and possibly change how information is used, stored, and even secured.
- **Impact on business**   Much like a store that was using a shoebox for a filing system changing to a database system, the impact an app can have on the processes and flow of the business' normal operations should be anticipated.

 EXAM TIP   Review what an app needs in the way of access to device and network resources before you install it.

REVIEW

Objective 1.7: Given a scenario, apply application installation and configuration concepts

- Before installing an application, you should check the device's hardware and software (including the operating system and other apps) for compatibility. Drive space can be an issue on mobile devices or on computers that use SSDs. Systems with non-upgradeable RAM might not be able to run some apps.
- Applications can have specific system requirements that go beyond those required by the OS.
- Applications may require a 64-bit or 32-bit system and compatibility with specific OS versions.
- The distribution methods most commonly used for applications are physical media, downloaded installation files, and mountable .ISO content.
- New application installations should be reviewed for their impact on the device, the network, the operations, and the business on the whole, where applicable.

- To avoid compatibility issues with apps, Windows includes compatibility features to enable older apps to run on newer versions of Windows and newer hardware.

- Most current systems use network-based installations, either via direct download, app stores, or software repositories. Checking permissions needed by an app is useful to determine if an app is a security risk.

1.7 QUESTIONS

1. A user is trying to install a 64-bit Windows app on a system running a 32-bit version of Windows. Which of the following recommendations should you make?

   A. Use the Program Compatibility Wizard.

   B. Create a Program Files (x64) folder for the program.

   C. Use the Compatibility tab.

   D. Install a 32-bit version of the app.

2. You are preparing a laptop for a trip that involves 12 hours of flight time. You have purchased a software key card from a retail store to use on the trip. When should you install the app?

   A. On the flight

   B. Before leaving for the airport

   C. While waiting for the flight

   D. Any of the above are acceptable

3. Your department is preparing to evaluate a new app that has a minimum requirement of 4 GB of RAM but recommends 8 GB of RAM. The systems you want to use have 4 GB of RAM and are expandable to 16 GB. Which of the following will help you evaluate the software most fairly?

   A. Set up a large pagefile on each system.

   B. Install the software on all computers and see how slow it runs.

   C. Install upgrades to 8 GB on some systems and install the app on all systems for comparison.

   D. Look for software that runs with 4 GB of RAM.

4. Although your department is now running Windows 10, it relies on an application made for Windows 7. It doesn't run properly on Windows 10. Which of the following could be used to help it run correctly?

   A. Device Manager

   B. System Properties

   C. Compatibility tab

   D. Virtual memory

5. Your employer wishes to install a multifactor authentication (MFA) system to control physical access into the company's IT center. Which of the following methods would be perhaps the most convenient way for employees to learn and work with the new system and also be the most secure?

   A. One-time passwords (OTPs)

   B. External hardware token (key fob)

   C. Password

   D. Issue keys for new locks on the IT doors.

1.7 ANSWERS

1. **D** A 32-bit app will work on 32-bit and 64-bit operating systems, but you cannot install a 64-bit app on a 32-bit operating system.

2. **B** If you wait to install the app until you go to the airport or while onboard the plane, you might not have access to an Internet connection or might need to pay a lot for a connection (which might be very slow) to download and configure the software.

3. **C** By upgrading some systems to 8 GB and running the app on all systems, you can determine if the performance difference between systems with 4 GB and 8 GB of RAM justifies upgrading all computers in the department.

4. **C** The Compatibility tab in the application's Properties dialog box provides access to the Program Compatibility Troubleshooter and to compatibility settings you can select manually.

5. **B** While all of the methods listed have one or more faults, using an external hardware token may be the easiest method for employees to work with, although there is still the issue of the token being lost.

Objective 1.8 **Explain common OS types and their purposes**

Operating systems (OSs) have many forms and perform a wide range of tasks, services, and functions. We tend to think of an OS as software on a PC, but in the digital world, many other types of devices have an operating system, including smartphones, cameras, video game consoles, and television set-top boxes, among others. Virtually any digital device that performs an automatic function of some kind has some form of an operating system.

This objective discusses the various types of standalone PC and network workstation (client) operating systems, looks at smartphone and mobile device operating systems, and briefly covers the issues of OS compatibility. It also describes and compares the file system types supported by the different operating systems and examines the problems that occur at the end-of-life point of an OS.

Operating systems fall into one of four basic types, each defined by the purpose and use of the computer on which they are installed:

- **Home workstations**   This type of OS is configured to serve the needs of a standalone PC or a network client in a small office/home office (SOHO) environment.
- **Business workstations**   This type of OS is more robustly configured than the home client and better serves the needs of a workstation in a centrally managed business, domain, or enterprise network.
- **Network servers**   This type of OS is configured to run as the centralized OS in business and enterprise networks.
- **Smartphones and tablets**   This is a more flexible type of OS that typically has a touch-screen interface and personal communication interactions.

Workstation Operating Systems

CompTIA includes four different operating system families in its objectives: Windows, Linux, macOS, and Chrome OS. There are others, but these are the ones you need to know for the CompTIA A+ Core 2 exam. The Core 2 objectives also emphasize workstations.

So, what is a workstation OS? In a standalone environment, a PC is just a PC for all intents and purposes. However, when that PC is connected to a network or server of some kind, it becomes a workstation, a node, a host, or a client. Regardless of what term is used, in a networked environment, the endpoint of a connection is, in the CompTIA A+ world, a workstation. A workstation is, as its name implies, a station for work, and, as such, it needs an OS that can support all the activities required by that work.

Okay, with all this in mind, let's look at the four operating systems CompTIA wants you to know.

Windows

The Windows OS is a graphical user interface (GUI) designed to simplify the interaction between the user and the hardware and software. Windows is known by its standard features, such as the Start menu, Desktop, taskbar, Task Manager, Control Panel, Recycle Bin, and Settings app. Each of these features and tools provides a user-friendly way to use and control a PC.

The various editions of the Windows OS provide one or more versions for each of the OS types listed earlier. Table 1.8-1 lists the Windows versions currently available by application.

Linux

The essential Linux OS is an unlimited open source OS kernel developed by Linus Torvalds, based on the UNIX OS. Unlike Windows and macOS, Linux is available from a wide variety of publishers, each of which produces one or more distributions (called *distros*) that range from basic functionality offerings (meaning the kernel plus a few additional features) to fully capable troubleshooting and diagnostics bundles, such as Kali Linux.

TABLE 1.8-1   Windows OS Versions

OS Usage Type	Windows Versions
Home workstation	Windows 10 Home Windows 10 Pro Windows 11 Home Windows 11 Pro Windows 11 Mixed Reality
Business workstation	Windows 10 Pro Windows 10 Pro for Workstations Windows 10 Enterprise Windows 11 Pro Windows 11 Pro for Workstations Windows 11 Enterprise
Network servers	Windows Server 2016 Windows Server 2019 Windows Server 2022

An open source OS is available for download to anyone who wishes to install it and perhaps even modify it for personal use or to share with the world. Windows and macOS systems are proprietary to Microsoft and Apple, respectively, and are restricted to purchased licenses. The source code for Linux is readily available, but this is not true of Windows and macOS.

Linux OS distros such as SUSE, Red Hat, Debian, Ubuntu, and Mint are some of the more commonly installed. Each is licensed differently. For example, Red Hat and SUSE are available via subscriptions, whereas Ubuntu is completely free to install for individual users, but enterprise-level use has support-agreement contracts. Others, like Debian and Mint, have no fee-for-service attachments and are supported by their installed communities. In virtually all Linux OS distros arrangements, the fee is for documentation and support. The Linux OS itself is still primarily open source.

Linux OS distros use two models for releasing new versions:

- **Standard release**   This model uses version numbers to distinguish update and version releases.
- **Rolling release**   When a distro provider believes an update is stable and ready for release, the update is made available to users. Some providers use their installed base to test updates by providing update packages on a voluntary basis. Rolling releases may have identification numbers, but the numbers are not considered benchmarks.

Linux can be installed for use as a workstation OS or a network server OS. Many schools use a Linux distro as their standard OS in student labs, and Linux is the leading OS for web servers. In addition, Linux distros are perhaps the most commonly used OSs for Internet of Things (IoT) networks and devices.

macOS

The macOS operating system is available for and only runs on Apple devices and is supplied as a standard component of each Apple computing product, including Apple Mac desktops, Apple iMac systems, and Apple MacBook laptops. Apple doesn't make the macOS available for purchase for non-Apple computers, but versions of the macOS can be installed on a PC using a virtual machine or a VM emulator, such as Oracle's VirtualBox.

The macOS operating system is built on a UNIX kernel and supplemented with proprietary routines for interfacing with its GUI and system utilities. Updates to macOS are released periodically at no cost to Apple device owners and are designated with both a number and a product identification name, such as version 10.15 (Catalina), 11 (Big Sur), and 12 (Monterey).

Virtually all Apple products, including macOS, are contained in what is called a "walled garden," which means that its products are confined to only its products. Products that have some compatibility with a variety of other brands and models, such as the Windows and Linux OSs, use the original equipment manufacturer (OEM) model.

Chrome OS

The Chrome OS is another operating system based on UNIX and, in this case, Linux as well. In fact, Chrome OS is essentially a Linux distro, named Chromium, which was developed by Google for use with web applications and as the OS on Chromebooks and Chromebox hardware. It is not a basic network workstation client but can be installed on compatible hardware.

In a web application environment, the web server performs most of the work, so the web client really doesn't need to have much in the way of processing power. Chrome OS provides a much reduced thin-client operating environment in which there are minimal system elements to interfere with the web browser and its interactions. Chrome OS can run Android applications.

Smartphone/Tablet Operating Systems

The top two operating systems for cellular phones, many tablets, and other handheld devices are Google Android and Apple iOS. There are others, but these two essentially dominate the mobile device OS market. In fact, in June 2022, according to the StatCounter.com website, Android had 72.11 percent of the global marketplace, Apple iOS had 27.22 percent, and several others had less than 1 percent each. The mobile device market will continue to expand with its key drivers likely being 5G, foldable devices, data content, and device capabilities.

ADDITIONAL RESOURCES   Visit the StatCounter website at https://gs.statcounter.com/ for more information about smartphones and mobile device OS market shares.

Android

Android is a mobile device operating system based on the Linux OS kernel. It also contains special-purpose open source software for touch screens and other touch devices that provides the interface for touch operations and gestures. Although most associated with Google, Android was developed by a consortium, Open Handset Alliance, and is primarily maintained by the Android Open Source Project (AOSP) under an Apache License. Google remains as Android's commercial sponsor. Android is deployed on devices with application support products, such as Google Mobile Services, Google Chrome, and Google Play, which are proprietary products. However, the licensing and end-of-life support for Android and its associate components are issued by the device manufacturers individually.

iPadOS

The Apple iPad handheld mobile tablet runs the iPadOS, which is essentially a variation of the Apple iOS operating system used on Apple's iPhones. At one time, iPadOS and iOS were very close in function and features, but as the phone and tablet products developed separate functions and features, the two OSs became more divergent.

iOS

The iOS operating system runs on Apple's iPhone smartphones and many of the older versions of the iPad. Like macOS, iOS is based on UNIX, but it's actually a closed source OS, proprietary to Apple.

 EXAM TIP Know which operating systems are closed source and which are open source. Windows, macOS, iOS, and iPadOS are all closed source. Open source platforms include Android, Chrome OS, and most Linux distributions.

The most basic feature of iOS is its user interface, which is a direct manipulation interface. A *direct manipulation interface* provides a variety of touch, motion, and directional gestures to indicate the choice or action requested, such as a swipe, a tap, a pinch, and others. The iOS interface also includes control objects such as sliders, switches, buttons, and the like.

The iOS starts up to an initial display or home screen, much like a Windows or macOS PC. Peripheral devices built into the smartphone, such as a camera, and apps, such as the flashlight and measuring tools, have their own hardware interfaces or application software that interfaces with the iOS in the same way applications interface with an OS on a PC.

 EXAM TIP Be able to explain the common OS types, their purposes, and their differences. Workstation OSs include Windows, Linux, macOS, and Chrome OS, while smartphone/tablet OSs include iPadOS, iOS, and Android.

Various File System Types

A file system defines the directory/folder organization of a physical storage device. File systems provide an organizational structure and the metadata describing the location and logistical characteristics of the elements stored within it. The basic function of a file system is to control the processes that locate, store, or retrieve data files. Operating systems support a variety of file systems, but each typically has one specific default file system.

Windows File Systems

The primary Windows file systems used on PCs are the *New Technology File System (NTFS)* and *File Allocation Table 32 (FAT32)*. These file systems have been in use for some time and have proven to be reliable.

New Technology File System

New Technology File System (NTFS) is a journaling file system, which means it logs all transactions performed against individual files, such as reads, writes, and deletes. This log information can then allow NTFS to recover parts or all of the file system.

 NOTE The repair tool for Windows NTFS is the chkdsk command.

NTFS is commonly the file system provided by remote data storage vendors. Because NTFS is the most common file system employed by corporate data centers, providing this file system on a remote storage service allows users to retain their file permissions, encryption, and compression, among other features.

NTFS provides the following benefits over other file systems, including the FAT variations and others:

- **Compression** Increased storage space on the storage medium.
- **Access control** Files and folders can be configured with permissions to restrict access.
- **Reliability** NTFS is consistent, so restoration, if needed, is quick and accurate.
- **Journaling** An audit trail is maintained in the Master File Table (MFT).

File Allocation Table 32

The File Allocation Table 32 (FAT32) is the 32-bit evolution of the FAT standard and is preceded by FAT, FAT12, and FAT16. The data width for FAT32 is 32 bits, which means it has the capability to address 32 bits, as opposed to NTFS, which is a 64-bit system. The FAT32 file system is capable of addressing 268,435,456 disk sectors and has a maximum cluster size of 32 KB.

The advantages of the FAT32 file system are as follows:

- **Compatibility** Many otherwise incompatible devices exchange data using FAT32.
- **Size** FAT32 supports partitions of up to 2 TB.
- **Efficiency** FAT32 has a minimum cluster size of 4 KB for partitions under 8 GB.

exFAT

The Extensible File Allocation Table (exFAT) is the version of FAT optimized for USB drives (flash memory) and Secure Digital (SD) cards. exFAT is a good substitute for NTFS, where NTFS cannot be used, and has a higher file size than FAT32 at 4 GB. sxFAT, a version of exFAT, is the standard for Secure Digital eXtended Capacity (SDXC) cards larger than 32 GB. exFAT is supported as a native system in Windows 10/11.

 EXAM TIP Know the differences between FAT32 and exFAT!

Linux File Systems

The basic file system of virtually all Linux distros is the extended (ext) file system. Currently, the two most commonly used file systems for Linux systems are *ext3* and *ext4*. The ext3 file system is a 64-bit file system that includes journaling support. The ext4 file system is considered a more efficient and faster file system.

The ext3 file system supports individual file sizes of 16 GB to 2 TB and volume sizes of 4 TB to 32 TB. However, one drawback of the ext3 file system is that deleted files cannot be undeleted. The ext4 file system enlarges individual file size to 16 TB, volume sizes to 1 exabyte (EB), and is able to support as many as 4 billion files. Perhaps its biggest drawback is that for all of its efficiencies and capacities, ext4 uses slightly more resources.

Apple File Systems

Apple workstations and laptops use the Apple-proprietary Apple File System (APFS), which like Windows NTFS, supports journaling, snapshots and imaging, user and group ownership and permissions, and encryption.

 EXAM TIP Be able to distinguish between file system types. Know that NTFS is the secure Windows file system. Linux file systems include ext3 and ext4. Modern Apple workstations and laptops use APFS.

Vendor Lifecycle Limitations

There are no standards for the policies and procedures an OS and application developer, provider, or vendor must follow. Each company defines and applies its own policies and procedures regarding the lifecycles of its products. However, here's a list of the lifecycle phases involved and recognized in most policies and procedures:

- **Product planning and feedback**   Vendors may refer to this phase as pre-release, alpha or beta testing, or insider activities. These activities, along with market release field testing, provide information and feedback to the vendor.
- **Product release and active marketing**   The product is made available for subscription or retail sale, and operational issues and security problems that require immediate remedy are monitored.
- **Extended support**   Once replacement editions or products enter the product planning and testing phases, a vendor may extend the product support period of the active releases but discontinue their active sales.
- **Product end-of-life**   When the product provider no longer wishes to offer support for a product, that product has reached its *end-of-life (EOL)* phase and support is ended, which includes security, operational, and features updates. One example of an EOL situation is Microsoft announcing that all support for Windows 10 will end in May of 2023. This provides a typical amount of time for users to plan for a move to another OS or Windows version.

Compatibility Concerns Between OSs

In a computing environment that involves hardware from a variety of different manufacturers, the compatibility of their various OSs and components can be a serious issue. Some manufacturers work to produce products that are compatible with competing products and, in some cases, even interchangeable. Other manufacturers work to keep their products proprietary and completely incompatible with similar and competing products. Compatibility issues fall into several different categories:

- **OS compatibility**   Having multiple OSs or OS versions can really complicate maintenance and support processes, which can include support for users, applications, and peripheral devices. However, on a local network, network nodes with different OSs can connect to an Ethernet network, because the OS interacts with its network adapter, which is the component connected to the network and servers.
- **File system compatibility**   Some Windows file systems, as shown in Table 1.8-2, are fully or partially compatible with Linux or macOS, or both.
- **Hardware compatibility**   Some hardware devices and peripherals may not have device drivers and support applications that are compatible with all OSs.

TABLE 1.8-2	OS and File System Compatibilities			
File System	**Windows**	**Linux**	**macOS**	**Comments**
NTFS	Yes	Yes	Read-only	
FAT32	Yes	Yes	Yes	
exFAT	Yes	Yes	Yes	
ADFS	No	Yes	Yes	Linux requires third-party software.
ext3/ex4	Yes	Yes	No	Windows requires Bootcamp app.

- **Software compatibility**   Applications, especially specific-purpose applications, tend to be developed for particular OSs, which may complicate enterprise standard operating procedures (SOPs).
- **Network compatibility**   Due to hardware and software incompatibilities, network devices may not be able to interact.

REVIEW

Objective 1.8: Explain common OS types and their purposes   Operating systems have many forms and perform a wide range of tasks, services, and functions. This objective covers the elements, definitions, and technologies for the most popular PC operating systems.

- Operating systems come in four basic types: home workstations, business workstations, network servers, and smartphones and tablets.
- The four different operating system families are Windows, Linux, macOS, and Chrome OS.
- A workstation is a computer with an OS that can support the activities required by the work.
- Windows is a GUI OS designed to simplify the interaction between the user and the hardware and software.
- Windows is known for its features, including the Start menu, Desktop, taskbar, Task Manager, Control Panel, Recycle Bin, and Settings app.
- The Linux OS is an open source OS kernel based on the UNIX OS.
- Linux is available as distros that range from basic functionality offerings to fully capable troubleshooting and diagnostics bundles.
- Linux OS distros use two release models: standard and rolling.

- The macOS operating system is closed source and available for Apple devices only.
- The macOS operating system is built on a UNIX kernel and supplemented with proprietary routines for interfacing with its GUI and system utilities.
- Windows and Linux OSs use the OEM model.
- The Chrome OS is a Linux version named Chromium, developed for use with web applications, Chromebooks, and Chromebox hardware.
- Chrome OS can run Android applications.
- The top two operating systems for smartphones and tablets are Google Android and Apple iOS.
- The Apple iPad tablet runs iPadOS, a variation of iOS.
- iOS runs on iPhone smartphones. iOS is based on UNIX but is a closed source OS.
- The most basic iOS feature is its direct manipulation interface.
- Android is an open source mobile device OS based on the Linux OS kernel.
- File systems provide an organizational structure as well as metadata describing the location and logistical characteristics of the elements stored within it.
- Windows file systems are NTFS, FAT32, and exFAT.
- NTFS is a journaling file system that logs all transactions performed against individual files.
- FAT32 is a 32-bit evolution of the FAT standard.
- exFAT is optimized for USB drives and SD cards.
- The basic Linux files systems are ext3 and ext4.
- Apple workstations and laptops use APFS.
- The lifecycle phases for OSs and applications are product planning and feedback, product release and active marketing, extended support, and product end-of-life (EOL).
- Compatibility issues are OS compatibility, hardware compatibility, software compatibility, and network compatibility.

1.8 QUESTIONS

1. What type of OS is more robustly configured than a home OS and better serves the operating needs of nodes on a centrally managed network?
   A. Home workstations
   B. Business workstations
   C. Network routers
   D. Smartphones and tablets

2. You have been delegated the task of picking an operating system for the endpoint workstations of your company's LAN. You wish to ensure that the applications that run on this OS are compatible with the applications running on the networks of the company's product partners. What OS would you recommend?

    A. Windows

    B. Linux

    C. macOS

    D. Chrome OS

3. What is the operating system that the macOS is based on?

    A. Windows

    B. Android

    C. UNIX

    D. Chrome OS

4. Which of the following are the most popular OSs for smartphones and tablet PCs? (Choose two.)

    A. Windows Mobile

    B. Google Android

    C. Apple iOS

    D. Linux Mobile

5. Which of the following are the most common file systems for the Linux OS? (Choose two.)

    A. exFAT

    B. ext3

    C. NTFS

    D. ext4

    E. APFS

1.8 ANSWERS

1. **B** A business operating system is better suited for the needs of workstations on larger networks.

2. **A** Any of the choices could be the answer, but if you are attempting to be compatible with other users or systems, your best bet is likely Windows.

3. **C** macOS is based on the UNIX OS.

4. **B C** Android and iOS are the most popular OSs for mobile devices. Windows Mobile has been deprecated, and there isn't a Linux Mobile product.

5. **B D** The two file systems most common on Linux OSs are ext3 and ext4.

Given a scenario, perform OS installations and upgrades in a diverse OS environment

One of the most common tasks for a computer technician is performing an operating system (OS) installation or upgrade. There are many ways to perform this task, and this objective discusses how these methods work and helps you determine when to use a particular one.

Boot Methods

A variety of boot methods are available for installing or upgrading Windows, macOS, or Linux. The following sections cover the boot methods you need to understand for the CompTIA A+ 220-1102 exam. (The installation choices are described a bit later in the "Types of Installation" section, later in this objective.)

External Drive/Flash Drive (USB)

To boot from a USB drive, follow this procedure:

1. Start up the computer and configure the BIOS/UEFI settings to boot from the desired drive.
2. With the bootable OS drive connected or inserted, restart the computer.
3. Follow the onscreen prompts to boot from the drive and start the installation process.

To perform an upgrade install from a USB flash drive, follow this procedure:

1. Open the OS USB flash drive in the file navigation app of the current operating system.
2. Open the installation app on the USB flash drive and follow the prompts to perform the upgrade.

Optical Disc (CD-ROM, DVD)

To perform a clean install from an optical disc, follow this procedure:

1. Make sure the target computer is configured to boot from the optical disc.
2. With the bootable OS disc inserted, restart the computer.
3. Follow the onscreen prompts to boot from the disc and start the installation process.

To perform an upgrade install from an optical disc, follow this procedure:

1. Open the OS optical disc in the file navigation app of the current operating system.

2. Open the installation app on the disc and follow the prompts to perform the upgrade.

 EXAM TIP Be familiar with the processes of booting from an optical disc, an external/hot-swappable drive, a USB flash drive, the network (PXE), the Internet, an internal hard drive, and a hard drive partition.

Network Boot (PXE)

Network boot is supported by Windows, Linux, and macOS. Windows and Linux refer to this feature as PXE, and macOS (and OS X) uses the terms NetBoot and NetInstall.

The *Preboot Execution Environment (PXE)* can boot from a network location using protocols such as IP, TFTP (Trivial FTP), DHCP, and DNS. If your network interface card (NIC) supports PXE, you can enable it in the BIOS/UEFI system setup utility from whichever screen has other options for your NIC (see Figure 1.9-1). While you're there, move network locations to the top of the boot sequence.

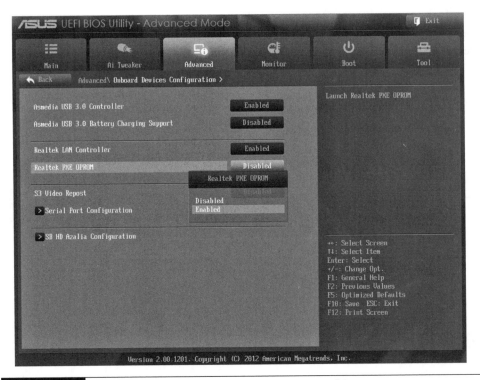

FIGURE 1.9-1 Selecting the PXE boot ROM option for a built-in Ethernet port

EXAM TIP PXE (Preboot Execution Environment) refers to network boot.

On a Windows or Linux system, when you reboot, somewhere along the familiar boot process you'll see the instruction "Press F12 for network boot." (It's almost always F12.) If the system can find and connect to a server, you'll be asked to press F12 again to continue booting from the network (see Figure 1.9-2), at which point you'll see a selection screen (if there are multiple images) or be taken directly to the Windows installer (if there's just one).

ADDITIONAL RESOURCES To learn more about configuring PXE with Windows 10, go to https://docs.microsoft.com/en-us/windows/deployment/configure-a-pxe-server-to-load-windows-pe. To learn more about using PXE in Linux, go to https://linuxconfig.org/network-booting-with-linux-pxe.

Legacy macOS systems can boot from a stored image on a network through a NetBoot server. A user can cause this boot process by pressing the N key at startup, which will select the default NetBoot image. The user could also use the Startup Disk preference pane to select the desired image. Current macOS models that include the Apple T2 security chip don't support NetBoot or NetInstall, and macOS Server no longer includes user interface (UI) tools for configuring either of these tools. As an alternative, Apple recommends using the open source NetSUS and BSDPy tools.

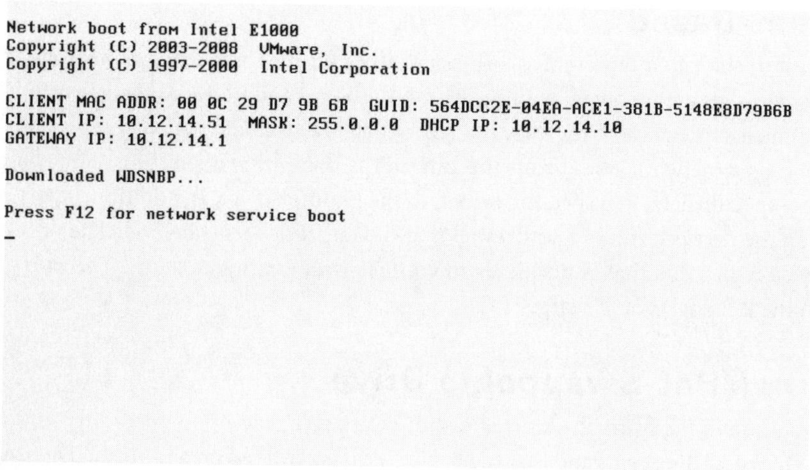

```
Network boot from Intel E1000
Copyright (C) 2003-2008  VMware, Inc.
Copyright (C) 1997-2000  Intel Corporation

CLIENT MAC ADDR: 00 0C 29 D7 9B 6B  GUID: 564DCC2E-04EA-ACE1-381B-5148E8D79B6B
CLIENT IP: 10.12.14.51  MASK: 255.0.0.0  DHCP IP: 10.12.14.10
GATEWAY IP: 10.12.14.1

Downloaded WDSNBP...

Press F12 for network service boot
_
```

FIGURE 1.9-2 Network boot using PXE

ADDITIONAL RESOURCES To learn how to create a NetBoot, NetInstall, or NetRestore volume and to learn which computers support booting from network volumes, see https://support.apple.com/en-us/HT202770. For a change list for macOS Server 5.7.1 and alternatives to no-longer-provided functions, see https://support .apple.com/en-gb/HT208312.

Solid-State/Flash Drives

A *solid-state drive (SSD)* can be an alternative boot source to a hard disk drive (HDD). With the SDD installed and configured in the PC, you clone the HDD to the SSD using a disk management or cloning tool like *AOMEI Partition Assistant, EaseUS Partition Master,* or *Macrium Reflect* to migrate the OS files from the HDD to the SDD. Then you reboot into the BIOS/UEFI and set the SSD as the primary boot source.

NOTE You may need to disable Secure Boot to be able to see the SSD as a bootable drive. The SSD should also be empty and free from partitioning.

A USB flash drive can also be used as a boot source. Preparing a USB boot drive involves using the *Windows Media Creation Tool, iSunshare ISO Genius, Rufus,* or the like to add the bootable image to a formatted USB drive. After creating the boot drive, set the BIOS/UEFI boot drive sequence priority.

Internet-Based

If you wish to start up a remote network node either on the same LAN or over the Internet, some prerequisites are involved: mainly, the motherboard and network adapter or NIC of the target PC must support *wake-on-LAN (WOL),* which is also called *remote wake-up.*

Starting up a network node from the Internet is done by transmitting a "magic packet" containing specific data, in a specific format, to the remote device. In addition, a port must be opened on the network router and firewall that the target node sits behind. The port number should be a high value that is not likely to conflict with existing systems. The port must be linked to the IP address of the target PC.

External/Hot-Swappable Drive

Before you boot a PC from an external or hot-swappable drive, you need to ensure that the BIOS/UEFI "sees" the device and that the device itself is powered on and ready. Then you need to set the boot device sequence or priority so that this drive is the first option in the boot device sequence. Finally, set the boot method to use what should be a USB-connected device as the priority option.

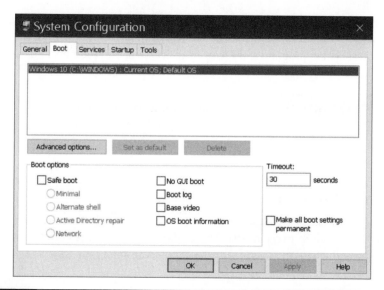

FIGURE 1.9-3   The Boot tab of the System Configuration dialog box

Internal Hard Drive (Partition)

If an internal partition of a hard disk has a bootable version of an OS, the system will ask which of the available boot versions you'd like to use to start the OS. However, since the BIOS/UEFI deals with drives and not partitions, you can configure the partition you want to boot from using the Windows System Configuration utility (msconfig). This utility configures how a computer starts up and the programs, applications, and services that are to load when Windows starts up.

The easiest way to open the msconfig.exe utility is to use the Start menu search and to select the System Configuration option from the results. On the System Configuration dialog box that displays, select the Boot tab (see Figure 1.9-3). The example shown in Figure 1.9-3 has only one entry, but if disks or partitions had bootable OSs available, they would be listed and you would be able to choose the one you wish to set as the boot partition.

Types of Installation

Operating systems can be installed using a variety of different methods. You need to understand these methods so that you can choose the right one for a particular situation (or exam question scenario).

Upgrade

An *upgrade* installation, also called an *in-place upgrade,* replaces an existing OS with either a newer version or, in the case of a damaged existing installation, a clean installation of the same version. On Windows systems, an upgrade enables users of Windows 8/8.1 or 10 to upgrade to Windows 11 without losing data or the need to reinstall applications.

To start an upgrade on a Windows system, start the computer normally, insert the installation media (DVD or USB flash drive), or connect to the network source of the ISO image file. Start the installation program and follow its instructions and prompts until the process is complete.

 EXAM TIP   In-place upgrades are also used to repair installations.

Recovery Partition

Some prebuilt systems come with a factory *recovery partition,* additional recovery media, or the capability to create recovery media. These recovery tools can restore the active system partition or the entire hard drive to fresh-from-the-factory condition using a *recovery image.*

 EXAM TIP   A recovery partition, recovery media, or the Reset This PC/Remove Everything setting of some systems should be regarded as a last resort for fixing a computer, as it wipes out all apps and user data.

Clean Install

A clean installation, or *clean install,* usually starts with an empty hard drive, but since the process partitions and formats the hard drive, it can also erase and install over an existing installation. This installation process is considered "clean" because it removes everything from the targeted medium and, as a result, doesn't inherit or carry over problems from an old OS. However, you will likely have to reconfigure the system and reinstall application or utility software not included in the OS. Begin by booting from an up-to-date installation media.

 EXAM TIP   A clean install wipes out all existing operating system files, apps, and user data.

Image Deployment

Image deployment saves tons of time when you manage many systems. An image is a complete copy of a hard drive volume that includes an operating system and often includes preinstalled apps. You can use special software to set up a fully loaded system by copying the image over from removable media or the network.

EXAM TIP   An image used for image deployment can also contain software.

Repair Installation

An in-place upgrade can be used to repair an existing installation without losing data or rein-stalling apps. A *repair installation* on a Windows system begins by booting from the instal-lation medium (ISO image file, DVD, or USB flash drive) that contains the same version of the OS as the version being repaired. Start the computer, boot from the installation media, and select Repair Your Computer (see Figure 1.9-4). Follow the prompts until the installation process is complete.

 EXAM TIP   Repair installations in Windows start the same way as in-place upgrades, but the user must select the Repair option when prompted. A repair installation is called a *reinstallation* in Linux.

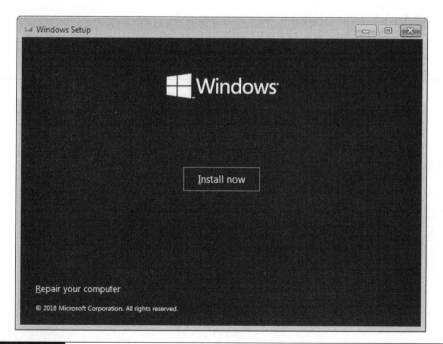

FIGURE 1.9-4   Repairing Windows from the installation media

Linux refers to a repair installation as a *reinstallation*. This option is available on some distributions, such as Ubuntu, when you start the computer with the same version of Linux on a Live CD or USB drive. The installation program detects the existing Linux install and asks you if you want to reinstall (keeping files and programs) or erase and install.

With macOS, start macOS Recovery (turn on the computer and immediately press COMMAND-R). From the macOS Utilities menu, select Reinstall macOS. You must have a working Internet connection to use Reinstall macOS.

Remote Network Installation

A *remote network installation* uses a network location as the installation media. Larger organizations may use this along with special scripts to automatically select options and answer all the prompts that us mere mortals have to deal with manually during the installation process. Unattended installations can even install applications once the OS is in place.

 EXAM TIP Remote network installations use a network location as the identity of the installation media and can be scripted to run automatically.

Third-Party Drivers

In computing, any hardware or software not developed by the original equipment manufacturer (OEM) is considered to be "third party," with the user as the first party and the OEM as the second party. When you add a peripheral device, and even some onboard components, it's common that the device has its own proprietary device driver, or *third-party driver*.

Microsoft requires third-party device drivers to be submitted for testing and approval. If approved, a "signed" third-party driver can be installed, but unsigned drivers cannot. The same processes goes for macOS. Linux, on the other hand, requires changing some Secure Boot parameters.

Partitioning

Partitioning is the process of electronically subdividing a physical drive into one or more units called *partitions*. Windows supports three partitioning schemes: the older *master boot record (MBR)* partitioning scheme, its own proprietary *dynamic storage partitioning* scheme, and the newer *GUID partition table (GPT)*. Microsoft calls an MBR-partitioned or GPT-partitioned drive a *basic disk* and a dynamic-storage-partitioned drive a *dynamic disk*. Windows doesn't mind if you mix schemes on different drives.

 EXAM TIP A *globally unique identifier (GUID)* is a number with an almost-impossible chance of duplication that's used to uniquely identify different objects.

Master Boot Record

Master boot record (MBR) basic disk partition tables support up to four partitions. The partition table supports two types of partitions: primary and extended.

Primary

Primary partitions support bootable operating systems (extended partitions don't). A single basic MBR disk supports up to four primary partitions, or three primary partitions and one extended partition. The partition table stores a binary *active* setting for each primary partition on the drive; at boot, the MBR uses it to determine which primary partition to boot to.

 EXAM TIP A primary partition can be bootable.

Extended

Each partition needs a unique identifier to distinguish it. Microsoft operating systems traditionally assign a drive letter from C: to Z:. Extended partitions do not get drive letters, but an extended partition can contain multiple logical drives, each of which can get a drive letter.

 EXAM TIP An extended partition can contain one or more logical drives.

Logical Drives   After you create an extended partition, you must create logical drives within that extended partition. A logical drive traditionally gets a drive letter from D: to Z:.

Note that when you create partitions and logical drives in Windows, the OS prompts you to create *volumes*. Further, it creates logical drives automatically after you exceed four volumes on a single drive.

 EXAM TIP Logical drives are found within extended partitions.

With the exception of the partition that stores boot files for Windows (always C:), primary partitions and logical drives can be assigned a drive letter or mounted as a folder on an existing primary partition. A *volume mount point* (or simply *mount point*) is the folder on one volume that points to another volume or partition. The mounted volume functions like a folder, but files stored in it are written to the mounted volume.

Globally Unique Identifier Partition Table

MBR-partitioned disks have tangible limits, such as a capacity no larger than 2.2 TB and no more than four partitions. The GUID partition table (GPT) partitioning scheme effectively overcomes these limits. GPT drives are basic drives, though you need a UEFI motherboard and a UEFI-compatible OS to boot to one.

 EXAM TIP GPT drives can have more than four partitions, compared to the MBR limit of four. Know the differences between GPT and MBR!

Drive Format

Formatting adds a file system to the drive—like a big spreadsheet that organizes each partition in such a way that the OS can store files and folders on the drive. Current Windows versions support these file systems: FAT32, NTFS, and exFAT/FAT64. Each has its own merits and limitations. Other file systems you need to understand for the CompTIA A+ Core 2 certification exam are ext3, ext4, and APFS.

Cross-Reference

For more information on file systems, refer back to Objective 1.8.

The default format type for a Windows drive is a quick format. A *quick format* (also known as a high-level format) saves time by creating a FAT (file allocation table) and a blank root directory. A *full format* tests every drive sector for read/write integrity, marking unusable ones in the FAT, and can take many minutes when performed on a hard drive.

 EXAM TIP Make sure you can describe the differences between quick format and full format.

Upgrade Considerations

When applying upgrades to an existing OS version or upgrading to a newer OS version, you should make certain considerations before proceeding with the upgrade. The following are the major considerations you should undertake:

 EXAM TIP Remember that upgrade considerations include backing up important files and user preferences, app and driver support/backward compatibility, and hardware compatibility.

- **Backup files and user preferences**   Before you begin an upgrade process, and especially before beginning a clean installation upgrade, all user files, applications, and settings (preferences) should be captured on a backup, just in case.

- **Application and driver support**   If RAID controllers or Ethernet or Wi-Fi adapters are in use, these devices may not be accessible by the installation software and should be uninstalled and replaced, if necessary, with versions compatible with the new system.

- **Backward compatibility**   An OS upgrade may not replace all of the drivers and certainly not the application software in place on a system. While attempts are made to remain backward compatible, this goal isn't always reached. Incompatible software and drivers must be uninstalled before the OS upgrade can complete in many cases.

- **Hardware compatibility**   Not only should you verify that the OS versions are compatible with the files and data on the system, but you should also check to see that the CPU, memory, and other system components are sufficient in size and technology to run the newer version. For example, virtually all desktop operating systems now require a 64-bit CPU. Many of the newer OS versions have higher RAM requirements than their predecessor as well.

Feature Updates—Product Lifecycle

The Windows 10/11 product lifecycle and the Windows Update function can be used to add new features or make changes to the desktop environment and any bundled applications. Although these changes seldom impact hardware compatibility, it's wise to deal with the updates like all other updates and verify their compatibility before applying them to a production system.

REVIEW

Objective 1.9: Given a scenario, perform OS installations and upgrades in a diverse OS environment

- Boot methods that can be used for installing an OS include optical media, external SSD drive or USB flash drive, network boot (PXE), Internet-based, external/hot-swappable drive, optical media, and internal hard drive partition.

- If installation media is not available, bootable optical media, USB flash drives, or hard drives can be created from downloadable OS ISO image files.

- Use an in-place upgrade to replace an older version of an OS with a newer one. Unlike a clean install, existing apps and files are preserved.

- To perform a clean install of Windows or Linux, the computer needs to be set to boot from the installation media (optical media or USB). To create installation media for Windows or Linux, download the appropriate ISO disk image file and use a special image burner/transfer utility to create the installation USB drive or optical disc.

- An in-place upgrade can also be used for a repair install to fix problems with the OS. To perform a repair install, use the same version of the OS as is currently installed.
- A remote network installation uses a network location for the installation media and can be scripted.
- Windows supports MBR partitions for drives up to 2.2 TB and GPT partitions for larger drives. MBR drives support no more than four partitions (one primary and up to three extended), while GPT supports many more partitions. Both are known as basic disks in Windows. Basic disks are bootable.
- Primary partitions are bootable, but extended partitions and the logical drives within them are not bootable.
- A quick format clears out the file allocation table, and a full format rewrites all sector markings and determines if any sectors are unusable.
- Load alternate third-party drivers when necessary to support nonstandard drive/host adapter hardware such as RAID.
- Back up files and user preferences and check the prerequisites/hardware compatibility issues before installing an OS.
- Check application and driver support/backward compatibility with the OS before buying/downloading/installing an app.
- Consider feature updates during the product's lifecycle.

1.9 QUESTIONS

1. You are upgrading a PC from Windows 10 to Windows 11 and have executed the Microsoft PC Health Check, which indicates that the hardware requirements for Windows 11 are met. What should now be the next step in the process?
   A. Proceed with the upgrade.
   B. Remove all unsigned drivers.
   C. Back up all user data and settings.
   D. Run the PC Health Check again to verify its results.

2. Which of the following is required for a network boot?
   A. USB boot media
   B. PXE-compatible network adapter
   C. Remote network installation server
   D. BIOS/UEFI boot priority for a flash memory device

3. What is the form of copy of an existing installation saved as one file?
   A. Image
   B. Full copy
   C. Incremental backup
   D. Differential backup

4. What type of partitioned disks have the tangible limits of capacity not larger than 2.2 TB and no more than four partitions?
   A. MBR
   B. GPT
   C. GUID
   D. FAT32

5. What type of disk partition is assigned a drive letter such as C:, E:, or X:?
   A. Extended
   B. Physical
   C. Logical
   D. Virtual

1.9 ANSWERS

1. **C**   It's always a good practice to back up user files and settings before proceeding with an installation or upgrade of any kind.

2. **B**   A network boot configuration requires, among other components, a PXE network adapter.

3. **A**   An image is a copy of an existing installation saved as one file.

4. **A**   An MBR partition has tangible limits of 2.2 TB and not more than four partitions.

5. **C**   A logical partition is assigned a drive letter.

Objective 1.10 Identify common features and tools of the macOS/desktop OS

Although macOS is not as popular as Windows, chances are increasing that you'll run into this operating system (OS) at some point. macOS and Linux have essentially the same underpinnings and some features in common, and they both differ a lot from Windows. This objective highlights the features, tools, and best practices of the macOS you need to know and understand for the CompTIA A+ 220-1102 exam.

Cross-Reference

Objective 1.11 covers the Linux OS.

macOS Applications

Unlike Windows, for which application and utility software can be found virtually everywhere, macOS is largely limited to two main sources for software: the *Apple App Store* and downloads from macOS application vendors.

File Types

The applications downloaded from a software vendor or the App Store have one of three primary file extensions to identify the type and content of the file. Here are the three types you will encounter on the CompTIA A+ Core 2 exam:

- **Disk image (.dmg)**   This macOS file format contains mountable disk image files that are opened (or mounted) with the Finder app (the equivalent of the Windows File Explorer), which is the default file management tool in macOS.
- **Installer file (.pkg)**   The Installer app included in macOS contains the compressed files used to install an application.
- **Application bundle (.app)**   An .app file is the equivalent of an .exe file in Windows and Linux. This file type is used for a single executable application.

 EXAM TIP   For the CompTIA A+ Core 2 exam, remember what the macOS file types (.dmg, .pkg, and .app) do.

App Store

Apple computers have only one official source for applications—the App Store. However, some very popular apps aren't included in the App Store and must be installed from the developers' websites.

The App Store is a central repository for Apple and macOS app developers to offer their apps to macOS users. The App Store is also used by Apple to distribute updates to macOS and to provide new versions of the OS. Users are required to have an identification token, called an Apple ID, to access the App Store.

 EXAM TIP   The App Store gives users a central place to discover, install, and update software.

Installation and Uninstallation of Applications

macOS only installs apps downloaded from the App Store by default. Installing an app from the App Store is virtually foolproof. Find the app you want, pay for it, if required, and it will install automatically into the Applications folder.

Some apps, like Microsoft Office for Mac, the Adobe Create Cloud, and other non–Apple-proprietary apps aren't offered in the App Store. These apps, and others, must be downloaded and installed from the developers' websites. Once the downloaded file is in the Finder, the .dmg or .pkg file is opened and its content is simply placed into the Applications folder using drag and drop.

To uninstall an app on macOS, use the Finder to delete the .app file or drag the application's icon to Trash.

Apple ID and Corporate Restrictions

An *Apple ID* is merely an account identifier, much like the user name and password used for the Microsoft Store and other account-related websites. It is also very much like single sign-on (SSO) in that the same ID code is used for virtually all Apple online sites and services, including iTunes and iCloud. The Apple ID includes your name, address, and shipping or download information, and it keeps track of what you have purchased in case you encounter problems later.

Under the heading of *corporate restrictions,* another service offered by Apple to business and corporate accounts is a formalized *mobile device management (MDM)* program. The Apple MDM program includes software and device updates, device monitoring for compliance with organizational policies, and tracking for lost devices, along with wiping and locking services. Employees can enroll personal devices, and company-owned devices are automatically enrolled by the Apple Business Manager.

Best Practices

As with a Windows system, macOS computers require best practices such as scheduled backups, antivirus software, system updates, and more.

Backups

macOS uses scripting tools to control and run a variety of tasks in the background automatically. One example is the macOS tool *launchd* (yes, it's spelled like that), which is a service framework similar to the *Service Control Manager (SCM)* in Windows or *systemd* in Linux. Using the Linux/UNIX convention, macOS appends the letter *d* to a function name to indicate that it works with *daemons,* or special-purpose services.

macOS provides two primary ways to back up the user files and settings: using the Time Machine app and moving or copying files to the iCloud. Either of these tools can be included in a launchd script to run in the background at a specific time. Time Machine creates full system backups (see Figure 1.10-1) called *local snapshots,* and it can write its backups to an external HDD or SSD or to a shared network drive.

FIGURE 1.10-1 The macOS Time Machine app is used to take snapshots of the system.

Antivirus

Apple offers a three-layer approach to antivirus and anti-malware protection. The three layers in this approach are as follows:

- **Prevention** Elements of the App Store and the Gatekeeper, which is the equivalent of Microsoft's signed apps, using Notarization, work to prevent the launch or execution of malware. Notarization is an Apple malware-scanning service.
- **Blocking** This layer ensures that any malware appearing on a macOS system is identified and blocked.
- **Protection** XProtect is used to remediate any harm caused by malware that was able to execute.

Updates and Patches

On a macOS system, the App Store checks for new updates, patches, and releases for the OS and any installed applications each day. Whenever a new item related to the app becomes available, the App Store icon is altered to indicate that it's available for download, and this information is added to the Software Update pane (see Figure 1.10-2). Similar to the Windows

FIGURE 1.10-2   Software Update pane for macOS updates

Update app, this Software Update pane shows the updates or releases available for the apps and features installed on the system. At this point, you have the choice of updating or installing one or all of the updates and apps available.

 EXAM TIP   Understand macOS best practices for backups, antivirus, and updates/patches.

System Preferences

The System Preferences panel of a macOS system is very much like the Settings app on a Windows system. Like the Windows Settings app, it centralizes settings, network options, and configuration options for a macOS system. Among the settings and configuration options on the System Preferences panel, shown in Figure 1.10-3, are Displays, Network, Print & Scan, Accessibility, and more.

Displays

On the System Preferences panel, the Displays option is used to open the Display Preferences panel, where you can set the configuration of the video display. What settings and options are available on the Display Preference panel depends on the type of display in use. On MacBooks and other video-included systems, the panel will look like the one shown in Figure 1.10-4. On iMacs and most of the larger systems, the options include resolution and scaling settings.

Network

The Network panel, which is accessed from the System Preferences panel, is used to configure the network connections for a macOS computer. The Networks Preference panel on a macOS with an Ethernet and/or Wi-Fi connection will display both connections in the available

FIGURE 1.10-3 The System Preferences panel on a macOS system

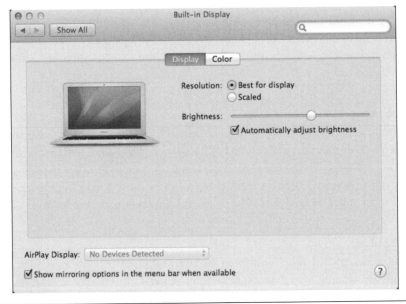

FIGURE 1.10-4 The Built-in Display panel of a MacBook

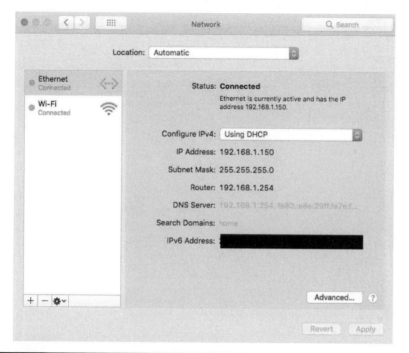

FIGURE 1.10-5   The Network panel of a macOS system

networks list (see Figure 1.10-5). Other connections that could be included in the list of available connections are FireWire, Thunderbolt, USB, and Bluetooth. For each of the connection types, the following settings can be configured: IP and MAC addressing as well as automatically or manually configuring the network adapter or connection. If you choose to configure a connection manually, you have the choice to set it with a standard or custom configuration that can include a custom maximum transmission unit (MTU) setting.

Printers & Scanners

The Printers & Scanners panel, shown in Figure 1.10-6, provides information on connected printers and scanning devices, including what the device is, where it's located, and its current status. Options on this panel allow you to set the printer style, paper size, and other printer-specific features. You can also add or remove a printer/scanning device and control the queue for an active device. On a macOS system that is connected to a network, a printer or scanner can be shared on the network.

Security & Privacy

Figure 1.10-7 shows the Security & Privacy panel for a macOS system. The available options on this panel are spread across four tabs: General, FileVault, Firewall, and Privacy. The objectives of the CompTIA A+ Core 2 exam focus on the Privacy tab's settings.

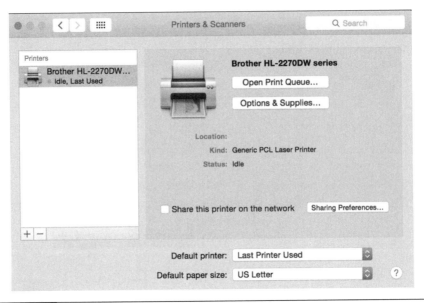

FIGURE 1.10-6   The Printers & Scanners panel

FIGURE 1.10-7   The macOS Security & Privacy panel

The Privacy tab includes options to control what data is collected for analysis, what personal information can be collected, and capabilities for setting location tracking. You can also control the privacy of camera images and data stored as contacts and in the calendar.

An area in the Privacy settings specifically included in the A+ Core 2 objectives is *Accessibility*. This preferences area is used to configure accessibilities features for assistance for users with limitations in vision, hearing, or physical abilities. The specific settings in these areas are as follows:

- **Vision**   These features allow the user to enlarge or reduce the display screen, increase the size of the menu bar and mouse pointer, change color filters, and have a voice read the content on the screen.
- **Hearing**   These features are used to display captions and to initiate and receive telephone calls using the Real-Time Text protocols.
- **Mobility**   These features allow the use of spoken commands and the use of a voice-controlled onscreen keyboard, pointer, or other device.

EXAM TIP   Objective 1.10 lists many macOS system preferences, including Displays, Network, Print & Scan, Security & Privacy, Accessibility, and Time Machine. Be sure you are familiar with each of these.

Features

Apple computers and the macOS are feature rich and provide users with several user-experience and task-oriented apps. For example, macOS supports a user having multiple full-screen apps open simultaneously. The Mission Control feature combines the features of Exposé, Dashboard, and Spaces to let a user view all open windows, desktop spaces, and apps in either full or split view on the Mac desktop. This allows the user to quickly move between views and apps. The following list describes a few more of the better macOS features and the ones you need to know for the CompTIA A+ Core 2 exam:

- **Multiple desktops**   Multiple active desktops can run on a macOS system using the Mission Control feature. Each of the desktops has its own identity and can be running a unique set of apps. Mission Control is activated with the F3 function key, and placing an app onto a new desktop is done by dragging the app onto the desktop you want it on.
- **Keychain Access**   This macOS app stores passwords and account details. Passwords and login credentials from any secured element, such as a website, e-mail account, or application, when saved on a macOS system, are saved to the Keychain Access app.
- **Spotlight**   This app is a search tool that indexes the contents of the hard drive, as well as information frequently visited on the Web, to make it easier to locate information when it's needed.

- **iCloud** You can use this Software as a Service (SaaS) app to store securely almost anything you wish to keep—photos, data files, system backups, and more. iCloud is the equivalent of the Dropbox and Microsoft OneDrive apps.

- **Gestures** macOS supports a set of apps for using gestures, including *Multi-Touch* (for the trackpad) and *Magic Mouse* (for mouse devices). Multi-Touch is a user interface technology that is not exclusive to Apple devices and can also be found on non-Apple devices. Multi-Touch accepts input from a variety of touch pressures and gestures on a touchpad, touch screen, and even electronic whiteboards and walls. The Magic Mouse device is a Multi-Touch mouse.

- **Finder** This macOS app is an inherent part of every Apple computer and is the equivalent of the Windows File Explorer. Finder is used to administer, organize, and manage files on a macOS system.

- **Remote Disk** Using this app, you can access optical disc storage media from a macOS device not configured for CDs or DVDs. However, this access doesn't include playback capabilities, only file or content access.

- **Dock** On a macOS computer, the Dock is the bar of icons at the bottom of the display screen that can be used to launch, manage, or stop applications.

- **Disk Utility** The macOS Disk Utility is used to manage (meaning *verify*) and repair the condition or state of a disk or an entire file system. Another common use of this app is to erase a hard disk using security settings for when the computer is sold, traded, gifted, or otherwise disposed of. However, its more common uses are for tracking storage status and configuring or formatting disk volumes.

- **FileVault** This macOS feature is used to encrypt disk storage. It is very similar to the BitLocker feature of Windows.

- **Terminal** Much like the Terminal app on a Linux system and the Command Prompt window of a Windows system, the macOS Terminal feature is used to open a command prompt environment that offers either a Bash shell or a Z shell (zsh). The zsh command prompt is the default on later macOS versions.

- **Force Quit** If a macOS app stops responding and the spinning "wait" cursor remains on the screen for a longer period of time than is normal for that particular app or function, it can be closed (killed) and, if necessary, restarted. The Force Quit feature is used to forcibly stop an app, similar to the Task Manager in Windows and the kill command (and others) in Linux.

 EXAM TIP You can be sure the CompTIA A+ Core 2 exam is going to test your knowledge of the various macOS features, including the Disk Utility, FileVault, Terminal, and Force Quit. Be ready!

REVIEW

Objective 1.10: Identify common features and tools of the macOS/desktop OS

- Software for macOS is generally limited to the App Store and downloads from macOS application vendors.

- macOS applications have three primary file extensions: disk image (.dmg), installer file (.pkg), and application bundle (.app).

- The App Store is the one official source for macOS applications. Apps not in the App Store must be installed from a developer's website. macOS only installs apps from the Apple App Store by default.

- An Apple ID is an account identifier that includes name, address, shipping or download information, and data on App Store purchases.

- Corporate restrictions fall under the Apple MDM program.

- macOS uses scripting tools like launchd to control and run a variety of tasks automatically in the background.

- macOS provides two ways to back up user files and settings: Time Machine and iCloud.

- Apple uses a three-layer approach to antivirus and anti-malware protection: prevention (Notarization), blocking, and protection.

- The System Preferences panel centralizes settings, network options, and configuration options that include Displays, Network, Print & Scan, Accessibility, and more.

- The settings for Security & Privacy are spread across four tabs: General, FileVault, Firewall, and Privacy.

- The Privacy settings control what data and personal information are collected as well as manage location tracking and other privacy issues.

- Accessibility preferences configure access for limitations in vision, hearing, and physical abilities.

- macOS features include Mission Control, Keychain Access, Spotlight, iCloud, Multi-Touch gestures, Magic Mouse, Finder, Remote Disk, Dock, Disk Utility, FileVault, Terminal, and Force Quit.

1.10 QUESTIONS

1. A macOS user needs to search for a specific file. Which utility should he use?

  A. Spotlight

  B. Finder

  C. Remote Disk

  D. Dock

2. A macOS user needs to stop an unresponsive app. What macOS feature can be used to stop the application?

   A. Finder

   B. Force Quit

   C. Terminal

   D. Mission Control

3. What is the macOS app used to create backups and snapshots?

   A. Time Machine

   B. Spotlight

   C. Dock

   D. Disk Utility

4. Which of the following is a macOS scripting tool used to create scripts used for running an app in background?

   A. Time Machine

   B. Dock

   C. Spotlight

   D. launchd

5. What macOS app stores passwords and account details?

   A. Dock

   B. Finder

   C. Keychain Access

   D. iCloud

1.10 ANSWERS

1. **A**   Spotlight is the macOS search and indexing tool.

2. **B**   Force Quit is used to stop unresponsive apps.

3. **A**   Time Machine is the backup app for macOS.

4. **D**   One of the tools available to create scripts in macOS is launchd.

5. **C**   Passwords and login credentials from websites, e-mail accounts, and applications are saved to Keychain Access.

Objective 1.11 Identify common features and tools of the Linux client/desktop OS

Although Linux systems are not nearly as popular as Windows in most offices, chances are increasing you will run into at least some computers that use these operating systems (OSs). Linux differs in many ways from Windows. This objective covers the essential best practices and tools you need to understand for the CompTIA A+ 220-1102 exam.

ADDITIONAL RESOURCES Before beginning your study of the Linux commands listed in this objective, it may be helpful for you to have access to or to create a Linux environment on which you can try out these commands. If you don't have access to a Linux system, navigate to https://geniusgeeks.com/install-linux-windows-10/ for the article "How to Download & Install Linux (Ubuntu) in Windows 10 PC."

Common Linux Commands

Table 1.11-1 lists some common Linux commands run from Terminal. To get help with a specific command, enter **man <command name>** to open the man page (or manual page) for that command.

EXAM TIP Make sure you know all the common Linux commands in Table 1.11-1 and the scenarios in which you would use them.

TABLE 1.11-1 Common Linux Commands

Command	Use	Examples/Notes
ls	Lists files and folders in a directory	**ls -a** (lists hidden as well as normal files in the current folder)
pwd	Displays the full path or working directory	**pwd** (displays current directory)
mv	Moves or renames files	**mv myfile.txt /home/user** (moves myfile.txt to the /home/user directory)
cp	Copies files	**cp *.doc docfiles** (copies all .doc files to the docfiles subfolder in the current folder)

TABLE 1.11-1   Common Linux Commands *(continued)*

Command	Use	Examples/Notes
rm	Permanently deletes files	**rm thisfile.doc** (removes thisfile.doc) **rm *.doc** (removes all .doc files in the current folder)
chmod	Changes permissions for specified files	**chmod 664 thisfile.doc** (changes the permissions of the owner and group to read/write and others to read-only)
chown	Changes ownership	**chown user thisfile.doc** (changes ownership of thisfile.doc to user)
su	Switches user to the specified user account	**su user** (switches to user's account and home folder)
sudo	Runs commands using root user access	**sudo apt-get update** (runs higher-level commands; must enter your password)
apt-get	Updates and maintains a list of software packages on Debian-based distributions	**sudo apt-get install newpackage** (installs newpackage) **sudo apt-get upgrade** (upgrades all installed packages)
shutdown	Brings down the system	**shutdown -r** (reboots machine)
yum	Package manager and installer	**yum install syncthing** (installs the syncthing package)
ip	Used for configuring network interfaces	**ip -4 addr** (lists IPv4 addresses)
df	Displays the number of 1K blocks of free disk space	**df** (displays the number of 1K blocks of free disk space on all mounted file systems)
grep	Searches text files or command output	**grep 'thistext' myfile.doc** (searches myfile.doc for thistext)
ps	Lists processes	**ps** (displays all active processes and their PIDs)
man	Displays manual (help) pages for a command	**man printf** (displays the manual pages for the printf command)
top	Shows running processes and kernel-managed tasks	**top -u user** (displays all running processes for user)
find	Searches for files and directories	**find ./User -name sample.txt** (searches for the file sample.txt in the ./User directory)
dig	Queries DNS servers for information	**dig totalsem.com** (requests all DNS information for totalsem.com)

Command	Use	Examples/Notes
TABLE 1.11-1 Common Linux Commands *(continued)*		
cat	Displays or concatenates files	**cat /etc/hosts/*** (displays the contents of the files in the /etc/hosts directory) **cat file1.txt file2.txt > combinedfile.txt** (combines two files into a new file)
nano	A command-line text editor	**nano filename.txt** (opens filename.txt for editing)

Best Practices

As with Windows, Linux computers require best practices such as scheduled backups, anti-malware, disk maintenance, system and application updates, and more.

Backups

Linux distributions can use a third-party app to create backups, but users can also write scripts using copy functions to write specific files and directories to a backup medium as well as schedule and control the use of these scripts through a *cron* (chronologically executed) statement.

Antivirus

Antivirus/anti-malware software packages are available from a variety of vendors, each of which provides updates. Depending on the specific app, updates might be automatic or manual.

 ADDITIONAL RESOURCES   For more information on Linux antivirus/ anti-malware apps, go to https://www.security.org/antivirus/best/linux/ for the article "The Best Antivirus Software for Linux."

Updates/Patches

First of all, remember that Linux is primarily open source. Therefore, if you install only a particular distro and download apps from the distro's provider, the updates and patches you'll need will be available from that provider. However, if you download open source apps and systems from general sources, such as Git, SourceForge.net, and the like, you may be on your own for updates and patches. Updates and patches may be available for the open source apps you use, but you'll probably need to track them down on your own.

FIGURE 1.11-1   Software Updater in Ubuntu Linux

Most Linux distro providers take an automated approach to patching and will alert you when their software needs an update. Some also provide two methods for posting updates and patches: the apt command-line tool and an updating software tool such as the *Software Updater* for Ubuntu (see Figure 1.11-1) or the *Update Manager* for Linux Mint.

EXAM TIP   Be familiar with Linux best practices, including backups, antivirus, and updates/patches.

Tools

Use the tools described in the following sections to keep Linux systems in top working order.

Shell/Terminal

The Linux Terminal is a non-GUI, text-based app that provides a command-line shell for entering Linux commands. Linux Terminal is similar in function to Bash and Z-shell (macOS) and PowerShell (Windows). Figure 1.11-2 shows a screen capture of the Linux Mint Terminal.

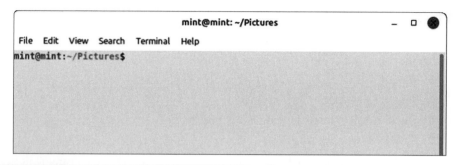

FIGURE 1.11-2   A screen capture of the Linux Mint Terminal app

Samba

Samba is an UNIX/Linux open source software application used to open communication with a Windows, Linux, or macOS system via a network. Samba uses the Common Internet File System (CIFS) and the Server Message Block (SMB) protocol. Samba provides the capability for a UNIX/Linux system to share files and resources with a Windows system. However, Samba is also able to support communication between Linux systems.

    EXAM TIP   For the Core 2 exam, practice entering Linux commands in Terminal and know that Samba allows file sharing and print services between macOS, Linux, and Windows systems.

REVIEW

Objective 1.11: Identify common features and tools of the Linux client/desktop OS

- The common Linux commands you should know are ls, pwd, mv, cp, rm, chmod, chown, su, sudo, apt-get, yum, ip, df, grep, ps, man, top, find, dig, cat, and nano (refer to Table 1.11-1).
- Linux distros use cron to launch a process based on clock time.
- Distro-sourced apps and updates are available from the distro provider. Open source apps and systems may require individual actions for updates and patches.
- Antivirus/anti-malware updates are provided by the software vendors. Depending on the specific app, updates might be automatic or manual.
- Linux backup tools differ by distro.
- Linux uses its Terminal to display a shell in which command-line functions can be entered.
- Samba is a UNIX/Linux open source software application that is used to open communication with a Windows system.

1.11 QUESTIONS

1. A Linux user is trying to update her system's apps with the command **apt-get update**, but the command doesn't work. What did the user forget to do?

   A. Restart in Safe Mode.

   B. Run the command from Terminal.

   C. Run the command as the root user with sudo.

   D. Create an image backup first.

2. A Linux user needs to stop a process but doesn't know its PID. Which command from a Terminal command line would provide this information?

   A. ifconfig

   B. ps

   C. ls

   D. kill

3. A backup script created on a Linux system is to run at a particular time of the day. Which Linux command can be used to ensure this occurs as scheduled?

   A. backup

   B. cron

   C. dd

   D. grep

4. What Linux command can be executed from a Terminal command line to display the amount of free disk space available on a file system?

   A. free

   B. chkdsk

   C. df

   D. ls

5. What system protocol can be used to allow a Linux system to interact with a Windows system to share files and other resources?

   A. apt-get

   B. dig

   C. Samba

   D. top

1.11 ANSWERS

1. **C**   Many Linux commands must be run as the root user (superuser) with sudo.

2. **B**   The ps command lists active processes and their PIDs.

3. **B**   The cron command is used to control the start of a script using the time of day, day of the week, and so on.

4. **C**   The df command displays the amount of free disk space in 1-K blocks available on a Linux system.

5. **C**   Samba is used to connect a Linux system with a Windows system for interactions.

Security

DOMAIN 2.0

Summarize various security measures and their purposes

This objective includes the various security concepts, vulnerabilities, and countermeasures used to mitigate or prevent security events. This includes implementing physical security to protect the facilities as well as authorized employees, agents, or other persons; applying and configuring logical security methods to prevent unauthorized access; using mobile device management for tracking and securing mobile devices; and using Active Directory to secure content and users.

Physical Security

Physical security might seem like a mundane topic in a tech-oriented certification, but it's a vital first step in the security process. Physical security methods range from door locks to privacy tokens and beyond. These methods are implemented for protection and to prevent any tampering, theft, or misuse that may come from physical access and proximity to a building, its contents, and especially the assets of the computing function of a home, office, or organization.

 EXAM TIP Make sure you understand the role that each of the physical security measures covered in this objective has in the overall physical security scheme.

Access Control Vestibule

An *access control vestibule (ACV),* a patented security screening system of Novacomm, Inc., is a weapons detection system intended to prevent unauthorized individuals from carrying firearms, knives, explosives, and other weapons into a facility. An ACV is essentially an enclosed chamber in which a person entering the space is held between two doorways while being scanned for weapons. Should a weapon be detected, the doors of the ACV are automatically locked, trapping the person inside of its bulletproof walls so that security personnel can deal with the situation. ACVs are common in banks and secured facilities, including large data centers, co-hosting facilities, and areas working with sensitive information.

An ACV is an extension of a mantrap security arrangement. A *mantrap* is a small room with a set of two doors, one to the outer, unsecured area and one to the inner, secure area. The mantrap's outer door must be closed before the inner door can be opened, and the entrant must present authentication before the inner door is opened. The mantrap is often controlled by a security guard who tracks entries and exits on an *entry control roster*. Using an ACV or a mantrap at the entrances to sensitive areas can also keep intruders from tailgating (closely following) authorized entrants.

Badge Reader

A *badge reader* is a fundamental physical security measure that uses radio frequency ID (RFID), magnetic strip, barcode, or Quick Response (QR) code technologies to read ID badges. The use of a badge reader, especially when combined with a mantrap, makes getting into secure areas much more difficult.

Video Surveillance

A *video surveillance* system, also called a closed-circuit television (CCTV) system, consists of video cameras, positioned in key observation locations, video monitors, and, typically, video recording equipment. While the equipment in a video surveillance system can be either digital or analog, the best results come from a digital system because of its capture, transmission, and storage advantages. These system offer both interior and exterior surveillance that can oper- ate 24/7/365. They can be set to record non-stop or only when movement within the cameras' range causes the system to activate.

Figure 2.1-1 illustrates the primary devices in a typical video surveillance system: video cameras, a surveillance system server that receives the captured images from the cameras, a disk storage device, and one or more display monitors that allow security personnel to observe the areas covered by the cameras. A video surveillance system is a closed system, meaning that the captured images are not broadcast beyond the system itself.

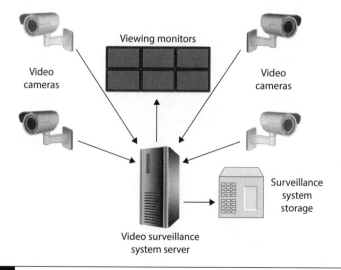

FIGURE 2.1-1   The devices in a video surveillance system

Alarm Systems

In the context of physical security, an alarm system is any system that is designed and installed for the prevention, detection, and warning of an intrusion. An alarm system can also include these same purposes for other situations or events, such as fire, water levels, temperature changes, and perhaps medical emergencies. However, the A+ Core 2 objectives focus on the former definition and the alarm systems for physical security.

An *alarm system* is typically made up of detection devices, typically sensors, a video processor or server, viewing monitors, and a video recording storage device. Security system detection devices and sensors are engineered specifically for a particular location, fit, and purpose. The next section describes the sensors and detectors listed in the A+ Core 2 objectives.

Motion Sensors

The purpose of a *motion sensor* is simple: if anything within its sensing range moves, the event causes an alert. Motion sensors, which are also known as *motion detectors,* are intrusion detection devices that sense when an object enters their scanning range. There are several types of motion sensors, each using a different technology.

Home and small office sensors:

- **Active sensor**   This type of motion sensor is also called a *radar-based sensor* because it uses ultrasonic waves. When the returning wave pattern is disturbed, an alarm is triggered.
- **Passive sensor**   This type of motion sensor absorbs heat emitted by bodies entering its monitored range.
- **Magnetic sensor**   This is a contact sensor, typically used on windows and doors. An event is triggered when the contact sensor's magnetic connection is broken.
- **Photo-sensor**   This type of detector uses a light beam and triggers an event if the beam is interrupted. While this can be used to detect entry or exit through a doorway or an area, these sensors are also used for safety reasons, such as with a garage door opener.

 NOTE   Active and passive motion sensors are also used for fire and smoke detection systems, to turn on or off lighting, HVAC systems, and video surveillance cameras.

Commercial and industrial sensors:

- **Microwave sensor**   This type of sensor emits microwave pulses that are reflected back to the device. Alterations in the wave patterns are used to determine the position and movement of an interfering object.
- **Tomographic sensor**   This type of sensor uses radio waves, which can penetrate walls and furniture, to detect an intruder or motion.

Motion sensors can be exterior or interior. The difference is that exterior devices are designed and constructed for use outdoors, as they can be mounted to fences, buildings, poles, and other exposed surfaces.

Locks and Applications

One of the most basic types of physical security is the lock. The following sections cover the lock types you need to understand for the CompTIA A+ Core 2 exam.

 EXAM TIP   Be sure to know the different types of locks covered in this objective, including door locks, biometric locks, cable locks, server locks, and USB locks.

Door Lock

Keyed *door locks* won't deter a determined intruder with a lock pick, but they will stop casual snoopers. Keyed door locks are also vulnerable if (when) keys are lost. Rekeying door locks can become quite expensive over time. A door lock combined with an access control vestibule improves security.

Biometric Locks

Biometric door locks typically use fingerprint or hand readers to determine identity. These are very useful for controlling access to highly secure areas. Biometric door locks vary in the number of fingerprints or handprints they can store for recognition, how they are programmed, the physical lock type, and water-resistance factors.

Cable Locks

A *cable lock* (see Figure 2.1-2) provides good physical security for portable devices such as laptop computers and external drives that have Kensington security lock connectors (see inset in Figure 2.1-2). Cable locks for individual users have combinations, while those made for use in organizations have keyed locks.

USB Locks

The ease of use and omnipresence of USB ports make them a security headache. While Group Policy settings can be used to prevent certain types of USB devices from being connected to servers, it might be easier to use a physical *USB lock* that inserts into a USB port and locks in place. These locks are available from many vendors. They are also available for USB flash drives and other types of external storage devices.

Equipment Locks

Locks are an essential part of the physical security of computing equipment and other types of equipment as well. Most of the locks described thus far can also be applied to secure rackmount

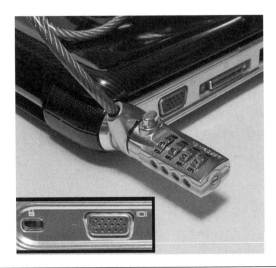

FIGURE 2.1-2   A cable lock on a laptop (inset shows Kensington security lock connector)

cabinets and other computing equipment. One particular category of equipment locks is *server locks,* which are used to limit access to a server's ports and drives. Locks can be used to prevent access to the front or back of a server rack. Server rack doors are available with support for electronic locks, keyed locks, and padlocks, and they can even support TCP/IP interfacing to inform the network of status or breaches.

Guards

Even if your organization uses badge readers, key fobs, or smart cards, the presence of one or more *security guards* provides an extra level of security and deterrence. A security guard with an entry control roster is needed to make an access control vestibule truly effective.

Bollards

Because vehicles crash into fencing and buildings frequently, *bollards* can provide some protection against physical damage or a physical breach of a secured facility. Protective bollards are used to prevent accidents and intentional attempts to use a car or truck for crashing into a facility and possibly gaining unauthorized access. Some bollards are capable of stopping cars and medium-duty trucks going at a rate of as much as 50 miles per hour (mph), or at least reducing the damage of such a crash.

Traffic bollards range from plastic tubes intended for traffic direction and control to hydraulic steel cylinders (security bollards) that can be retracted when necessary. The types of bollards used for the protection of secure facilities depends on the nature and level of protection needed and the budget available. For most data center installations, the type of bollard used is known as a *ram-raid bollard,* which is a solid metal rod securely fastened to a sidewalk or roadway. Figure 2.1-3 shows an example of this type of bollard.

FIGURE 2.1-3   The use of ram-raid bollards at a sports stadium

Fences

The three primary considerations when selecting a *security fence* to enclose a secured facility are as follows:

- Can it be climbed?
- Can it be penetrated?
- How much does it cost?

The answers to these questions define the fencing the facility should use. The fence should be tall enough and possibly have climb-prevention materials or hazards at the top or where necessary. The fence should be made of material that cannot be easily penetrated, cut, or torn, yet compatible with local zoning codes and the aesthetics of the facility. The cost should be considered against the risk potential of a breach of the facility.

Physical Security for Staff

Physical security programs must include policies that define who is and isn't authorized to enter a facility. These policies often define the control mechanisms, methods, and devices that are used to implement a policy's restrictions. The following sections describe many of the devices and mechanisms used to enforce these policies.

Smart Cards and Key Fobs

Single-factor authentication (SFA) policies typically require a user name and password (something you know), which are considered by security policies to be a single factor. The username is the link to the password, which is the verified security factor. Multifactor authentication (MFA) adds a possession factor (or something you have), which creates a two-factor authentication (2FA). A *smart card,* like the one shown in Figure 2.1-4, is about the size of a credit card and contains circuitry to identify the card's bearer and provides "something you have."

FIGURE 2.1-4 Keyboard-mounted smart card reader being used to verify an employee badge (image courtesy of Adesso, Inc.)

Another device that can serve the same function as a smart card is a *security token,* commonly in the form of a *key fob.* It's used to store digital certificates, passwords, biometric data, and more.

Hard Tokens

A *hard token* (see Figure 2.1-5), also called an *RSA token* or an *authentication token,* is a small physical device that can be used to provide a second factor in an MFA procedure. There are three basic types of hard tokens:

- **Connected**   This type of hard token is inserted into a token reader and automatically transfers security and authentication information to a system. Connected hard tokens are commonly implemented as key fobs and USB tokens.
- **Disconnected**   This type of hard token doesn't have to be physically inserted into a reader; instead, it generates a one-time access code that is passed as a signal to a receiver. Using this technology, a smartphone can be a disconnected hard token.

FIGURE 2.1-5   RSA hard token (image courtesy of EMC Corp.)

- **Contactless**   This type of hard token is a proximity device, meaning that by using Bluetooth or an RF signal, the security or authenticated codes are passed to the security system.

Typically the code or data passed to the receiving system by a hard token is constructed using an initial random seed to generate a time-based passcode that the user enters or the token passes to authenticate.

 ADDITIONAL RESOURCES   Navigate to https://expertinsights.com/ insights/ for more information on the leading providers of MFA solutions.

Keys

Keys and *digital lock key codes* are used by authorized individuals to enter secured physical spaces. The security aspect of a key policy must include the following:

- All persons to whom one or more keys are issued must be trained in the proper handling and security of the keys and the locks to which they are associated.
- All keys must be controlled and accounted for at all times.
- All keys are to be inspected and inventoried on a regular basis.

Where locks are opened using digital or physical code entries, the knowledge of the code must be treated as a physical key under the security policies.

Biometrics

Biometrics is the use of a physical, most commonly a physiological, measurement made on a person's hands, eyes, or face. In fact, these are the three biometric measurements used in the systems implemented as a part of a physical security program.

The three biometric technologies most commonly used are as follows:

- **Hands (hand and fingerprints)**   A *fingerprint* or *palm print scan* performs two tasks: It captures an image of a section of a finger or a palm to record its characteristics and determines if the pattern of the characteristics is an exact match to pre-scanned and stored captures of the same hand or finger.
- **Eye (retina and iris)**   Also called a *retina scan,* an *eye scan* captures the pattern of the retina and iris parts of a person's eye. The pattern is formed by blood vessels in the eye and is as unique as a person's fingerprint.
- **Facial**   A *facial scan* captures the image of a person's face and analyzes the structure of the cheek bones as well as the shape of the eyes, nose, mouth, lips, chin, and jaws. The geometry of these features yields a highly unique result that can be used for authenticating a person.

Lighting

Security lighting is used to prevent intrusions and to provide a safe environment for employees, the public, and first responders, when necessary. Security lighting can be active at all times, during dark hours, or as required when triggered by motion detectors. Lighting can be a major element in a physical security program.

Magnetometers

A *magnetometer,* also known as a *walk-through metal detector,* measures the strength and direction of the magnetic field emitted by a metallic object. As a person walks through the magnetometer, a complete scan of the person is made that will locate any ferrous and some non-ferrous metals the system is configured to identify. A magnetometer is either a single-zone or a multi-zone device. A single-zone scan focuses on a single fixed area, and a multi-zone scan focuses on several areas in each pass.

Logical Security

Logical security is the application of software- and technology-based measures to create a protected and secured environment for users, computers, and data. The logical security elements covered in the CompTIA A+ Core 2 objectives include the security measures that are implemented through software or operating system (OS) services.

Logical security focuses on the application of the AAA (authentication, authorization, and accounting) model to protect the programming and data stored on computing equipment. This includes user identification elements such as logins, user names, account numbers, and associated personally identifiable information (PII) as well as the verification of a supplicant's identification using biometrics, tokens, and passwords. The following sections describe the elements of logical security you should know for the CompTIA A+ Core 2 exam.

Principle of Least Privilege

The number-one consideration in logical security and access control is the *principle of least privilege,* which says that the permissions and rights assigned to a user account should be no higher than those needed by the user to perform their assigned tasks. This would limit the user to only the resources absolutely required to complete their tasks.

 EXAM TIP   Expect to encounter the principle of least privilege on the exam and know that users should have permission to access only the resources they need to perform their jobs.

Access Control Lists

There are two basic types of *access control lists (ACLs)*:

- A list stored on the boot drive of a file system that provides the basis for user and group permissions
- A list of the MAC addresses permitted (an allowed list) from a wireless network that is stored on a wireless access point (WAP)

These two ACL types work differently, but both share an ability to permit or block access to a resource.

Multifactor Authentication

As discussed earlier in this objective (see "Smart Cards and Key Fobs"), single-factor authentication (SFA) is less secure and because it's typically made up of only a user name and password (the single factor), it can possibly be defeated in a variety of ways. Adding one or more additional factors to the "login" credentials adds nearly exponential complexity to an attacker's ability to break its security.

Some examples of the factors that can be used in a *multifactor authentication (MFA)* scheme are:

- **Something you have**   A physical device in possession of the user that provides a security, account, or user ID code, such as a bank card, a key fob, a badge, etc.
- **Something you know**   A remembered code or phrase, such as a passcode, PIN, or the answer to a security question.
- **Something you are**   This is really something about you, such as a finger or hand print, iris details, voice, gait, and other physical demonstrations.
- **Somewhere you are**   This could be a GPS reading or locations in a facility where you are authorized to access.

Commonly, MFAs are just 2FA (two-factor authentication) schemes, such as a bank card (something you have) and a PIN (something you know). Facial recognition and a password is another example of a 2FA method.

E-mail Security

E-mail is by far the largest target for several types of attacks, including phishing attacks and malware transfers. Because e-mail is used to transmit sensitive information at times, its security should be a high priority for individuals and companies alike. It contains several areas that can be attacked, including its header, body, URL, address, and, in many cases, attachments. All of these elements can be an attack surface.

Cross-Reference

For more information on phishing and other malware attacks, see Objectives 2.3 and 2.4.

The following are the best defenses for protecting e-mail:

- **Encryption** The use of public key infrastructure (PKI) and other encryption methods turn the contents of an e-mail and its attachments into unreadable cipher text.
- **Spam filter** Usually contained in most anti-malware packages, this tool can detect unwanted or dangerous e-mail and senders and then quarantine or destroy detected messages.
- **Anti-malware software** E-mail is perhaps the most used way to transmit malware. In addition to scanning for spam, this tool can detect messages carrying dangerous attachments or content.
- **User training** E-mail recipients, whether SOHO or corporate employees, should be trained to detect social engineering attacks, such as phishing and spoofing, and the process of reporting and blocking these attempts.
- **Secure e-mail gateway (SEG)** An SEG is a form of firewall that logically sits between a user's e-mail account and the outside world. Both inbound and outbound e-mail are scanned for illicit content or attachments to enforce the organization's security policies.

Soft Tokens

In the context of computer security, a token is a device used by a user to verify their identity for the purpose of gaining access to a system and its resources. Hard tokens were discussed earlier in this objective (see "Hard Tokens"). *Soft tokens* perform essentially the same function, but through programs and apps rather than a handheld device. The use of a soft token typically involves two or more steps, much like an MFA process. In addition to a user's identifying data (user name, password, PIN, and so on), a soft token system may require the use of a one-time password (OTP) that is valid for only a short period of time, such as one minute. Some soft token systems also integrate with smartphones and biometric devices.

 ADDITIONAL RESOURCES For a definition and examples of soft tokens, visit https://searchsecurity.techtarget.com and search for "soft token."

Short Message Service

The bottom line on *short message service (SMS)* messaging is that it is not private, nor is it secure. In fact, SMS security can be compared to that of a fax machine that sends its content in the open. Using SMS on a cell phone is not secure, and the messages are not encrypted over its entire path. Cell service providers have access to the message content and hold it for days at a time. The short answer for keeping SMS messaging secure is to not use it. However, if you do choose to use it, Apple's iMessage, Android's Rich Communication Services (RCS), and the open source chat service Signal offer partial or end-to-end encryption.

Voice Calls

In today's world, cellular *voice calls* are by far the most used type of telephone service, with landline service virtually disappearing. However, because of its inherent end-to-end circuit technology, landline service is by far the more secure. Hacking into a landline can be done, but it's not easy and, in most cases, not worth the effort. This is especially true when cellular voice calls are so much easier to intercept.

The security measures most commonly used to protect cellular and VoIP voice calls are Transport Layer Security (TLS), Session Initiation Protocol (SIP) with TLS, and Secure Real-time Transport Protocol (SRTP). These protocols provide encryption for the voice signal and data in transit to protect the message's authentication and integrity as well as to guard against replay attacks.

Early cell phone transmissions were easily intercepted and the identity of the call exposed, including user IDs, phone numbers, and the like. However, 4G and now 5G have added technologies to secure a voice call end-to-end. Security for 4G used a group of transmission protocols that had some vulnerabilities that could be exploited by smart attackers. However, 5G uses one cohesive set of protocols to secure the call, making it much harder, if not impossible, to intercept and interpret.

Authenticator Application

An *authenticator application* applies two-factor authentication (2FA) to the accounts that you wish to protect beyond their simple login credentials. Using an authenticator app, the user must enter a generated key value into the authenticator app to gain access to the account. The codes can be valid for varying time periods—as short as a few minutes or as long as forever (although this latter option is not recommended). The use of changing codes and 2FA authentication create the security for the account.

Mobile Device Management

Mobile device management (MDM) is implemented typically through software and provides an organization with the capability to manage and monitor the use of mobile devices that connect to an internal network. MDM is conducted from a central location, with the objective of limiting the loss of proprietary data. The results of several recent studies show that about 75 percent of a company's employees use a personal communication device in the workplace. Businesses hoping to reduce their workstation costs have a bring-your-own-device (BYOD) policy for employees or provide employees with company-owned devices. However, mobile devices that can connect to an internal network and then disconnect to leave the premises present a range of security issues.

NOTE The common acronyms for mobile device schemes are BYOD or Bring Your Own Device, COPE or Company Owned/Personally Enabled, and COBO or Company Owned/Business Only

MDM software helps the organization control the connection, use, and location of mobile devices capable of accessing its internal or virtual private network (VPN) networks. MDM systems push the security policies and monitor compliance with those policies on mobile devices that are on the premises or at remote locations, regardless of their type. The software also allows IT administrators to automate device management processes, which can greatly reduce their workload. It also helps IT admins to manage diverse device types remotely, without the need for manual configuration.

 ADDITIONAL RESOURCES To learn more about MDM, go to https://www.fortinet.com/resources/cyberglossary/mobile-device-management and read "Mobile Device Management (MDM)."
For an example of a mobile device policy, go to https://spearstone.com/mobile-device-management-policy-examples/.

 EXAM TIP Be sure you know that MDM provides control over company devices and can be used to update devices, track devices, and enforce policies.

Active Directory

Active Directory is an integral part of Windows Server. It provides directory services to a Windows Server domain. Active Directory centralizes user accounts, passwords, and access to resources on a network via a domain controller. Valid domain accounts log in once to the domain and have access to all resources on the domain. This is called single sign-on (SSO).

 EXAM TIP Be sure you can identify each of the Active Directory security features (login script, domain, group policy/updates, organizational units, home folder, folder redirection, and security groups) covered in this section.

 ADDITIONAL RESOURCES To learn more about Active Directory, go to https://www.comparitech.com/net-admin/active-directory-step-by-step-tutorial/ and search for "What is Active Directory? A step-by-step tutorial."

Login Script

A *login script* (aka *logon script*) runs every time the user logs in to an Active Directory domain and is used to set up variables for the user, such as mapping folders to drive letters, setting a default printer for a specific user, capturing information about the user or device that is logged in, and much more.

 ADDITIONAL RESOURCES To learn more about Active Directory login scripts, go to https://redmondmag.com and search for "Exploring Logon Scripts for Active Directory." Even though this article is a few years old, it's still one of the best explanations for this topic.

Domain

Larger networks use domains, in which a server running Windows Server controls access to network resources. An administrator creates a domain on the Windows Server system and makes it the domain controller (DC). The DC can then be used to create new domain accounts for users. A DC must have the Active Directory Domain Services (AD DS) server role installed (see Figure 2.1-6).

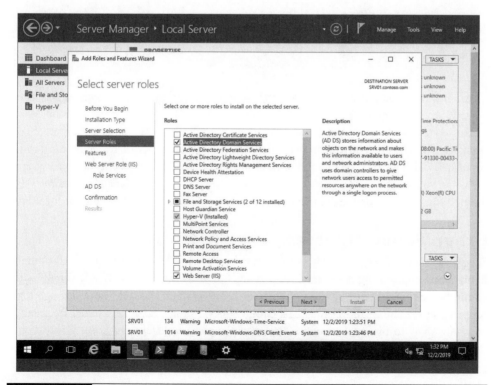

FIGURE 2.1-6 Adding Active Directory Domain Services to Windows Server

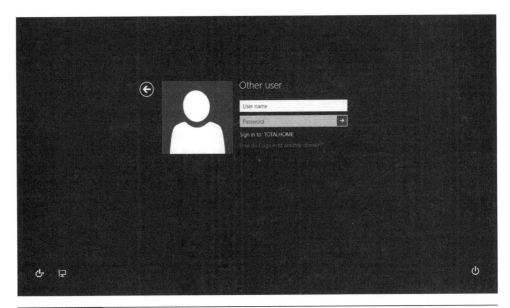

FIGURE 2.1-7   A domain logon screen

EXAM TIP   Login scripts and home folders are two common methods for setting up user accounts. Be sure you understand the differences between these two methods.

A networked computer can be a member of either a workgroup or a domain, but never both. When a system joins a domain, it's automatically removed from its workgroup. When you log on to any computer in a domain, Windows prompts for a user name (see Figure 2.1-7), which is used to log you directly in to the domain. All user accounts are stored on the domain controller, which functions as the authentication server, though each system still creates a local user directory when you log on. You can log on using <domain>\<domain user name>. For example, the user Jane on the domain totalhome.local would log on with totalhome.local\Jane.

Group Policy/Updates

To apply granular (detailed) policy settings en masse, you need to set a Windows AD domain-based group policy using the Local Group Policy Editor (see Figure 2.1-8). AD simplifies the admin burden by configuring group policy on the server and pushing it out through login scripts. This is not the same as the Local Group Policy Editor, where the settings are granular and only apply to the local machine. For example, you would use the Local Group Policy Editor in a workgroup. You would use AD group policy and login scripts to push updates and policy to many systems in a domain.

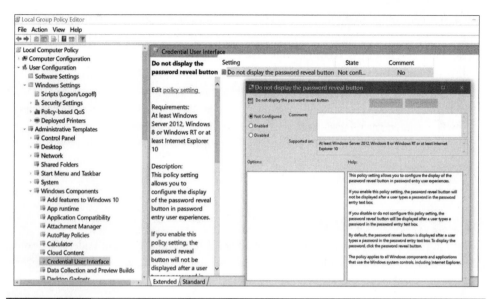

Using the Local Group Policy Editor to disable the ability to display a password

For the CompTIA A+ Core 2 (220-1102) exam, you should have a basic understanding of the concept of group policies. Policies can be used to establish the rules and guidelines for setting a variety of restrictions or permissions, including actions like preventing a user from editing the Registry, accessing a command-line prompt, and installing software; defining who can and cannot log in to or shut down a system; enforcing minimum password length; configuring account lockout after a set number of failed attempts; and enabling users to browse for printers on the network, among dozens of other settings.

Organizational Units

An organizational unit (OU) is an Active Directory container that holds users, groups, and computers. A domain can manage multiple OUs, and each OU can have its own group policies. An OU can be used to collect the members of a department or division, and an OU can have its own administrator.

ADDITIONAL RESOURCES   To learn more about the role of an OU in an Active Directory domain, go to https://www.windows-active-directory.com and search for "The Structures and Benefits of Organizational Units."

Home Folder

A home folder is used to store personal files on an Active Directory network. It can be used in place of login scripts to set up drives for users. One of the benefits of using a home folder is that each user's files can be stored in their own home folder on a remote server rather than having some files stored in each computer's Documents folder, as users log in to different computers in a domain. This feature is known as *folder redirection.*

 ADDITIONAL RESOURCES For a discussion of the pros and cons of login scripts versus home folders, see https://community.spiceworks.com/topic/77593-login-script-vs-home-folder-connect and read "Login Script vs. Home Folder (Connect:)." Microsoft doesn't provide guidance as to which method is recommended, so you should be familiar with both methods.

Folder Redirection

Folder redirection is used to redirect users of a known folder to a different folder—for example, from a local Documents folder to the user's home folder on an Active Directory network. Folder redirection can be performed using group policy or manually.

Security Groups

Active Directory provides two types of security accounts: user accounts and computer accounts. Each of these account types represents either a person or a computer on the system. User accounts tend to be associated with service accounts and applications, whereas computer accounts are, well, for computers. Both of these account types can be collected into and controlled by a security group to create a unit that can be managed as one entity.

The use of security groups on a Windows system provides an administrator with several benefits and efficiencies, including the ability to assign user rights to an entire security group and to configure access permissions to a system resource to the elements of a security group.

REVIEW

Objective 2.1: Summarize various security measures and their purposes Physical security is a vital security program that includes measures that range from door locks to privacy tokens. Physical security measures help prevent and protect against unauthorized entry and access to a building and its assets.

Physical security measures include the following:

- An access control vestibule (ACV) is a weapons-detection system intended to prevent unauthorized individuals from carrying weapons into a facility.
- A mantrap limits access to only authorized persons and prevents tailgating.
- A badge reader uses RFID, a magnetic strip, a barcode, or a QR code to identify a specific person or entity.

- A video surveillance system uses video cameras (positioned in key observation locations), video monitors, and video recording equipment.
- An alarm system is designed and installed to prevent, detect, and warn of an intrusion.
- A motion sensor is an intrusion detection device that senses when an object enters its scanning range and then issues an alert.
- Biometric door locks use fingerprint or palm readers to determine the identity of a person.
- A cable lock provides physical security for portable devices.
- Physical USB locks insert into USB ports and lock in place to prevent their use by unauthorized USB flash drives and other devices.
- Server locks limit access to a server's ports and drives and can also prevent access to the front or back of a server rack.
- Even with security devices in place, the presence of a security guard provides an extra level of security and deterrence.
- Bollards provide protection against physical damage or breach of physical security by preventing accidents and intentional attempts to use a vehicle to crash into a facility.
- A fence can provide a security barrier to help prevent intrusions into a facility.
- Physical security programs must extend to include policies that define who is and isn't authorized to enter a facility.
- Multifactor authentication (MFA) adds something you have to create, at minimum, a two-factor authentication (2FA) process.
- A smart card contains circuitry to identify the card's bearer and satisfies the "something you have" factor of MFA.
- A security token, commonly a key fob, stores digital certificates, passwords, biometric data, and more.
- A hard token (aka RSA token or authentication token) provides a factor to an MFA procedure. There are three types of hard tokens: connected, disconnected, and contactless.
- Keys and digital lock key codes are used by authorized individuals to enter secured physical spaces.
- Biometrics use physiological measurements of a person's hands, eyes, or face to verify the person's identity.
- Security lighting can prevent intrusions and help to provide a safe environment for employees, the public, and first responders.
- A magnetometer (aka walkthrough metal detector) measures the strength and direction of a magnetic field from what may be a weapon.
- Smart cards, key fobs, and hard tokens can all be used as part of a 2FA scheme.

Logical security measures include the following:

- Logical security is the application of software- and technology-based measures to create a protected and secured environment for users, computers, and data.
- The principle of least privilege applies permissions and rights to a user account that are no higher than needed to perform assigned tasks.
- Access control lists (ACLs) are based on allowed addresses or blocked addresses to protect system or network resources.
- The best defenses for protecting e-mail are encryption, spam filters, anti-malware software, user training, and secure e-mail gateways.
- A soft token uses programs and apps to provide authentication for the person presenting the token.
- 4G and 5G technologies secure a voice call from end to end.
- An authenticator application applies 2FA to the accounts beyond just login credentials.
- Mobile device management (MDM) provides an organization with the capability to manage and monitor the use of mobile devices that connect to its network.
- Active Directory is an integral part of Windows Server that centralizes user accounts, passwords, and access to resources on a network via a domain controller. Active Directory provides two types of security accounts: user accounts and computer accounts.
- A login script runs each time a user logs in to an Active Directory domain and sets up operating variables for the user. A domain controls access to network resources. A networked computer can be a member of either a workgroup or a domain, but never both.
- Windows AD domain-based group policies simplify the administrative burden by pushing policies through login scripts. Organizational units (OUs) hold users, groups, and computers.
- A home folder stores personal files on an Active Directory network. Folder redirection redirects users of a folder to a different folder.

2.1 QUESTIONS

1. Which of the following is a useful feature in the use of access control vestibules (or mantraps) and entry control rosters?
   A. Key fob
   B. Security guard
   C. Biometric lock
   D. Cable lock

2. An organization has contacted you for help in stopping security breaches on its servers. The latest breach involved the use of a flash drive to steal credentials. Which of the following is designed to stop this type of security breach?

   A. Privacy screen

   B. Server lock

   C. Cable lock

   D. USB lock

3. RFID, magnetic strip, barcode, and QR code technologies can all be used by which of the following?

   A. Badge reader

   B. Smart card

   C. ACLs

   D. Biometric lock

4. A Kensington lock connector is used by which of the following devices?

   A. Door lock

   B. USB lock

   C. Cable lock

   D. Biometric lock

5. A company wishes to allow its employees to connect their personal devices to its internal network. What software-provided management system should the company consider implementing?

   A. Soft tokens

   B. Biometric security

   C. Mobile device management

   D. Smart cards

2.1 ANSWERS

1. **B**   A security guard is helpful in making an access control vestibule (or mantrap) more effective and to maintain the entry control roster.

2. **D**   A USB lock prevents unused USB ports from being "borrowed" for data theft.

3. **A**   Different types of badge readers use these technologies.

4. **C**   The cable lock connector was developed by Kensington, hence the name.

5. **C**   Mobile device management (MDM) is software used to manage and control mobile devices that connect to a network.

Objective 2.2 # Compare and contrast wireless security protocols and authentication methods

Although it's widely understood that wireless networks need to be secured, many people don't realize the huge differences in protection between technologies and authentication methods. After reviewing this objective, you'll be able to choose the best protocols and methods for your situation.

Protocols and Encryption

Security protocols and encryption standards help safeguard wireless networks. The following sections will help you to understand the differences between the wireless security protocols you need to know for the CompTIA A+ Core 2 (220-1102) exam.

EXAM TIP   Be familiar with the differences between WPA2 and WPA3 and how they use TKIP and AES.

WPA2

Wi-Fi Protected Access 2 (WAP2) is a network security protocol for Wi-Fi networks. It was developed as an improvement of and replacement for the WPA protocol, which was a replacement for the less secure WEP. WPA2 is based on the IEEE 802.11i standard and has been a standard for certified Wi-Fi hardware since 2006. WPA2 implements the Advanced Encryption Standard (AES), which is a very strong encryption method.

A feature of WPA2 is the *pre-shared key (PSK),* which is a very long series of alphanumeric characters generated when a Wi-Fi device connects to a network through a wireless access point (AP). To connect to a Wi-Fi network, the *service set ID (SSID)* and passcode are used. A PSK, which is 8 to 63 characters in length, is the combination of these two data elements. There are two levels of WPA2-PSK: *WPA2-Enterprise* and *WPA2-Personal,* and their names indicate the best application of each.

WPA2 also uses *Counter Mode with Cipher Block Chaining Message Authentication Code Protocol (CCMP),* which provides added security over the *Temporal Key Integrity Protocol (TKIP)* used with WPA. CCMP provides for data confidentiality, user authentication, and access control.

Cross-Reference

AES and TKIP are discussed later in this objective.

WPA3

Wi-Fi Protected Access 3 (WAP3) improves on (and is the replacement for) WPA2 by simplifying the protocol's use and increasing its encryption strength. WAP3, which also has enterprise and personal versions, provides stronger authentication and encryption methods. It also provides a fix for the WPA2 *KRACK (key reinstallation attack)* flaw and is secure for use in *Internet of Things (IoT)* networks.

WPA3 replaces the PSK technology of WPA2 with *Simultaneous Authentication of Equals (SAE),* which is a password-based authentication and key establishment protocol. SAE provides a strong authentication process that is resistant to the most common password attacks. WPA3 also implements the *Protected Management Frames (PMF)* standard, which provides for transmitted packet privacy and protection.

Most wireless access points have onboard configuration apps. For example, Figure 2.2-1 shows the Wi-Fi Settings page used to configure a wireless access point with the WPA3-Personal protocol.

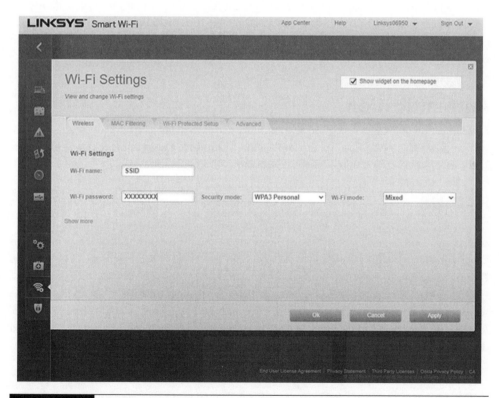

FIGURE 2.2-1   Configuring a wireless access point with WPA3-Personal

TKIP

Temporal Key Integrity Protocol (TKIP) was used with WPA2 to protect against attacks to which WEP was vulnerable. This protection is provided by an individual encryption key for every transmitted packet. TKIP also provides encryption key integrity checking and user authentication through the industry-standard *Extensible Authentication Protocol (EAP)*. TKIP is a deprecated standard that has largely been replaced by CCMP and SAE.

AES

WPA2 and WPA3 use the *Advanced Encryption Standard (AES)* to secure transmissions over Wi-Fi networks. AES is a symmetric key algorithm, which means that the same key is used to encrypt and decrypt the encrypted cipher text. AES works by applying a substitution permutation network (SPN) algorithm, which uses multiple encryption rounds to encode data to create a multilayered cipher text that has been impossible to crack.

The AES symmetrical keys can be one of three sizes: 128 bits, 192 bits, or 256 bits. Each of these is able to provide a large number of keys, but the longer the key is, the more keys it can provide. For example, a 128-bit AES key provides for 3.4×10^{38} (or 157,108,198,082,446,748,462) keys. AES keys using 192 bits provide 6.2×10^{57} keys, and AES keys using 256 bits produce 1.1×10^{77} keys.

Authentication

Authentication on wireless networks is commonly performed using an authentication protocol, such as RADIUS, TACACS+, or the application of multiple-factor authentication processes. These tools are described in the following sections.

RADIUS

Larger wireless networks, such as those with a domain server, require some form of a centralized user authentication process. One of the most commonly used authentication standards on larger wireless networks (as well as wired and dial-up networks) is the *Remote Authentication Dial-In User Service, or RADIUS,* protocol.

On a RADIUS network, users log in with their user names and passwords, and a RADIUS server provides access to only the requestor credentials it can verify as authorized for access. RADIUS is considered to be more secure than PSK because the user only enters a standard domain/network login to request access. RADIUS is partially encrypted and uses User Datagram Protocol (UDP).

TACACS+

Another centralized authentication protocol used on larger wireless networks is the *Terminal Access Controller Access-Control System Plus (TACACS+)*. TACACS+ is primarily used for device administration. Thus, both RADIUS and TACACS+ are likely to be used on enterprise networks.

ADDITIONAL RESOURCES To learn more about RADIUS versus TACACS+, go to https://www.cisco.com/c/en/us/support/docs/security-vpn/remote-authentication-dial-user-service-radius/13838-10.pdf and download the PDF file "TACACS+ vs. RADIUS Comparison."

 NOTE WPA2 and WPA3 use AES encryption, and RADIUS and TACACS+ are both used for authentication on enterprise networks.

Kerberos

Kerberos, which gets its name from a three-headed dog in Greek mythology, provides an intermediate point between an end user and a web server. Its primary purpose is to authenticate a user without the need to transmit a password over the Internet. Kerberos supports a variety of authentication functions, including single sign-on (SSO), and it is the primary authentication protocol for many websites.

Kerberos uses symmetrical key encryption and a key distribution center (KDC), which is a service that verifies the session keys of connection entities. The Kerberos authentication process involves four primary parts:

- The client requesting the content
- The server hosting the requested content
- The authentication server (AS), which performs the client authentication and issues a ticket-granting ticket (TGT) or a user authentication token to verify the client is authenticated.
- The KDC, which is a server on which the AS operates. The AS has three components: the AS itself, a ticket-granting server (TGS) that issues the service (authentication) tickets, and a Kerberos database.

Multifactor Authentication

The most common and simplest form of user authentication is *single-factor authentication (SFA)*, which requires only a user name (account ID) and a password (or "something you know"). The combination of the user name and the password is considered to be a single factor, as the user name is used to look up and verify the password entered. In addition, the user name and password are both considered to be knowledge factors that make up a single entry. On a Wi-Fi network, SFA is commonly a PSK, which is the encryption code used by the network. A user attempting to log on to a Wi-Fi network must provide the correct PSK to gain access to the network.

Multifactor authentication (MFA) aims for better security by adding an additional factor. MFA is commonly referred to as *two-factor authentication (2FA)*, meaning that it combines the user name and password with an additional factor that is generated by the authenticating device and sent to the user or entered by the user in response to a demand for a particular type of factor. The additional types of factors used for the second factor in MFA are commonly either something you have (such as a smart card, badge, or token) or something you are (via a fingerprint, eye, or facial scan).

Wireless security authentication uses one or more *authentication factors*:

- Something you know (for example, a password, user name, or name of your first childhood pet) is a *knowledge* factor.
- Something you have (for example, a smart card, key, or driver's license) is an *ownership* or *possession* factor.
- Something you are (for example, your voice, fingerprint, or retinal pattern) is an *inherence* factor.

 NOTE   Less common factors exist, such as "somewhere you are," which is a *location* factor. *Temporal* factors may restrict authentication to given times or specify time relationships between different steps (like in the movies, when two people must turn their respective key simultaneously).

REVIEW

Objective 2.2: Compare and contrast wireless security protocols and authentication methods

- Wireless security protocols include WPA2 and WPA3, both of which apply the AES encryption technology.
- Authentication methods use the following factors:
  - Something you know (such as user name and password)
  - Something you have (smart card)
  - Something you are (voice or fingerprint)
- Single-factor authentication is the most commonly used type of authentication, but multifactor authentication is increasingly employed for added security.
- The RADIUS protocol is used to authenticate larger wireless networks.
- Pre-shared keys (PSKs) are used for authentication on SOHO networks.
- TACACS+ is primarily used for device administration.
- Kerberos is an authentication process used commonly for web requests.

2.2 QUESTIONS

1. If you log in to a server with your user name and password, which type of authentication is being used?

   A. Multifactor

   B. TACACS+

   C. Single factor

   D. WEP

2. WPA3-Enterprise uses which of the following for authentication?

   A. SAE

   B. TKIP

   C. AES

   D. WPA2

3. What is the authentication technology used to authenticate a user web content request without needing to send a password over the Internet?

   A. SAE

   B. TACACS+

   C. Kerberos

   D. MFA

4. Entering a code sent to a device along with a user name and password constitutes which type of authentication?

   A. RADIUS authentication

   B. Multifactor authentication

   C. Single-factor authentication

   D. WEP

5. Which of the following statements is true of AES encryption? (Choose two.)

   A. It features 128-bit, 192-bit, and 256-bit encryption.

   B. It is easily defeated.

   C. It is the strongest wireless encryption standard.

   D. It is the weakest wireless encryption standard.

2.2 ANSWERS

1. **C** This is single-factor authentication because the user name and password together are considered to be a single knowledge factor.

2. **A** WPA3 replaced PSK with SAE.

3. **C** Kerberos is used to authenticate web requests over the Internet and Web.

4. **B** This is multifactor authentication because the user name/password combo is one factor (knowledge) and the code is the second factor (possession).

5. **A C** AES encryption offers 128-, 192-, and 256-bit encryption and is by far the strongest wireless encryption standard.

 **Objective 2.3**

Given a scenario, detect, remove, and prevent malware using the appropriate tools and methods

Malware is like a multipurpose tool, with every blade and gizmo designed to disrupt the computers, devices, and data you are responsible for. In this objective, we review the major types of malware and how to stop them.

Malware

Malware, short for *malicious software,* is any program or code designed to do something on a system or network that you don't want done. Let's examine the forms and features of malware.

 EXAM TIP Malware types include worms (which replicate themselves through networks), viruses (which infect executable or data files), rootkits (which hide in protected parts of drives or operating systems), keyloggers (which record keystrokes), Trojans (malware disguised as useful programs), ransomware (which encrypts data until a ransom is paid), boot sector viruses (which prevent or alter the boot sector data), cryptominers (software that mines for cryptocurrency deposits), and spyware (which collects information for misuse). Some types of malware can convert infected systems into "zombies," which are controlled remotely and can be used as a botnet to attack other computers. Know these types of malware for the exam.

Cross-Reference

For details on the removal of malware, see Objective 3.3 in Domain 3.0.

Trojan

A *Trojan (Trojan horse)* doesn't replicate. Instead, it tricks users into installing it by appearing to do something useful such as scan for malware (Trojan.FakeAV) or update a media player (Petya), when in reality it does something malicious.

Rootkit

A *rootkit* is a program that exploits root-level access to burrow deep into the system's operating system (OS) or hardware, where it can often hide from all but the most aggressive anti-malware tools. Rootkits like ZeroAccess and Necurs can be used to turn your computer into a cryptocurrency miner, a zombie in a botnet used to send spam, a ransomware launcher, and more.

Virus

A *virus* is a type of malware that performs two tasks: replicating itself and activating its payload. When executed, a virus copies itself into existing executables or data files. A user action (such as opening a file, as with the ILOVEYOU virus, or inserting infected auto-run removable media, as in the case of Stuxnet) triggers the initial infection. Most viruses have a malicious payload capable of damaging the system or stealing data, but the payload may not be activated until the virus has had time to quietly spread.

Spyware

Spyware, which often sneaks in alongside legitimate software being downloaded, collects information on the system and its users. Many associate it with a subtype, *adware,* which attempts to make money by explicitly showing ads, redirecting searches, or replacing ads from other providers with its own. However, this association is largely because most adware is obvious. The most dangerous spyware (such as Matcash) quietly collects private information without detection.

Ransomware

Ransomware encrypts all the data it can gain access to on the system and its mapped network drives and then demands a ransom payment (often in Bitcoin) in exchange for the decryption keys. To encourage fast payment, ransomware may present a countdown to the deletion of the encryption keys, which renders the scrambled data unrecoverable. Ransomware such as WannaCry has targeted both individual PC users and enterprise business and governmental networks.

 NOTE   Bitcoin is a digital currency that supports global transactions and lacks the governmental control of most other currencies. These features make it a popular choice for ransomware payouts.

Keylogger

A *keylogger* records your keystrokes and is used to capture login information, banking or e-commerce transactions, and anything you do with a keyboard on your computer.

Boot Sector Virus

A hard disk drive has a reserved space that holds the coding and data used to start up an OS on a PC. A *boot sector virus* infects this space or, on many PCs, the master boot record (MBR) by replacing all or some of the code with malicious code. When the infected PC boots up, the malware code seeks to infect other disk and storage devices on the system.

Cryptominers

The rapid growth of the value of Bitcoin and other cryptocurrencies didn't go unnoticed by attackers and evildoers. Therefore, to "cash in" on the opportunity to capture some of the wealth available, *cryptominers* were developed and launched. Cryptomining software, which is used in most cases to legitimately generate new cryptocurrency, can also be used by attackers to illegally access enterprise servers and install cryptocurrency miners. A cryptominer is a large piece of software that consumes significant amounts of electrical power. The damage done to an organization and its servers is that power demands are increased, along with the electric bill.

 ADDITIONAL RESOURCES   To learn more about the use of cryptominers and "cryptojacking," go to https://www.malwarebytes.com/cryptojacking and read the article "Cryptojacking – What is it?"

Tools and Methods

There are plenty of different types of malware threats, and it's not surprising that there are several different types of tools and methods you can use to fight back.

Recovery Mode

The need to recover or restore a system can arise from a variety of actions, but most commonly this need comes immediately after the installation of a new operating system version or major update. Installing an app doesn't typically create a situation where the entire system needs to be recovered. The *recovery mode* option is available on virtually all devices with an OS, including Windows, macOS, iOS, and Android. However, on a Windows 10/11 system, recovery mode is actually a set of options, each specific to a particular situation or fault.

The options available on a Windows 10/11 system for recovery include removing an OS update, using the Startup Repair function, reinstalling the OS, reverting to the previous OS version, and others. The Android Recovery Mode can be used to free up a frozen display, mitigate malware damage, and improve device performance. The Apple Recovery Mode reloads the iOS or macOS operating system to correct for system issues. The recovery mode on a Linux system varies somewhat with the distro, but essentially it's an OS reload.

Cross-Reference

To learn more about the special boot options in Windows 10/11, see the "Reboot" and "Restart Services" sections in Objective 3.1 of Domain 3.0.

Antivirus and Anti-Malware

A classic *antivirus* program can actively scan for lurking malware or operate as a *virus shield* that passively monitors your computer's activity, checking for viruses in real time as your system runs programs or downloads files.

 EXAM TIP Viruses are only a small component of the many types of malware. Many people continue to use the term *antivirus* as a synonym for *anti-malware*. However, CompTIA identifies antivirus and anti-malware as separate types of tools and expects you to know the differences.

Anti-malware programs use different techniques to combat different types of viruses:

* Because most boot sectors are the same, anti-malware programs detect boot sector viruses simply by comparing the drive's boot sector to a standard boot sector. If they detect a virus, most replace the infected boot sector from a copy.

* Executable viruses are difficult to find because they can lurk in any file, so the anti-malware program compares files against a library of signatures to identify the code pattern of a known virus. From time to time, a perfectly clean program will match a signature, in which case the anti-malware program usually issues a patch to prevent further false alarms.

* Anti-malware programs search for *polymorphic malware* (malware that changes its signature to evade detection) by computing and storing a *checksum* from the contents of each executable file. Every time a program runs, the anti-malware program calculates a new checksum to see if the executable has changed.

Software Firewalls

Software firewalls such as Windows Defender Firewall, shown in Figure 2.3-1, provide a variety of security features for computers, including the ability to block malware attacks originating from the network or the Internet. If you enable Windows Defender Firewall with Advanced Security or install a third-party firewall that checks inbound and outbound network traffic, you can provide even more protection against malware for your network.

Cross-Reference

For more information about the Windows Defender Firewall, see the "Windows Defender Firewall" section in Objective 1.4 of Domain 1.0.

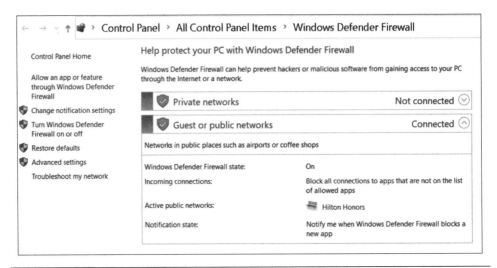

FIGURE 2.3-1   Windows Defender Firewall applet

Anti-Phishing Training

Phishing attacks attempt to take advantage of basic human nature, which is commonly over-trusting. *Anti-phishing* or *phishing-awareness training* can help an organization's employees to recognize a phishing attempt and provide them with the appropriate actions they should take when one is detected. The training should help them to understand that any malware attack that focuses on people most always starts with some form of a phishing attack.

User Education Regarding Common Threats

In any organization, the knowledge or ignorance of the end users can be the key to success or failure, respectively. The success of any security program that focuses on the detection and prevention of malware and other attacks is very much dependent on the awareness of the network users concerning the characteristics and actions of malware and hacker attacks.

Even the best anti-malware software is imperfect and often becomes a rarely tested second line of defense. The first line of defense is educating end users. Users should be trained to be cautious with e-mail from senders they don't recognize and to never click an attachment or URL in an e-mail unless they are 100 percent certain of the source. Explain the dangers of questionable websites, and teach your users how to react when a site is trying to manipulate them or is triggering their browser's built-in attack page warning (see Figure 2.3-2).

Depending on how much say your users have over their systems, you may need to reinforce the importance of having an anti-malware program, scanning regularly, and enabling the virus shield to automatically scan e-mail, downloads, running programs, and so on. Tell your users

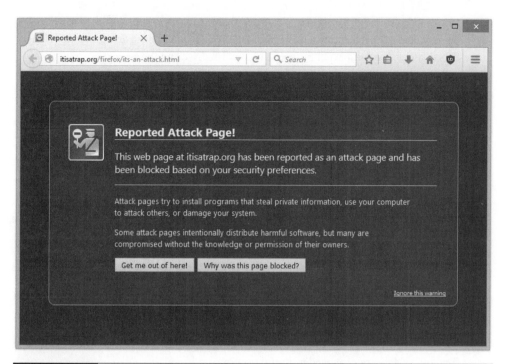

FIGURE 2.3-2 Attack page warning

to only install apps from trusted sources, such as the manufacturer's website, or well-known app stores, such as Valve's Steam service—and teach them how to both identify and avoid untrusted software sources, such as free registry cleaners from some .support domain.

Likewise, if your users have a say in whether their anti-malware software and its definitions automatically update, make sure they know how to enable these automatic updates to defend against new malware.

 NOTE The best-laid security plans include end-user education.

OS Reinstallation

Often, the simplest solution to resolving OS performance or malware issues is to reinstall the OS. While doing so shouldn't always be the first solution to any problem, reinstalling the OS on any system can have a variety of benefits:

- **Improved system performance** Provided that the files and apps you wish to keep have been backed up, performing a clean install of the OS can wipe out any unnecessary disk files that may have impacted the speed of the disk drive and the system.
- **Elimination of malware** Without the user knowing it, their system can accumulate a variety of malware and viruses when they're browsing the Web or perhaps even sharing files with coworkers. Reinstalling the OS can help to wipe out any malware on the system, provided, of course, that the malware or infected files aren't on the backup medium.
- **Elimination of junk files** Over the course of using a computer for any length of time, a variety of "temporary" or task-related files are accumulated on a system. These files, which can be managed somewhat with a disk cleanup app, can be removed by a clean install of the OS.

REVIEW

Objective 2.3: Given a scenario, detect, remove, and prevent malware using the appropriate tools and methods

The types of malware include the following:

- **Trojans** Malware disguised as useful programs
- **Rootkits** Hide in protected parts of drives or OSs where they are very hard to find and remove
- **Viruses** Infect executable or data files
- **Spyware** Collects information for misuse
- **Ransomware** Encrypts data until a ransom is paid
- **Keyloggers** Record keystrokes to steal information
- **Boot sector viruses** Infect the boot sector or MBR of a disk drive
- **Cryptominers** Infect servers with cryptomining software

Here are some tools and methods to fight against malware:

- **Antivirus programs** Block virus infections and scan systems
- **Anti-malware programs** Perform antivirus tasks, detect boot sector viruses and rootkits, create checksums for executable files, and compare stored checksums when a file is run to determine if it has been infected
- **Recovery mode systems** Help to restore an OS on most systems
- **End-user education** Essential for avoiding attacks from e-mail, links to dangerous websites, and other user-triggered threats

- **Software firewalls (such as Windows Defender Firewall)** Can stop malware attacks from other computers on the network or Internet
- **OS reinstallation** Can resolve issues related to OS performance and unnecessary files

2.3 QUESTIONS

1. A client calls you for help: the company files are encrypted and they'll be deleted unless the company sends a payment in cryptocurrency. What type of attack has happened to your client?

   A. Malware

   B. Trojan

   C. Worm

   D. Ransomware

2. Instructing individuals in your company not to click URLs in suspicious e-mails is an example of what?

   A. Social engineering

   B. Paranoia

   C. End-user education

   D. Untrusted software

3. If anti-malware software is a second line of system defense, what would be an organization's first line of defense against malware and social engineering attacks?

   A. Antivirus software

   B. Third-party consultants

   C. Risk assessment policies

   D. End-user training and education

4. A company's electrical power costs have suddenly increased significantly without any major equipment changes to the system. What could one possibility be for this increase?

   A. Hardware failures

   B. Rogue cryptominers

   C. Software failures

   D. Faulty distribution equipment

5. Which of the following OSs provide some form of a recovery mode?

   A. Windows

   B. Android

   C. macOS

   D. All of the above

2.3 ANSWERS

1. **D** A ransomware attack combines file encryption and a demand for payment of a ransom before the files will be decrypted.

2. **C** Instructing users in how to avoid e-mail traps is an example of end-user education.

3. **D** User training and education should be the first line of defense and first-level priority to protect an organization from malware and social engineering attacks.

4. **B** One sign of the presence of a cryptominer is an increase in electrical power use.

5. **D** All of these OSs, plus Linux and iOS, provide a recovery mode of one form or another.

 **Objective 2.4** Explain common social-engineering attacks, threats, and vulnerabilities

Social engineering is used to attack networks by tricking users into providing access. Threats attack technological vulnerabilities found in networks. Understanding the differences among social engineering, threats, and vulnerabilities is an important part of improving security.

Social Engineering

Attackers use social engineering to trick or manipulate people inside the organization into giving up access to its network or facilities. Social-engineering attacks are rarely used in isolation.

Attackers may infiltrate facilities by posing as cleaning personnel, repair technicians, or messengers. Once inside, they may snoop around or talk with people to gather more information. Passwords are obvious targets, but information such as employee names, office numbers, and department names could all be useful for further social-engineering attacks later. Social engineering can take place in person, via telephone calls, or via e-mail or messaging.

Phishing

The term *phishing* got its name during the telephone scam days—not that they are completely gone. Phishing is perhaps the most common form of social engineering and is the act of tricking a person into voluntarily providing their personally identifiable information (PII), such as names, user names, passwords, financial information, credit card numbers, and the like, to someone they believe to be a legitimate requestor but in reality is not. Commonly, the subterfuge is through e-mail, a web page, social media, or sometimes even snail mail.

A more targeted type of phishing is *spear phishing*, which focuses on a specific group or personal characteristic, with the same objective as any regular phishing attack. For example, the attacker or thief may launch a spear phishing attack on students in a particular field of study at a university or people who have accounts at a certain financial institution. Regardless of the target, the objective is to focus the fraud on a common characteristic of the members of the group.

Vishing

Another type of phishing is *voice phishing*, or *vishing*. Vishing is simply phishing returning to its roots: the telephone, but more specifically Voice over IP (VoIP). Like phishing, vishing is criminal fraud perpetrated through social engineering with the same goal: gaining private, financial, and personal information. Vishing is most commonly carried out with voice messages that express an urgent need for certain information by someone posing as a representative of a reputable company.

Shoulder Surfing

Shoulder surfing simply involves an attacker observing a user's screen or keyboard for information such as passwords—usually over the user's shoulder. Privacy is the first line of defense against shoulder surfing, but placing screen filters on displays and conducting user education on this and other social-engineering attacks can help to prevent and remedy shoulder-surfing attacks.

Whaling

Yet another form of phishing is *whaling*. In effect, a whaling attack pits an attacker (perhaps masquerading as a highly placed company officer or professional) against an authentic, important individual who is in a senior position within an organization or company. The intent of the attacker is to mislead the "whale" into disclosing sensitive information, granting access to an internal network, or paying money to the fraudster.

Tailgating

Tailgating, also called *piggybacking*, is another social-engineering breach that is carried out physically. Tailgating occurs when an unauthorized person enters a secured facility by physically sharing an authorized space with an authorized individual. In other words, tailgating involves walking directly behind one or more people being admitted to a secure area and often includes impersonation techniques. For example, if an employee must present MFA credentials to use a turnstile or revolving door, a tailgater just jumps into the same space as the allowed entrant. Figure 2.4-1 illustrates how an impersonator piggybacks on an employee to gain entry into a building through a revolving door. Organizations use an access control vestibule (or mantrap, described earlier in Objective 2.1) to keep intruders from tailgating into the facility behind authorized entrants.

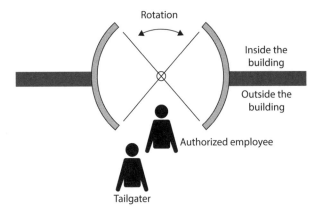

FIGURE 2.4-1   An impersonator enters a secure space by piggybacking or tailgating an employee.

Impersonation

Impersonation can take a variety of forms. For example, the attacker in a telephone scam attempts to impersonate someone inside the organization to gain information (such as a phone number, user name, blackmail material, or schedule) or help (perhaps a password reset or wire transfer). Impersonation can also rely on disguises such as cleaning personnel, repair technicians, messengers, employees with fake badges—anything that will help the attackers snoop around desks, chat with people inside the organization, and gather names, office numbers, and department names. These might be little things in and of themselves, but they are powerful tools when combined later with other social-engineering attacks.

Dumpster Diving

Dumpster diving is the generic term for searching through refuse for information. This is also a form of intrusion. Make sure unneeded documents are immediately shredded to reduce your vulnerability to dumpster diving. The best practice is to not throw away documents that could have sensitive or private information. Instead, use a licensed shredding or document disposal company, many of which can provide a *certificate of destruction (COD)*.

Evil Twin

An *evil twin* attack is not really a social-engineering attack, but rather a technological intrusion into a Wi-Fi network. This attack occurs when an attacker inserts a rogue access point into a wireless network with the intention that network users will connect to the rogue device instead of the legitimate AP.

The rogue AP, the evil twin, is then able to intercept all of the network traffic from users, including their login credentials, sensitive data, personal data, and the sites they visit. An evil twin can also be set up with a smartphone or another type of Wi-Fi–capable device, but typically a wireless network AP is used. A best practice to prevent or detect evil twins and other device insertion attacks is to contract for a professional site survey to be performed periodically at random.

 EXAM TIP Know the common social-engineering attacks and remember that user education is the best defense!

Threats

Threats are potential security events that could occur on a system or network. A threat is only possible when a vulnerability or weakness exists and could be exploited. Security systems must mitigate threats to avoid them becoming risks or security events. Vulnerabilities in a system include weaknesses in firewalls and internetworking devices, weak passwords, and insecure data and information.

Cross-Reference

Vulnerabilities are discussed later in this objective. See the "Vulnerabilities" section later in this objective.

 EXAM TIP Be able to compare and contrast all the threats and vulnerabilities listed in the following sections.

DoS and DDoS

A *denial of service (DoS)* attack is an attempt by a single device to disable another device by overwhelming ("flooding") its Internet connection with connection requests such as rapidly repeated pings, page requests, and so on. A *distributed denial of service (DDoS)* attack uses multiple coordinated devices to perform the attack. Devices involved in a DDoS attack often are compromised by malware that has turned them into zombie members of a botnet.

Zombies and botnets are often the purveyors of DoS and DDoS attacks. The term *botnet* is a combination of *robot* and *network*. A botnet is an ad hoc network of computers in homes and offices that typically don't know they've been infected and turned into a "zombie." Actions performed on a botnet are under the control of a *bot herder* who activates scripts installed on the zombies to launch an attack.

 NOTE A botnet includes a large number of infected computers (bots). The bots then flood the target computer or network with transmissions.

Zero-Day Attack

A *zero-day attack* exploits a vulnerability that was previously unknown to the software's developers—in other words, they've had zero days to fix it. Systems running the software will be vulnerable until the developers release a patch and it is installed.

Spoofing

Spoofing is the process of pretending to be someone or something you are not by placing false information into your packets, such as a user name or MAC, IP, e-mail, or web address, in order to trick other systems or users into aiding the attack.

 EXAM TIP   Be sure to know the difference between impersonation (pretending to be someone you are not—in person or by phone, e-mail, or messaging) and spoofing (adding false information to network data).

On-Path Attack

An *on-path attack* is carried out by an on-path attacker. While that may seem obvious, it's the attacker that is the threat as a result of what they do. An on-path attacker inserts themself somewhere between a user and what the user is attempting to contact over a network. In most cases, the attacker is attempting to intercept and steal user data. However, the attacker may impersonate or spoof either the site to the user or the user to the site. Typically, an on-path attack focuses on a website, but such attacks can also be on e-mail, DNS requests, and quite often on public Wi-Fi hotspot connections.

An on-path attack is a form of what is commonly called a *man-in-the-middle (MITM)* attack. In an MITM attack, like the on-path attack, the attacker taps into the communication stream between two systems to intercept traffic thought to be private. The attacker can then read or modify the data before sending it to its intended recipient. In either of these attack forms, the recipient is unaware of the intrusion.

Brute-Force Attack

Brute force is technically any attempt to find a useful value by trying many or all possibilities (typically with a program), but it most often refers to discovering a password by trying many possibilities. You can also use a brute-force search to find open ports, network IDs, IP addresses, or user names, or even to try a long list of known vulnerabilities.

Dictionary Attack

A *dictionary attack* is a form of brute-force attack that essentially guesses every word in a dictionary. Don't think only of *Webster's* dictionary—a dictionary used to attack passwords might contain every password ever leaked online. A dictionary attack uses a list of possible matches for passwords. Since many users who create their own passwords often recycle old passwords in whole or in part, a list of old passwords can be very useful in the hands of an attacker.

Insider Threat

The largest threat any workplace network has is from internal users. An *insider* is any author-ized, and typically authenticated, user who is aware of an organization's data resources, but also knows about other employees, the buildings, security systems, and operations.

The U.S. Cybersecurity and Infrastructure Security Agency (CISA) defines *insider threat* as "the threat that an insider will use his or her authorized access, wittingly or unwittingly, to do harm" to an organization's resources, data and information, and even its other employees, and physical assets.

ADDITIONAL RESOURCES   Visit the CISA's website at https://www.cisa .gov/defining-insider-threats for more information on defining insider threats.

SQL Injection

When an attacker inserts malicious SQL statements into the coding of a web page, an *SQL injection (SQLi)* attack occurs. The purpose of this attack is to access and likely manipulate data stored on the back-end database (the part of a website that a user typically can't see). An SQLi attack can be catastrophic for a business in that the attacker may have access to customer lists as well as financial records and data. The attacker could even gain administrator rights to the database and more.

Depending on the knowledge or needs of the attacker, the injected SQL statements can query specific data or cause error messages that provide data or better knowledge for the attack. The attacker can use SQL statements to gain a better understanding of a database for other attacks. These attacks can be carried out over the same communication link for the inser-tion and the response (called "in-band"), or they can trick a server into using DNS or HTTP responses to provide the sought-after information.

EXAM TIP   Although the industry no longer refers to SQL as meaning "Structured Query Language," the CompTIA A+ Core 2 exam objectives still use this full name. Understand that SQL and Structured Query Language represent the same coding scheme on the CompTIA A+ Core 2 exam.

Cross-Site Scripting

In a *cross-site scripting (XSS)* attack, the attacker inserts malicious coding statements, typically in JavaScript, into a web page. The inserted code (script) executes when the web page is dis-played in a browser along with the legitimate coding of the page. An XSS attack is commonly performed in one of two ways: the script is added as a string to the end of the URL or it's injected into the page's HTML or JavaScript coding. Because an XSS attack is carried out by the user's browser after it's downloaded, it is considered a *client-side attack.*

An XSS attack using a URL (called a "reflected" attack) may be sent to a user in an e-mail message, asking the user to click a link to claim a prize or some other inducement. The link would be something like this:

```
http://your.bank.com/index.htm?user=<script>inserted script goes here</script>
```

Also, XSS code can be inserted into a page via a persistent attack mode in which code is injected into a data field. For example, an attacker might enter the following into a name field in a web page form:

```
John Doe <script>inserted script goes here</script>
```

Vulnerabilities

A *vulnerability* is a flaw or weakness in the physical or logical systems, controls, or processes that could possibly be exploited for malicious purposes by an attacker. (Understand that the key words here are *could* and *possibly.*) Vulnerabilities lead to threats, which can lead to risk and harm. The following sections describe the vulnerability types you need to know for the CompTIA A+ Core 2 exam.

Noncompliant Systems

A *noncompliant system* is a system that has not had operating system updates and security patches, anti-malware updates and patches, or driver updates applied. A noncompliant system is not only vulnerable to attack itself but could be used as an *attack vector* (method) against other computers and devices on a network.

Unpatched Systems

An *unpatched system* is an operating system, application system, database system, or any computer-based system that is not up to date with the latest security-related patches, fixes, or upgrades. A bug or flaw in a system, especially a zero-day flaw, that goes unresolved when a patch or fix is available makes that system highly vulnerable to attack. Several studies have found that unpatched systems are the primary targets for major attacks such as ransomware.

An unpatched system may sound very much like a non-compliant system, but remember that version updates, addendums, and/or refreshed databases can also affect the security of a system. The failure to post patches and bug fixes results in an unpatched system, and failing to update any element, software, and features of a system results in a non-compliant system.

Unprotected Systems

An *unprotected system* is a computer, whether a server or a workstation, that doesn't have an anti-malware, antivirus, firewall, or other form of intrusion detection installed. In other words, an unprotected system is completely vulnerable to an attack.

EOL OSs

When an OS has been designated by its provider as *end-of-life (EOL)*, all updates, fixes, and patches are no longer issued and the user is essentially on their own. Any flaws or bugs that may be discovered following the EOL designation will not be corrected, which creates a vulnerability that can be exploited. This is also a serious problem for open source software (OSS) that is no longer supported.

BYOD

Bring-your-own-device (BYOD) policies allow users to connect their personal devices to the internal network. BYOD policies save an organization on end-user device costs, but they also create vulnerabilities on the organization's network that attackers could exploit to steal data, capture stored user credentials, or manipulate or destroy data. The primary vulnerability types created by BYOD are data leakage and malware infections.

REVIEW

Objective 2.4: Explain common social-engineering attacks, threats, and vulnerabilities

- Social engineering can use any of the following methods, and often uses them in combination:
  - **Phishing**   Pretending to be someone else electronically, via e-mail, social networks, and so on, to get user names, passwords, and so on
  - **Spear phishing**   Hackers attempt to steal sensitive information from specific victims with an attack that is highly targeted and difficult to prevent
  - **Vishing**   Phishing on VoIP or telephone systems
  - **Shoulder surfing**   Sneaking a peek at confidential information or a user's login process
  - **Whaling**   A phishing attack that targets high-profile executives attempting to gain access to the network, passwords, or other user information
  - **Tailgating**   Walking in behind someone who has access to a secure area
  - **Impersonation**   Using phone deception, disguises, or just walking around to get information
  - **Dumpster diving**   Picking up discarded information
  - **Evil twin**   Inserting an AP into a wireless network to intercept personal data

- Denial of service (DoS) and distributed denial of service (DDoS) are attacks on a network or Internet resource.
- Exploiting a vulnerability before its publisher has the opportunity to fix it is a zero-day attack.
- Spoofing places false information (MAC addresses, IP addresses, and so on) into network packets to trick other systems.
- On-path attackers insert themselves between a user and a resource the user is attempting to reach.
- Brute-force attacks try all possible passwords, user names, open ports, or other values.
- A dictionary attack is a form of brute-force attack that essentially guesses every word in a dictionary.
- Insider threats are posed by authorized users on an internal network.
- An SQL injection attack occurs when an attacker inserts malicious SQL statements into a website to gain or modify data in a database.
- Cross-site scripting (XSS) is an SQL injection type of attack in which script (JavaScript) code is inserted into a web page.
- Vulnerabilities are exposures to attacks and include the following:
  - Noncompliant systems have not been brought up to standard concerning OS patches and updates, anti-malware updates, or driver updates and are vulnerable to being turned into zombies in a botnet.
  - Unpatched systems are vulnerable to attack due to unmitigated bugs and flaws.
  - Unprotected systems don't have anti-malware, firewalls, or other intrusion protections installed.
  - End-of-life (EOL) operating systems are vulnerable because any flaws are no longer repaired.
  - Bring-your-own-device (BYOD) policies allow employees to connect their personal devices to the internal network, which can make the network vulnerable to attack.

2.4 QUESTIONS

1. A client reports that the organization's wireless network is being flooded with pings and page requests far beyond normal limits. The pings and page requests are coming from a wide variety of locations. Your client is dealing with what type of attack?

    A. DDoS

    B. Impersonation

    C. DoS

    D. Social engineering

2. You receive an e-mail purporting to be from the head of IT that is asking you to install a piece of malware. Which type of attack is being used?

   A. Impersonation

   B. Spoofing

   C. Evil twin

   D. Brute force

3. Security cameras reveal that someone is walking by the server room and pulling reports out of the trash. What is going on?

   A. Dumpster diving

   B. Shoulder surfing

   C. Phishing

   D. Vishing

4. The same day that your accounting software vendor is informed of a security vulnerability, you discover it was used to attack accounts payable. What type of attack is being attempted?

   A. Phishing

   B. On-path

   C. Zero day

   D. Cross-site scripting (XSS)

5. The RADIUS authentication server on your wireless network has been hacked and a list of old passwords has been leaked. Although none of the passwords are current, the list could still be used for which of the following attacks?

   A. Brute force

   B. Whaling

   C. SQL injection

   D. Dictionary

2.4 ANSWERS

1. **A**   A distributed denial of service (DDoS) attack comes from multiple locations, seeking to overwhelm a network resource so it can't respond.

2. **B**   The use of a false sender on the e-mail makes this an example of spoofing.

3. **A**   Dumpster diving involves taking discarded information from any location, not just a dumpster.

4. **C**   A zero-day attack takes place before or immediately after the software vendor discovers or has been provided knowledge of a vulnerability. It's called zero-day because the vendor has had zero days to patch the vulnerability.

5. **D**   A dictionary attack uses a list of possible matches for passwords. Since many users who create their own passwords often recycle old passwords in whole or in part, a list of old passwords can be very useful in the hands of an attacker.

Objective 2.5 Given a scenario, manage and configure basic security settings in the Microsoft Windows OS

The operating systems (OSs) on PCs and mobile devices include several security features, but due to the inherent nature of these devices, it's virtually impossible for the developers to anticipate all of the ways these devices will be used. However, each OS includes many security features and countermeasures to help users protect their data and information. This objective discusses the basics of the security settings and features of the Windows 10/11 operating systems.

Defender Antivirus

Defender antivirus, as it's referred to in the CompTIA A+ Core 2 objectives, is officially Virus & Threat Protection in Windows 10/11 (Settings | Windows Security). For this discussion, we'll use the Defender antivirus name, but you should also be aware of its actual title and how to find and configure it.

The Defender antivirus tool applies several advanced technologies as a built-in component of Windows 10/11. Defender antivirus is also anti-malware that can work in the background with several third-party anti-malware/antivirus systems. Defender antivirus can be configured into three modes:

- **Active mode**   In this mode, Defender antivirus is the primary antivirus tool of the Windows OSs. This tool scans files for viruses, malware, and threats. Any attacks or threats found are reported to the organization's security information and retained in the data kept by the Windows Security application.
- **Passive mode**   In this mode, Defender antivirus works in the background behind other antivirus software. It scans files, and any detected malware or threats are reported to the organization's security information and to Windows Security. However, it doesn't perform any remediation, leaving that task to the foreground antivirus application.
- **Disabled mode**   In this mode, no actions take place, no files are scanned, no data is reported, and no remediation takes place.

Microsoft refers to its malware and antivirus database as its Security Intelligence Definition, which provides up-to-date descriptions and signatures of known malware and virus attacks.

This data includes intelligence gathered from third-party information and is constantly updated from the cloud to provide the best detection profiles for identifying threats.

Virus & Threat Protection is activated by default. However, should you wish to deactivate (or reactivate) this tool and all of its individual protection areas (real-time, cloud-delivered, and sample submission), use the following steps:

1. Use the Start menu to search for "group policy."

2. Select the option Edit Group Policy to open the Local Group Policy Editor.

3. In the left-side navigation pane, under Computer Configuration, select Administrative Templates.

4. From the list opened in the center pane, select Windows Components to display a components list.

5. Scroll down and select Microsoft Defender Antivirus and click Turn off Microsoft Defender Antivirus to display its dialog box, shown in Figure 2.5-1.

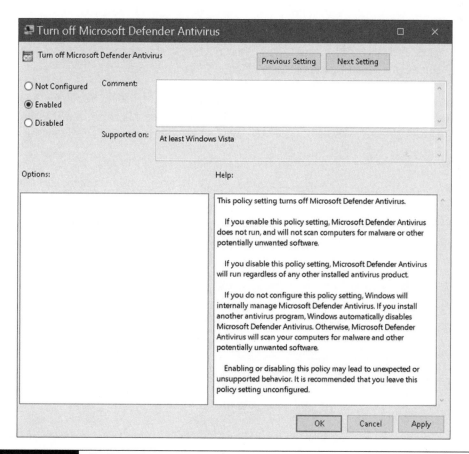

FIGURE 2.5-1   The Turn off Microsoft Defender Antivirus dialog box

6. Remember that you are enabling or disabling the "turn off" option. Therefore, if you choose to activate this option, you are turning off the antivirus app. Choosing Disable or Not Configured, you are actually choosing that you want this tool to continue running, meaning that you want to turn off the "turn off" option. To disable this tool, choose the Enable option. Got it?

7. Click Apply and OK to save this setting.

To update the definitions, you can use one of three different methods: automatic updates, triggering updates, and manual updates. The default setting is automatic updates, but if you want to be sure you have the latest updates, you can use the following method to trigger an update:

1. Open the Settings app and choose the Updates and Security option.

2. Choose Windows Security from the navigation pane on the left side of the page.

3. Click the Virus & Threat Protection option in the center pane.

4. Under the Virus & Threat Protection Updates heading, click the Check for Updates link to open the Protection Updates page.

5. Click the Check for Updates button. Any updates not already installed are uploaded and the status dates are updated (see Figure 2.5-2).

You can also manually download the latest definitions from Microsoft. Search for "Security intelligence updates for Microsoft Defender Antivirus and other Microsoft anti-malware" on the Microsoft Updates website to locate the latest update download. Follow the instructions on the web page.

FIGURE 2.5-2   The Protection Updates page

EXAM TIP   Know how to activate/deactivate Defender Antivirus. Also know how to update virus definitions.

Firewalls

A *firewall,* whether hardware or software, if configured with the proper rules, permits author-ized (meaning approved) inbound and outbound network traffic and denies traffic that the firewall's rules specifically exclude.

Windows Defender Firewall with Advanced Security (its full name) can be configured into one of four basic designs, each with specific goals and defined filtering and restrictions:

- **Basic**   Allows only the network traffic that is needed and authorized by firewall rules.
- **Domain isolation**   Blocks unsolicited messages from devices that aren't domain members from reaching devices that are. Security zones can be created within a domain and define rules that apply to specific devices. For example, a boundary zone enables a device to receive messages from non-domain member devices, and an encryption zone is used for the protection of devices that store sensitive information.
- **Server isolation**   Access to a particular server is limited to only those devices designated as being authorized to do so. The server itself may be designated as a member of a domain isolation zone.
- **Certificate-based**   This design policy can be used with either domain or server isolation designs. It applies certificates for authenticating clients and servers, including devices running OSs other than Windows.

Cross-Reference

More information is available on the Windows Defender Firewall in Domain 1 and Objective 1.4.

Activate/Deactivate

Use the following steps to turn on or off Windows Defender Firewall:

1. Select the Update & Security link from the Settings app and choose Windows Security.
2. On the Windows Security page, select the Firewall & Network Protection option in the left-side navigation pane.
3. On the Firewall & Network Protection page (see Figure 2.5-3), you have three choices for firewall location:
    - **Domain network**   The computer is connected to a domain controller.
    - **Private network**   This profile is used for SOHO networks on which the users and devices are trusted.

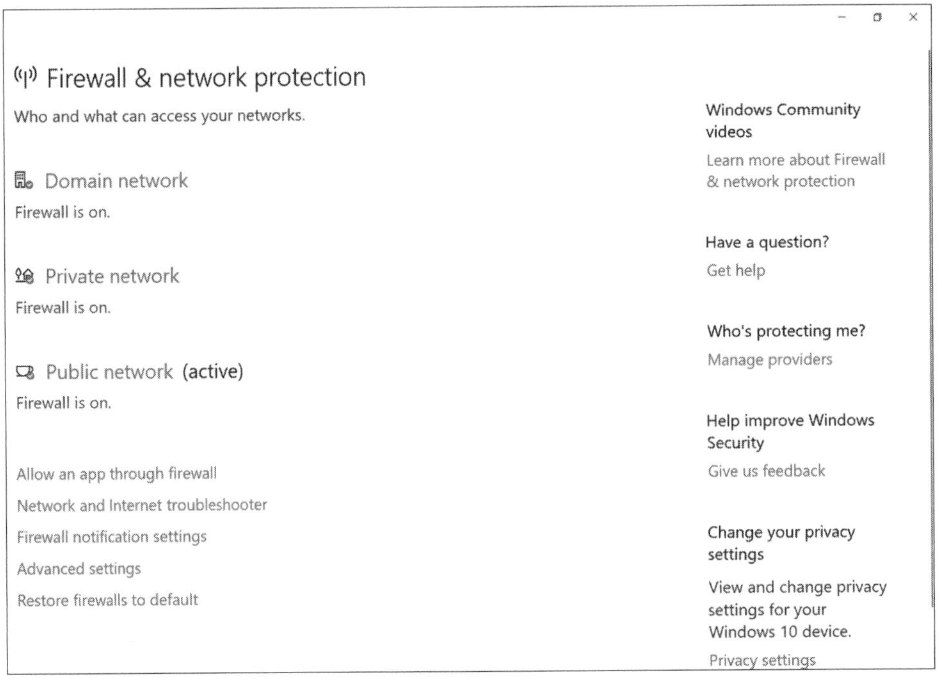

FIGURE 2.5-3   The Firewall & Network Protection page of the Settings app

- **Public network**   This is the default profile for new network connections and is initially the most secure of the three location profiles, with the assumption that a public network isn't secure.

  Click the name of the location profile you wish to use to open the configuration page for that profile. Figure 2.5-4 shows a screen capture of the Private Network page.

4. Under the Microsoft Defender Firewall heading, toggle the slide switch to On (switch turns blue) or Off (which may require additional steps). This is virtually the same process for activating the Domain Network and Public Network profiles.

Port Security

When a connection is made between two network devices, it is made through a TCP/UDP port, which is identified with a *port number*. The port number signifies how the message traffic that flows over the connection is to be handled, meaning which application or service is to process the messages. The default settings of Windows Defender Firewall block unsolicited traffic, but there may be traffic from a particular application you want to be allowed to pass. The way this is done is by "opening" the port associated with that traffic.

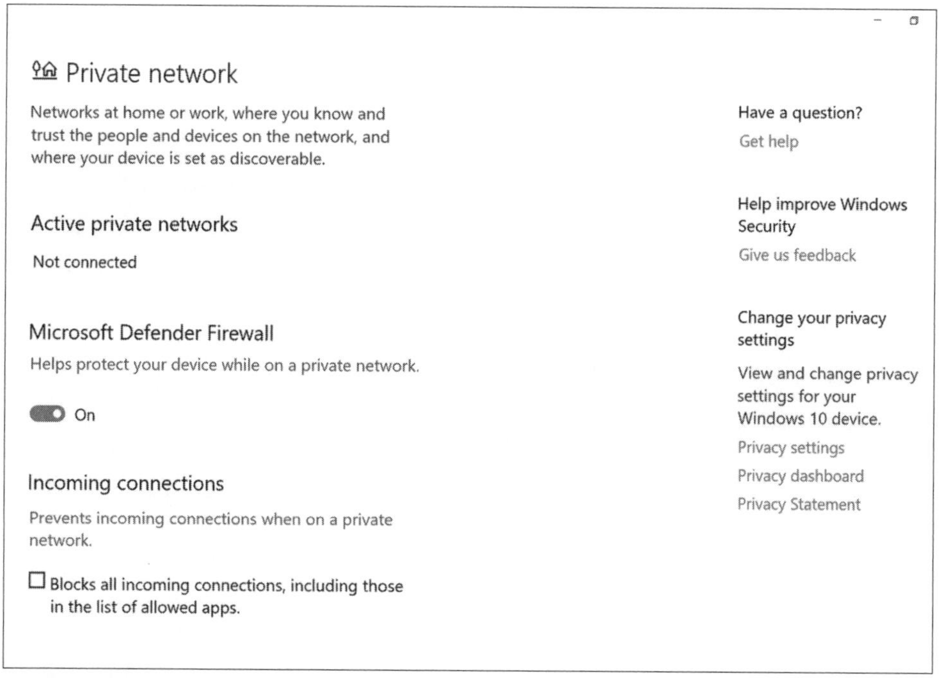

FIGURE 2.5-4   The Private Network page of the Windows Defender Firewall settings

There are two ways to open a port on Windows Defender Firewall: allowing a particular application (and its associated port) to pass and configuring the port directly using an inbound rule.

Security rules, including those that deal with ports, are the means for setting up *application security*. The rules that control the permit/deny of messages generated or destined for a particular application, typically identified by a port number, define not only which applications can pass in or out but also which applications cannot enter or leave. The next few sections describe the processes used to allow or deny application traffic.

Allow an App Through Firewall

To allow a particular application to pass through Windows Defender Firewall, use the following steps:

1. Using steps 1 and 2 of the process in the "Activate/Deactivate" section, access the Firewall & Network Protection page.

2. Select the Allow an App Through Firewall link located near the bottom of the center pane to open the Allow Apps to Communicate Through Windows Defender Firewall dialog box, shown in Figure 2.5-5.

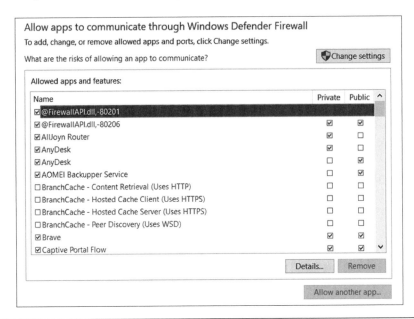

The Allow Apps to Communicate Through Windows Defender Firewall dialog box

3. Scroll down through the list of allowed apps to find the app you wish to allow to see if it may already be selected. An app can be allowed on a private or public network. Therefore, the app you want to allow may already be allowed, but not on the network you want.

4. If you find the app and wish to add or modify the network on which it's allowed, click the Change Settings button and click the checkbox you wish to alter. Click OK to save the change.

5. If the app is not in the existing list, click the Allow Another App button at the bottom of the box to open the Add an App dialog box, shown in Figure 2.5-6.

6. Use the Browse button to locate the application and then use the Network Types button to set the public/private network type. Click OK to complete the configuration.

New Inbound Rule

Another and more specific way to open a port on Windows Defender Firewall is to create an explicitly targeted inbound rule. Use the following steps to create a new inbound rule that allows traffic for a specific port number to pass through the firewall.

1. Access the Firewall & Network Protection page of the Settings app.

2. Click the Advanced Settings link located near the bottom of the center pane to display the Windows Defender Firewall with Advanced Security page, shown in Figure 2.5-7.

The Add an App dialog box

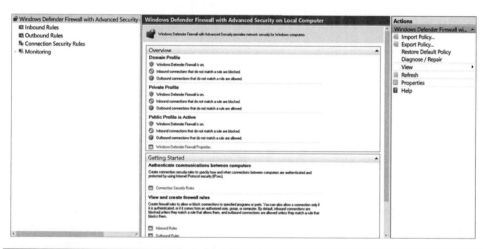

The Windows Defender Firewall with Advanced Security page

3. In the left-side navigation pane, click *Inbound Rules,* which lists the existing Inbound rules in the center pane. The Actions available for managing existing or new Inbound rules appear in the right-side pane, as shown in Figure 2.5-7. Click New Rule in the Actions pane to open the New Inbound Rule Wizard dialog box (see Figure 2.5-8).

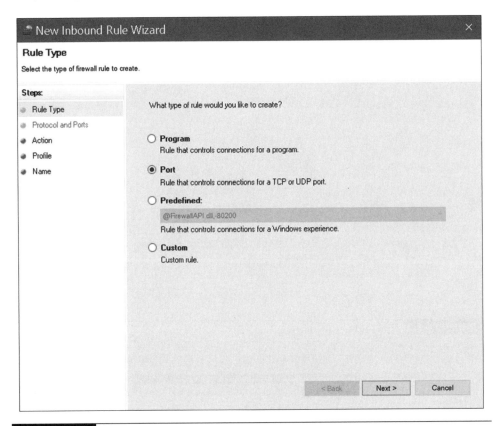

FIGURE 2.5-8 The New Inbound Rule Wizard dialog box

4. Select the Port option by clicking its radio button. Click Next to continue.

5. Choose whether the port to be configured is TCP or UDP and then enter the port number(s) in Specific Local Ports. If multiple ports are entered, separate them with commas. Click Next to continue.

 ADDITIONAL RESOURCES If you are unsure of whether the port number for a protocol or service is TCP or UDP (or both), refer to the article "Common Ports And Protocols List" at https://www.lddgo.net/en/network/port.

6. On the next page that displays, the default option is Allow the Connection, which is the option to be used if the port number and its associated protocol or service are trusted. However, if you wish to only allow messages to the port number to pass, select the option Allow the Connection If It Is Secure, which invokes IPSec to authenticate the connection and its traffic. The Block the Connection option is used to disengage an active rule. Click Next to continue.

ADDITIONAL RESOURCES   IPSec (Internet Protocol Security) is a suite of security protocols and encryption algorithms used to secure data in transit on the Internet and public networks. For more information, see "IPSec: A Comprehensive Guide" at https://techgenix.com/what-is-ipsec-internet-protocol-security/.

7. Choose the location policy to which this new rule should apply. Choose Domain, Private, Public, or all three. Click Next to continue.

8. The last step is to give the new inbound rule a name and, if you wish, a description. Click Finish to save the rule.

EXAM TIP   Given a scenario, be ready to activate/deactivate Windows Firewall and configure port and application security.

User Accounts

When the Windows OS is installed, it creates three user account types by default: a standard user, a guest account, and an administrator account. The administrator and guest accounts are created as inactive accounts. and the standard account is active for use to complete the installation and user-level configurations.

Windows 10/11 supports several account types for which user accounts can be created: local, Microsoft, administrator, standard/guest, and power user accounts. Table 2.5-1 briefly describes each of these account types.

Groups

A *group* is a container holding user accounts that defines the capabilities of its members, such as file/folder permissions, printer access, and so on. For example, if you make an Accounting group and add all users in the accounting department, you can easily grant or deny the whole group access to a given file or folder.

By creating groups with specified roles and users for each group, and by providing each group with access to only files or folders relevant to their jobs, you improve the data security of the organization. Windows provides built-in groups with predetermined access levels. Table 2.5-2 lists the groups you should know for the CompTIA A+ Core 2 exam.

Other groups that may be created by default or as required on Windows 10/11 systems include DHCP Administrators and DHCP Users (installed with DHCP Server service), Help Services, Network Configuration Operators, Performance Monitor Users, Performance Log Users, Print Operators, Remote Desktop Users, and Replicator.

TABLE 2.5-1 Windows 10/11 User Accounts

Account Type	Privileges and Rights
Local	Associates one user account with one specific system. Local accounts are limited to accessing resources to which permission has been granted.
Microsoft	A combination of any e-mail address (Outlook, Yahoo!, Gmail, and so on) and a password. Can be used to log in to Windows 10/11 as well as Xbox Live, Outlook.com, OneDrive, and nearly all Microsoft products and services. A Microsoft account is not linked to a specific computer, and a user can create multiple accounts.
Administrator	Total control of and full access to the Windows OS environment. A system can have multiple Administrator accounts.
Standard/guest	The user can perform normal functions and other actions not requiring administrator permissions. Limited to accessing only files created by the user or those publicly shared.
Power user	The user can create and manage local user accounts and groups, run legacy applications, customize system resources, and stop and start system services. The user cannot modify operating system files or install system services.

TABLE 2.5-2 Windows 10/11 User Account Groups

Group	Rights and Privileges
Administrators	Full control of system. Can assign user rights and access control. An Administrator account is a default member of this group.
Backup Operators	Back up and restore files. Cannot change security settings.
Guests	Temporary profiles that are deleted when user logs off. A Guest account (inactive by default) is a default member of this group.
Power Users	Create and modify user accounts and local groups. Cannot take ownership of files, backup or restore folders, install or disable device drivers, or manage logs.
Remote Desktop Users	Can remotely log on to a server.
Users	Can run applications as well as use local and network printers. Cannot share directories. Members of this group, by default, are the Domain Users, Authenticated Users, and Interactive groups. Any Domain User account is a member.

EXAM TIP Know the various Microsoft users and groups described in this section and what they can and cannot do.

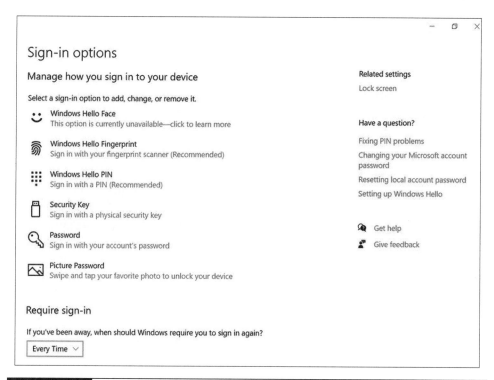

FIGURE 2.5-9   The Sign-in Options page of the Settings app

OS Login Options

The Password login (sign-in) option is the most commonly used of the options available for logging in to a Windows 10/11 system. The other options available, shown in Figure 2.5-9, provide other ways to log in to the OS that can be more secure, easier to negotiate, or just simpler to use. Table 2.5-3 lists and describes the login or sign-in options available on the Sign-in Options page of the Settings app.

 EXAM TIP   Remember that the Windows Hello feature requires a PC to have a Trusted Platform Module (TPM) chip.

The final option available on the Sign-in Options page is the Require Sign-In option, which controls whether a user returning to a Windows system that has been put into sleep or hibernation mode is required to enter a password to resume work. This option would be better named as Require Sign-in on Wakeup because that is the condition being configured. You have the choices of Never and When PC Wakes Up from Sleep.

TABLE 2.5-3	Sign-in Settings on the Windows 10/11 Sign-in Options Page

Login/Sign-in Options	Function
Windows Hello Face Windows Hello Fingerprint Windows Hello PIN	Log in to devices, applications, online sites, or networks using an image of your face, a scan of the iris in your eye, or a fingerprint, or by entering a PIN code. Note that pictures of your face or iris and fingerprint images are not stored on a Windows system.
Security Key	A security key is a hardware device, such as a USB key, that substitutes for the entry of a user name and password. Security keys are used in conjunction with a fingerprint or PIN. This is a secure sign-in because, even if the security is lost or stolen, an attacker must also know the PIN or have your fingerprint.
Password	Passwords are the most common of the sign-in options. In combination with a user name or account ID, a password completes a single-factor authentication key.
Picture Password	A picture password can be used to replace an entered text user name and password on a Windows 10/11 system. To sign in with this option, you can draw a shape or access a graphic image, touch or click preset positions on the graphic, or replicate a prerecorded series of gestures.

Single Sign-On

Single sign-on (SSO) is a feature that enables a single Windows account to log on to any system on a domain. SSO permits a user to access multiple applications or resources through the use of one user name and password combination. SSO eliminates the need for a user to have a separate local account for every computer they wish to access. User authentication through a single domain account enables the user to access all of the machines on a domain.

 NOTE Single sign-on (SSO) is an enterprise-level feature.

NTFS vs. Share Permissions

Each OS uses separate network sharing permissions to grant or restrict access to shared resources. Beyond these, file- or folder-level permissions (such as NTFS) also affect network shares. What are NTFS permissions? They are sets of rules that affect every folder and file in your system, and they define what any group or account can or cannot do with a file or folder.

Windows uses NTFS to authorize local and network users: even if you grant access via network share permissions, NTFS permissions still say what users can do with the resource.

If you share from an NTFS drive, you must set *both* network and NTFS permissions to grant access. The shortcut is to give everyone Full Control network permissions, and then you use NTFS permissions to precisely control who has what access.

File and Folder Attributes

By default, the Windows 10/11 File Explorer hides system files and folders to protect against a standard user accidentally or purposefully changing or erasing these files.

Hidden Files and Folders

Technicians and administrators need to view hidden files when they need to modify configuration settings for files and folders, investigate issues, and repair problems.

To make hidden files visible on a Windows 10/11 system, use the following steps:

1. Click the File Explorer Options icon on the Control Panel to display its dialog box.

2. On the File Explorer Options dialog box, select the View tab.

3. Find the Hidden Files and Folders attribute in the Files and Folders section of the Advanced Settings list. Then select the Show Hidden Files, Folders, and Drives radio button, as shown in Figure 2.5-10.

FIGURE 2.5-10   The File Explorer Options dialog box showing the Advanced Settings list

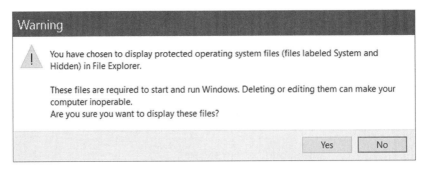

FIGURE 2.5-11 The message box that displays when you attempt to remove the Hide Protected Operating System Files (Recommended) setting

4. If the Hide Protected Operating System Files (Recommended) option (in the same section) is checked, you should clear it.

5. When you click the checkbox to clear this option, a warning message displays (see Figure 2.5-11). If you wish to continue with unselecting this option, click Yes; otherwise, click No to cancel this action.

6. If it was necessary to make those settings changes in order to make other necessary changes to the system, you should reverse the changes you made to the settings in the Control Panel to undo the changes and their effects to the system.

User Account File and Folder Attributes

Depending on the account level of the user who creates or modifies a file on a Windows 10/11 system, that user (or other users) may encounter restrictions as to what they can do with the file, if anything at all. To view or modify the attributes of a file or folder, use the following steps.

1. Use the File Explorer to navigate to the folder in which the targeted file is contained.

2. Right-click the file you want to view or modify.

3. To view the properties of this file, either click the Properties icon in the Open section of the Ribbon or right-click the filename and choose Properties from the pop-up menu. If you wish to view the properties of a folder, click it in the left-side navigation pane and click the Properties option on the Ribbon. The result of any of these actions is that the Properties dialog box for the file or folder is displayed. An example of the Properties dialog box is shown in Figure 2.5-12.

4. In the Attributes settings at the bottom of the General tab, you can alter the file's attributes to make it read-only or hidden, as shown in Figure 2.5-12.

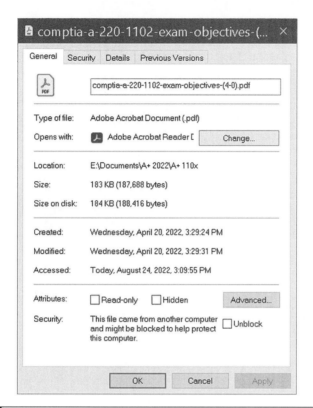

FIGURE 2.5-12   The Properties dialog box for a PDF file

Inheritance

Inheritance determines which NTFS permissions apply to new files or subfolders. The default rule is that new files or folders get the NTFS permissions of the parent folder. You can technically disable inheritance in the file or folder properties, but don't. Inheritance is good (and expected). Inherited permissions are dimmed and can't be changed (see Figure 2.5-13), but you can override them as needed with the Deny checkbox. These permissions are additive. For example, if you have Full Control on a folder and only Read on a file in it, you still get Full Control on the file.

 EXAM TIP   You should know how and where properties settings are changed on the Windows 10/11 File Explorer and understand the concept and application of file permission inheritance for the CompTIA A+ Core 2 exam.

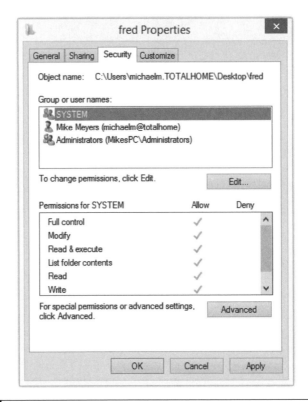

FIGURE 2.5-13   Inherited permissions

Run as Administrator vs. Standard User

On a Windows 10/11 system, the security settings prevent standard users from running some commands. To overcome this limitation, you can run most administrative commands at an elevated level by choosing the Run as Administrator option. To execute a command or app at the elevated level, right-click the command on the Start menu and choose Run as Administrator.

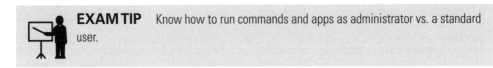

EXAM TIP   Know how to run commands and apps as administrator vs. a standard user.

User Account Control

The Windows 10/11 security feature User Account Control (UAC) helps users to prevent major system changes being made as well as keeps unauthorized or unsigned applications from being installed. The benefit of UAC, if configured properly, is to prevent malware

FIGURE 2.5-14 The UAC challenge/warning box

and other malicious software from being added to the system. When an attempt is made to install an unknown or unsigned application or service to the system, UAC displays a warning message to challenge a suspicious action, as shown in Figure 2.5-14. Choosing the No option cancels the installation and prevents a security breach.

The security level of UAC is configured through the User Accounts app on the Control Panel. To set the security level of UAC on a Windows 10/11 system, use the following steps.

1. Open the Control Panel with Administrator rights.

2. Select the User Accounts option to open the Make Changes to Your User Account page.

3. Under the Make Changes to My Account in PC Settings heading, click the Change User Account Control option to open the User Account Control Settings dialog box, shown in Figure 2.5-15.

4. As shown in Figure 2.5-15, the body of the UAC Settings dialog box is a vertical slide that lists, from top to bottom, the following options:

   - **Always notify me when** This option sets the UAC to always display a notification for any changes, including trusted Windows settings.

   - **Notify me only when apps try to make changes to my computer (default)** This is typically the default option and displays the challenge/warning box when an application attempts to make a change to a system setting or resource. A response is required before the system can resume operations.

   - **Notify me only when apps try to make changes to my computer (do not dim my desktop)** This option is essentially the same as the previous one, with the exception that processes running in the background continue to run (without dimming the Desktop).

   - **Never notify** Not a great choice, even for the most careful administrators. No notice or warning is given for any changes.

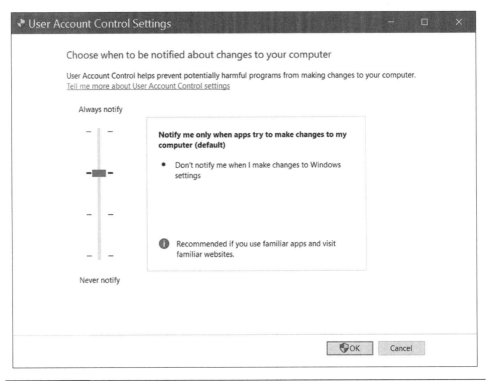

FIGURE 2.5-15 The User Account Control Settings dialog box

BitLocker and BitLocker To Go

Windows 10/11 Pro and Enterprise editions (meaning not the Windows Home editions) feature *BitLocker Drive Encryption,* which encrypts the whole drive, including every user's files. If the system has a *Trusted Platform Module (TPM)* chip, BitLocker Drive Encryption can enhance security by validating on boot that the computer has not changed. Create a recovery key or password when you enable BitLocker and keep it somewhere secure (like a safe). To enable BitLocker, double-click the BitLocker Drive Encryption icon in the Control Panel and then click Turn on BitLocker (see Figure 2.5-16). *BitLocker To Go* enables you to encrypt removable media (such as a USB flash drive) and require a password to access its data.

FIGURE 2.5-16 Enabling BitLocker Drive Encryption

EFS

The Pro and Enterprise editions of Windows 10/11 support the *Encrypting File System (EFS)*, an encryption scheme any user can use to encrypt individual files or folders. To encrypt a file or folder, just right-click it and select Properties, click the General tab, click the Advanced button, and then check Encrypt Contents to Secure Data (see Figure 2.5-17) in the Advanced Attributes dialog box. Close the open dialog boxes, and the file or folder is locked from other user accounts (unless you copy it to a non-NTFS drive).

CAUTION Data you encrypt with EFS is secure from prying eyes, but access to your encrypted files is related to specific individual Windows 10/11 installations. A lost password or one that is inadvertently reset can mean that a user and possibly the administrator are locked out of the encrypted files permanently. If you use EFS, it's a wise choice to make a password reset disk (see "Create a password reset disk for a local account in Windows" at https://support.microsoft.com/en-us/windows/create-a-password-reset-disk-for-a-local-account-in-windows-9a54a5ca-27bc-de72-244a-27b7d62951de.)

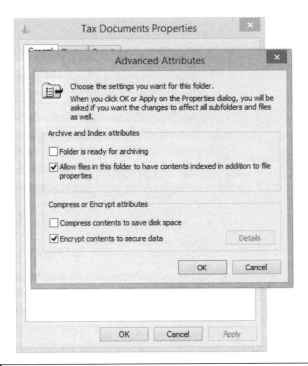

FIGURE 2.5-17   Selecting encryption

REVIEW

Objective 2.5: Given a scenario, manage and configure basic security settings in the Microsoft Windows OS

- Defender antivirus is the antivirus application for Windows 10/11 that scans files for viruses, malware, and threats.
- A firewall is hardware or software that permits authorized inbound and outbound traffic and denies traffic its rules specifically exclude.
- The filtering and restrictions of Windows Defender Firewall are basic, domain isolation, server isolation, and certificate-based.
- A connection between network devices is made through a port.
- The Windows OS creates three user account types by default: standard user, guest account, and administrator account.
- A *group* is a container for user accounts that defines the capabilities of its members.
- Windows provides these built-in groups: Administrators, Backup Operators, Guests, Power Users, Remote Desktop Users, and Users.

- Windows login options are Windows Hello (Face, Fingerprint, or PIN), Security Key, Password, and Picture Password.

- The Require Sign-In option controls whether a user must enter a password to resume work on an OS in sleep mode.

- A single sign-on (SSO) account logs a user into any system on a domain.

- Windows uses NTFS to authorize local and network users.

- Inheritance determines which NTFS permissions apply to a new file or subfolder.

- Windows security settings prevent a standard user from running some commands unless they are executed with Run as Administrator.

- User Account Control (UAC) helps to prevent major system changes from being made or unauthorized or unsigned applications from being installed. The UAC security levels are as follows:

  - Always notify me when

  - Notify me only when apps try to make changes to my computer (default)

  - Notify me only when apps try to make changes to my computer (do not dim my desktop

  - Never notify

- BitLocker Drive Encryption encrypts a whole drive, including user files. With a TPM chip, it can validate on boot that the computer has not changed.

- The Windows Pro and Enterprise editions support the Encrypting File System (EFS), which a user can use to encrypt files or folders.

2.5 QUESTIONS

1. You have been using a separate and unique login user name and password for several different Microsoft applications, including Xbox Live. You learn that you can use just one login account for all Microsoft products. What is it?

   A. Administrator account

   B. Remote user account

   C. Microsoft account

   D. Guest account

2. A client has called you needing help to find BitLocker on a Windows 10 Home edition PC. The client wants to encrypt a hard disk drive and was unable to find it. What is your response to this client?

   A. Set File Explorer to show hidden files.

   B. Search the Web for how to edit the Registry.

   C. Look in the PC's documentation.

   D. BitLocker is not installed with Windows 10/11 Home editions.

3. Which one of the following is not currently a Windows 10/11 sign-in option?

   A. Windows Hello

   B. Security Key

   C. Password

   D. Picture Password

   E. Spoken Password

4. What is the user sign-on type that authenticates a user only once on a device or network and allows access to multiple applications or services?

   A. Windows Hello

   B. SSO

   C. Security key

   D. Password

5. An administrator is suspicious that unknown and unsigned applications are being installed by a user on a network node. What UAC setting should the administrator use to block users from installing software on their computers?

   A. Always notify me when

   B. Notify me only when apps try to make changes to my computer (default)

   C. Notify me only when I make changes to my computer

   D. Never notify

2.5 ANSWERS

1. **C** A Microsoft account, while not universal, can be used to log in to most Microsoft applications and services.

2. **D** BitLocker is not installed with the Windows 10/11 Home editions. The user can upgrade to another Windows edition or purchase BitLocker directly from the Microsoft Store.

3. **E** At the present time, Spoken Passwords aren't available as a sign-in option.

4. **B** Single sign-on (SSO) authenticates a user over multiple applications.

5. **A** This option sets the UAC to always display a notification for any changes, including trusted Windows settings.

Objective 2.6 Given a scenario, configure a workstation to meet best practices for security

K eeping a workstation secure starts with protecting stored data, but it doesn't end there. Other considerations for securing a workstation, regardless of whether it is connected to a network, include following password best practices, applying techniques to maintain the physical and logical security of the device, and managing accounts. In this objective, you learn the methods for securing accounts and devices and when to use them.

EXAM TIP   Given a scenario, be ready to implement the appropriate security best practices listed in this objective.

Data-at-Rest Encryption

Data encryption is used to protect the confidentiality, integrity, and availability (the elements of the CIA model) of data while it's at rest (stored), in transit (transmitted), and in use (in memory). In this objective, the focus is on *data at rest,* meaning stored data on any permanent storage device.

NOTE   Data-at-rest encryption doesn't protect data when it's being transmitted or used by an app or service.

Data at rest is data that is not in use and is not being transmitted. It is idle on a storage device. Data at rest can be structured or unstructured and can be stored on multiple types of devices or services, including hard disk drives (HDDs), solid-state drives (SSDs), database servers, the cloud, mobile phones, USB devices, storage area networks (SANs), and networked-attached storage (NAS). Each of these and other storage devices have their strengths and weaknesses, but the goal is to protect the data regardless of where it's stored.

So, how is data at rest best protected in this essentially helpless state? The best answer (and the one you need to understand for the CompTIA A+ Core 2 exam) is *encryption.* As discussed many times throughout this book, encryption is the conversion of plain-text data into cipher text. Figure 2.6-1 illustrates the encryption/decryption processes. Data encryption is the best protection for data at rest.

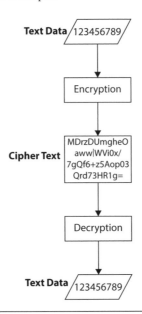

Text Data /123456789/

Encryption

Cipher Text MDrzDUmgheO aww|WVi0x/ 7gQf6+z5Aop03 Qrd73HR1g=

Decryption

Text Data /123456789/

FIGURE 2.6-1   The encryption/decryption processes

The most common encryption method used on data at rest is *symmetric encryption,* which uses the same encryption key to encode and decode the data. Four types of encryption can be applied to data at rest:

- **Application-level**   Data is encrypted by the same application that generates or modifies it on the client, workstation, or server. This method allows the encryption to include rules for user logon levels.
- **File system**   This type of data-at-rest encryption can target specific data, files, and folders. Access to the data can be tied to user accounts and may require a password or PIN.
- **Database**   The data written to a database is included when all or parts of a database are encrypted.
- **Full disk encryption (FDE)**   The entire contents of a storage device are encrypted. This is the most secure protection for data at rest. Access typically requires authentication.

 NOTE   Encrypting data at rest is commonly used to comply with regulatory requirements in PCI, HIPAA, and others.

The Windows 10/11 operating system (OS) provides *BitLocker* encryption and the *Encrypting File System (EFS)* for securing data at rest. With BitLocker engaged, a file stored on a disk drive (in other words, *data at rest*) can be encrypted through its Properties settings.

FIGURE 2.6-2   The Advanced Attributes dialog box includes the setting for encrypting files and folders.

To apply encryption to a specific file or folder, right-click the file/folder name, choose Properties, and then click the Advanced button to display the Advanced Attributes dialog box (see Figure 2.6-2). Check the box for Encrypt Contents to Secure Data and then click OK to encrypt the file.

Cross-Reference

For more information on BitLocker, BitLocker To Go, and EFS, see Objective 2.5.

Files or folders encrypted with EFS cannot be read unless an EFS certificate is available to the current user. For example, if User A uses EFS to encrypt a folder on their system drive, Administrator B cannot read the folder unless User A provides the EFS certificate to Administrator B.

 ADDITIONAL RESOURCES   For details about setting BitLocker and BitLocker To Go options, go to https://docs.microsoft.com and search for "BitLocker group policy settings."

 EXAM TIP   The best protection for data at rest is encryption.

Password Best Practices

What does CompTIA mean by password best practices? Simply put, if you set up password policies that enforce the following practices, you will reduce the likelihood that attacks against password-protected resources, such as user accounts, will succeed.

 EXAM TIP   Given a scenario, know how to implement the password best practices described in this section.

Set Strong Passwords

Strong passwords are passwords that are reasonably resistant to a calculated attack by password-guessing programs. Requiring strong passwords on Windows 10/11 systems involves the configuration of several security settings, as described in the following sections. These settings can be used individually or as a part of a comprehensive password security program.

Strong Password Requirement

A security policy can be set on a Windows 10/11 system that requires the use of "strong" passwords in conjunction with user names. To set a requirement for strong passwords, use the following steps:

1. Open a Run command box (WIN key-R) and enter **secpol.msc** to open the Local Security Policy app (shown in Figure 2.6-3).

2. In the left-side navigation pane, expand the Account Policies option and click Password Policy.

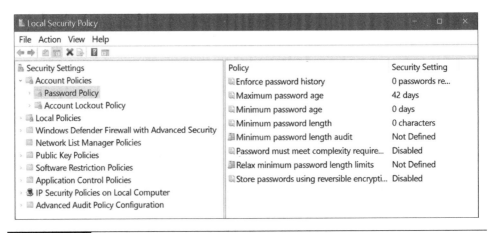

FIGURE 2.6-3   The Local Security Policy app's main page

The right-side pane of the Local Security Policy app displays the various security policies that can be included in a strong password policy. Here's a description of what each does:

- **Enforce password history**   This sets the maximum number of unique and not previously used passwords that must be associated with a user account before a previously used password can be reused. Without this setting, a user can continue to use the same password, regardless of any time limits set for it to change. Microsoft recommends a value of 24 for this setting, which means that before a password can be reused, 24 unique passwords must have been used and expired.

- **Maximum password age**   This setting is the length of time in days that after a password is changed, it must be changed again. For example, a value of 60 indicates that after 60 days, a password is required to be changed.

- **Minimum password age**   This setting defines the minimum number of days that a password must be used before it can be changed again. A value of 0 (zero) allows a user to change the password whenever they wish.

- **Minimum password length**   This setting creates a length requirement for any new password. A value of 8 in this setting requires a new password to be at least eight characters in length.

- **Minimum password length audit**   This setting turns on an audit function that creates a log file entry each time a user creates a password that is less than a certain value. For example, if this value is 12, but the minimum password length is 8, any time a password is created with a length more than 8 but less than 12, a log file entry is generated.

- **Password must meet complexity requirements**   This is perhaps the key setting for a strong password policy. This setting is a toggle, meaning that it is either enabled or disabled. We discuss how it's enforced a bit later in this section.

- **Relax minimum length limits**   This setting may seem unnecessary because the minimum length requirements could be set to 0, which would remove the requirement. However, what this setting does is to allow (enabled) or disallow (disabled) the minimum password length to be greater than 14 characters. A "not defined" status for this setting means it is not in effect.

- **Store passwords using reversible encryption**   Be sure this setting is Disabled (the default). A password stored with reversible encryption can be exposed by an attacker using advanced methods.

To change the value or setting for any of these policies, click its name under the Policy item in the right-side pane.

A strong password is a string of alphanumeric characters that is very difficult to guess or easily generate using a password cracking tool. There are myriad recommendations for how to create a strong password, but, in general, they all agree on five basic principles:

- At least 12 characters in length. Longer is better.
- Contains both upper- and lowercase characters, numbers, and special characters in no predictable order.
- Doesn't have any serial or memorable key sequences, such as QWERTY or zxcvb from a PC keyboard.
- Is unrelated to you, your family, your pets, any significant dates (birth, anniversary, and so on), phone numbers, or the like.
- A unique password is used for each login account for a user.

Complexity Requirement

Enabling the Password Must Meet Complexity Requirement setting on the Local Security Policy app turns on the requirement that a newly created password must meet certain construction requirements. These complexity requirements are not extensive, but they do establish a baseline upon which a secure password policy can be built. The complexity requirements for this setting are as follows:

- A password cannot contain the account's user name or any part of the user's full name.
- A password cannot be less than six characters in length.
- The characters in a password must contain at least three of the following four categories: uppercase alphabetic characters, lowercase alphabetic characters, decimal digits, and special characters. For example, on a U.S. English system, the characters in the four categories are A–Z, a–z, 0–9, and !, @, #, $, %, ^, &, *, (,), +, =, ?, <, >, ~ (and a few more).

Expiration Requirement

Setting passwords to expire regularly reduces the exposure of a user's password to random attacks. Two Local Security Policy settings, Enforce Password History and Maximum Password Age, combine to create a requirement that a user must change their password on a regularly prescribed basis. For example, a security policy with the password history policy set to 24 and a maximum age of 60 sets up the requirement that users must change their passwords at least every 60 days and cannot reuse an old password again for two years (24 months).

BIOS/UEFI Passwords

Without a *BIOS (Binary Input/Output System)* or *UEFI (Unified Extensible Firmware Interface)* password set, anyone can boot up a system using a boot disk or USB drive. A BIOS or UEFI password prevents that from happening, unless they know the password. A BIOS/UEFI password prevents all unauthorized, curious, or ill-intended users from booting a system at all, let alone accessing or modifying the BIOS/UEFI settings.

BIOS and UEFI are motherboard and ROM features and can vary with different manufacturers. However, setting or removing a password is essentially the same for all BIOS/UEFI providers. A BIOS/UEFI password provides a first line of security to a system and its data and other resources.

Any PC or mobile device that was purchased with Windows 10 or Windows 11 pre-installed most likely has the UEFI interface. Some newer systems and virtually all older systems have the BIOS interface. To set a password on either of these systems, follow the steps in the next section.

 NOTE   To find out which firmware your system is using, search for "system information" using the Start search. On the System Information page, the BIOS Mode setting will be either BIOS or UEFI.

Set a UEFI Password

Accessing the UEFI firmware on a Windows 10/11 system is very different from the process used to open the BIOS interface (see the next section). To open the UEFI interface, use the following steps:

1. Open the Settings app and click the Update & Security icon to open its configuration page.

2. Click Recovery to display the Recovery page (see Figure 2.6-4). Before proceeding, you should save any open documents and close all apps.

3. Click the Restart Now button under the Advanced Settings section.

4. On the Choose an Option page, click the Troubleshoot option.

5. On the Troubleshoot page, click Advanced Options.

6. On the Advanced Options page, choose the UEFI Firmware Settings item (see Figure 2.6-5). Then click the Restart button on the next page that displays to reboot the PC.

7. The system reboots into the UEFI interface, where you can create an administrator password.

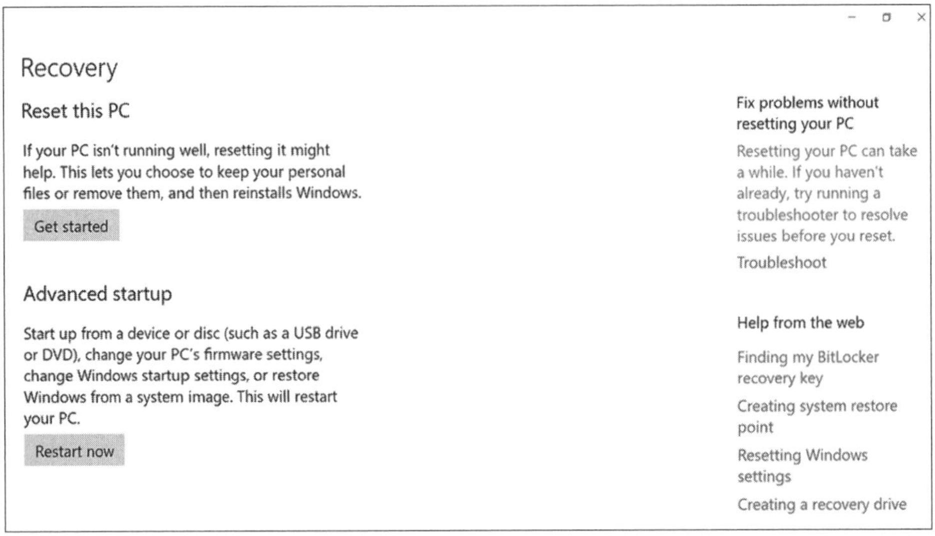

Recovery
Reset this PC
If your PC isn't running well, resetting it might help. This lets you choose to keep your personal files or remove them, and then reinstalls Windows.
Get started
Advanced startup
Start up from a device or disc (such as a USB drive or DVD), change your PC's firmware settings, change Windows startup settings, or restore Windows from a system image. This will restart your PC.
Restart now
Fix problems without resetting your PC
Resetting your PC can take a while. If you haven't already, try running a troubleshooter to resolve issues before you reset.
Troubleshoot
Help from the web
Finding my BitLocker recovery key
Creating system restore point
Resetting Windows settings
Creating a recovery drive

FIGURE 2.6-4 The Recovery page of the Settings app

Advanced options
Startup Repair
Fix problems that keep Windows from loading
Uninstall Updates
Remove recently installed quality or feature updates from Windows
Startup Settings
Change Windows startup behavior
UEFI Firmware Settings
Change settings in your PC's UEFI firmware
Command Prompt
Use the Command Prompt for advanced troubleshooting
System Restore
Use a restore point recorded on your PC to restore Windows
See more recovery options

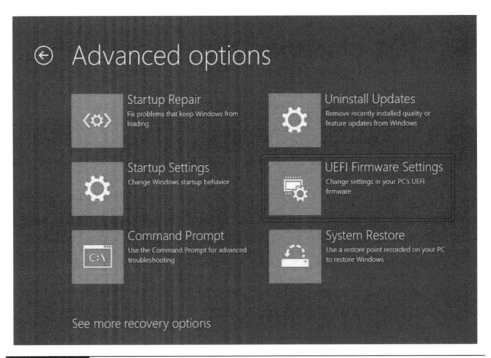

FIGURE 2.6-5 The Advanced Options page

Set a BIOS Password

Whereas accessing the UEFI firmware starts from within Windows, accessing the BIOS settings is an external process. To access the BIOS interface and create an administrator password, use the following steps:

1. Reboot the system and press the designated key for booting into BIOS. This key is usually one of the following, depending on the manufacturer of the motherboard: DEL, F2, ESC, F10, or F12. If you are unsure of which key to use, check the system's documentation for which key is right for your system.

2. When the BIOS interface opens, the password field will be named Set Supervisor Password, User Password (meaning BIOS user), System Password, or the like and be in the Security or Password section.

3. Press the appropriate key (noted on the BIOS page) to save the settings and reboot.

 NOTE If the BIOS interface has supervisor password *and* user password options, it's best to set both passwords. Yes, you will be asked for both when the system boots.

 CAUTION If you were to inadvertently change a setting in either BIOS or UEFI, it can change how the system starts up or performs after booting. Only access these interfaces when you have a specific purpose—and be careful.

End-User Best Practices

End users can apply and follow a variety of practices to help ensure the security of their accounts, data, and resources. The following are some of the more important of these practices:

- **Unique passwords** A unique password should be created for each Microsoft account as well as all other applications, websites, and any sensitive or valuable items stored on the computer (documents, photos, recordings, and so on).

- **Use screensaver locks** If you are to be away from your computer for almost any amount of time while it's active and logged in, it's wise to have a screensaver enabled with a timeout setting that will display the screensaver in a relatively short time period, and you should have a password requirement to close the screensaver.

 NOTE Windows doesn't enable screensavers by default but does include several from which to choose.

- **Login timeout** Enable a system logout after it idles for an extended period of time.

- **Security hardware** Laptop and notebook PCs that are used in a stationary location for any amount of time should be secured with a cable lock to prevent theft, cooled with a cooling pad, and/or secured with a laptop locker or security plate.
- **Personally identifiable information (PII) security** To protect your PII, you should be cautious about sharing it, know where it's stored, know where it's shared, and know its protections under the applicable laws, such as General Data Protection Regulation (GDPR) in the European Union (EU) and the data privacy laws of states like California, Virginia, Colorado, and others.
- **Password protections** Use a different strong password for each account and keep it private.

 EXAM TIP Remember the end-user best practices listed here. It is very likely you'll see them on the real exam!

Account Management

Account management refers to the creation and configuration of specific user accounts in Windows as well as the configuration of account settings, also known as *policies*. Policies can further restrict the actions a group or account can perform (such as opening a command prompt, installing software, or logging on at a given time of day). Every Windows client (except for Home versions) has a Local Security Policy app (see Figure 2.6-6), but local policies are a pain if you want the same settings on multiple systems.

Cross-Reference

To learn more about group policy settings, see the "Group Policy/Updates" section in Objective 2.1, earlier in this domain.

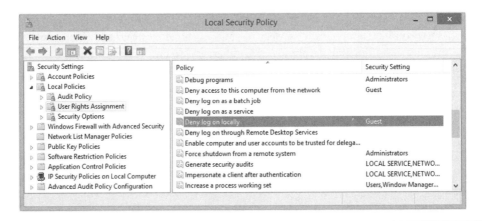

FIGURE 2.6-6 Local Security Policy

The Local Policy Editor also provides access to local security policies (see the upcoming examples). The aspects of account management you need to understand for the CompTIA A+ 220-1102 exam are covered in the following sections.

Restricting User Permissions

Users have three basic types of permissions that control what they can or can't do with a folder or the files in a folder: read, write, and execute. However, on the Security tab of a file's or folder's properties (see Figure 2.6-7), these permissions are expanded to Full Control (read, write, execute), Modify (write, includes delete), Read & Execute, Read (read-only), and Write. The settings for both the group or user names and the permissions for each group or user are administered by clicking the Edit button.

More advanced administration capabilities are available on the Advanced Security Settings dialog box for a file or folder (see Figure 2.6-8). This option is opened by clicking the Advanced button at the bottom of the Security tab of the Properties dialog box (refer back to Figure 2.6-7).

As stated earlier, user permissions can be governed by the groups to which a user account is assigned. To see the current policies and the groups affected, click Local Policies | User Rights Assignment and scroll through the list of policies. To learn more about a policy, double-click it and then click the Explain tab (see Figure 2.6-9).

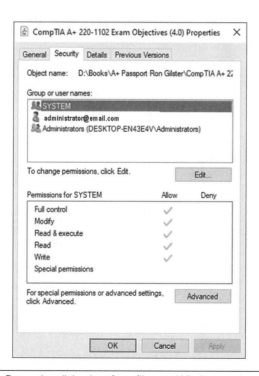

FIGURE 2.6-7   The Properties dialog box for a file on a Windows 10/11 system

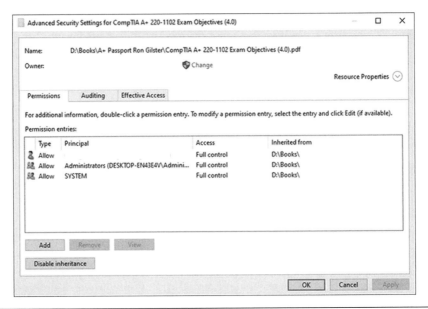

FIGURE 2.6-8   The Properties dialog box for a file on a Windows 10/11 system

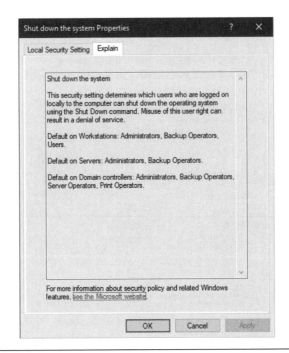

FIGURE 2.6-9   Viewing the description for the Shut Down the System policy

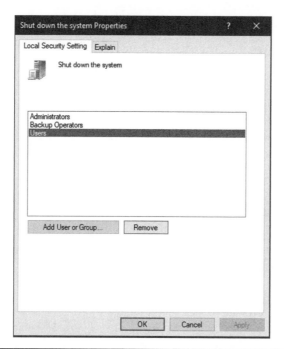

FIGURE 2.6-10   Preparing to remove the group Users from the Shut Down the System policy

To prevent a group from performing a task, open the Local Security Setting tab, click the group, click Remove, and then click Apply (see Figure 2.6-10).

Logon Time Restrictions

Logon time restrictions for specific users can be set up with group policy on a domain controller, or by using the net user command on a workgroup or individual PC using an elevated command prompt. For example, to limit the user Geeksy to logging in between 11:00 AM and 8:00 PM (20:00 hours) from Monday to Friday, enter the following from an elevated command prompt:

```
net user Geeksy /time:M-F,11:00-20:00
```

 ADDITIONAL RESOURCES   To learn more about using net user for this process, see www.makeuseof.com and search for "How to Set Time Limits for User Accounts in Windows."

To set time limits for children in Windows 10, you can set up their accounts as family members and use the Microsoft Account/Family dialog box available online to restrict logon days, times, and maximum hours of usage. The similar Parental Controls feature is available in Windows 11.

ADDITIONAL RESOURCES To learn more about family safety and parental controls in Windows, go to www.lifewire.com and search for "Microsoft Family Safety."

Disabling Guest Account

The Guest account in Windows represents a potential security risk. To prevent it from being enabled, go to Local Policies | Security Options, double-click Accounts: Guest Account Status, and set it to Disabled.

Failed Attempts Lockout

Set up account lockout policies to stop brute-force or dictionary attacks from going on endlessly. To enable a lockout duration or to set an account lockout threshold, go to Security Settings | Account Policies | Account Lockout Policy.

Timeout/Screen Lock

By enabling the system to lock the display screen after a period of inactivity and requiring a login to unlock the screen, you can protect the system from casual snooping. This feature is enabled in Windows 10/11 in the Personalize settings, which are accessed by right-clicking an open portion of the Desktop and selecting Personalize | Lock Screen (see Figure 2.6-11). The bottom of the Lock Screen page also has links for screen timeouts and screensaver settings.

FIGURE 2.6-11 The Lock Screen page

EXAM TIP   Best security practices for account management include restricting user permissions and login times, disabling the Guest account, using failed attempts lockout, and using timeout/screen lock.

Change Default Admin User Account/Password

As part of any operating system security best practice, it is recommended that you rename any default accounts, such as the default Administrator or Guest accounts created at installation, and apply strong passwords. This practice also applies to routers and any other devices that come "out of the box" with default accounts/passwords. It is also common practice to create a new account that has admin privileges and disable the default account.

Windows 10/11 offers an administrator account for use when making system-level configuration, user permissions, and file, folder, and application settings. However, this account is inactive by default. To activate the Administrator account, open a command prompt with the Run as Administrator option and enter the following command:

```
net user administrator /active: yes
```

Disable AutoRun and AutoPlay

On Windows 10/11 systems, two apps are available that are intended to provide convenience by automatically opening or executing the content of an optical disc: AutoRun and AutoPlay. AutoRun was initially intended for use when Windows was installed from optical disc media, and AutoPlay does the same, but with control given to the user.

AutoRun automatically starts a program (named in an autorun.inf file), plays a movie or music from a disc, and detects a USB device inserted into a drive. AutoRun also works with non-optical media, but instead of automatically starting its content, control is passed to the AutoPlay app.

AutoPlay, instead of automatically starting content from an inserted media, displays a dialog box that lists the options available to the user for the contents of the inserted medium (see Figure 2.6-12).

While AutoRun and AutoPlay can be convenient, they can also create security problems on a system. Automatically running or loading the content on inserted media can transfer malware or other forms of bad stuff onto a system. Therefore, it can be a good idea to disable or limit the use of both of these tools.

The quickest, easiest, and safest way to disable the AutoPlay feature on a Windows 10/11 system is outlined in the following steps:

1. On the Settings app, click Devices to open the Devices page.
2. On the Devices page, click AutoPlay to display the AutoPlay page, shown in Figure 2.6-13.

FIGURE 2.6-12   The AutoPlay dialog box

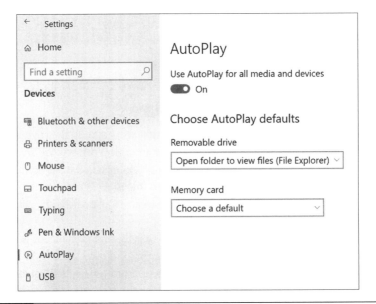

FIGURE 2.6-13   The AutoPlay page of the Settings app

3. Disable the AutoPlay tool by moving the Use AutoPlay for All Media and Devices slide switch to Off. Close the page to save this setting.

   However, if you only wish to change what AutoPlay does or disable it only for certain devices, leave the slide switch in the On position and continue to the next step.

4. Under the Choose AutoPlay Defaults heading, use the Removeable Drive and Memory Card pull-down lists to choose the action you wish AutoPlay to perform when it discovers the insertion of either of these media types.

REVIEW

Objective 2.6: Given a scenario, configure a workstation to meet best practices for security   Workstation best practices include the following:

- Encrypting data at rest
- Following password best practices, such as the following:
  - Setting complexity requirements, including length and character types
  - Using effective password expiration policies
  - Using BIOS/UEFI passwords to protect computer firmware
- Following end-user best practices, such as the following:
  - Using screensaver locks and requiring passwords when screensavers are activated
  - Logging off when the computer is not in use
  - Securing and protecting computer hardware
  - Securing PII
- Following account management best practices, such as the following:
  - Restricting user permissions
  - Restricting login times
  - Disabling guest accounts
  - Using failed logon attempts lockout
  - Using screen timeout and lockout
- Changing the default admin user account/password
- Disabling AutoRun and AutoPlay

2.6 QUESTIONS

1. You are considering using one of the following eight-character passwords. Which is the strongest password?

    A. 12345678

    B. 1Z$#7j!~

    C. 867530900

    D. My$$Name

2. Your client is being plagued by a series of brute-force logon attacks. Which of the following group policy settings would best help stop them?

    A. Account Lockout Policy

    B. Security Options

    C. Password Policy

    D. Logon Time Restrictions

3. Your department was recently attacked by malware that was automatically loaded from a consultant's USB drive when it was inserted for diagnostic purposes. Which of the following should be disabled?

   A. Plug and Play

   B. File Explorer

   C. AutoPlay

   D. BIOS/UEFI

4. You wish to prevent users from using the same password over and over. What setting do you need to configure to prevent the same password from being reused within a one-year period?

   A. Enforce Password History

   B. Maximum Password Age

   C. Minimum Password Length

   D. Relax Minimum Length Requirement

5. Data that is stored on a computer or mobile device, a database server, or an external backup medium is considered to be which of the following?

   A. Data in transit

   B. Data in use

   C. Data in suspense

   D. Data at rest

2.6 ANSWERS

1. **B**   The strongest passwords use a mixture of upper- and lowercase letters, numbers, and symbols without recognized words.

2. **A**   Account Lockout Policy prevents login attempts after a specified number of incorrect logins.

3. **C**   AutoPlay is the feature that opens an app or lists a choice of apps based on the contents of the removable media.

4. **A**   The Enforce Password History value sets the number of password changes that must occur before a password can be reused.

5. **D**   Data stored on any form of media is considered to be "at rest."

Objective 2.7 Explain common methods for securing mobile and embedded devices

*M*obile devices are convenient for carrying around data and apps and communicating via voice, e-mail, and text from anywhere in the world. But convenience means that if mobile devices are unsecured, they can be a wide-open malware target flashing a neon sign that says "infect me."

Embedded devices are objects containing programming or a single-purpose system. This system is completely contained within the object. Security issues arise when objects connect to a network of similar objects, referred to in general as the *Internet of Things (IoT)*, or to the Internet itself. Objects that are able to connect to other objects or the Internet are referred to as *smart,* as in smartphones, smart TVs, smart refrigerators, and so on. Not all embedded devices have user interfaces.

In this objective, you learn how to implement the appropriate methods to prevent mobile and embedded devices from becoming security headaches.

Screen Locks

Screen lock generally refers to any security mechanism used to prevent unauthorized users from viewing the display or using a mobile device. There are five types of screen locks you should know for the CompTIA A+ Core 2 (220-1102) exam, as described in the following sections.

 NOTE   Most mobile devices provide at least two different types of screen locks.

Facial Recognition

Facial recognition locks use a device's camera to capture an image of the user's face. The captured image is digitized and compared to a previously stored image of the user. If the two images match, the device is unlocked. Windows and Apple both have a facial recognition app.

The Windows facial recognition is a part of the Windows Biometric Framework (WBF) and is known as Windows Hello Face. This app requires the device to have a specially configured near infrared (NIR) imaging camera to capture the source image and the comparison image. An NIR camera captures images that are very close to what a human sees, but with all color (except shades of black and white) removed. A match of the images unlocks the Windows system and can also be used to unlock Windows Passport, which is a two-factor user authentication tool that can be used in place of the standard user account and password method.

Apple offers the Face ID app, which also uses NIR to capture and compare facial images on its X Series iPhones and iPad Pro tablets. The Android OS no longer includes its Trusted Face app but provides support for third-party facial recognition apps available for smartphones and tablet devices.

To enable Windows Hello Face, use the following steps (you must have a Windows Hello–compatible camera and have created a PIN code before you can set up the face recognition feature):

1. Open the Settings app and select the Accounts option.

2. On the Account page, select Sign-in Options to display its settings page (see Figure 2.7-1).

3. In the Manage How You Sign In to Your Device section, select the Windows Hello Face option and click the Set Up button.

4. On the Welcome to Windows Hello message box that displays, click Get Started.

5. A Making Sure It's You box displays. Enter your PIN code to continue.

6. The Windows Hello image capture box opens next. This box captures your face as the comparison image. Your face needs to be centered in the image frame, and you need to hold your position until the capture is completed.

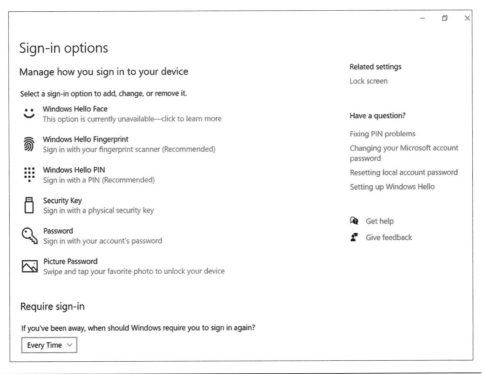

FIGURE 2.7-1   The Sign-in Options page of the Settings app

7. If you think you may want to redo the capture, click the Improve Recognition link on the All Set! message box. Otherwise, click Close to return to the Sign-in Options page.

8. The last step in setting up the Windows Hello Face option is to use the slide switch for the Automatically Dismiss the Lock Screen If Windows Recognizes Your Face setting to turn it on or off. Turning it off reverts the sign-in back to the PIN code. You can also access the Improve Recognition action from this area, or you can remove the entire setup.

After you've completed the Windows Hello Face setup, your facial image will log you in to Windows the next time you log in to the system.

PIN Codes

A *PIN code* (which is an abbreviation for *personal identification number,* although that meaning is rarely used anymore) is a short, typically four-digit series of numbers that serves in place of a password for user logins. Virtually all mobile devices accept a PIN code or a password, whichever is the user's choice. On most devices, the PIN code is the primary authentication value, with all other sign-in lock options being alternatives. At a minimum, a PIN or passcode is four digits, but some are six or eight digits. Some even allow alpha characters to make the PIN harder to crack. Figure 2.7-2 shows the Passcode settings screen for an iPhone.

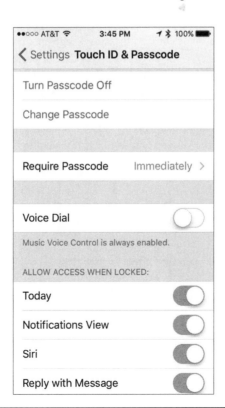

FIGURE 2.7-2   Passcode options in Settings on an iPhone

Fingerprints

A fingerprint lock requires the user to touch a fingerprint sensor button or screen area to have their fingerprint scanned. If the scanned fingerprint image matches the pre-scanned and stored fingerprint image, the device is unlocked. Typically, this feature is used in conjunction with a PIN code. Should a user not be able to provide a valid readable fingerprint, the user may have the option to enter a PIN code to unlock the device. The following describes the processes used to set up a fingerprint lock on Windows, Android, and macOS, respectively.

- Implementing a fingerprint lock on a Windows 10/11 system follows about the same setup process as that used for the Hello Face option, with the camera replaced by a fingerprint scanner. Open Settings | Accounts | Sign-in Options and then select Set Up in the Windows Hello fingerprint section and follow the prompts (you must have a PIN enabled to use Windows Hello).
- To implement a fingerprint lock on an Android device, open Settings | Lock Screen and Security | Fingerprints and then follow the prompts.
- To implement a fingerprint lock (known as Touch ID) on an iOS device, open Settings | Touch ID & Passcode and then follow the prompts.

Pattern Locks

Virtually all smartphones provide lock patterns as a sign-in option. *Pattern locks* are most commonly used in place of other forms of security locks. In particular, they are used to prevent accidental dialing or app starts. A pattern lock requires a user to record a continuous line that connects a series of dots, which are usually in a grid of nine points. A grid of nine points provides 362,880 different grid patterns. Figure 2.7-3 shows three examples of grid patterns.

Using an easily drawn simple pattern can create a security risk. To create a strong lock pattern, consider the following rules: never use any of your initials as a pattern; use multiple

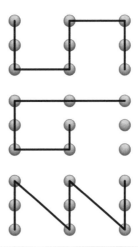

FIGURE 2.7-3   Three examples of pattern lock patterns

crossovers (lines crossing other lines); the pattern should be complex and use as many of the nodes as possible; and a simple pattern will typically be too simple to be secure.

Swipe Lock

A *swipe lock* compares the motion and direction of a finger-sweeping (a swipe) pattern across the screen of a mobile device (typically a smartphone). If the swipe matches the pattern stored by the user when the swipe lock was configured, or if it matches a prescribed pattern of a swipe lock app, the device is unlocked. Swipe locks, when available, are configured through Settings | Security.

Remote Wipe

If you back up the data on your mobile device frequently and completely, you're safe to *remotely wipe* the device to prevent your data from being accessed if the device is lost or stolen. Your personal data, which may include credit card numbers, account credentials, and other sensitive information, is very much at risk if the device is lost or stolen, in many cases regardless of the sign-on method you use. True, some devices, such as Apple iPhones and iPads, are a bit more difficult for someone else to crack (including you possibly), but for the most part, it's a good security practice to keep a backup of your device and know how to perform a remote wipe.

Although this may be obvious, a remote wipe is done remotely. If a remote wipe needs to be done, you won't likely be with (or at) the device when you need to do it. Therefore, this must be set up beforehand. The capability to perform a remote wipe on a mobile device, such as a smartphone or tablet, is built in or available through an associated service. On Apple devices, a remote wipe is available through the Find My iPhone on the iCloud service. On Android and Microsoft devices, third-party mobile device management (MDM) tools or services, such as Microsoft Intune, include apps to remotely lock or wipe a device. The remote wipe capability is especially important where mobile devices are used in a bring-your-own-device (BYOD) environment.

 EXAM TIP Know how to implement mobile device screen locks and remote wipes.

Locator Applications

Locator applications and services (such as Android Device Manager or Find My Device, Lookout for iOS or Android, Find My iPhone, and Find My Device in Windows 10/11) enable users to find lost devices (see Figure 2.7-4 for an example). When enabled in a device, the locator app periodically sends the device's location to the OS vendor so you can locate a lost device using an app from the vendor, typically named something like "Find My Device." These apps, which are available from nearly all mobile device providers, work in a variety of ways that range from GPS tracking, cell-tower connections, and connections to synched devices.

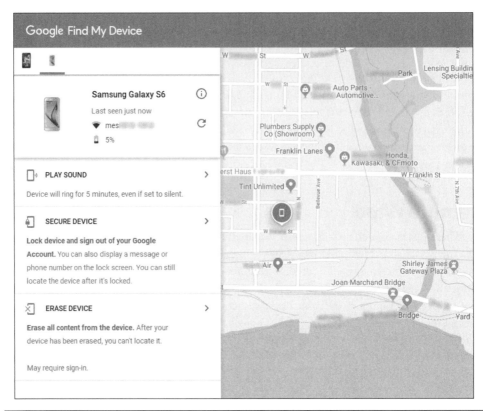

FIGURE 2.7-4 Locating an Android smartphone using Find My Device

On Windows 10 systems, the settings for the Find My Device feature is on the Update & Security section of the Settings app. On a Windows 11 system, use the Privacy & Security option on the Settings app. In iOS, open Settings, tap your Apple ID, tap iCloud, and tap Find My iPhone or Find My iPad and then slide its switch to on. In Android, open Settings and look for Android Device Manager (on older devices) or Find My Device or Find My Mobile (although the name of this app varies across Android versions). You may need to download Find My Device or Find My Mobile from Google Play. Follow the prompts to enable it or set it up.

OS Updates

Windows 10/11 mobile devices and iOS devices have updates available from Microsoft and Apple, respectively, on a regular basis. However, Android smartphones and cellular-equipped tablets receive OS and firmware updates from mobile service providers (iOS devices receive cellular-specific updates from mobile telecom vendors).

Android tablets without cellular service, unlike Windows 10 and iOS devices, are updated only by the device vendors. Some vendors provide updates, whereas others do not.

Device Encryption

iOS devices automatically apply full device encryption when you assign a passcode to your device. Windows 10/11 mobile devices use *BitLocker* or *BitLocker To Go* to encrypt storage and removable storage, respectively.

Cross-Reference

More information on the use of encryption for data at rest (that is, stored data) is in Objective 2.6.

Android devices apply Gilster's Law: "You never can tell, and it all depends." Encrypting an Android device depends on the versions in use and may require you to set up a PIN or password beforehand or it may allow you to go straight to encryption. Many of the more recent Android devices automatically encrypt their contents, but many Android devices require you to apply the encryption. Just be sure that your Android device is fully charged before you start the encryption process, which can take an hour or so.

Remote Backup Applications

Remote backup applications are built into iOS, Android, and Microsoft Windows. For Apple devices, you back up and restore using services such as iCloud and iTunes. The Apple Configurator can be used to back up the Apple devices of an enterprise. Android devices use Google Sync to back up and restore. Windows 10 mobile devices can use OneDrive for file backup and restore.

 ADDITIONAL RESOURCES To learn more about setting up OneDrive and your documents or other folders for automatic backup, go to https://www.howtogeek .com/720851/how-to-automatically-back-up-windows-folders-to-onedrive/ and read the article " How to Automatically Back up Windows Folders to OneDrive."

Failed Login Attempts Restrictions

System lockout occurs when the number of unsuccessful login attempts exceeds the threshold value in the system's defaults or settings. The primary purpose behind this security measure is to protect a device (mobile or not) from any type of brute-force attack. Both iOS and Android devices have built-in default values for failed login attempts. On Windows 10/11 devices, a group policy can be used to set a cap for the number of failed login attempts as well as an account lockout duration.

With Android devices, options to change these settings vary with the version of the Android OS and whether the OS is a stock or modified version.

With iOS, the lockout duration increases with each unsuccessful attempt that is made and eventually finishes with a total lockout. When you enable the Erase Data option in Settings | Passcode, the device will be completely erased after ten failed passcode attempts.

Antivirus/Anti-Malware

Windows 10/11 mobile devices include the Windows Defender application for antivirus and anti-malware protection. iOS and Android don't include antivirus/anti-malware protection as native apps. However, antivirus and anti-malware apps are available for both iOS and Android from virtually all of the major security software providers. Some of these products are free, and others are offered in free detection-only versions and paid virus- and malware-removal versions.

Firewalls

Software firewalls protect individual mobile devices from network-based threats. For the most part, a mobile device doesn't require a firewall because it rarely interacts with the traffic that a typical firewall blocks. Cellular and Wi-Fi networks typically employ firewalls to protect the devices connecting to their networks. There are firewall apps available for individual or enterprise use to filter specific traffic coming into the host, which may also include anti-malware and basic intrusion detection. Figure 2.7-5 shows an example of an Android firewall app.

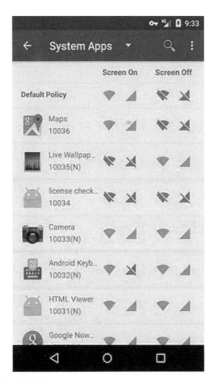 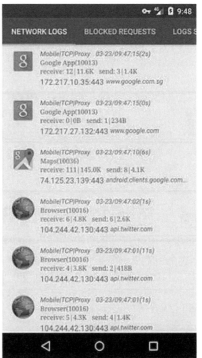

FIGURE 2.7-5   The Netpatch Firewall is an open source Android app.

Policies and Procedures

Policies and procedures relating to mobile devices can be more complex than those for other types of computing devices because of the following questions:

- Who owns the device (the user or the organization)?
- Who manages the device?

BYOD vs. Corporate-Owned

With the omnipresence of mobile devices in the workplace, companies generally take one of two approaches to the subject: bring your own device (BYOD) or corporate-owned devices.

A *BYOD* policy covers if and how individually owned devices can be used within the organization. Some companies prohibit access to corporate data and resources using personal devices, particularly in high-security environments; others encourage the use of personal devices to cut costs and keep employees happy. Most fall in the middle. The BYOD policy answers questions such as who pays for device service, who owns and can access the device's data, and how privacy is handled.

For organizations that prefer to own their employees' mobile devices, an alternative to BYOD is *corporate-owned personally enabled (COPE)* devices. Organizations that use this model provide their employees with mobile devices such as smartphones, tablets, or laptop computers but permit employees to use them as if they personally own them.

 EXAM TIP   The two critical issues with BYOD are personal data privacy versus protection of corporate data as well as the level of organizational control versus individual control. Know the difference between BYOD and corporate-owned.

Profile Security Requirements

A *profile* is a collection of configuration and security settings that an administrator can create to apply to almost any user or device category (see Figure 2.7-6). Profiles, created through the mobile device management (MDM) software or a program such as Apple Configurator, are typically saved in eXtensible Markup Language (XML) format and pushed out to the correct devices. A common use is to restrict or grant access to apps, connections, and servers based on whether the user is a manager, executive, or external contractor, works in a given department, and so on. Profiles for a given device or OS can address device- or platform-specific risks.

Cross-Reference

For more details about MDM, see the "Mobile Device Management" section in Objective 2.1, earlier in this domain.

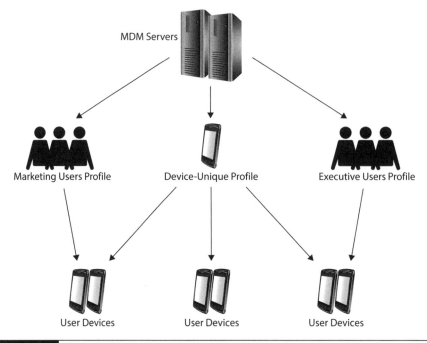

MDM Servers

Marketing Users Profile

Device-Unique Profile

Executive Users Profile

User Devices

User Devices

User Devices

FIGURE 2.7-6 Applying profiles to different device and user groups

Internet of Things

The *Internet of Things (IoT)* is a nexus network of devices that communicate and exchange data that each has collected or needs to pass on without outside intervention. The communication between a large majority of these devices actually occurs between embedded devices and may or may not include the Internet. An *embedded device* is commonly a microcontroller or microprocessor on an integrated circuit (IC) that also contains an operating system. Embedded devices and systems are built into cars, phones, appliances, and network communication devices and can be as simple as an on/off lighting control or as complicated as the guidance system of a missile or airliner.

Windows and Android both have apps for working with IoT apps: Windows IoT Core for Windows 10/11 and Android Things, respectively. Each of these apps is optimized for use and interaction on and with smaller devices. Apple, while considered a leader in IoT because of the Apple Watch, iPhone IoT interfaces (like Square and myriad medical apps), and many other products, relies on third-party developers for its consumer and industrial IoT products. Windows and Android have interaction and software development kit (SDK) apps for IoT product development.

Another aspect of IoT is its security. You can't really enforce policies that secure a refrigerator by not allowing anyone to access it or padlocking it and selectively distributing the keys (well, maybe you can). IoT devices are secured by keeping their firmware up to date and isolating devices on their networks as much as possible, meaning limiting access to them from the outside.

REVIEW

Objective 2.7: Explain common methods for securing mobile and embedded devices
Mobile devices are secured by screen locks. Types of lock screens include the following:

- Facial recognition
- PIN code
- Fingerprint
- Pattern
- Swipe

Other mobile devices' security features include the following:

- Remotely wiping device data
- Using locator applications to locate lost or stolen devices
- Posting OS updates
- Encrypting devices
- Backing up systems remotely to ensure device data is recoverable
- Restricting failed login attempts to counter brute-force password guessing
- Adding antivirus/anti-malware protection
- Implementing firewall apps
- Using policies and procedures covering BYOD versus company-owned devices and profile security requirements
- Being aware of IoT apps

2.7 QUESTIONS

1. An Android phone with confidential company information was lost. The information on the phone began to be used for attacks on company resources, although the user had set up a passcode. Which of the following Android settings could have prevented attacks using the information in the phone? (Choose two.)

    A. Remote wipe

    B. Firewall

    C. Device encryption

    D. BYOD

2. A client is attempting to sign on to his iPhone but cannot remember the passcode. He has tried eight times and the wait time keeps getting longer between attempts. What would you advise him to do?

   A. Keep trying to log in.

   B. Stop trying until he can get back home and check to see if he has the information available there.

   C. Use a hacking tool.

   D. Run antivirus.

3. You are part of a team developing a BYOD policy for smartphone usage. Which of the following topics is most likely to be part of the policy?

   A. Approved case colors

   B. Ownership of private data stored on the device

   C. Ownership of charging cables

   D. Ownership of company data stored on the device

4. What biometric method compares a camera-captured image of a user's face to an image previously captured from a scanned photograph and stored?

   A. Facial recognition

   B. Faceprinting

   C. Image matching

   D. Pattern matching

5. The Internet of Things (IoT) is a communications network of devices. What is the primary component in each device for its operations and communications?

   A. Embedded device

   B. Modem

   C. Microcontroller

   D. Integrated circuit

2.7 ANSWERS

1. **A C** Remote wipe could wipe out the device's contents after it was determined to be lost or stolen; device encryption (a manual process on many devices) could prevent the device's contents from being accessed.

2. **B** If the option to wipe data after ten unsuccessful logins has been enabled in Settings | Passcode, the user is very close to losing his data, which is hopefully backed up to iCloud.

3. **D** Who owns company data on a BYOD device is an important issue in a BYOD policy.

4. **A** Facial recognition locks compare a previously captured image to a real-time image.

5. **A** The operations and communications of an IoT device are controlled by embedded devices, which typically include a microprocessor, operating system, and a network adapter.

Objective 2.8 Given a scenario, use common data destruction and disposal methods

Although a device might have reached end-of-life (EOL) status, the data it contains can still be valuable—and ready to be exploited by thieves or hackers. Data that is no longer needed on a device should be rendered inaccessible, and in this objective you learn the methods to use and when to use each one.

Physical Destruction

If you want to make sure that absolutely nobody can recover data from a magnetic, optical, or flash storage device, physical destruction is the way to go. The following sections describe the methods you can use.

> **EXAM TIP** Know the appropriate data destruction or disposal method, described in this section, to use in a given scenario.

Drilling

If you don't want to take your devices to a third-party data disposal facility, a power drill does a great job of rendering them unusable. Drilling multiple holes through the disk drives, motherboard, memory boards, expansion cards, and any other onboard devices, except the power supply, pretty much makes a PC and any of the devices inoperable. Remember that power supplies include capacitors that store electrical power, so you shouldn't drill them. There's no data stored there anyway.

Shredding

A few heavy-duty office paper shredders can make hash out of optical media, but certified data destruction firms who offer certificates of destruction have shredders that can also take on hard drives, flash drives, magnetic tape, and any other type of storage around.

Degaussing

Degaussing tools reduce or remove the magnetization used to store data on hard disks, magnetic tape media, and other forms of magnetic data storage. Using a degausser is great for situations in which you want to have a device that looks intact but no longer has readable magnetic data.

Incinerating

Incineration (burning) is a good alternative to shredding for paper, magnetic tape, and optical media. For medium-to-large volumes of disposable matter, incineration should be performed by a third-party data disposal facility. Don't try this at home—or in an office wastebasket!

Recycling and Repurposing Best Practices

An alternative to destroying data storage devices is recycling or repurposing. Just as with destroying devices, the objective is to make sure that no one else can use the device or access its data.

Erasing/Wiping

Simply deleting data from a storage device doesn't actually remove the data from the device, which is why undelete functions work. There are two primary ways to use software to completely wipe all data from a storage device:

- **Data destruction software**   Also called *hard drive eraser software* or *drive wiping software*. This type of software, which is generally available for free, writes over all data on a device with strings of gibberish (or junk data) several times. This process obliterates any data that originally existed on the device.

 NOTE   The most commonly used apps for wiping a disk are ATA Secure Erase (supported by many SATA magnetic and SSD drives) and Darik's Boot and Nuke (DBAN).

- **Low-level formatting**   Also called *physical formatting* or *zero-fill*. This type of formatting is used to prepare a new disk for use by setting up the sectors and tracks of the disks, without which the data could not be addressed. However, low-level formatting can also be used to completely erase a disk. This process overwrites all of the bits on the disk with zeroes. Low-level formatting is not available to a standard user; therefore, a third-party app may need to be used.

 NOTE   The wear-leveling feature on SSDs may leave some data on small portions of a drive.

ADDITIONAL RESOURCES   For the latest National Institute of Standards and Technology (NIST) recommendations for sanitizing data, download Special Publication 800-88, Rev. 1, "Guidelines for Media Sanitization," from https://csrc.nist.gov.

Low-Level Formatting vs. Standard Formatting

As described earlier, a low-level format overwrites the data and sector markings on the media. This is possible with some types of removable media, but not with modern SATA drives.

A standard format leaves data in place but inaccessible if requested through the file system. Keep in mind, though, that many third-party apps and data-recovery services can be used to retrieve data from a standard formatted drive.

Outsourcing Concepts

Some businesses choose to use an outside vendor for the destruction and disposal of their data and devices. This is okay, except when the company falls under the *Fair and Accurate Credit Transactions Act (FACTA)* regulations. FACTA rules say that the business must use a data destruction and disposal service that adheres to the FACTA regulations regarding the proper disposal of consumers' private information. Regardless, the business remains responsible for the proper destruction and disposal of its data.

Third-Party Vendor

An organization has data security exposure when a third party, whether it's a private party or a company, is hired to dispose of data storage devices or records. This exposure can also include the individuals whose data is at risk.

An organization that uses third-party disposal companies should perform a background check on the vendor, monitor the vendor's employees if or when they are on the organization's premises, and inspect the vendor's operating sites for security, privacy, and the methods used.

Certificate of Destruction or Recycling

Organizations that record and electronically store data that includes confidential information about their clients, customers, or applicants must be able to prove that if this data is destroyed, it was done in accordance with the regulations or requirements of its industry or the government. The same holds true if an organization disposes of or recycles hardware devices on which this data was stored. The proof that the organization is following the applicable requirements or laws is a *certificate of destruction*.

REVIEW

Objective 2.8: Given a scenario, use common data destruction and disposal methods
Physical data destruction methods include the following:

- Drilling
- Shredding
- Degaussing
- Incinerating

Recycling or repurposing best practices include the following:

- Erasing/wiping
- Low-level formatting
- Standard formatting

Outsourcing concepts include the following:

- Using a third-party vendor
- Obtaining a certification of destruction/recycling

2.8 QUESTIONS

1. A 64-GB flash memory card contains confidential information. Which of the following methods ensures that data cannot be read from the card and that the card cannot be reused?

   A. Drilling

   B. Zero-fill

   C. Drive wiping

   D. Degaussing

2. After the completion of a government contact, your firm must prove that the media used to store data have been destroyed. Which of the following do you need?

   A. Drill

   B. Certificate of destruction

   C. Shredder

   D. Degausser

3. Your client is panicking because a disgruntled employee performed some type of command on an important hard drive before leaving the premises. Which of the following would make the data the most difficult to recover?

   A. Standard format

   B. Zero-fill

    C. Drive wiping

    D. Low-level format

4. You are in charge of a project to remove hard drives from end-of-life systems and prepare them for donation to schools for reuse. You discover that one of your assistants is running the Format command on each drive before removing it. Which of the following is the best reaction to this discovery?

    A. "Good job! No one can get to that data now."

    B. "Did you use quick or standard format?"

    C. "Using Format isn't drive wiping."

    D. "You should be using a drill."

5. Your firm has a large amount of magnetic tape from old mainframe systems. Which of the following is the quickest way to render this tape unreadable?

    A. Drilling

    B. Zero-fill

    C. Drive wiping

    D. Degaussing

2.8 ANSWERS

1. **A**   Drilling through the memory chip(s) will render the contents unrecoverable.

2. **B**   A certificate of destruction from a third-party data destruction facility is what you need; the facility will decide the best methods and tools to use.

3. **C**   Drive wiping would be the biggest concern.

4. **C**   Formatting doesn't remove or overwrite data, so it is no substitute for drive wiping.

5. **D**   Degaussing is the only suitable method of those listed for destroying data on magnetic tape.

Objective 2.9 # Given a scenario, configure appropriate security settings on small office/home office (SOHO) wireless and wired networks

A network without security is like leaving the doors and windows of your home or office open at all hours: anyone can enter and help themselves to whatever they can find. In this objective, you learn the methods you can use to secure your small office/home office (SOHO) network.

EXAM TIP Know how to configure the home router wireless and wired network security–related settings in this objective.

Home Router Settings

The configuration and settings of a *router* in a home or SOHO installation has many elements that must be considered to provide the best optimized performance for its network. Not all SOHO networks have a specific device called a router.

There is a difference between a home network and a SOHO network in today's small network environments. Home networks have become primarily wireless. SOHO networks have remained wired, but some also include wireless devices. The CompTIA A+ Core 2 (220-1102) exam objectives specially include home network topics, as covered in this objective.

Changing Default Passwords

Any router, regardless of wired or wireless, has a user name and a *default password* assigned by the manufacturer. In nearly every case, manufacturers' devices have the same or very similar login credentials. For example, Netgear routers right out of the box, with a few exceptions, have a user name of *admin,* a password of *password,* and an IP address of 192.168.0.1. Other manufacturers may not use these exact values, but they are likely to be very similar.

A best practice when installing and configuring a new router on a home network, or any network for that matter, is to change the user name and password almost immediately. In fact, most new SOHO routers today require you to change the default user name and password during installation. Otherwise, the router will have a published user name and password that is readily available on the Web. Changing the login credentials of a home router is done through a network interface on the router that can be accessed via a browser. Figure 2.9-1 shows an example of the main screen from an ASUS router. This page is addressed using the default IP address of the router. You must use the default credentials to access this page the first time you access the router, but you should, before you do anything else, change the router's user name and password.

NOTE Configuration utilities, like the one shown in Figure 2.9-1, vary by vendor and product model.

IP Filtering

IP filtering is a router or firewall function that screens incoming and outcoming network traffic based on source or destination IP address. Users (administrators) can set up rules that specify what the device is to do with packets arriving with certain IP addresses. A rule may

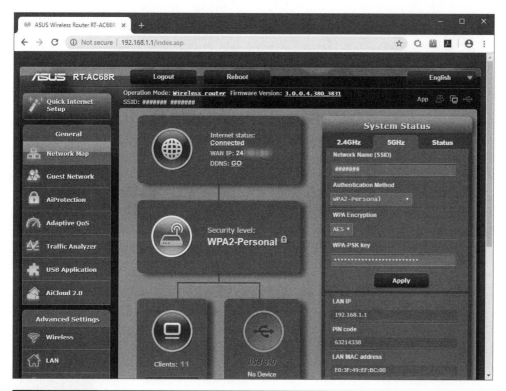

FIGURE 2.9-1   ASUS wireless main setup screen

allow or deny an entire network (such as a filter on 15.0.0.0), subnets (such as 128.152.254.0), or a single host (such as 218.250.158.101). On some more complex home or office networks, IP filtering rules can be deployed in tandem, with generic filters applied by a firewall and more specific filtering done by a router.

There can be a downside to IP filtering caused by the rules not being in logical order and causing an allowable address to be denied (for example, placing a deny all before the rule that allows the address).

Firmware Updates

Like any firmware-based device, a router's basic hardware operations are controlled by its firmware, and the firmware of a router can be updated. Keeping the firmware of a router up to date helps the device perform better and most likely improves its security. Most *firmware updates* fix bugs, add new features, and improve the security functions of the router, and most of the better routers update firmware automatically. However, the automatic firmware update feature can be disabled, or the router might not have this feature, in which case the updates can be made manually. Firmware updates are typically made available on the manufacturer's website for download.

ADDITIONAL RESOURCES   A very good guide for how to update the firmware on a home router for Windows, Android, and macOS networks is provided in the article "How To Update Router Firmware?" at https://bcca.org/how-to-update-router-firmware/.

CAUTION   A firmware update can kill (or "brick") your router, so be careful to follow all of the instructions and make sure you choose the correct firmware update for your router brand, model, and revision. Many mass-market routers use different hardware for the different revisions of the same model. Therefore, choosing a firmware update for revision 1.0 of a router when you have revision 2.0, for example, could destroy the router.

Content Filtering

Content filtering is an important user access control feature for many institutions and families. Using content filtering can limit a user's exposure to potentially harmful or undesirable online content. Adding this feature can be done at the client or network level, by using a web-based service (such as Windows Family) or configuring a proxy server or a router with this feature.

Physical Placement/Secure Locations

The *physical placement* of a router on a wired network requires a few considerations. Perhaps the most important consideration is physical access, meaning its accessibility by unauthorized and perhaps unsupervised individuals to prevent tampering and theft.

However, on a wireless network, several service, range, and performance issues must be considered. The most important of the physical location considerations for a wireless router or an access point (AP) are listed here:

- **Signal path obstructions**   Radio frequency (RF) signals can be obstructed, deflected, refracted, or blocked by certain objects and materials in their path (items such as metal cabinets, mirrors, thick walls, ceilings, and heavy wooden objects). A router should be placed such that its path to network nodes is affected only minimally by these objects.
- **Radio frequency and electromagnetic interference**   Nearby wireless networks using the same frequency or channel, RF transmitters (like a TV or radio transmitter), and noisy devices (those that emit strong electromagnetic interference, or EMI) can interfere with a home network's wireless signal. Changing the wireless channel to 1, 6, or 11 may help. You can also change the frequency (move from 2.4 GHz to 5 GHz or higher). However, any of the other problems are solved by moving the router or using other, more costly solutions.

NOTE   On a 2.4-GHz or 5-GHz wireless network in a populated area, you may want to try using a 20-MHz band. In a less populated area, a 40-MHz band may improve service.

- **Site survey**   Prior to the installation or expansion of a wireless LAN in a larger organization's office space, a best practice is to perform a *site survey*. This exercise, whether performed by employees or a third-party consultant, will typically identify any potential obstruction, interference, and range issues before the network is installed.

EXAM TIP   Most access points (APs) have physical Ethernet ports that are not password-protected or encrypted. Place the AP where unscrupulous folks can't get to it.

Dynamic Host Configuration Protocol Reservations

Nodes or workstations on a network obtain their IP configuration through requests to a *Dynamic Host Configuration Protocol (DHCP)* server either directly or over a network relay. It isn't that important that network hosts have the same IP address day in and day out. However, there are devices on a network that shouldn't be a moving target when it comes to their IP configuration, such as printers, smart hubs and switches, and scanners. Assigning static IP addresses to these devices can solve this problem, but it also limits the flexibility DHCP offers.

Address reservations provide a solution to this dilemma. This process uses a DHCP server to assign permanent addresses. Address reservations are a rarely used capability of virtually all home routers. Address reservations are configured by tying the MAC address of a device to a single IP address, which is removed from the DHCP address pool. One of the benefits of using the address reservation method is that it eliminates the chance that an address is issued to two different devices.

Static Wide Area Network IP

A router, which is the external edge device of a home or SOHO network, can be configured with a single *static IP address* in much the same way that the address reservation configuration can be used for a network's internal devices. However, it does require coordination with the Internet service provider (ISP) for the router's connection to the Internet, along with DNS server and gateway addresses, which can be static or dynamic. Once the router is configured and the ISP is on board, the router will operate with a single configuration.

CAUTION   Setting up a static wide area network (WAN) configuration is a relatively advanced process. Any user who is uncomfortable with this process should work with an ISP or bring in a technician set it up.

Universal Plug and Play

Universal Plug and Play (UPnP) is not quite the same as Plug and Play (PnP), but it does essentially work the same. Whereas PnP automatically configures an added device to a PC or mobile device, UPnP works with standard network protocols like TCP, IP, HTTP, DHCP, and others to automatically perform the following network configuration process:

1. Configure a network device with an IP address.
2. Build convergence with existing devices on a network.
3. Create a web page interface for viewing device status.

UPnP works with virtually all networking technologies, including Ethernet, Wi-Fi, and Bluetooth, without the need for the user to install drivers. The best use cases for UPnP are network printers and other network-capable peripheral devices.

Screened Subnet

A *screened subnet* is another name for a triple-homed router or firewall, which is another name for a router that has been configured as three completely separate subnetworks: an access router, an internal router, and a perimeter router. An *access router* is an external router that provides a separation between an external router and a perimeter router. An *internal router,* also called a *choke router,* separates the perimeter router from the internal router. The *perimeter router,* also called a *border router* or a *DMZ,* provides routing services to servers or bastion hosts. The screened subnet creates a secured network that can be placed between an internal network and a presumed hostile network, such as the Internet.

Wireless-Specific Security Settings

Some security settings apply only to wireless networks, such as the SSID and security settings and processes. For details, keep reading.

Changing the Service Set Identifier

Wireless devices want to be heard, and APs are usually configured to broadcast their *service set identifier (SSID),* or *network name,* to announce their presence. Unfortunately, the default SSID can give away important clues about the AP's manufacturer (and maybe even the model of the AP), which can make it easier for attackers to exploit known vulnerabilities in the AP hardware.

Always change the default SSID and the password on the AP to something unique. Default SSID names and passwords are well known and available online. When picking an SSID, think about whether the name could make your network an easy target or give an attacker information that could be used to physically locate the AP. Newer APs require you to create a unique SSID, user name, and password during installation.

Disabling SSID Broadcast

Although CompTIA, in its objectives, sees disabling the SSID broadcast on an AP as a method for securing a wireless network, in practice, even simple wireless scanning programs can discover the name of an "unknown" wireless network. Disabling the SSID broadcast is useful only as a way to avoid the attention of someone targeting known vulnerabilities with specific hardware and default settings.

Encryption Settings

Use the strongest encryption protocols and settings supported by the devices on your wireless network (in order from strongest to weakest: WPA3, WPA2, WPA, and WEP). You probably won't encounter the last two on the CompTIA A+ Core 2 exam, but you should definitely know the first two.

Cross-Reference

> To learn more about wireless encryption, see the "Protocols and Encryption" section in Objective 2.2, earlier in this domain.

Disabling Guest Accounts

A *guest mode* is commonly available on wireless routers and APs. Guest mode on a wireless router is actually a separate wireless network that can be configured with a different SSID and passcode. However, in spite of this, guest mode is not always secure, depending on the router manufacturer or model. Therefore, unless you expect to have many guests using your home wireless network, your best bet is to disable guest accounts or networks in the router's configuration.

Changing Channels

As mentioned earlier, one of the causes for interference on a wireless network is conflicting or overlapping wireless channel transmissions. *Changing the channel* for a wireless network can lessen the interference, as can adjusting the location, power, and more. In the United States, the primary non-overlapping channels are 1, 6, and 11. In a congested area, such as a city neighborhood, adjacent wireless networks may be using the same channel, which can cause interference. Moving to a different channel, or reducing power, may possibly improve the performance of the wireless network.

To change the channel configuration, use the administration tools on the router or AP. This isn't a difficult change and, in most cases, is an easy-to-find and easy-to-change action.

 EXAM TIP   Know how to change wireless-specific settings, including changing the SSID, disabling SSID broadcast, setting encryption (WPA2 or WPA3), disabling guest access, and changing wireless frequency channels.

Firewall Settings

A *firewall,* whether software or hardware, protects a home or SOHO network from outside threats by filtering packets before they reach the nodes of an internal network. Most local network routers also include firewall functions that can be configured using the router's browser-based settings utility (see Figure 2.9-2). Firewalls or the firewall functions on a router use *stateful packet inspection (SPI)* to examine individual packets and block or allow incoming traffic that isn't a response to outgoing traffic. You can even disable some ports entirely, blocking all traffic in or out a port.

Disabling Ports

Enabled (open) ports on a router that aren't used and are unnecessary can be an attack waiting to happen. On any router, unused *ports* should be *disabled.* Typically, a wireless router provides the capability to disable these ports. One example is the Ethernet RJ-45 connection and its associated port available on most routers. However, be sure that this is an action you need to take, because it's generally safer to administer a router using the Ethernet connection than doing so over the wireless network.

FIGURE 2.9-2 SPI firewall settings

EXAM TIP   Disabling ports can refer to Ethernet ports or TCP/UDP ports on a firewall as well as a router. On the CompTIA A+ Core 2 exam, carefully read any questions regarding enabling or disabling a port on these devices to be sure which ports and which device are being addressed.

Port Forwarding/Mapping

Since *Network Address Translation (NAT)* hides the true IP address of internal systems, a common configuration task is to enable devices outside of your LAN to reach a server inside it. *Port forwarding* (see Figure 2.9-3) enables you to open a port in the firewall and direct incoming traffic on that port to a specific IP address on your LAN.

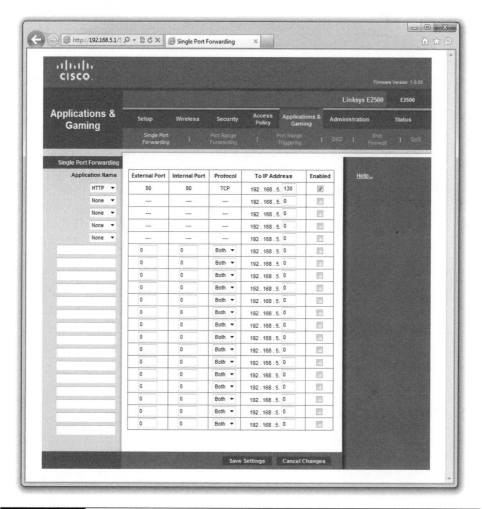

FIGURE 2.9-3   Port forwarding configured to pass HTTP traffic to a web server

EXAM TIP Port mapping is a synonym for port forwarding, and CompTIA may use either term.

REVIEW

Objective 2.9: Given a scenario, configure appropriate security settings on small office/home office (SOHO) wireless and wired networks The following are the home and SOHO router and AP security settings and configurations you should know for the CompTIA A+ Core 2 exam:

- Change the default user name and password immediately during installation.
- IP filtering screens incoming and outgoing network traffic based on their source or destination IP address.
- Keeping firmware up to date improves security.
- Content filtering limits a user's exposure to potentially harmful or undesirable online content.
- The physical placement of a router on a wireless network can prevent path obstructions and interference.
- DHCP address reservations can be used to provide a static address to a device.
- Universal Plug and Play (UPnP) works with standard protocols to automatically configure a network device and create an interface for device status.
- A screened subnet configures three separate subnetworks to create a secured network.
- Always change the default SSID and the password on the AP to something unique.
- Disabling the SSID broadcast is a way to avoid attacks.
- Guest mode is a separate wireless network, but it may not be secure.
- Changing the channel for a wireless network can lessen interference.
- A firewall protects a network from outside threats by filtering packets before they reach the nodes of an internal network.
- Open ports that are unnecessary can be an attack risk.
- Port forwarding enables a firewall port to direct traffic to a specific IP address on a LAN.

2.9 QUESTIONS

1. What settings on a new wireless router or AP should be changed immediately after installation? (Choose all that apply.)

   A. Brand and model

   B. Default administrator login name

   C. Default administrator password

   D. Location

2. Which of the following programs are you most likely to use when you set up your SOHO router?

   A. Web browser

   B. Paint program

   C. FTP program

   D. Word processor

3. What enables you to open a port in the firewall and direct incoming traffic on that port to a specific IP address?

   A. Port forwarding

   B. Screened subnet

   C. Disabling ports

   D. Changing channels

4. Which one of the following is *not* a role fulfilled by a screened subnet on an internal network?

   A. Access router

   B. Internal router

   C. Perimeter router

   D. WAN router

5. A local insurance agency wants to block both incoming and outgoing network traffic addressed to one or more specific IP addresses. What feature should the agency configure on its router or firewall?

   A. DHCP

   B. IP filtering

   C. Encryption settings

   D. Content filtering

2.9 ANSWERS

1. **A B D**   These settings are not only standard to the devices but are publicly shared by the manufacturers.

2. **A**   Using a web browser is the standard method for configuring and managing a router's settings.

3. **A**   Port forwarding/mapping enables you to open a port in the firewall and direct incoming traffic on that port to a specific IP address on your LAN.

4. **D**   A screened subnet does not include the role of WAN router.

5. **B**   IP filtering blocks incoming or outgoing messages based on their source and destination addresses.

Objective 2.10 Given a scenario, install and configure browsers and relevant security settings

Web browsers have become the go-to app on essentially all devices able to connect to a network, and especially to the Internet. The task of configuring a browser with the look and feel, apps, and security desired by an individual or an organization requires knowledge of what each setting controls, limits, or provides. It's also important to know how this is done on any particular browser.

This objective discusses the browser features, functions, and settings identified in the CompTIA A+ Core 2 objectives that you should know, understand, and apply for the exam.

Browser Download/Installation

All new computers and smart devices include one or more browsers, which are typically associated with the operating system (OS) on the device. Although browsers tend to be OS independent and can be installed on the most popular OSs, each OS has a default browser, typically provided by the same provider. Windows 10/11 systems come with the *Edge* browser, Android systems include the *Chrome* browser, Apple devices include the *Safari* browser, and many Linux distros, such as Ubuntu and Debian, include *Firefox* as the default browser. However, there are literally a dozen or more independent browsers, most of which will run on one or more of the major OSs.

Trusted Sources

To add a Web browser that meets your needs to a PC or a mobile device, you should download the browser's installation files from a *trusted source* or site. The best trusted source for a browser is its developer's website. Some third-party sites may also offer browsers for download, but some of these are considered to be *untrusted sites,* meaning that files downloaded from them may be infected with malware or tricks that cause you to download more files than you want. You should only download and install apps from trusted sources, such as the manufacturer's website, or well-known app stores, such the Apple App Store, the Microsoft Store, Ninite, and Softpedia (more on this a bit later).

```
PS C:\> Get-FileHash -Path C:\ubuntu-22.04.1-desktop-amd64.iso -Algorithm MD5

Algorithm         Hash                                                           Path
---------         ----                                                           ----
MD5               8C651682056205967D530697C98D98C3                               C:\ubuntu-22.04.1-desktop-amd64.iso
```

FIGURE 2.10-1   An example of the PowerShell command Get-FileHash

There are several ways to verify that a downloaded file itself can be trusted, but one of the most commonly used methods, beyond downloading the file from a trusted source, is to run a *checksum* or *hashing* total on the file. In many cases, a hash total, either in MD5 or SHA256, or both, is available from the trusted source. This string can be compared to a hashing total you generate on the downloaded file. For example, on a Windows system, the PowerShell command Get-FileHash will generate a hash total for comparison with the hash value provided by the trusted source. Figure 2.10-1 illustrates this command in action.

 EXAM TIP   Be sure you know the difference between a trusted and an untrusted source and how hashing can be used to verify a downloaded file.

Untrusted Sources

In the Microsoft world, an *untrusted source* is any source that is not from the Microsoft Store or sites that Microsoft has listed as trusted. Android labels apps or content that is not obtained from Google Play as being from an *unknown source*. Apple designates files not from the App Store as being *unknown developers*. In each case, the restriction placed on the unknown or untrusted file denies its installation or use.

However, the designation of a file being from an "unknown" source, which blocks its use or installation, can be overridden. On a macOS system, an unknown developer file can be installed through the System Preferences and Security and Privacy. On an Android system, the process is performed with the Security and Unknown Sources app. On Windows 10/11, the restriction on an app from an unknown source can be removed using the Settings app and the Apps & Features option to designate which sources you are willing to trust. Figure 2.10-2 shows the Choose Where to Get Apps section of the Apps & Features page.

Apps & features

Choose where to get apps

Installing apps only from Microsoft Store helps protect your device.

Anywhere, but warn me before installing an... ∨

FIGURE 2.10-2   The Choose Where to Get Apps section of the Apps & Features page of the Windows Settings app

Extensions and Plug-Ins

The terms *browser extensions* and *plug-ins* are often used interchangeably (another commonly used term is *add-ons*), and they basically refer to the same thing. In either case, the object is typically a compartmentalized feature or app that can be added or connected to a browser in a standalone manner, an enhancement to a browser feature, or used to enable an existing browser feature.

Browser extensions are software enhancements that add new features or functions to a browser. On the other hand, a plug-in provides a link or conduit between a browser and an application, such as QuickTime, Adobe Reader, Microsoft Office, and so on. A plug-in can provide support for viewing videos, opening PDF files, working with a spreadsheet, and more.

However, there are also malicious extensions and plug-ins. An extension or plug-in that appears to be highly desirable, may, in fact, be adware, spyware, or another form of browser attack. Malicious extensions and plug-ins are often piggybacked with an extension or plug-in that appeared, at least from its description, to be something you could really use. Once installed or attached, they can be very difficult to remove.

 NOTE A browser extension runs outside of the browser to which it's attached, and a browser plug-in runs inside the browser into which it is inserted.

A best practice is to only download, install, or attach extensions and plug-ins from trusted sources, such as the application store of each OS provider. However, if you do want to install an add-on from an untrusted source, be very careful with the questions and other prompts that are displayed—and even more careful with the answers you give. Remember that browser extensions and plug-ins don't typically install or attach themselves; you can always say no.

 EXAM TIP Know the difference between browser extensions and plug-ins and how they relate to the browser when executed.

Password Managers

Virtually all of the current browsers available include some form of a *password manager*. This tool is like a cabinet that stores the user names and passwords created and used on web pages downloaded by the browser. Typically, the user has a choice as to whether or not they want the browser to store their credentials. Most users see this function as being extremely convenient. Figure 2.10-3 shows an example of the Firefox Logins and Passwords app. Operating systems also provide password managers. Windows 10/11 offers the Credential Manager, and macOS provides Keychain for storing web and OS credentials.

FIGURE 2.10-3   The Firefox Logins and Passwords app is very similar to the password managers in most browsers.

In addition to browser password managers, there are a variety of standalone apps and online services that provide additional features to protect more than just your login credentials to websites. These tools, such as Bitwarden, LastPass, and 1Password, are password manager apps that secure your identity and login credentials as well as provide data safes for sensitive data. In addition, they generate strong passwords and monitor their use to make sure you don't use the same password in too many places. As browsers continue to incorporate more features, their built-in password manager apps are adding many of these same functions or connecting with trusted source websites that provide these services.

 ADDITIONAL RESOURCES   To learn more about password manager apps, visit https://www.passwordmanager.com/.

Secure Connections/Sites

In many respects, the Internet has become a mine field, with any number of threats and risks, many of which are hidden from view. The only defense a user has to navigate through this battlefield is to use a *secure connection*.

A secure connection encrypts network traffic before it is transmitted over a communication medium. Most browsers provide secure connections by applying SSL or TLS encryption for the requests they send to web servers over an HTTPS (HTTP over SSL/TLS) link. A non-secure connection is easily identified by the lack of the *S*, as in HTTP instead of HTTPS. Browsers also indicate when a secure connection is in use by including a padlock symbol on their address bar (see Figure 2.10-4).

| **FIGURE 2.10-4** | The padlock symbol on a browser address bar indicates a secure connection. |

| **FIGURE 2.10-5** | The security certificate information displayed by clicking the padlock icon |

HTTPS can also be used to secure websites and the transmission of the content in a user's request data back to the user's device. SSL/TLS provides three layers of protection for the web page transmitted back to the user: encryption, authentication, and integrity. Encryption keeps the data private; authentication ensures the data is from the same site the user requested it from; integrity ensures the data isn't altered in transit.

Another way to provide security assurance to users and validate that a site is real and not a fake is with a *security certificate*. The security certificate can itself be verified, which validates and authenticates a site's ownership and its domain name. To view information about the security certificate in use for a web page, click the padlock icon on a browser's address bar (see Figure 2.10-4). Figure 2.10-5 shows an example of the information that displays.

 EXAM TIP Be sure you know the difference between a trusted and an untrusted site and what makes a site trusted.

Settings

The settings on most browsers are essentially fairly uniform for basic configuration concerning what they enable, disable, or control. In general, these settings enable/disable features and functions such as pop-up and ad blockers, browsing history, and other basic functions. The following sections describe these and a few other settings on browsers.

Pop-up Blockers

A *pop-up* is generally considered a nuisance object that displays over the top of a web page (which it may or may not be associated with) to present an advertisement, show a message while malware is being transferred, or present a survey, among other purposes. However, not all pop-ups are bad. Many legitimate websites required that pop-ups be allowed in order for the site to function.

Virtually all browsers have a setting for blocking pop-ups, typically in their privacy settings. The following sections provide a review of how to block pop-up messages in the more popular browsers.

Chrome

1. Click the three-dot icon (…) at the top right of the browser.
2. On the menu that opens, click Settings.
3. On the Settings page, choose Privacy and Security and scroll down to the Content section.
4. Click Pop-ups and Redirects and choose the options you wish to use for your default setting. Figure 2.10-6 shows the Pop-ups and Redirects settings for Chrome.

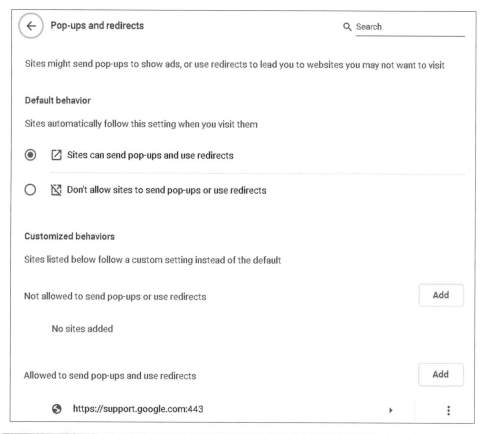

FIGURE 2.10-6   The Pop-ups and Redirects page for the Chrome browser

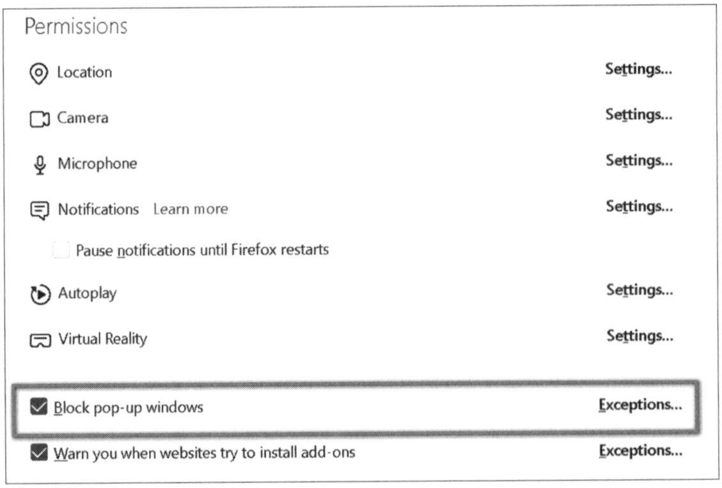

Permissions

⊚ Location		Settings...
▢ Camera		Settings...
▯ Microphone		Settings...
▤ Notifications Learn more		Settings...
☐ Pause notifications until Firefox restarts		
▶ Autoplay		Settings...
▭ Virtual Reality		Settings...
☑ Block pop-up windows		Exceptions...
☑ Warn you when websites try to install add-ons		Exceptions...

FIGURE 2.10-7 The Permissions section of the Firefox browser's Privacy page

Firefox

1. Click the three-bar icon in the top-right corner of the page.
2. Scroll down in the menu that displays and click Settings to open the General Settings page.
3. In the left-side navigation pane, click Privacy & Security.
4. On the Browser Privacy page, scroll down to the Permissions section (see Figure 2.10-7).
5. Check the box for Block Pop-up Windows.
6. Close the page to save the setting.

Microsoft Edge

1. Click the three-dot symbol (…) in the upper-right corner to open a menu of administrative options.
2. Scroll down and select the Settings option.
3. On the Settings page, click the three-line symbol in the upper-left corner and select Cookies and Site Permissions.
4. Scroll down on the page that displays to the All Permissions section and click the Popups and Redirects option.
5. To block all pop-ups and redirects, move the slide switch to the right to turn on this blocker. You also have the options to block only certain sites and to allow only certain sites.
6. Close the page to save the setting.

Clearing Browser Data

Browsers retain certain data as a means to provide convenience to the user and to promote efficiency to the Internet and Web. A browser saves two types of data: caching data and browsing data.

Caching data is data that produces a website's image. Caching data is stored ("remembered") by a browser in anticipation of you visiting that site again. If the data that was cached has everything needed to completely display the site, the cached data can be used to reproduce the page without the browser needing to redownload the data from the source server. In some cases, a page may include dates, news scrolls, and the like, so only these items are downloaded to be merged with the cached date to display the site in a browser.

Browsing data (aka browser history) is a historical record of the websites you've visited and downloaded during a recent period of time. Its contents provide a record that includes the titles, URLs, the time and date of each visit, and in some instances, data you provided in each visit. The records for your download history, cookies, and cache can all be removed from the system, should you wish to do so.

The first decision you need to make when deleting browsing data from your system is what data you want to delete and what point in time is the cut-off date, after which the history is to be deleted. For example, as shown in Figure 2.10-8, the Chrome browser's settings include an option to manage the browser history.

Figure 2.10-9 shows the pull-down list on Chrome's History settings from which you can decide the time period of the browsing data to be removed. After you've indicated how much of the history to delete, the next designation is the type(s) of data to be removed. Although other browsers may have a different look and feel for this function, they all perform in essentially the

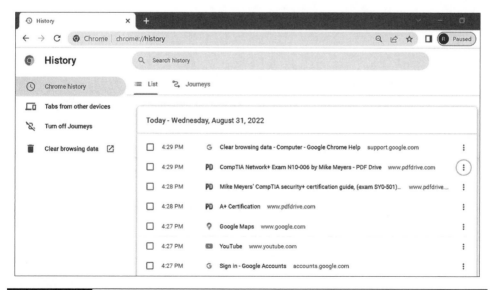

FIGURE 2.10-8   The Chrome browser's History page

FIGURE 2.10-9   Clearing browsing data in Chrome

same manner, with the time period and the file types needing to be selected before the browsing data is removed.

   NOTE   Browsing data, once removed, cannot be undeleted.

Private Browsing Mode

Virtually all web browsers provide a privacy or hidden mode for accessing the Web. Chrome offers an *Incognito mode,* Firefox and Safari provide a *Private window,* Microsoft Edge has an *InPrivate window,* and other browsers include a similar option. This feature is very consistent across all browsers that offer it. A private browser option doesn't record the user's online activities and doesn't cache downloaded files. However, private browsers don't mask who the user is and in some cases, such as on a smartphone, may record a small amount of browsing history. This private browsing history can contain enough information for some apps to use without your knowledge.

Sign-in/Browser Data Synchronization

Synchronization in the context of web browsers and mobile devices means that a user is able to coordinate browser software and settings between devices. For example, after the browsers on a PC and another device are configured for synchronization, any action on either browser is duplicated on the other. Even multiple devices of the same kind can be synchronized. This feature is now an integrated service of virtually all browsers and mobile device OSs. Many third-party apps are also available that offer higher levels of security and privacy in their synchronization processes.

Ad Blockers

An *ad blocker* is essentially just what its name says it is: an ad blocker blocks ads. However, there is a bit more to it. When you visit a website that contains advertisements, an ad blocker removes the coding from the downloaded web page file that would display the ad or advertising content. At this point, ad blockers haven't been incorporated into browsers as a feature, but there are several free and for-fee ad blockers available for download that can be added to a browser as an extension. However, you may find yourself working around websites that won't display when an ad blocker is active.

 EXAM TIP You may see a question on the CompTIA A+ Core 2 exam specifically about one or more of the browser features in this section. You should also expect questions that reference these features.

REVIEW

Objective 2.10: Given a scenario, install and configure browsers and relevant security settings This objective looked at the installation and configuration of web browsers and the pertinent settings that support key user features, functions, and security. The following key points were covered:

- Web browsers are standard software apps on any device with access to a network.
- Browsers and other security-related software should be downloaded from a trusted source.
- Software downloaded from an untrusted site may be infected with malware.
- Hashing is used to verify the authenticity of a downloaded file.
- Browser extensions and plug-ins add features or apps to a browser.
- Adware and spyware are common forms of browser attacks.
- A password manager stores the usernames and passwords used to access web pages.
- A secure connection encrypts network traffic before it is transmitted over a communication medium. Secure connections are created by applying SSL/TLS.
- A security certificate verified to both the owner and the domain name validates the ownership of a website.

- A pop-up is a browser object that displays over the top of a web page.
- Cache data is stored in anticipation of a site being visited again.
- Browsing data is a historical record of websites visited and files downloaded over a specific period of time.
- Privacy or hidden modes provide for unrecorded browsing.
- Two or more devices can be set up to have their actions and processes synchronized.
- Ad blockers remove the coding in a website that displays ad content.

2.10 QUESTIONS

1. A client downloaded a relatively unknown browser called WebWeave, which claims to provide higher security than other, better-known browsers, from a software download site called Apps2Bad.us. He says that since he installed the browser, he is unable to open files in his Windows User folder. What is likely contributing to this situation? (Choose two.)
   A. A possibly untrusted site
   B. Malware
   C. Improper installation
   D. User permissions

2. What is the term for software enhancements that add new features or functions to a browser?
   A. Add-ons
   B. Apps
   C. Extensions
   D. Plug-ons

3. What browser-related program is an additional feature that becomes a part of a browser for functions like viewing specific types of information?
   A. Extension
   B. Plug-in
   C. Attachment
   D. Upgrade

4. Before you fill in the data requested by a form on a web page, what indicator should you look for on the browser's address bar?
   A. An anchor symbol
   B. A heart symbol
   C. A padlock symbol
   D. A crossed out insect symbol

5. Sheila wants to be able to access her e-mail account using the same client as she uses on her desktop computer. She receives consulting engagement assignments via e-mail and wants to be able to respond as quickly as possible, even when she is away from her office. What process should she use?

   A. E-mail forwarding

   B. Synchronization

   C. Separate e-mail addresses for her desktop and mobile devices

   D. Mirroring

2.10 ANSWERS

1. **A** **B**   It's safe to assume that the software obtained from what is obviously an untrusted site contained malware.

2. **C**   An extension adds a function to a browser that is executed externally to the browser itself.

3. **B**   A plug-in executes within the browser as an additional feature.

4. **C**   A padlock symbol on the address bar indicates a site is trusted.

5. **B**   Synchronization establishes a link between devices and apps to keep data up to date on the synched devices.

Software Troubleshooting

Domain Objectives

- **3.1** Given a scenario, troubleshoot common Windows OS problems.
- **3.2** Given a scenario, troubleshoot common personal computer (PC) security issues.
- **3.3** Given a scenario, use best practice procedures for malware removal.
- **3.4** Given a scenario, troubleshoot common mobile OS and application issues.
- **3.5** Given a scenario, troubleshoot common mobile OS and application security issues.

Objective 3.1 # Given a scenario, troubleshoot common Windows OS problems

Microsoft Windows is, by far, the most commonly used family of desktop operating systems in homes, small offices, and enterprises. Keeping Windows working is essential to not only knowledge workers, SOHO workers, and gamers but also to the support personnel and technicians responsible for making sure it does. This objective discusses the common problems and their symptoms and solutions you can expect to encounter on the CompTIA A+ Core 2 (220-1102) exam.

Common Symptoms of Windows Problems

The following sections discuss the common Windows 10/11 problems and their symptoms identified in the objectives of the CompTIA A+ Core 2 exam.

Blue Screen of Death

Besides a solid blue background, the Windows Sudden Restart or Shutdown screen, aka the blue screen of death (BSOD), displays what can appear to be gibberish (it's not) when a non-maskable interrupt (NMI) or stop error occurs (see Figure 3.1-1). The BSOD appears when a system error occurs and Windows isn't able to recover. The BSOD is an error notice and report that may or may not contain the actual cause of the problem. On the BSOD is an error code. Look up this code on the Microsoft Support website or by using the Windows Event Viewer to view the system log files to learn what may actually be causing the problem.

 NOTE If Windows restarts automatically before you can read the information on a BSOD, you should disable automatic restarts by running sysdm.cpl in the Run command box and disabling restarts after system failures.

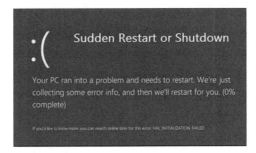

FIGURE 3.1-1 The Windows Sudden Restart or Shutdown screen, aka the blue screen of death (BSOD)

ADDITIONAL RESOURCES   A good site for more information on BSOD error/stop codes is "Windows Error Codes: Blue Screen Of Death" on the MiniTool website at https://www.minitool.com/news/windows-error-codes-blue-screen-fix.html.

Sluggish Performance

Here are some of the causes for Windows to perform sluggishly:

- Too many startup applications and processes, consuming high CPU, RAM, or hard disk resources
- Running too many applications or services in limited RAM, causing RAM contents to be swapped to virtual memory frequently
- Insufficient RAM
- Device infested with viruses or malware
- Windows updates and patches not applied
- Fragmented disk drives
- Out-of-date or misapplied device drivers

These system performance problems and other common problems are discussed later in this objective in the "Common Troubleshooting Steps" section.

Boot Problems

If a Windows 10/11 system powers on and the *POST (power-on/self-test)* succeeds, the operating system (OS) tries to load. A boot failure can be caused by hardware, the BIOS/UEFI firmware configuration, or Windows system faults. The challenge is figuring out the actual cause.

Error messages like "Operating System Not Found" and "No Boot Device Detected" may mean that the hard drive does not have proper connectivity and power, which could be caused by a faulty power supply unit or cable. Other messages, equally as unclear as to the actual problem, such as errors from missing critical boot files or components and corrupted or damaged boot files, may indicate a disk drive problem, when the issue may actually be a configuration, malware, or mechanical issue.

The specific boot files and settings you should know for the CompTIA A+ Core 2 exam are the Boot Manager (Bootmgr) and Boot Configuration Data (BCD) and the boot device order in the BIOS/UEFI firmware. The Boot Manager is a small software file that is a part of the boot device's volume boot record. It gets the data it needs to complete the boot-up from the BCD, which is essentially a small Registry-like database. The priority of boot devices is a configuration in the BIOS/UEFI configuration data that lists the devices, in order of priority, on which the system is to look for a volume boot record.

Frequent Shutdowns

Every so often, a Windows system will suddenly restart itself, which is no real cause for concern if it's truly infrequent. However, should sudden shutdowns (see Figure 3.1-1) or restarts become frequent, there are several areas you should look at to resolve the underlying problem. There really isn't a single fix for this problem, but the areas that may contribute to it include the following:

- **Sleep mode**   This can be a desirable feature, especially if you are frequently away from your work area. However, sleep mode can also initiate a shutdown on occasion.

- **Fast startup**   This feature increases the speed of the system during startup, but it can also cause problems during shutdown. It's enabled by default, but it can be disabled by navigating to the Control Panel | Power Options | Choose What the Power Buttons Do | Change Settings That Are Currently Unavailable and removing the check from the box next to Turn On Fast Startup (Recommended), as shown in Figure 3.1-2. Save the change and reboot to activate the setting change.

- **The processor's temperature**   If a processor, either the CPU or GPU, should overheat, it may cause the system to shut down. The motherboard protects itself by turning off any component that threatens it. A frequent example of this problem is a laptop PC that's used for gaming but is not engineered for it. Also, on overclocked PCs, overheating can be a recurring issue. Several freeware apps are available to test the temperature of the processor as well as several other internal components of a PC.

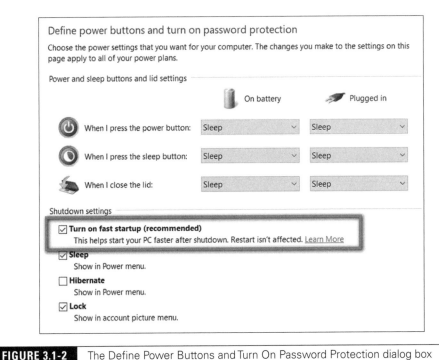

FIGURE 3.1-2   The Define Power Buttons and Turn On Password Protection dialog box

- **The advanced power settings**   Seemingly unrelated power settings can be the cause of system shutdowns. However, adjusting the power settings can be a guessing game or trial-and-error process. Typically, the power settings that may contribute to the problem are in an active power plan. Examples of the settings for review and possible adjustments are the Minimum Processor State setting in the Processor Power Management group (try setting it to 0) and the Turn Off Hard Disk After setting in the Hard Disk option (try setting it to Never).

Although not for the faint of heart, updating the firmware of the BIOS/UEFI could also resolve this issue, especially after new technology devices are added to the system. The instructions for this process can typically be found on the website of the motherboard manufacturer.

Services Not Starting

Windows uses a wide variety of services, some of which start automatically when Windows starts, while others are started only when they have been configured to start either automatically, after a delay, or when called upon to start by an application or event. They can even be configured to never start.

When Windows services fail to start, the feature provided by the service fails. Depending on the service, you might see an error message at system startup, or the problem might not be noticed until you attempt to use a service. For example, if the services used for wireless networking don't start, you can't connect to a wireless network. Services might fail to start if they depend on other services that didn't start, if a specific user account used to run the account has a different password than the one used when the service was set up, and for other reasons.

 ADDITIONAL RESOURCES   To learn more about why Windows services might not start, go to www.coretechnologies.com and search for "Why doesn't my Windows Service Start at Boot?"

Applications Crashing

Some programs, often games that were rushed to market near the winter holidays, are released with code errors that can render them unstable. These errors can produce symptoms such as a crash to desktop (CTD), a freeze, and even an unexpected shutdown or restart. These improper shutdowns can cause other problems, including damage to open files and folders. Keep an open mind, because hardware or driver problems could also be the cause; think in terms of what the system is using.

Think about what could cause this scenario: your whole system freezes while you're playing a huge, graphically intensive game that eats RAM like candy. For starters, it could be an error in the game code, an overwhelmed video card, a problem with the video card driver, a hardware problem on the video card, or a bad section of RAM. But what if the system didn't freeze; what if it was just slow and jerky? After checking for malware, check other possibilities such as poor programming and hardware that just isn't powerful enough to run the game properly.

Low Memory Warnings

Should a low memory warning display, as shown in Figure 3.1-3, there's no doubt that the system is running out of RAM. This could be caused by the fact that the system doesn't have enough RAM installed to begin with, but it could also be that one or more processes are using too much memory. The easiest solution to this problem is to shut down some of the jobs running on the system, such as apps and their associated services running in background. Another interim remedy is to increase the size of the virtual memory. You should also run the **sfc /scannow** command to check for and replace incorrect or corrupted operating system files.

USB Controller Resource Warnings

When the warning message "Not Enough USB Controller Resources" displays, the cause of this problem may be hard to pin down. This message typically appears when an application looking for a USB device, such as a graphics package or an audio recorder, starts up. And just as typically, the problem is caused by a lack of available endpoints.

A USB *endpoint* is a data buffer. USB controllers have a limited number to make available, and different USB devices and software require a varying number of endpoints. For example, a USB Bluetooth adapter needs three endpoints, but a USB digital-to-analog converter (DAC) needs ten or more endpoints. USB controllers commonly have 32 endpoints that are divided into 16 inputs and 16 outputs that are fixed in their functions. Should an application need more endpoints than are available, the "Not Enough USB Controller Resources" message or an equivalent message is displayed.

Theoretically, a USB hub is able to support up to 128 devices, but if the USB standard in use has fewer endpoints than that, you could eventually see the warning message. For example, a USB 3.0 controller is limited to 96 endpoints that are equally divided into input and output. However, multiple USB controllers are supported by most motherboards, and installing additional controllers can be a solution to this issue.

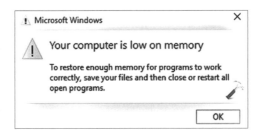

FIGURE 3.1-3   The low memory warning message on a Windows system

System Instability

A Windows system doesn't just go instable all by itself. Instability is a condition that shows up on a Windows system usually after a major change has been made, such as an update or fix is applied, a new cutting-edge hardware device is installed, or, rarely, when a large application is installed. Any one of these and many other events can make increased demands on the hardware and software of the system and cause its performance to change.

So, what is an instable system? There's no definitive answer to this, but a system that frequently reboots, has application crashes, has lots of instances of the BSOD, and has multiple "Unexpected Store Exceptions," among other odd occurrences, is considered to be instable. In other words, the system shows just about all of the problems being discussed in this objective.

Reverting to a "last known-good" image is one way to resolve the issue, but if that isn't an option, you can use the **sfc /scannow** command, the Deployment Image Servicing and Management (DISM) tool, and the System Update Readiness tool to scan for issues on the system.

No Operating System Found

The message "An operating system wasn't found" can be a real attention getter. Essentially, this message is saying that there is no operating system to be found, the hard disk is missing or has crashed with an error, or malware has eaten your boot records. Any one of these conditions could be the problem, but there could also be others.

Should this warning message show up during a startup process, your first action is to boot into the BIOS/UEFI to check on the boot device settings. If all is well there, shut down the system and check the hard disk connections. At this point, if you've found no problems, chances are that either the hard disk has failed, has been erased, or no OS was ever installed.

Slow Profile Load

Windows creates a profile for a user the first time the user logs in to the system. Each time the user logs on, the profile is loaded and used by the Windows components to configure the user's operating environment based on the information in the profile. A *user profile* contains information about the icons on the Desktop, the folders and files the user owns or has permissions for, and other environment elements. When a user is logged on to a Windows system, anything added to the system adds information to the user's profile. A bloated profile can take a while to load. A user profile is loaded when the user logs in, and it's updated when the user logs off. If the user is the only one on a particular computer, the slowness of the profile loading may not be noticeable. However, a user with a Roaming profile is possibly dragging a bloated profile around with them. The default user profile is around 280 MB, but there really is no upper limit for the size of a user profile. One example is shown in Figure 3.1-4. To view the size of your user profile, type **syspl.cpy** in the Run command box (WIN-R), open the Advanced tab, and click the Settings button in the User Profiles section.

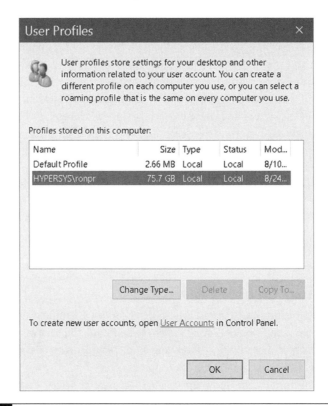

FIGURE 3.1-4 The User Profiles dialog box

Time Drift

On any system are several processes that require the clock time to be accurate (for example, authentication, time-dependent apps, and backup creation). In many cases, the clock time of a local PC must closely synchronize to the time on another device, such as a server. Most coordinating services have some flexibility for small time differences, such as 30 to 60 seconds or so. However, security functions, such as authentication services, are usually less tolerant of time differences between systems.

A PC motherboard has a battery-powered real-time clock (RTC) that speeds up or slows down with the strength of the CMOS battery. Because of this, the clock time on the RTC becomes less of an accurate time source. Using the internal RTC time leads to servers and clients experiencing time drift, especially if the client is remote.

The solution to the time drift issue is to create a Group Policy Object (GPO) on remote devices that uses one or a pool of GPS-synchronized time sources on both remote devices and the servers, which then allows the remote devices to use the servers as authoritative time sources.

EXAM TIP   Be sure you know the symptoms and possible causes for the events discussed in this section.

Common Troubleshooting Steps

Finding a solution to a problem first requires that you know what the problem is, which is where *troubleshooting* comes in. As you probably know from experience or have learned when preparing for the CompTIA A+ Core 1 exam, CompTIA endorses a six-step troubleshooting methodology to resolve problems. This or any structured process is meant for mysterious, troublesome, and hard-to-diagnose problems on servers, workstations, and peripheral devices. However, as you also know from experience, finding the source of a problem can also be simple and, in many instances, obvious. This section of the objective discusses the troubleshooting processes used with the common issues you are likely to encounter on the CompTIA A+ Core 2 (220-1102) exam.

ADDITIONAL RESOURCES   Access and read the article "A Guide to Network Troubleshooting: Basic Steps, Tips and Tools" at https://www.comptia .org/content/guides/a-guide-to-network-troubleshooting for more information on the CompTIA troubleshooting steps.

EXAM TIP   You should know the tools and techniques used for troubleshooting common Windows system problems, including reboot, restart, and uninstall/reinstall/ update application processes.

Reboot

One of the simplest solutions to any type of Windows or hardware problem is rebooting the system. If Windows or application code is corrupt, devices are incorrectly set, or memory is being filled up, rebooting the system provides a clean workspace to use after a restart.

- Be sure to close all apps before rebooting.
- If an app is still open, this prevents the system from rebooting. Windows displays a warning if there are open files when you select the reboot option, so you can choose to close them (recommended) or force a reboot.
- Forcing a reboot could cause the app to become corrupted, or you could lose unsaved data.

EXAM TIP   For a Windows troubleshooting scenario, be sure to know common solutions such as defragmenting, rebooting, killing tasks, and restarting services.

Restart Services

If a service has stopped running or is not working properly, open Services, select the service you want to restart, stop it, and then restart it. You can also use the Services dialog box to start a service that failed to start automatically.

Cross-Reference

More information on using the Windows Task Manager or the services.msc to manage services can be found in Objective 1.3 of Domain 1.

Uninstall/Reinstall/Update Applications

Windows apps can become corrupt for a variety of reasons, including disk errors, poor coding, errant updates, or apps left open when Windows is shut down or restarted. To get a faulty application working again, repair the application.

You can repair an application through Control Panel's Programs and Features applet. To start the process, click the application and then click Uninstall/Change. If a repair option is available, select it to repair the app. If an app lacks a repair option, uninstall the app and reinstall it instead.

In Windows 10/11, you can also open Apps & Features in Settings, choose an app, and click Modify to start the process.

 NOTE   The Windows 10 Apps & Features menu doesn't always offer repair options for apps that have them. Try the Programs and Features applet in Control Panel instead.

Add Resources

If Windows or an application is performing slowly, use the Task Manager, Resource Monitor, and perhaps the Performance Monitor to determine what the issue may be. If the problem is a system resource issue, you can free up the resource by stopping any competing processes. However, this is likely a temporary solution. Your best bet is likely to be adding additional resources. If the resource issue involves the CPU, RAM, disk storage, or network resources, it's time for a hardware upgrade or expansion.

Verify Requirements

If an application is not working properly or if an OS upgrade either won't install or fails to complete, chances are that the hardware or supporting services required by the software are either not sufficient or not present.

Before installing an application, visit the provider's website (or simply read the information regarding the system requirements on the packaging, if applicable) to learn what the system requirements are for its installation and proper operations. To upgrade to a new version of Windows, such as upgrading from Windows 10 to Windows 11, you should use the PC Health Check app to verify if your system has the resources to support Windows 11.

 ADDITIONAL RESOURCES Before upgrading from Windows 10 to Windows 11, visit https://support.microsoft.com/en-us/windows/windows-11-system-requirements-86c11283-ea52-4782-9efd-7674389a7ba3 and read the article "Windows 11 System Requirements."

System File Check

The *System File Check (sfc)* utility, which is executed from a command prompt, is used to verify and, if necessary, replace system files for the Windows 10 and 11 OSs. The sfc command is used in many system troubleshooting procedures. Its primary purpose is to examine system and protected OS files for performance issues. Here are some common uses of this command:

- **sfc /scannow**   Checks the integrity of Windows system files.
- **sfc C:**   Scans the C: hard disk drive or the boot volume.
- **sfc C: /f**   If errors are identified with the previous command, this command attempts to repair them.

Repair/Restore/Reimage Windows

On occasion, Windows may not perform as it should or just not work at all. When either of these conditions occur, Windows provides tools to help you diagnose, analyze, and repair the problem. The following sections discuss these tools and when and why they are used.

Windows Repair

Windows needs two critical files to boot: Bootmgr and BCD. If they are damaged, you can fix them with the bcdedit tool from a command prompt. Figure 3.1-5 shows a bcdedit listing of the current settings of a BCD file. Each of the settings shown can be edited using this tool. To list the edit options available, run the command **bcdedit /?**.

```
C:\WINDOWS\system32>bcdedit /v

Windows Boot Manager
--------------------
identifier              {9dea862c-5cdd-4e70-acc1-f32b344d4795}
device                  partition=\Device\HarddiskVolume2
path                    \EFI\Microsoft\Boot\bootmgfw.efi
description             Windows Boot Manager
locale                  en-US
inherit                 {7ea2e1ac-2e61-4728-aaa3-896d9d0a9f0e}
default                 {3ac04e9e-8425-11eb-a8bf-cb868190b301}
resumeobject            {3ac04e9d-8425-11eb-a8bf-cb868190b301}
displayorder            {3ac04e9e-8425-11eb-a8bf-cb868190b301}
toolsdisplayorder       {b2721d73-1db4-4c62-bf78-c548a880142d}
timeout                 30

Windows Boot Loader
-------------------
identifier              {3ac04e9e-8425-11eb-a8bf-cb868190b301}
device                  partition=C:
path                    \WINDOWS\system32\winload.efi
description             Windows 10
locale                  en-US
inherit                 {6efb52bf-1766-41db-a6b3-0ee5eff72bd7}
recoverysequence        {a92dba00-1e7d-11eb-aa54-e73bad0e24de}
displaymessageoverride  Recovery
recoveryenabled         Yes
isolatedcontext         Yes
allowedinmemorysettings 0x15000075
osdevice                partition=C:
systemroot              \WINDOWS
resumeobject            {3ac04e9d-8425-11eb-a8bf-cb868190b301}
nx                      OptOut
```

FIGURE 3.1-5   The output of a bcdedit /v command

EXAM TIP   For the CompTIA A+ Core 2 exam, know that the Boot Configuration Data (BCD) contains information about installed operating systems.

Windows Restore and Recovery

If you are unable to boot a computer or access its startup options (see Figure 3.1-6), try using the installation media, a repair disk, or a recovery drive, which may require that you change the BIOS/UEFI settings to make the recovery drive the priority boot source.

If your installation media is lost or damaged, you can create a system repair drive—but you must do it before you have problems. To create a repair drive, access Settings | Update & Security | Recovery | Creating a Recovery Drive.

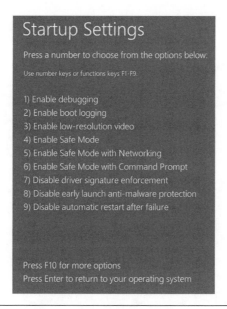

FIGURE 3.1-6   The Windows Startup Settings options list

Advanced Options   After you boot in to the WinRE recovery system, choose the Trouble-shoot option and then select Advanced Options (see Figure 3.1-7). Depending on the recovery or repair action needed, you can choose from the following options:

- **System Restore**   Restores the computer to a previous state.
- **System Image Recovery**   Restores a computer to a previous disk image.
- **Startup Repair**   Scans for and fixes issues preventing a computer from starting.
- **Command Prompt**   Opens a command line for access to volumes, folders, and files.
- **Startup Settings**   Opens the Startup Settings menu with the following options:
  - **Enable Debugging**   Turns on debugging for the Windows 10/11 kernel.
  - **Enable Boot Logging**   Starts the OS in normal mode and creates a log file to track future boots.
  - **Enable Low-Resolution Video**   Starts the OS in normal mode with the display resolution set to 800×600.
  - **Enable Safe Mode**   Starts the OS in Safe Mode.
  - **Enable Safe Mode with Networking**   Starts the OS in Safe Mode with networking services and drivers.
  - **Enable Safe Mode with Command Prompt**   Starts the OS in Safe Mode with a command prompt UI.

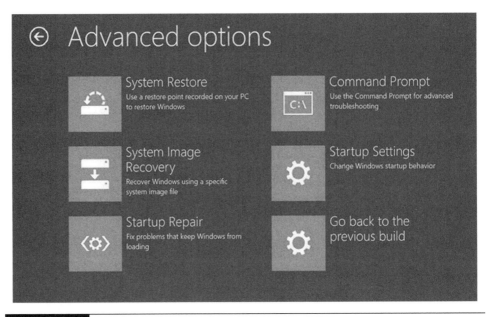

Windows 10 WinRE Advanced Options main screen

- **Disable Driver Signature Enforcement** Non-signed device drivers are allowed to be installed.
- **Disable Early Launch Anti-Malware Protection** The Early Launch Anti-Malware driver, typically loaded during the boot cycle, is disabled.
- **Disable Automatic Restart After Failure** Blocks restarts after major failures, like a BSOD stop.
- **Launch Recovery Environment** Returns to the Advanced Startup Options page.
- **Go Back to the Previous Build** This option may not be available if Windows was updated more than 10 days ago. If it's available, it reverts Windows to the build/version that was replaced and removes all apps or packages installed after the upgrade.

WinPE The *Windows Preinstallation Environment (WinPE* or *Windows PE)* is a limited graphical OS that is started directly from the Windows installation media. WinPE provides access to troubleshooting, diagnostic, and repair tools collectively called the *Windows Recovery Environment (WinRE* or *Windows RE)* that includes automatic repair, reset to factory default settings, system image recovery, and a few troubleshooting tools.

 NOTE WinPE can also assist unattended installations, network installations, and booting diskless workstations on a network.

EXAM TIP   Most prebuilt systems come with a *factory recovery partition,* other recovery media, or the ability to create recovery media. These can restore the active system partition or the entire hard drive to fresh-from-the-factory condition using a *recovery image*.

Reimage Windows

If your computer is not running as well as it should be, you can reimage Windows 10 to fix the issues. For example, if your operating system gets damaged or corrupted, or you sense some ransomware or spyware virus has infected it, then a reimage is necessary to get rid of the issue.

Depending on a whole host of reasons, most of which relate to the actions of the users, Windows can become messed up and perform sluggish, erratically, or just plain strange and needs a start over. *Reimaging* Windows simply means removing everything (everything!) on the hard disk drive and performing a clean install of Windows. This resets Windows back to its default settings. The reimage process restores the OS files; removes all installed apps, updates, and settings; and changes to the Registry and all user-created GPOs. The upside of a reimage is a faster and cleaner system. The downside is that, if not backed up, any apps or features you wanted to keep must to be reinstalled and all settings and configuration changes must be reapplied.

As mentioned, reimaging requires you to reformat the hard drive in order to get rid of some nasty issues. If you do not want your valuable data lost during the process, you can create an offline backup of your hard drive and selectively restore your data after the reimage process.

Roll Back Updates

If Windows malfunctions can be traced back to right after an update was installed, the update is almost certain to be the cause. System Restore is the key to rolling back updates that don't work because it records the system configuration as part of a restore point so that you can go back to it if an update fails.

Another important rollback function is the capability to roll back a device driver. For any number of reasons, but mostly compatibility issues, if a newly installed device driver doesn't work properly (or at all), it will need to be backed out of the system and the previous driver reactivated. To do this, you'd use these general steps:

1. Access the Device Manager by right-clicking the Start menu icon or pressing WIN-X to open the Power User menu and choosing Device Manager.
2. Locate the device for which you want to roll back its driver. You probably need to open a device category to find the specific device.
3. Right-click the device and click Properties.

FIGURE 3.1-8 The Roll Back Driver function is accessed on the Properties dialog box of a device.

4. On the Properties dialog box that displays, click Roll Back Driver (see Figure 3.1-8) and select Yes to proceed.

5. When the rollback completes, close the Properties dialog box and click Yes to restart the system.

Cross-Reference

For more information about System Restore, see Objective 3.3.

Rebuild Windows Profiles

If a corrupted user account profile prevents you from logging in to your system, you have two ways to fix it:

- You can fix the user profile settings in the Registry with Regedit.
- You can create a new user account and copy the files from the corrupt one to the new one.

ADDITIONAL RESOURCES   To learn more about rebuilding Windows profiles, see https://www.easeus.com and search for "Fix a Corrupted User Profile."

REVIEW

Objective 3.1: Given a scenario, troubleshoot common Windows OS problems   Common symptoms of Windows 10/11 problems include the following:

- Blue screen of death (BSOD)
- Sluggish performance
- Boot problems
- Frequent shutdowns
- Services not starting
- Applications crashing
- Low memory warnings
- USB controller resource warnings
- System instability
- No OS found
- Slow profile load
- Time drift

The following are some common troubleshooting steps:

- Reboot
- Restart services
- Uninstall/reinstall/update applications
- Add resources
- Verify requirements
- Use System File Check
- Repair/restore/reimage Windows
- Roll back updates
- Rebuild Windows profiles

3.1 QUESTIONS

1. To change the boot order, which of the following is necessary?
   A. Starting Windows in Safe Mode
   B. Restarting the system and opening the BIOS/UEFI firmware setup
   C. Using the Task Manager
   D. Using MSConfig

2. Which of the following is the best way to recover from a bad device driver update?
   A. Rolling back the system
   B. Restarting the system and opening the BIOS/UEFI firmware setup
   C. Rolling back the device driver
   D. Restarting in Safe Mode

3. Your client needs to restart a system to solve a problem. Which of the following should be done first?
   A. Creating a registry backup
   B. Running System Restore
   C. Creating a full system backup
   D. Unplugging USB drives

4. Your personal computer used to load your Desktop in about ten seconds. Now it takes ten minutes. Which of the following is *not* a likely cause?
   A. Too many tasks running
   B. Malware
   C. System file corruption
   D. User profile corrupted

5. Which of the following is not an option for the WinRE Troubleshooting Advanced Options?
   A. System Restore
   B. System Image Recovery
   C. System Startup Repair
   D. Safe Mode Repair

3.1 ANSWERS

1. **B**   You must use the BIOS/UEFI firmware dialog box to change the boot order.

2. **C**   Rolling back the device driver will not affect other parts of the system, so it is the preferred method.

3. **D**   USB drives that are plugged in could prevent the system from restarting.

4. **A**   The other items listed are likely causes; the number of tasks running has a small impact on load time, but not as much impact as the others.

5. **D**   Safe Mode Repair is not a WinRE troubleshooting advanced option.

 **Objective 3.2** # Given a scenario, troubleshoot common personal computer (PC) security issues

Security issues, regardless of the effectiveness of e-mail filters and anti-malware apps, are likely to be around for a long time. In this objective, you will learn about common symptoms of PC security issues, from pop-ups and slow performance to invalid security certificates and "access denied" errors. This objective sets the stage for Objective 3.3, where you learn how to remove malware, a frequent cause of security issues.

Common Symptoms

PC problems are typically software problems, but, then again, some PC problems are absolutely hardware problems. Also, some software problems can be caused by hardware problems, and vice versa. The keys to resolving PC problems are to recognize the symptoms you see, hear, or smell and to know where to begin troubleshooting to verify their cause. The following sections describe how to identify common PC security problems.

Unable to Access the Network

If a network host cannot connect to a network, you should check for the following issues:

- **Windows issues**   The first thing to check is whether the network connection is properly configured. Review the status of the network connection on the Internet Network Connections page of the Control Panel and Network and Internet settings.

- **APIPA address**   If the host is configured with an APIPA IPv4 address (169.254.0.1 to 169.254.255.254), it should be able to connect to the local network, but not beyond that. Use the ipconfig command at a command prompt to verify this condition. If this is the case, the issue is not with the host.

- **No IP configuration**   If the host has no valid IP configuration (no IP address assigned), the problem may be the network connection (for example, the cable of a wired connection or the settings of a wireless connection).

- **DHCP configuration**   If the IP configuration supplied by a DHCP server to a host appears to be good, the issue is not with the host or the network devices. Check the gateway device(s) for connection issues using ping and tracert.

Cross-Reference

You can find information on the use of ipconfig, ping, and tracert in Objective 1.2.

EXAM TIP Know the different causes for a PC to be unable to connect to a network and some of their possible solutions.

Desktop Alerts

Five basic types of messages can be displayed by an operating system's user interface (UI): confirmation, information, warning, error, and service.

A *confirmation message* asks "Are you sure?" types of questions to verify a requested action. An *information message* informs the user that an action has been completed successfully, such as a file was successfully deleted. A *warning message* cautions against the consequences of a requested action and asks the user to confirm that the requested action should proceed. A warning message has an icon (for example, the Windows yellow triangle with an exclamation mark, as shown in Figure 3.2-1) and typically asks something like "Do you want to continue?"

An *error message* is meant to alert the user of an action or condition that violates a validation or business rule (for example, "This page cannot load an unsigned control" or "Unable to connect to the network"). The user can clear the message but must correct the condition to continue.

Service messages are caused by errors that occur within an application or service. The message notifies users of a condition caused by an interruption or failure in a process, protocol, or application. Examples of service messages in a browser are HTTP 403 (forbidden), 404 (not found), and 503 (no service).

EXAM TIP Know the general causes for a browser's service messages.

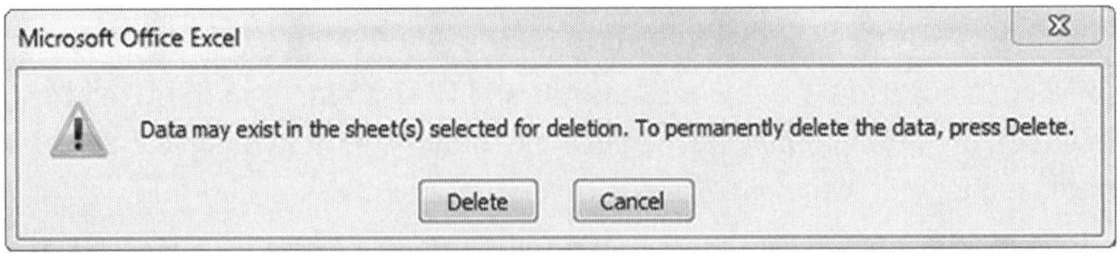

Microsoft Office Excel	⌖

⚠ Data may exist in the sheet(s) selected for deletion. To permanently delete the data, press Delete.

[Delete]   [Cancel]

FIGURE 3.2-1   An example of a Windows 10/11 warning message

False Alerts Regarding Antivirus Protection

A *false alert,* typically in the form of a displayed warning or error message, is caused by an antivirus program erroneously flagging legitimate and secure software as malware, creating what is called a *false positive.* Virtually all antivirus and anti-malware programs create false positives at some point.

An example of a false positive, which causes a false alert, is a third-party password manager. These programs, because they create executable files and alter Windows Registry entries, look very much like a rootkit, which is a malware type scanned for by anti-malware software.

Altered System or Personal Files

One of the sure signs of a malware infection is system, application, or personal files that have been altered, renamed, corrupted, or are no longer there. Other signs of malware are new files with names that are very similar to system files (such as r3gedit.exe and expl0rer.exe), date stamps on some files that are later than the last known-good images, and access being denied to files that are used frequently.

Should any of these symptoms appear on stored files, especially system or personal files, a malware scan should be done immediately and any flagged files should be quarantined.

Unwanted Notifications Within the OS

Notifications are messages displayed in the Notification bar on the Windows 10/11 Desktop. Not all notifications are good, and not all notifications are bad; however, you can control which notifications you wish to see. As shown in Figure 3.2-2, using the Notifications & Actions page of the Settings app, a user can control whether or not to receive notifications, the type of notifications to receive, and which applications, in particular, can send notifications (if any).

OS Update Failures

OS updates don't typically fail for random reasons. The causes are similar to those that cause applications and other software services to fail. The following are the more common of the causes for an update process to fail.

- **Low storage**   On any operating system (OS), a low amount of available storage space can cause critical system functions from starting or completely finishing.
- **Multiple pending updates**   An OS has two layers of system elements: core system components and general system components. An update process posts updates and fixes to the core system elements before updating the general system elements. If these updates are applied out of sequence because there are several to be applied, a general system update may fail because it's depending on a core system update to have preceded it.
- **Corrupt files**   If the files in an update are corrupted, this can cause major issues for both the update and the OS.

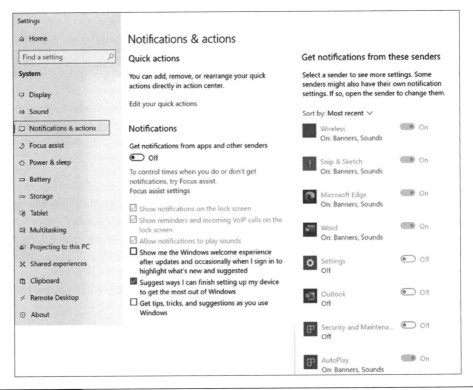

FIGURE 3.2-2 The Notifications & Actions page of the Settings app

- **Update software malfunction** This is perhaps the most common cause of an update to fail. If an error message displays to the effect of "Cannot check for updates," the update processing has failed.

If the update process for an OS fails, search the provider's web page for the appropriate recovery methods. For example, on a Windows system, you can run the **sfc /scannow** command.

 EXAM TIP You should be able to identify an OS update failure by its symptoms.

Browser-Related Symptoms

Web browsers are frequently the target of malware. Symptoms of a browser that's infected by malware, typically in the form of adware or spyware, are random and possibly frequent pop-ups, the appearance of additional toolbars, the default search engine changing, and search results that are not actually what was searched for. Other symptoms of malware infections can be slow performance and excessive crashes.

Random/Frequent Pop-Ups

Pop-ups are typically small browser windows that display inadvertently when you visit a site or click a site's elements At one time pop-ups were a common part of many websites. They were simple ad windows, and most still are. However, they have since become carriers of malware that masquerade as alerts from a server or an OS as a form of social engineering in an attempt to infect your host system. These infections try to get around anti-malware protections attempting to block drive-by (nefarious) downloads. Abuse of automatic pop-ups has led to the inclusion of pop-up blockers in virtually all antivirus, anti-malware, and browser software. Sketchy pop-ups now must trick the user into clicking something to open them.

Certificate Warnings

Digital certificates are used by web browsers and operating systems to validate websites and applications (in other words, to prove that the alleged owner or developer is actually valid). A digital certificate error can be caused by various issues, but one possible cause is that malware has attempted to sneak a bad certificate onto your system or has changed the system date (a date mismatch is the cause of many certificate errors). A web page/website displays whether or not it is protected by a certificate. On the address bar, a padlock icon indicates that the page is protected by a trusted certificate. However, if the padlock icon is replaced with an alert icon, in most cases, the URL is struck out and a warning message displays to the effect of "Untrusted certificated warning."

 EXAM TIP Know the significance of the padlock and alert symbols that display on a browser's address bar.

Certificate warnings are caused by a few other conditions, including the certificate was issue by an untrusted authority, the certificate is self-signed (not signed by a publicly trusted Certificate Authority, or CA), and the fully qualified domain name (FQDN) of the certificate the browser is requesting is not the same as the one on the certificate.

 ADDITIONAL RESOURCES To learn more about certificate errors in browsers, go to https://support.microsoft.com and look up "Certificate errors: FAQ."

Redirection

In browser *redirection,* an incorrect URL is opened when the user clicks what is believed to be a legitimate link on a web page. This is a common sign that malware has infected either the browser or the hosts file. A variation on browser redirection is when the official home page of a site is changed to a different home page (which may look very much like the original) by a malware action known as *home page hijacking.*

To stop browser redirection, use anti-malware apps. Keep your browser updated, and check whether your browser has an option to lock your home page.

REVIEW

Objective 3.2: Given a scenario, troubleshoot common personal computer (PC) security issues   Here are some common symptoms indicating possible PC security problems you should know for the CompTIA A+ Core 2 exam:

- Unable to access the network
- Desktop alerts
- False alerts regarding antivirus protection
- Altered system or personal files and missing or renamed files
- Unwanted notifications within the OS
- OS update failures

Here are some browser-related symptoms:

- Random/frequent pop-ups
- Certificate warnings
- Redirection

3.2 QUESTIONS

1. A user navigates to her bank's website, which opens with a padlock icon on the address bar. However, as the user navigates through the bank's website, she notices that the padlock icon has changed to an alert symbol. What is likely the cause for this change?

   A. Malware has caused the user to open a page without a trusted certificate.

   B. The user is no longer on the home page of the bank.

   C. The browser has an issue loading the page.

   D. There is a problem with the network router.

2. A user's network host computer is unable to contact any address on the Internet. The user sees that an IPv4 address of 169.254.0.1 is assigned to the computer. What could be the problem?

   A. The network adapter must be faulty.

   B. The gateway router is down.

   C. An APIPA address cannot be used beyond a local network.

   D. The URL is bad.

3. What is the term for a displayed warning or error message that results from an antivirus program erroneously flagging legitimate and secure software as malware?

  A. False flag

  B. False alert

  C. False negative

  D. True negative

4. Which of the following message types would be used to display an alert that warns against the consequences of an action and asks the user to confirm they wish to continue?

  A. Confirmation message

  B. Information message

  C. Warning message

  D. Error message

  E. Service message

5. A website keeps displaying small pages requesting information that isn't consistent with the site's content. What type of artifact is being displayed?

  A. Web page form

  B. Pop-up

  C. Hypertext link

  D. Web survey

3.2 ANSWERS

  1. **A** Malware has caused the user to open a page without a trusted certificate.

  2. **C** An APIPA address cannot be used beyond a local network.

  3. **B** A false alert occurs when malware erroneously identifies valid data or files as bad.

  4. **C** A warning message seeks confirmation that the user wishes to proceed.

  5. **B** Pop-ups are typically displayed by malware that has infected a web page.

Objective 3.3 **Given a scenario, use best practice procedures for malware removal**

Malware, including viruses and other malicious software, e-mail attachments, spoofed downloads, and several other types of ill-intended programming, is a major problem in the network-connected world of today. This problem has become so sophisticated that just deleting malware from a computer or device isn't typically enough. This objective discusses some of the best practices you need to know and use to remove malware.

Best-Practice Malware-Removal Process

Despite your best efforts, your computer (or a computer you are responsible for) is likely to become infected with malware. To get rid of computer viruses or other malware infections, follow the best-practice steps in this section.

Step 0: Preparation   Before beginning this process, be sure your antivirus/anti-malware software is fully updated. Since the system is infected, this may be difficult. You may need to remove the infected disk(s) from the system and perform the removal process on a different system.

Step 1: Investigate and verify malware symptoms   The first step is to recognize (verify) that a potential malware outbreak has occurred and to act swiftly to keep it from spreading. Network monitoring, security event logs, and user reports may all tip you off to the malware symptoms described in the previous objective. Many networks employ software such as third-party *network access control (NAC)* products that interact with Windows 10/11 Intune or open source products like PacketFence, Zabbix, and openNAC to monitor network traffic and automatically isolate systems that start sending suspicious packets.

Step 2: Quarantine infected systems   If you suspect that one or more hosts may be infected with malware, you should quarantine the host(s) before attempting to verify the infection. Your suspicion is enough reason to take precautionary steps to prevent the risk of an infection.

To quarantine a computer, take it off the network by disconnecting the network cable or disconnecting/disabling its Wi-Fi network adapter. Depending on how the malware spread, you may need to take additional steps to keep other systems from contracting it. For example, don't allow removable drives or media from that system to be connected to other systems unless the drives or media are scanned for malware first.

Step 3: Disable System Restore in Windows   Once you're sure the machine isn't capable of infecting other systems, disable *System Restore* to keep the malware from being included in (and potentially restored later from) saved restore points. To disable System Restore in Windows 10/11, use the following steps:

1. On the Control Panel, click the System icon.
2. On the System page, click the System Protection link under the Related Settings heading on the far right side of the page to open the System Properties dialog box.
3. In the Protection Settings section, for each drive, select the drive and click the Configure button to open the System Protection dialog box (see Figure 3.3-1).
4. Activate the Disable System Protection radio button.
5. Repeat steps 3 and 4 for each drive.

Step 4: Remediate infected systems   The main tool you should use to attempt to remediate an infected system is anti-malware/antivirus software. Although the software didn't detect the

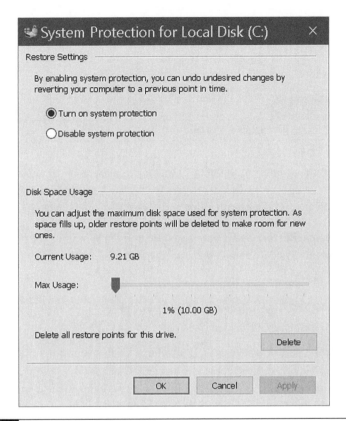

FIGURE 3.3-1   The System Protections dialog box displays for each storage drive.

malware to begin with, either an updated database or a completely different suite should detect the malware.

Follow these best practices to remediate a system:

- **Update anti-malware software**   Do this step before you begin the entire process (see Step 0). You can also obtain downloadable files from an anti-malware software provider that can be copied to media and then used on the infected system.

- **Scanning and removal techniques**   Scanning to detect the presence of malware and viruses and then removing that presence can be done, for the most part, using the most rigorous scans and removal processes of an anti-malware or antivirus app. More vicious malware, such as variants of ransomware, adware, Trojans, backdoors, and others, is more difficult to track down and remove. Booting a Windows system into *Safe Mode* removes virtually all of the system services an anti-malware app offers, including Windows Security apps. However, the good news is that malware cannot run either.

  To scan for and remove anti-malware from a system in Safe Mode requires the use of third-party antivirus and anti-malware software (such as GridinSoft) able to run in the Safe Mode environment.

Remediation sometimes requires a third step: Repair any damage done to the system. If you are unable to start Windows after this step is completed, boot into the Windows Preinstallation Environment (WinPE) and use the Windows Recovery Environment (WinRE)/System Recovery Options tools to repair the system.

Cross-Reference

See Objective 2.3 for more information on WinRE and WinPE.

Step 5: Schedule scans and run updates   One of the reasons systems become infected is because anti-malware updates and scans are perhaps disabled, not updated, or never set up. Set up a schedule for scans and the downloading and application of updates.

Step 6: Enable System Restore and create a restore point in Windows   By creating a restore point after re-enabling System Restore, you establish a new baseline to return to after cleaning up the system.

EXAM TIP   Remember to re-enable System Restore and create a new restore point once the system has been repaired.

Step 7: Educate the end user   After performing the steps of this process, you should be well aware that even the best anti-malware suite is imperfect and, at best, forms a rarely tested second line of defense. In all matters of system security, the first line of defense is educating users. Teach users to be cautious with e-mail from senders they don't recognize and to never click an attachment or URL in an e-mail unless they are absolutely certain of its source. Explain the dangers of questionable websites and teach users what to do when a site tries to manipulate them or triggers their browser's built-in attack site warning (see Figure 3.3-2).

Inform users that the following actions should be a part of a regular system maintenance/preventive program:

- Install, use, and update anti-malware programs regularly.
- Enable automatic updates for anti-malware programs.
- Install apps only from trusted sources.
- Avoid untrusted software sources (such as warez and registry cleaners from obscure websites).
- If a malware attack takes place, analyze weaknesses in prevention and work to improve user education.

EXAM TIP   Be sure you know the steps for best-practice procedures for removing malware.

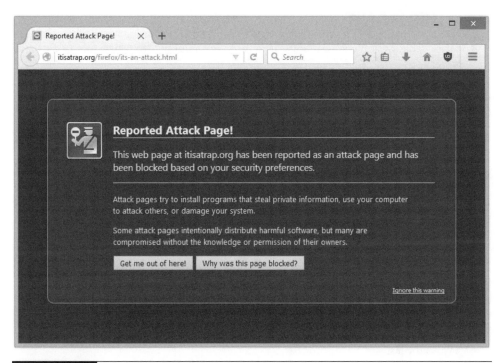

FIGURE 3.3-2 | Attack site warning

REVIEW

Objective 3.3: Given a scenario, use best practice procedures for malware removal

Removing malware involves a seven-step process:

1. Investigate and verify malware symptoms.
2. Quarantine infected systems.
3. Disable System Restore in Windows.
4. Remediate infected systems, which includes updating anti-malware software and using scanning and removal techniques (such as Safe Mode and the preinstallation environment).
5. Schedule scans and run updates.
6. Enable System Restore and create a restore point in Windows.
7. Educate the end user.

3.3 QUESTIONS

1. After updating anti-malware software and using scanning/removal techniques, what is another step that might be necessary in remediation?

    A. Educating the user

    B. Repairing damage from malware

    C. Re-enabling system restore

    D. Creating a restore point

2. Which of the following is a reason to use a clean boot environment in removing malware?

    A. It makes the computer run faster.

    B. It makes user education easier.

    C. It prevents reinfection.

    D. It helps prevent malware from interfering with removal.

3. When should you enable System Restore and create a restore point?

    A. Before removing malware

    B. Before scheduling scans and running updates

    C. After scheduling scans and running updates

    D. As the last step in the process

4. Determining that a system has probably been infected with malware is which step in the malware removal process?

    A. Step 7

    B. Step 2

    C. Step 3

    D. Step 1

5. After you have completed the seven-step malware remediation process, Windows will not start properly. What should be your next steps? (Choose two.)

    A. Boot into WinPE.

    B. Use WinRE.

    C. Boot into the anti-malware app.

    D. Repeat the seven-step process.

3.3 ANSWERS

1. **B**   Software can be damaged by malware, so repairing it may be a part of remediation on some systems.

2. **D**   Clean booting or booting from a USB or optical disc before running malware removal helps prevent malware from running and interfering with the removal process.

3. **C**   The restore point needs to remember the system configuration after it has been remediated and protected against threats.

4. **D**   Determining that a malware infection is present is included in Step 1: Investigate and verify malware symptoms.

5. **A B**   Boot into the Windows Preinstallation Environment (WinPE) and use the Windows Recovery Environment (WinRE) tools to recover the system.

Objective 3.4 Given a scenario, troubleshoot common mobile OS and application issues

Mobile operating systems (OSs) and applications have some issues in common with desktop and laptop OSs and applications, but because of how mobile devices work, some OS and application issues are unique. In this objective, you learn how to deal with them.

Common Symptoms

The following symptoms commonly plague mobile devices, operating systems, and applications. After each symptom is provided, you will also learn some typical solutions.

Application Fails to Launch

If a mobile device app is not loading, try these steps:

1. Start with a soft reset.

2. If the app still won't load, it may be incompatible with some combination of the mobile device's hardware, OS version, or vendor/carrier customizations to the OS.

3. Confirm the device meets the app's hardware requirements, including RAM, storage space, processor type, specific sensors or radios, required camera features, and so on.

Application Fails to Close/Crashes

Returning to the home screen on a mobile device doesn't stop the app you just left. The app may appear to close, in that it's no longer on the screen, but it continues to run in the background. There are also other situations where you attempt to close an app, but it just won't stop or it appears to stop but leaves associated services running in the background.

To close an app that fails to stop, the best remedy is to use *force stop*. Should an app crash, use force stop to stop any background services and then try starting the app again. To use force stop on different mobile device OSs, use the following steps.

Android:

1. Open Settings and choose Apps.

2. On the Apps list, select the app you wish to stop and use the Force Stop option to stop it or any background services. You can also use the Disable option to make the app unavailable.

iOS:

1. Open the App Switcher and swipe the display right or left to find the app.

2. Swipe up on the app to close it.

3. If this fails to close the app, restart the device.

Application/OS Fails to Update

Mobile devices are updated over wireless services typically. If a mobile device fails to update online, it can perhaps be updated by connecting it to another device and updating over a direct connection. For example, an iPhone or iPad that failed to update over a wireless connection can be connected to a macOS system with a Lightning or USB cable and updated with the iTunes app.

When an app fails to update itself automatically, typically the app rolls back to its previous, non-updated version and displays an alert that the update failed. The most likely cause for the failure is insufficient storage space, incompatibility with the device's OS, or a missing service now required by the app.

Slow to Respond

The general cause for a slow-performing mobile device is a lack of resources. This shortage could be caused by too many open apps or poorly constructed apps that use too much of one or more resources, but typically memory. In most situations, a restart of the device will cure the immediate problem, unless the same app or apps are started with the reboot.

Should the slow performance be a recent development, consider which app(s) has been added of late and discontinue its use or remove it from the system. Slow performance can be caused by too many apps running. Try closing running apps one at a time to try to identify which app may be the main culprit. Another approach is to install a system-monitoring app (yes, another app) to track and report resource utilization.

Other considerations include the following:

- A slow-performing mobile device often runs hot. However, a hot device could be using *thermal throttling* to protect its CPU. See if its performance improves as it cools.
- Performance issues can be caused by the storage space becoming full, which can make it inefficient. Free up some space and see if the performance improves.

- In most cases, a *system reset,* also known as a *soft reset,* will improve a system's performance. However, if the same apps or services are restarted, no gain will have been made. If this is the case, use an app-by-app approach to isolate the cause.

 EXAM TIP   Be aware of the symptoms a system reset can be used to resolve, such as apps not loading, slow performance, frozen system, and others.

Battery Life Issues

Modern mobile devices use Li-ion batteries, and it's important to manage them well to ensure the device lives a long life. Before good management can help, the user's power needs must be met. Know how long a given user's device needs to last on a charge and try to provide a device that can last at least 20 percent longer to account for dwindling capacity over the battery's lifetime.

Mobile devices are rated in terms of how long their battery should power them during "normal" use, how long the device can go between battery charges, and how much power the battery provides and needs to charge. Start with the device maker's numbers and follow up with benchmarks on mobile device review sites. If no devices meet the user's needs, make sure they have a removable battery and spares or a portable external battery recharger. You can plug a mobile device into a *portable battery recharger* (also called an *external battery, power pack,* or *portable charger*) to recharge.

There are two ways to think about battery life: how long it will last on each charge and how long the battery can meet your needs before you have to replace it. When you waste battery life on unused device features, you shorten both. Here's a list of power-hungry components with tips for managing them, but there's no need to guess; check your device's battery usage monitor (see Figure 3.4-1).

- **Display**   The fastest way to drain most modern mobile devices is leaving the screen on. Keep the display off when you can, and use the lowest acceptable brightness setting or automatic brightness. Other settings control how soon the screen turns off without input and whether notifications turn it on. Enable *power-saving modes*—some of which can even go grayscale. OLED displays, which use less power for darker colors, can reduce drain with black wallpapers and dark app themes.

- **Wireless communication**   Cellular voice, cellular data, Wi-Fi, Bluetooth, NFC, and so on all have a radio inside the device, and each draws power while enabled. Additionally, searching for a signal is expensive, and some apps will do more work when a radio is available. You may be able to dodge signal-search drain with settings to limit or disable device roaming and searching for new wireless networks. You can likewise restrict power drain from overeager apps with app or OS settings.

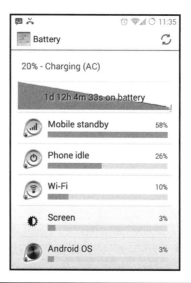

FIGURE 3.4-1   Battery usage display for an Android device

 EXAM TIP   Be sure to know how wireless connections can be turned off and affect battery life.

- **Location services**   The power drain caused by these services can vary widely between an app that occasionally checks low-accuracy location based on nearby cellular or Wi-Fi networks in the background and an app that constantly requests high-quality GPS updates. The simple solution is keeping location services off, unless needed, but you may find a happy medium with per-app restrictions. An app should prompt you to turn location services on when it needs them.

 EXAM TIP   Be familiar with the factors that can reduce battery power and battery life.

Randomly Reboots

Several issues can cause a mobile device to randomly restart itself. Although it may seem like this happens for no apparent reason, several technical issues can cause it. The following are the more common of these issues:

- **Bad app**   Perhaps the most common cause of random reboots is a bad app, meaning an app that is poorly constructed, overuses system resources, and is generally unreliable. While not in every case, e-mail and text messaging apps fall into this category. Some things you can do are switch to a more reliable app, uninstall apps you suspect or don't use, and make sure all apps are the latest revision or version.

- **Disabled services**   Sometimes system services are disabled by the user in an attempt to improve system performance. Review the turned off or disabled apps in the system settings for any services that are needed by the apps on the device.

- **Device overheating**   Most mobile devices will limit services or completely shut down if they are overheating. On a hot day, scale back on the brightness of the display, limit the use of 5G or 4G, and close any apps not really in use. You may want to check with the manufacturer of the device for known overheating issues.

- **Battery issues**   Devices with removeable batteries can experience the battery becoming slightly disconnected or not fitting tightly into the connectors. Sudden jolts or motion can cause the battery to disengage from the connectors and the system will shut down.

- **Malware**   Although at one time it was believed that mobile devices were essentially immune to viruses and malware, this is no longer the case. Install an anti-malware app to protect the system files.

- **Stuck buttons**   There are only a few mechanical features on most mobile devices, such as buttons, slides, and power switches, all of which can become stuck in their down position. Also, these are the entry ways for moisture, dirt, and other environmental threats.

Connectivity Issues

Connecting to a network is an area where there can be frequent problems. Connectivity issues on a mobile device can involve problems with connecting to Wi-Fi, Bluetooth, near-field communication (NFC), and other communication services. The first step is resolving the connectivity problems, which can be unique to the communication service in use. Then check for interference and configuration issues.

Bluetooth

The following are the primary reasons for Bluetooth connectivity issues:

- **Range**   Bluetooth devices are limited in range to about 30 feet.
- **Versions**   Bluetooth devices may have different versions that make them difficult to pair.
- **Power**   Bluetooth devices use a lot of power, and if sufficient power is not available on a device, it might not connect.

- **Enabled**   Bluetooth is a service that must be enabled on a mobile device and also configured for pairing.
- **Interference**   Wi-Fi and other RF devices emit radio frequency interference (RFI) that can impede a Bluetooth signal.

 **EXAM TIP**   Bluetooth range is about 10 meters, or 30 feet, which is less than Wi-Fi's range.

Wi-Fi

The biggest wireless connectivity problem for mobile devices is a weak signal caused by distance or interference. The symptoms are dropped connections, delays, slow transmission speeds, and frequent no-signal indicators. There's not much you can do on the device end except move. Cellular signal boosters exist, but they're best in a fixed, low-signal location.

Some tricky connectivity problems can occur despite a good signal:

- An *overloaded network* is common when large public events or emergencies cause a surge in network use, leaving users with a good signal unable to place calls, send texts, or transfer data.
- You may experience slow data speeds while roaming just because the carrier of the network you are roaming on limits data rates for nonsubscribers.
- Exceeding *data usage limits* your carrier sets can lead to slow data speeds, overage charges, or a hard data cap. To resolve this last problem, either pay your carrier to raise the data limits or monitor data use and disable cellular data (see Figure 3.4-2), as needed.

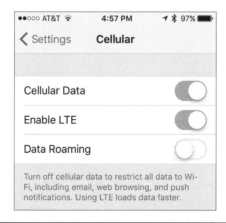

FIGURE 3.4-2   Option to disable cellular data in iOS

Symptoms depend on how the carrier handles the overage, so check these limits when dealing with unexplained good-signal connection problems.

If you have no cellular or Wi-Fi connectivity, regardless of your location relative to cell towers or Wi-Fi access points (APs), the problem might be with the mobile device itself: Airplane mode, when enabled, turns off all wireless connections. Airplane mode, developed originally to enable fliers with mobile devices to keep them on without interfering with navigation systems, can be easily triggered on some mobile devices.

To determine if your device is in Airplane mode, look at the status bar on your smartphone, tablet, or laptop for an airplane icon. To restore the connection, turn off Airplane mode and reconnect to a Wi-Fi AP (cellular reconnection is automatic).

Near-Field Communication

A *near-field communication (NFC)* connectivity issue typically occurs when a user is trying to use a payment or identity card to sign in or to make a payment on a contactless card reader. The most common problem is that the mobile device in use has not been unlocked, which enables NFC. To avoid NFC issues, verify the NFC sensor is enabled and that Airplane mode is disabled.

AirDrop

AirDrop is an Apple iOS feature that supports file transfers between an iOS device and a macOS device using a Bluetooth connection. AirDrop has a few rules for its use, though. The sender needs to be in the receiver's contacts, or the sender and receiver must both be configured to receive AirDrop transmissions from anyone/everyone.

 NOTE   Android has a feature that is similar to AirDrop called Nearby Share.

Screen Does Not Autorotate

Mobile devices, including smartphones, tablets, and most laptops and notebooks, have the built-in capability to rotate the display screen when the device is physically rotated 90 degrees in any direction. In effect, the rotation switches the view between portrait and landscape orientations. If the autorotation, as it's called, isn't working, there are a few possible causes for this: the autorotate feature is not enabled, the accelerometer sensor (called a G-sensor on Android devices) isn't working, an app or a finger is blocking the rotation, or the device just needs an update.

REVIEW

Objective 3.4: Given a scenario, troubleshoot mobile OS and application issues
Common symptoms of mobile OS and application issues include the following:

- Application fails to launch
- Application fails to close/crashes
- Application fails to update
- Slow to respond
- OS fails to update
- Battery life issues
- Randomly reboots
- Connectivity issues with Bluetooth, Wi-Fi, NFC, and AirDrop
- Screen does not autorotate

A common solution for some of these problems is a soft reset.

3.4 QUESTIONS

1. Which of the following issues can be helped by performing a soft reset of a mobile device?
    A. Extremely short battery life
    B. Slow performance
    C. Moisture
    D. Display too bright

2. Which of the following services, functions, or features can be used to stop an app or service running in background?
    A. Kill app
    B. Quit app
    C. Force stop
    D. Cancel app

3. A mobile device app is failing to update. Which of the following conditions could be the cause? (Choose all that apply.)
    A. Insufficient storage space
    B. Required service is missing
    C. Incompatible with device's OS
    D. Conflicts with competitor's app already installed

4. A client has brought a smartphone to you requesting help in determining the battery that should be installed in the device. You consider how the user will use the device and the amount of operating time required to come to the amount of power required. How much additional power should be added to your findings to cover the reduction in the power capacity over the battery's lifetime?

   A. 10 percent

   B. 20 percent

   C. 30 percent

   D. 50 percent

5. Your tablet PC cannot establish a connection with a Wi-Fi network. You have checked that the network is configured on the device and is within range for a connection. You are puzzled because you were able to make this connection before a recent airline trip. What should be your next action?

   A. Check the network adapter configuration

   B. Ping the gateway router

   C. Disable Airplane mode

   D. Reboot the system

3.4 ANSWERS

1. **B**   The performance of a mobile device may be improved by a system reset.

2. **C**   A force stop stops an app and any supporting services.

3. **A B C**   Any or all of these conditions could be the issue.

4. **B**   But more may be better in certain instances.

5. **C**   Most likely the Airplane mode is still enabled.

Objective 3.5   Given a scenario, troubleshoot common mobile OS and application security issues

With mobile devices becoming more and more common as primary computing devices, mobile operating system (OS) and application security issues are more important than ever. With the rise of BYOD (bring-your-own-device) policies, it can be harder than ever to keep mobile devices working securely.

Security Concerns

The following sections discuss common symptoms of mobile OS and application security issues and their corresponding solutions.

Android Package Source

Android apps are released in containers called *Android Package (APK)* files, which are *Java archive (JAR)* files in a ZIP file format. The folders and files in an APK file provide all of the components and elements required for an app to be installed, configured, and executed.

An Android system can be configured to allow APKs to be downloaded from third-party (and even untrusted) sites, a process called *sideloading*. Sideloading can weaken a device's security by installing untrusted and possibly unintended apps on the device. Android apps have a setting called "Install unknown apps," which, if enabled, allows apps to install apps (for example, a browser can install an app). A best practice for enterprises to prevent the installation of apps from untrusted stores and the use of sideloading is to use mobile device management (MDM) software.

Cross-Reference

For more information on MDM (mobile device management), see Objective 2.1 in Domain 2.

Developer Mode

Putting a mobile device into *developer mode* opens advanced configuration settings and diagnostic/log data files. Developer mode typically doesn't weaken the security configuration of a device, but it should only be used for app development or modification and remain disabled for the most part. The security risk of using developer mode is its possible misuse to install untrusted or bootleg apps. MDM systems can be used to block the interfaces with external devices with developer mode enabled.

Rooting/Jailbreaking

The Android OS runs on a Linux kernel, and access to its top-level (that is, its root) directory essentially gives a user access to the OS and all its components. Accessing the root directory of the OS is an exploit called *rooting*, which, if done, voids the warranty of the device by tripping an internal switch.

Virtually the same action on an iOS system is called *jailbreaking*. With an iOS device that has been jailbroken, a user can access the device's storage and its file system and get around the features that normally block downloading apps from untrusted/alternative stores or directly from the Internet.

Bootleg/Malicious Application

Virtually all legitimate, trusted, and official software is licensed either by its developer or by an official store, such as the Apple Store, Google Play, or the Microsoft Store. However, just like fake clothing, recordings, and other products that are sold with copies or facsimiles of a manufacturer's brand, labeling, or trademark, *bootleg software* apps can be found on the Web, especially on warez sites, which often carry pirated software, music, and more. The protection against installing a bootleg version of an app, which is likely full of malware, is to use only trusted or official app stores.

While a *malicious app* can also be a bootleg, there are malicious apps that are just plain malicious. A malicious app is strictly designed to do bad things. Most have the capabilities to evade detection, and most malicious app developers keep their apps up to date with security developments. Downloads from the Web or Internet are typically *application spoofing* (app spoofs) that can appear to be the desired app or feature but are anything but.

 EXAM TIP Know how to identify and avoid malicious apps and bootlegs.

Common Symptoms

Although anti-malware apps are available for the various mobile device OSs, their performance isn't always consistent or reliable. You should be the first line of defense by being aware of how your mobile device performs, which is generally altered by malware running on the device. The following list describes the symptoms to watch for:

- **High network traffic**   An unusually high level of network activity may be a symptom of malware. Bootleg apps are commonly Trojans that may run the app the user believed was downloaded, but its hidden parts are malware, such as spyware that's copying data and files and transmitting them to the attacker. A higher-than-normal network volume or high bandwidth utilization should be investigated. Data usage logs, high data transfer bills, and higher-than-normal data usage could be symptoms of a malware infection. Data usage apps can monitor how data is being used.

- **Sluggish response times**   Another symptom that malware is active on a mobile device and is actively gathering data in the background or is engaged in cryptomining is slower-than-normal response and performance times on the device.

- **Data-usage limit notifications**   Most mobile devices include an app for monitoring data usage that allows the user to set a threshold limit for the volume of data transferred up or down the network. When the amount of data usage reaches the limit, a notification is displayed. Data usage should be checked, including the data usage of each application, to spot irregularities.

- **Limited Internet connectivity/no Internet connectivity** Malware can corrupt a DNS server or search app into performing a redirection attack, which replaces the actual results with a spoofed site that redirects users to malicious sites or content. Legitimate sites can be modified to issue fake certificate warnings and typically cause slow network performance.

- **High number of ads** Freeware apps typically display ads as a means to remain free, and a higher number of ads being displayed isn't necessarily an indication of anything bad (other than the annoyance). However, if there is an unusually high number of ads, pop-ups (that are difficult to close), or changes in the personalization of your display that you didn't make yourself, it's likely that some form of malware is active.

- **Fake security warnings** The type of malware known as *scareware* attempts to trick users into downloading and installing a security, cleanup, or scanning app, which is likely to be a Trojan that the user is tricked into giving additional permissions.

- **Unexpected application behavior** An app introduced to the device as a bootleg, spoofed app, or Trojan may appear to be the game or app the user was expecting. However, in the background, it's a rootkit or spyware that is modifying, destroying, or gathering data and files from the device and sending them back to the attacker.

- **Leaked personal files/data** Leaked personal files and data pose a direct privacy or security risk resulting from an ongoing security issue and, in most cases, can provide clues as to what the issue may be. Whether the data is personal or corporate, the device(s) should be quarantined and scrubbed.

 EXAM TIP Be prepared for questions that describe one or more symptoms for problems on mobile devices.

REVIEW

Objective 3.5: Given a scenario, troubleshoot common mobile OS and application security issues This objective covered the following mobile device OS and application security issues you may encounter on the CompTIA A+ Core 2 (220-1102) exam:

- Android Package (APK) files contain the components required for an app to be installed and configured. Downloading an APK from an untrusted site is called sideloading.
- Developer mode opens advanced configuration settings and diagnostic/log data files.
- Root access (or rooting) may void the warranty of a mobile device.
- Jailbreaking allows a user to access iOS storage and bypass features that block downloading apps from untrusted sources.
- Bootleg software and malicious apps are likely full of malware.

The following may be symptoms of a mobile device being infected by malware:

- High network traffic
- Sluggish response times
- Data-usage limit notifications
- Limited Internet connectivity
- No Internet connectivity
- A high number of ads
- Fake security warnings
- Unexpected application behavior
- Leaked personal files/data

3.5 QUESTIONS

1. High resource utilization when no apps are open could be a sign of which of the following?
   - **A.** Dying battery
   - **B.** Malware
   - **C.** Airplane mode
   - **D.** GPS enabled

2. A client has discovered what appears to be a very advanced app that performs data analysis on a mobile device, but the APK must be downloaded from an untrusted site using a URL from a foreign country. If the client downloads this file, what action is being used?
   - **A.** Phishing
   - **B.** Sideloading
   - **C.** Jailbreaking
   - **D.** Rooting

3. What advanced configuration setting should only be used in the creation of apps and should not be routinely enabled?
   - **A.** Root access
   - **B.** Sideloading
   - **C.** AirDrop
   - **D.** Developer mode

4. Jane is experiencing extremely slow performance on her smartphone. She explains that this has just started about a week ago and just after she let her younger brother use her phone while she was busy. She suspects that he downloaded a game from an untrusted site. What tool can she use to verify her suspicions that the game was a Trojan and her phone is infected with malware? (Choose two.)

   A. Data usage monitor

   B. Anti-malware app

   C. Developer mode

   D. Troubleshooting app

5. The act of rooting (accessing the root of) a smartphone may have which of the following results?

   A. Releasing the actions of a rootkit

   B. Voiding the device's warranty

   C. Erasing certain apps

   D. Nothing

3.5 ANSWERS

1. **B**   Malware can use a lot of resources because it captures and sends data without the user's permission or knowledge.

2. **B**   Sideloading occurs when a system file is loaded from an untrusted site.

3. **D**   Developer mode opens several apps and files not usually available to a standard user.

4. **A B**   These tools can be used to detect and profile the actions of a malware infection.

5. **B**   Rooting can void a device's warranty.

Operational Procedures

DOMAIN
4.0

Objective 4.1 **Given a scenario, implement best practices associated with documentation and support systems information management**

Y̶ou should always document a service environment and include its logical, physical, and environmental elements. The documentation should identify and describe every asset that could be the subject of a service support action and serve as the record of how any issue is reported, diagnosed, and resolved. Documentation of any kind, whether formal system development documentation or service tickets, must be written clearly, concisely, and with the intention that someone else will be reading it. Even in the case of a one-technician shop, it is never guaranteed that the writer of the documentation will be the next one to read it.

Many networks and individual workstations don't have documentation at all. This objective helps you to understand the best practices needed to create accurate and useful documentation and how to manage it.

EXAM TIP   Be ready to compare, contrast, and implement best practices for the various types of documentation listed in this section.

Ticketing Systems

When a user makes a service request, they expect the request to be written down, tracked, acted upon, and the results of the service support actions recorded. These expectations describe the actions of a *ticketing system*. The complexity or sophistication of a ticketing system typically matches the size of the organization and the number of devices supported, but it can be whatever works. The key here is that the ticketing system must work.

Ticketing systems are used to support both internal or on-premises end-user devices and external or remote end-user devices. When an end user requests service or reports a problem, a ticket (aka a trouble ticket, service request ticket, maintenance call, and so on) is initiated. The pertinent information regarding the user request is recorded, which usually includes name, contact information, device ID, and a description of the problem. Depending on the reported issue, the ticket may be assigned to a category.

Categories

A *category*, and possibly a subcategory, is typically based on the severity or urgency of the reported problem and perhaps the type of device involved. Ticket categories are used for technician assignments as well as for tracking, reporting, and analysis. Common category types include the following, in no particular order:

- **Provisioning**   This category could include new user accounts, installs, setups, configurations of new hardware or software, and other routine tasks.
- **Incident**   This category may include failures, errors, or situations end users are unable to resolve themselves. Subcategories may be based on severity, urgency, or device type.
- **Problem**   This category records reports of incidents that need further investigation. These tickets are generated by the support staff.

Severity

An important element of a support ticket is the *severity* of the reported issue. A three-level severity scale typically provides enough information to determine the priority of a service ticket in relation to others. The severity scale has the following levels:

- **Critical**   These issues or incidents usually affect more than a single workstation and can impact more than one end user (for example, a network device failure, a possible data breach, or the results of a disaster).
- **Major**   These issues or incidents may have an effect on a limited number of end users or a specific group of end users or they may concern an in-house security event.
- **Minor**   These issues are typically not the result of an incident. Rather, they are problems that affect only a single end user and were reported as non-critical.

Severity can also be divided into impact and urgency to further indicate the priority of a reported service problem or incident.

Escalation Levels

Regardless of the service ticket's category, once a ticket is initiated, it must be acted upon and all the actions taken to troubleshoot, resolve, and test should be recorded. At each stage, the ticket must be managed and tracked by the owner(s), recording the who, what, when, and how and the processing steps for each issue. If the ticket is escalated (assigned to a higher authority or responsible agent), that must be recorded and tracked as well.

The specific issue on a problem report or trouble ticket cannot always be resolved by the initial reviewing agent or authority. In cases where the ticket needs to be referred to a higher level of authority or expertise, an escalation policy is required. This policy defines the authority levels or tiers designated to handle and resolve different reported issues. A successful trouble ticket program must be able to escalate a ticket as fast as possible.

A successful escalation plan should include the following elements:

- A definition of the issues that require escalation
- Documentation of the escalation of a ticket

- The tracking process of an escalated ticket
- An effort to keep ticket initiators informed
- Documentation of the resolution of the issue
- Tracking of the history of escalated tickets
- Ticket initiator feedback

Depending on the organization's size and the complexity of its systems, these elements may need to be expanded or reduced.

 EXAM TIP Be sure you understand the need, purpose, and objectives of an escalation process for trouble tickets.

Clear and Concise Written Communication

It has been said many times that the IT service field is more of a communication field than a technical field. When it comes to service support tracking, this statement could not be truer. A weakness of many standard service report forms is the inclusion of checkboxes, text boxes, or free-form text fields. These elements can give the impression that only a limited or short message can be or should be entered. A service report should fully explain the actions taken clearly and completely. Here are the three primary ticket fields that must be completed during the life cycle of a ticket:

- **Problem description**   This field must contain a full and detailed description of the problem that includes all of the information available as collected from the reporting party (commonly an end user).
- **Progress (notes)**   This field has multiple entries in many cases, but each entry must describe and report the troubleshooting, diagnostic, and testing performed to identify, verify, and isolate the reported or associated and subsequently discovered problems related to confirming the issue to be resolved.
- **Problem resolution**   This field describes the action plan to be used to resolve the issue, the progress and results of the action plan, the testing performed to verify the resolution applied, and the results of a full system test. An entry should also report the end user's acceptance as well as document any residual or lingering issues. If the resolution actions fail to resolve the issue, that fact should be recorded as well. If a new ticket should be issued, a reference to the new ticket needs to be recorded.

The fields of a service ticket require clear and concise language that is as technology-neutral as possible. *Clear* means using plain language that is devoid of jargon. *Concise* means the use of as few words as possible. The challenge for nearly everyone is to accomplish both goals.

Service tickets are likely to be reviewed, analyzed, and possibly sent to the end user who reported the issue. Anyone reviewing a service ticket, technical or not, should be able to understand the events in its lifecycle.

EXAM TIP   Be sure you understand the purpose and importance of using clear and concise language when completing a service ticket for the CompTIA A+ Core 2 exam.

Asset Management

The assets of an information system include all hardware, software, humans, and especially data involved in the information system's input processing, storage, and output processing—essentially everything. Asset management involves the cataloging, classifying, provisioning, maintaining, and retiring of the assets. Most assets are tangible, meaning physical and touchable, but many are intangible (such as software and software licenses, storable data, and intellectual property). Virtually all IT departments, along with the accounting departments, keep an *inventory list* of their assets.

Database Systems

Asset information is commonly stored in an *asset management database system,* which serves the needs of the IT department and the other departments of a business or organization. The information stored for an information system asset typically includes asset class (identification of accounting rules that apply, such as depreciation, leased, bought, and so on), asset type (hardware, software, intellectual property, and so on), manufacturer/source, model, serial number, inventory ID number, location or device ID, acquisition cost, acquisition date, end-of-life (EOL) date, and perhaps service history.

Cross-Reference

Objective 1.8 in Domain 1 provides more information on vendor lifecycle limitations and end-of-life (EOL).

For example, for a computer used as a server platform, the information could be something like class=A (that is, depreciable), type=hardware, source=Dell, model=PowerEdge T150, and so on. For software or intellectual property, the information might be class=B (that is, intangible), type=software, source=Microsoft, model=Server 2022, and so on. Field-replaceable units (FRUs) and peripheral devices, such as disk drives, power supplies, printers, and memory, would each have its own asset record.

Asset Tags and IDs

To properly track and account for a physical asset, the owner needs to assign it a unique identity. Most system components have a serial number that is intended to uniquely identify them.

However, there is very little uniformity between manufacturers for these numbers. Assigning an *asset ID* and associating it with an asset through an *asset tag*, sticker, or label provides a unique identity to the asset within a single organization.

Procurement Lifecycle

Another vital part of an asset's documentation is a schedule for the asset's procurement lifecycle. Physical assets are depreciated over time as a means to fund their eventual replacement. Software assets may have an expected end of life that can be planned for. At some point, either asset type will need to be retired, replaced, or deprecated. An asset's *procurement lifecycle* plan typically includes the procedures for requesting an improvement, upgrade, or replacement asset; the identity of a trusted supplier; and the budget for the replacement, if necessary, and procedures and methods of the various departments involved with the use, replacement, or disposal of the asset.

Warranty and Licensing

The records kept for an asset should include any documents or information pertaining to its warranty or licensing, which could include its original purchasing, invoicing, receiving, and installation records. Records for a software asset should include the licensing details and any seat allocations or usage limitations.

Assigned Users

Some assets, typically hardware assets (computers, mobile devices, telephones, and so on), can be assigned to a single person or department for specific use. Others may also be shared assets (used by all users). Examples include servers, network devices, and security software.

 EXAM TIP   You should understand the meaning and purpose of each of the topics covered in this section.

Types of Documents

The documentation of an organization's information system should include all or most of the preceding elements, but other types of documents can and in many cases should be a part of the documentation as well. These are described in the following sections.

Acceptable Use Policy

It's common for an enterprise or academic institution to require employees or students to sign or commit to an *acceptable use policy (AUP)*. An AUP defines the permissible actions users can perform, and those that they cannot perform, while using the equipment and systems of that authority, including its computers, phones, printers, and the network itself—and possibly more. Often this agreement is included in the login process to the systems.

EXAM TIP   You might see a question on an acceptable use policy. An organization's AUP defines what actions employees may or may not perform when using the organization's property.

The enforcement of an AUP protects the organization from the misuse of organization-owned equipment and systems. To reinforce the user's knowledge of the conditions of the AUP, often a digest of the policy's principal points is displayed on a "splash screen," which is the screen that displays as the login screen.

ADDITIONAL RESOURCES   The SANS Institute provides a boilerplate AUP at www.sans.org. Search for "Information Security Policy Templates" to find the link.

Network Topology Diagrams

A *network topology diagram* provides a visual guide to the hardware on the network, from routers and switches to workstations, printers, and wireless access points (WAPs). A simple diagram is useful for showing how the components connect and interact. More complex diagrams can provide connection types, speeds, and specific component brand/model information. Figure 4.1-1 illustrates a simple network diagram created with Microsoft Visio and Cisco network diagram icons.

Regulatory and Compliance Requirements

Larger organizations, such as government entities, benefit greatly from organizing their data according to its sensitivity and minimizing surprises by keeping computer hardware and software as uniform as possible. This also helps maintain *compliance* with government and internal regulations; common examples are rules on approved software and regulations on how you must handle *personally identifiable information (PII)* such as health or academic records. Templates for regulatory and compliance policies are widely available online.

Cross-Reference

Objective 4.4 provides more information on compliance with government regulations.

Incident Reports

Incident reports, aka after-action reports (AAR), are essentially documentation of lessons learned from an incident or event. An incident report solicits the input and opinions of users, customers, technicians, and stakeholders who are participants or interested parties of a service,

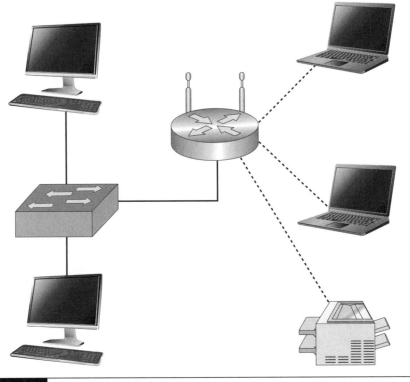

FIGURE 4.1-1 A simple network diagram

process, or product or the recipients of their outcomes. Incident reports are used to identify the underlying causes of an incident or event for use in developing preventive or remediation measures to avoid a repeat of the event.

EXAM TIP To track inventory items using wireless devices, RFID asset tags are the way to go. You may even see a question on this on the exam.

Cross-Reference

To learn more about the full scope of incident response and use of documentation, see the "Incident Response" section in Objective 4.6, later in this domain.

Standard Operating Procedures

In any company, the rules and restrictions for an employee to use a computer, network resource, and other related equipment is documented in a *standard operating procedure (SOP)*. An SOP is a written guideline on how an organization expects its employees and agents to perform tasks that are critical to the operation of the business. An SOP normally includes the following elements, among others:

- A statement defining the intent of the policy governing an action
- The action steps required to complete an activity in compliance with a policy

 EXAM TIP   Each IT process should be controlled by an SOP.

- Guidelines providing direction for policy areas for which no procedures exist or where it's necessary to deviate from standard procedures and procedures for the custom installation of software packages.

New-User Setup Checklists

A *new-user setup checklist* is an SOP that provides the official process or guideline steps for a new user to successfully complete a procedure necessary for a new employee to accomplish a required activity. Examples are a checklist for the onboarding of new employees for the human resources (HR) office, a computer/workstation setup checklist for the IT department, and how to establish secure credentials for logging in to the company network for new employees.

End-User Termination Checklists

End-user termination checklists are SOPs that detail the steps, privileges, and rights that must be revoked and deleted when an employee ends their employment with an organization. Essentially, end-user termination checklists are the reverse of new-user setup checklists in that they undo the assignments, rights, and privileges of the user.

Knowledge Base/Articles

A network topology diagram is just the beginning of your company's *knowledge base*—a collection of documents that identifies the equipment and software in use, problems detected, and solutions to those problems, along with links to vendors and third-party websites with relevant information.

Every time a technology-related event happens in an organization, there's an opportunity to build up your knowledge base. Ideally, an organization's knowledge base should start with pertinent documentation for each computer, component, and peripheral. In nearly every case for newer devices and components, this information is almost always available for download.

ADDITIONAL RESOURCES   If you need to identify the specific motherboard, CPU, GPU, and other components in a custom-built system, a number of free and commercial apps are available that can help, such as Belarc Advisor at https://www.belarc.com/products/belarc-advisor.

Add documentation for the operating systems and apps used, supplemented by third-party ebooks and patch and update information. To track down the information you need, make sure you have searchable PDF or ebook versions of your documentation.

Make sure you identify the device(s) or software affected, the theories that were discarded and the one theory that was accurate, how the solution/resolution was applied, and what has been implemented to avoid similar problems in the future.

To summarize, here's what your organization needs in its knowledge base:

- Official documentation, including patch and update information
- Third-party resources (websites, forums, ebooks)
- Documentation of the organization's own troubleshooting solutions

REVIEW

Objective 4.1: Given a scenario, implement best practices associated with documentation and support systems information management   The best practices for documentation and support systems information management covered in this objective of the CompTIA A+ Core 2 exam include the following:

- A ticketing system supports both internal end-user devices and remote end-user devices by tracking the information of a user service request.
- Depending on the issue, a ticket may be assigned to a category, based on the severity or urgency of the reported problem. Categories can include provisioning, incident, and problem resolution.
- Severity levels are important to a support ticket. The levels of a severity scale are critical, major, and minor. Severity can be divided into impact and urgency.
- Clear and concisely written communication is the key element of a service ticket.
- The assets of an information system include the hardware, software, humans, and data used in the input, processing, storage, and output phases of the information system's operations.
- Data is commonly stored in and accounted for in an asset management database.
- Acceptable use policies define the permissible actions users can and cannot perform on equipment and systems of a company or school.

- A network topology diagram provides a visual guide to the hardware on the network.
- Incident reports are the documentation of lessons learned from an incident or event.
- The rules and restrictions to guide the use of a computer, network resource, and other related equipment are documented in a standard operating procedure (SOP).
- A knowledge base is a collection of relevant information concerning an organization's systems, including compliance with regulatory requirements, splash screens, incident reports, new-user setups, end-user terminations, and installations of customer software.

4.1 QUESTIONS

1. At a minimum, a network topology diagram should record which of the following?
   A. Connections between network components such as routers, switches, and WAPs
   B. User names and accounts
   C. Routing details
   D. DHCP address ranges

2. You have been tasked with creating a knowledge base for the Windows-based equipment in your department. Some of the computers were hand-built by a computer shop, and you need to find out the motherboard, chipset, CPU, and RAM information. Which of the following will enable you to find the most information about each system?
   A. Contacting the computer shop
   B. Dismantling each custom-built PC
   C. Running a third-party system information app
   D. Viewing the System Properties dialog box

3. Which of the following is *not* likely to be covered in an acceptable use policy (AUP)?
   A. Password handling
   B. Keyboard lighting
   C. Using e-mail
   D. Personal print jobs

4. You are creating an asset tag design for your employer, which plans to use a handheld scanner as part of the company's inventory system. Which of the following must be on the asset tag?
   A. Company slogan
   B. Manufacturer's serial number
   C. Company logo
   D. Asset number

5. Which of the following should be in an organization's knowledge base? (Choose two.)

   A. Office floorplan

   B. Equipment inventory with descriptions and identification details

   C. Network topology diagram

   D. End-user login credentials

4.1 ANSWERS

1. **A**   A network topology diagram must record the network's physical layout. The other items are desirable to know but not essential.

2. **C**   A third-party system information app can provide much more information than the System Properties dialog box in Windows.

3. **B**   Keyboard lighting is a feature found mainly on gaming keyboards and some laptops and won't affect typical operations covered in an AUP.

4. **D**   The asset must be identified with a unique asset identification number.

5. **B C**   The network diagram and the installed equipment information are considered key operational knowledge.

 **Objective 4.2** **Explain basic change-management best practices**

"Change" is a frightening word to most organizations. Whether it's a change from one brand of computer to another, from an older Windows version to Windows 11, or from local to cloud-based apps, people are usually comfortable with the status quo and tend to resist change. Managing change helps ease the shock of the new and makes it easier for an organization to cope with the inevitable.

Change Management Best Practices

Change includes actions and activities that add, alter, or delete content, processes, or authorities from a standard operating procedure (SOP), guideline, policy, or documentation. The purpose for a change management policy is to ensure that the application of a change doesn't adversely impact the operation of an organization. Typically, changes are generated by a new service or product, process improvement, or correcting errors or mistakes in existing procedures.

Cross-Reference

For more information on SOPs, see Objective 4.1.

The change management best practices you should know and understand for the CompTIA A+ Core 2 exam are discussed in the sections that follow.

EXAM TIP   Be familiar with the actions and need for the documented business processes as well as the elements and actions of change management in the change management best practices included in this objective.

Documented Business Processes

A change to the infrastructure or processes of an organization is typically initiated from some form of a change request. This request may be in the form of a formal written document or a directive from upper management. In any case, the first step in a defined change control or change management procedure is determining which existing documented processes, procedures, or guidelines may be impacted by the as-yet-undefined scope of the requested change.

For example, a change request may propose a redesign of the existing disaster recovery plan (DRP), changing the process for taking backups, or just rewording an existing SOP. Regardless of the scope of the proposed change, the management process used should be consistently and completely applied.

Rollback Plan

Some people believe that a change always equals an improvement, but in the real world, changes don't always improve a situation. Having a *rollback plan,* sometimes referred to as a *backout plan,* is a change management best practice. Its purpose is to be able to return to the pre-change condition if needed.

Some parts of a rollback plan might include the following:

- Backing up the operating system, apps, and data before applying a change
- Using restore points, versioning, snapshots, or other options to capture the state of the system before and during changes.
- Creating a checklist of expectations for the change; if the change doesn't meet expectations, the checklist also needs to establish at what point changes should be backed out.

EXAM TIP   You should know and understand that the general purpose of a rollback plan is to provide an emergency fallback that restores a process or a system to its "last-known good" state.

Sandbox Testing

Before you fully implement a software or process change, it's always a best practice to test it fully before taking the change live. Procedural changes that are not software or automated processes can be tested with dry runs or scenario-based testing. However, relatively major hardware or software changes, especially those that alter the supporting procedures, should be tested in a safe environment, such as a sandbox.

A *sandbox* is a software testing environment that is isolated from a production operating environment. A sandbox is commonly a virtual machine (VM), a cloud Platform as a Service (PaaS) or Infrastructure as a Service (IaaS), or a cloned environment not connected to or interfaced with an organization's live production network. A sandbox provides for siloed execution of software as well as independent analysis and monitoring of test results.

 ADDITIONAL RESOURCES For an expanded definition of a sandbox, visit https://www.techopedia.com/definition/27681/sandbox-software-testing.

Responsible Staff Member

After sandbox testing, end-user testing, and the test results are approved, the next step is to implement the change. In addition to the planning that preceded it, implementation requires a detailed plan of its own. With an approved implementation plan in hand, a *responsible staff member* (aka a change coordinator or change manager) is appointed to manage and oversee its completion.

Change Management

Earlier in this objective, the phases of a change management project were listed and a few were discussed. In the following sections, the steps that constitute the general flow of a change project are discussed.

Request Forms

Change request forms have different names, including system modification requests, software change requests, and system revision requests. Regardless of whether it's a paper form or online web page form, a user fills it in to request a change to a system, process, or method. All formal change management programs begin with the submission of the data on the form.

A filled-out change request form seeks for a proposed procedure or process to be created, for modifications or additions to be made to an existing process, or for an existing process to be abandoned. The change request needs to provide the information described in the following sections.

Purpose of the Change

The obvious purpose of a change request is to request a change. However, the purpose statement provides the reasons or requirements (including the details of new laws, guidelines, or procedures) that make the change requested necessary.

Scope of the Change

In all forms of project management, including change management, it's necessary to define limits on what the requested change affects. Without a definitive scope statement, policies, procedures, and project tasks can experience "scope creep" or the gradual change in the boundaries and the areas affected by the change.

The scope statement on a change request should delineate as closely as possible exactly what is to be changed or affected by the change. For example, a change request to add a field to a form on a web page for the purpose of gathering data now required by law will also cause changes to the backend database, processing, and the interface to a credit card processor. This description would be the basis of the scope statement.

Date and Time of the Change

On occasion multiple changes can be made in a relatively short period of time, which can make the time element important to establish the sequencing of the actions. However, in most cases, the date of a change is most important to establish when a change was made.

Affected Systems Impact

The scope statement is typically the source of this information, as it defines the breadth and width of the requested change. In the *affected systems impact* statement, the external elements impacted by the change to the primary area, either directly or indirectly, are identified and the specific effect of the change is detailed. This statement provides a basis for a testing plan and perhaps a revised scope statement.

Risk Analysis

One of the criteria for whether a change request should be approved is that it must be proved that the change will not create a security risk. *Risk analysis* has two approaches: quantitative analysis and qualitative analysis. *Quantitative risk analysis,* a numerical measurement, focuses on the potential loss value for each area of the requested change. *Qualitative risk analysis,* a measure of a risk's characteristics, attempts to identify the likelihood of potential exploitations and the impact of any attack.

 ADDITIONAL RESOURCES   For more information on quantitative vs. qualitative analyses, access the article "Qualitative vs. Quantitative" at https://www.diffen.com/difference/Qualitative_vs_Quantitative.

The purpose of the risk analysis is to identify the *risk level* of proceeding with the requested change. The risk level can be specified as high, medium, or low. A high risk level doesn't necessarily kill the change request, but it should identify that those affected by the change be made to understand that additional security countermeasures may be required. Regardless of the risk level, risk analysis/assessment should be repeated at several points of the project.

Change Board Approvals

If the impact of a requested change is minor or routine, the change may be approved by a department supervisor or manager. However, a major change that has a broad impact must be scrutinized by a group or committee consisting of management, technical experts, and impacted stakeholders. This committee is typically called a *change advisory board (CAB)* or *change control board (CCB)*. The CAB's role is to analyze the technical benefits, disadvantages, and risks of a proposed change.

End-User Acceptance

A very important finalizing step of any change project is *end-user acceptance*. Gaining the acceptance of users who say that the old way was "just fine" or that "it worked before" can be difficult, as they resist adapting to the new process. Gaining end-user acceptance should be a formal phase of the implementation plan of a requested change. Here are three strategies for gaining the end-user acceptance:

- Include non-supervisory stakeholders on the CAB to represent the concerns and needs of the end users.
- Incorporate user acceptance testing (UAT) in the testing plan to allow end users to work with the post-change system in a sandbox environment.
- Conduct training for end users before the change is implemented.

REVIEW

Objective 4.2: Explain basic change-management best practices

- Elements of basic change management best practices include the following:
  - Identify the documented business processes affected.
  - State the purpose of the change.
  - Set the scope of the change.
  - Analyze the risk of making the change.
  - Plan for and test the change.
  - Achieve end-user acceptance.
  - Prepare a change board and gain approvals.
  - Develop a rollback plan.
  - Document the activities and results of each step.

- A change request may be in the form of a formal written document or a directive from upper management.
- A rollback plan addresses a return to the pre-change condition, if needed.
- Before a change is implemented, a best practice is to fully test it in a sandbox environment.
- Change request forms provide the following information: purpose of change, scope of change, impacts on affected systems, risk analysis, change board approvals, and end-user acceptance.
- Quantitative risk analysis focuses on the potential loss value of the requested change, and qualitative risk analysis identifies the likelihood and impact of an attack.
- Three strategies for gaining end-user acceptance are including stakeholders on the CAB, including UAT in the testing plan, and providing training for end users.

4.2 QUESTIONS

1. A rollback plan is used to perform which of the following tasks?
   A. Gaining change board approval
   B. Analyzing the effects of change
   C. Returning to pre-change conditions
   D. Aiding end-user acceptance.

2. Which of the following would be an action in a good change management policy?
   A. End users are introduced to a new technology without training.
   B. The change board is not consulted during the process.
   C. Rumors abound about the reasons for the change.
   D. Risk analysis is performed.

3. Six months after a software change was made in a department, you are asked to troubleshoot a problem. The only related information you can locate refers to the old software system. Which of the steps in change management was not performed?
   A. Document changes
   B. End-user acceptance
   C. Risk management
   D. Plan for change

4. Your organization is proposing a change that will have a big impact on its salespeople in the field. Which of the following steps is most likely to enable the field reps to provide input about the proposed change?
   A. Plan for change
   B. Risk management
   C. End-user acceptance
   D. Document changes

5. What individual should be appointed to manage and oversee the implementation plan's activities?

A. Programmer

B. IT manager

C. Change board member

D. Responsible staff member

4.2 ANSWERS

1. **C**   A rollback (backout) plan is designed to help an organization return to pre-change conditions if a change has an adverse impact.

2. **D**   Risk analysis is a necessary part of change management. The other choices, not so much.

3. **A**   Without documenting changes, the knowledge of what has changed will fade over time

4. **C**   End users and other stakeholders must have the opportunity to review proposed changes and how they may affect their tasks.

5. **D**   A responsible staff member should be appointed to oversee the implementation.

Objective 4.3 # Given a scenario, implement workstation backup and recovery methods

Often an A+ certified technician faces a situation where troubleshooting and repairing a hardware problem could result in the loss of the data stored on a user's system. Because user data is one of if not the most valuable assets of any computing system, you know that the data must be backed up to a restorable medium before you can begin working on a computer and its issues. This objective of the CompTIA A+ Core 2 (220-1102) exam discusses the importance, methods, and procedures that define backup, recovery, testing, and scheduling for data backups.

NOTE   This objective focuses on workstation backups, which don't typically include backup media rotation. In addition, the objective doesn't specifically mention Windows backup apps, which back up only a single device.

Backup and Recovery

Creating a system backup is a relatively easy and routine task. The purpose of a backup is to protect against the loss of the software, data, and other soft assets of a system due to some unforeseen event. Should a breach, catastrophe, or human error result in the loss of some or all of the software and data on a system, a backup provides a safety net that can be used to restore the system, at least to the point at which the backup was created.

 EXAM TIP   A backup protects against loss of data, and recovery enables a restoration of the backed-up data.

Backup Types

Two primary criteria are used to define a backup policy: frequency and retention. *Frequency* defines how often a backup is made (and typically the type of backup). *Retention* defines how long a backup is to be kept before it's destroyed or abandoned.

Most backups are created in sets that combine different levels of completeness. This means that a baseline backup is followed by a number of partial backups over a specific period of time.

Before we get too deep into the types of backups and when a file or folder is included in the different types of backups, let's look at the role of the *archive bit*. Files and folders have an attribute called an archive bit that flags whether or not it's a candidate for inclusion in a backup. Figure 4.3-1 shows the Advanced Attributes dialog box of a file with its archive bit (file attribute) indicating that it should be included in certain types of backups or archives

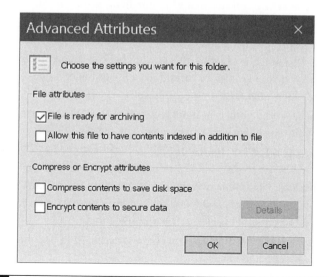

FIGURE 4.3-1   The Advanced Attributes dialog box of a file

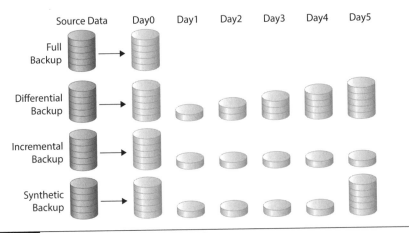

FIGURE 4.3-2 The four basic system backup plans.

(more on that later). Whenever a file or folder has been modified or perhaps replaced (using the same filename), the archive bit of the file (and its folder) are turned on. Figure 4.3-1 shows the file attribute "File is ready for archiving" is selected as a result of the archive bit being set on.

The following four primary backup models (illustrated in Figure 4.3-2) are used:

- **Full backup** This type of backup captures everything on a storage device and results in the backup being the same size (volume) as the source data (unless it's compressed and/or encrypted). A *full backup* requires the most space and takes the most time of any of the backup models. However, it also provides the simplest recovery process. A full backup also turns off the archive bit for all of the files or folders backed up.

- **Incremental backup** An *incremental backup* copies only those files and folders modified since the last full or incremental backup. For example, if a full backup is made on Friday, only files affected after the full backup (or an incremental backup) are included on the next incremental backup. As a file or folder is added to an incremental backup, its archive bit is turned off.

- **Differential backup** Only files modified or created since the last full backup are included in this type of backup. For example, any file modified or created since a full backup made on Sunday evening are archived. A differential backup doesn't reset the archive bit, so the size of the backup continues to grow until the next full backup.

- **Synthetic backup** This type of backup is essentially a full backup, but not quite. Whereas a full backup is made directly from an original data source, a synthetic backup is made from other backups. It works like this:

  1. A normal full incremental backup chain is executed to begin the synthetic backup process.

2. When the chain is to repeat, an additional incremental backup is made.

3. The synthetic full backup is then built from the normal full backup and the incremental backups.

4. The synthetic backup then becomes the full backup for the next cycle.

Remember that the purpose of a backup plan is to provide as complete a recovery as possible.

Recovery

Although you hope it never happens, a catastrophe, such as a lightning strike, hurricane, tornado, fire, flood, or earthquake, could occur. Therefore, a blueprint for recovering shelter, power, operations, and computer systems should be detailed in a disaster recovery plan (DRP). A proper DRP details the processes, steps, contacts to use, and the responsibilities of the members of the disaster recovery team.

The computer systems recovery part of a DRP identifies standby computers and devices to be used as well as the process to be used to restore the software and data to the system. The process used to restore the system depends on the scheme used to create the backup(s).

The DRP should also define two very important time and date designations:

- **Recovery point objective (RPO)** The RPO defines the maximum amount of data loss that can be tolerated without causing a serious impact on an organization's operations. In other words, how old can the backups be and still allow an organization to restart its operations successfully?

- **Recovery time objective (RTO)** The RTO designates the length of time allowed to restore the organization's operations. For example, for an online sales company that depends on its database, the RTO may be just a few hours, but for a document archive database, the RTO could be a few days or weeks.

Restoring from an Incremental Backup Scheme

Restoring the system from an incremental backup scheme uses the following steps:

- Restore the last reliable full backup. A full backup can be unreliable due to a variety of factors, including unnoticed failures to complete as well as portions of the backup sources being offline. A reliable backup has been tested for completeness and recoverability.

- Restore all incremental backups. An incremental backup captures only those resources modified since the last incremental backup. Therefore, restoring the system requires each of the incremental backups be individually restored to the required point of recovery designated in the DRP.

Restoring from a Differential Backup Scheme

Restoring the system from a differential backup scheme uses the following steps:

- Restore the last reliable full backup. This step is exactly the same as that used in the restoration of the full backup in an incremental scheme (see previous section).
- Restore the differential backup taken at the recovery point designed by the RPO and RTO in the DRP.

Restoring from a Synthetic Backup Scheme

Restoring the system from a synthetic full backup scheme involves two steps:

1. Restore the last synthetic full backup, assuming the recovery occurs after the first synthetic backup cycle.
2. Restore the incremental backups to reach the RPO.

Synthetic backups are full backups that simplify the restoration process.

Frequency

Frequency sets how often a backup is taken. Activity or volume is the driver of frequency. If a system experiences a high volume of activity, it most likely needs more frequent backups. However, a higher frequency typically means more backup capacity is required. Therefore, the type of backup and its frequency should be balanced out in any backup policy.

A commonly used plan sets the frequency and backup types with a full backup at the beginning of a time frame and then incremental or differential backups as frequently as needed. The frequency of the backups taken during the period between full backups directly impacts the recovery time and process should it become necessary.

 EXAM TIP Be sure you understand the importance of properly configuring and testing backup and recovery procedures.

Backup Retention

It's usually not necessary to keep backups of all data types for the same amount of time. A data retention policy defines the duration, storage, and disposal requirements for each different type of data.

Data retention policies are governed by two primary criteria: laws/regulations and the owner's specific needs (typically, the recovery point). In most cases, the law and needs apply to only specific types or classes of data. Each data class is defined by external forces (the law) or internal forces (operational needs). External data may be product, service, purchasing, shipping, and disposal records. Internal data is more commonly operational in nature, such as personnel, inventory, sales, and the like. External data is kept for reporting, and internal data is kept for reference, but primarily for recovery.

However, the most important aspects of a data retention plan define how long each class of data is kept, where it's kept, how it's kept, and when it no longer needs to be kept. External data may have specific requirements for each of these criteria. Internal data retention policies are strictly up to the organization.

 ADDITIONAL RESOURCES   A good general description of what is included in a data retention plan is available at https://bigid.com/blog/data-retention/.

Backup Testing

Whatever backup scheme is chosen for use, before it's actually used in a security or disaster recovery plan, it must be tested to verify that it's reliable and will provide the required data should it be needed. A test plan for a backup scheme should include the following:

- Restoring a sampling of different types of data from a full backup into a test folder/directory to avoid overwriting production data. A good choice for this testing is a virtual machine.
- A feature common to most backup and restore schemes is verification that uses hashing to confirm that the copy (to or from the backup media) is valid.
- Verification that the backup/restoration contains the expected files.

A backup program should include a definitive schedule of testing, typically by data class or type. Critical data should be tested more frequently than less important data. The standard rule of thumb is that the backup plan should be tested every six to nine months.

 EXAM TIP   For the A+ Core 2 exam, be sure you understand backup plans and the processes used to restore the various backup schemes, including how to test the restore process.

Backup Rotation Schemes

A backup policy must also include a *backup rotation plan* in which older backup media can be reused after its retention period has expired. Backup rotation addresses the use and reuse of the backup media as much as it does the data it holds. In situations where the data itself requires a longer retention period than the rotation of the media, synthetic backups may be used to consolidate the required data onto a medium that is not in the rotation. Certain accounting and recordkeeping points may also require a backup medium to be excluded from a rotation plan.

A few different backup rotation schemes are generally used, but the most widely used is the *grandfather-father-son (GFS)* scheme. The GFS rotation is based on the age (or sequence) of the backup media, meaning the oldest to the newest. GFS designates the backup media (usually removeable media) as grandfather (the oldest), father (second oldest/newest), and son (newest). Here is an example of the GFS rotation, assuming all backups require only a single volume:

1. A full backup is made every week, typically on Sunday evening, and labeled as "Father." In some months, there can be five fathers.

2. Incremental backups are made during the following week to the same tape, disk, or cloud medium. It is labeled as "Son."

3. A full backup is made on the last calendar date of each month to the medium labeled as "Grandfather."

Therefore, in terms of the number of the medium units required, you have four or five fathers, one son, and 12 grandfathers. The fathers and sons are reused in the following weeks and days, respectively. Depending on the business, certain grandfathers may need to be retained, such as those at the end of a quarter, half year, or year. Otherwise, the first grandfather of a previous year is overwritten to be the first grandfather of the next year.

Another backup rotation scheme is the 3-2-1 rule, which is designed to provide a better safeguard against disasters or catastrophic failures. In simple terms, 3-2-1 requires three copies of production and backed-up data, on two different media, with one copy of the current backup stored offline and offsite.

Onsite storage means that that the production system and the backed-up data are stored in the same place, typically the data center. Obviously this means there is a real chance of losing both in the same event. *Offsite storage* (not to include cloud storage) means that the current father and son are stored outside of the building in a secured and environmentally safe facility that can be easily and quickly accessed.

An online backup, typically on a cloud Backup as a Service (BaaS) provider, is a convenient way to store backups, regardless of the rotation or retention scheme in use. However, the cloud still has a few issues to overcome before it can be considered failsafe, so it's a best practice to also keep physical media copies.

 EXAM TIP Be sure you know the differences between onsite and offsite storage, GFS, and the 3-2-1 backup rule. Backups, recovery, testing, and backup rotation schemes are often targeted on the exam!

REVIEW

Objective 4.3: Given a scenario, implement workstation backup and recovery methods

The key points in this objective are the following:

- A backup protects against the loss of software, data, and other soft assets in an unforeseen event.
- A backup plan focuses on two primary policies: frequency and retention.
- An archive bit indicates files and folders that are candidates for backup.
- The backup models you can expect to see on the CompTIA A+ Core 2 exam are full, incremental, differential, and synthetic.
- A backup chain is a scheduled sequence of backups over a specific time period.
- Frequency sets how often a backup is taken.
- A data retention policy defines the duration, storage, and disposal requirements for different types of data based on laws/regulations and the owner's specific needs.
- External data is kept for reporting purposes, and internal data is operational or administrative.
- A backup scheme must be tested and verified for reliability and integrity.
- A backup rotation plan addresses the use/reuse of backup media.
- The two primary backup rotation schemes are grandfather-father-son (GFS) and the 3-2-1 rule.
- Onsite storage means the production system and the backed-up data are stored in the same place, and offsite storage houses backup data outside of the building in a secured facility.
- An online backup is convenient but may have security issues.

4.3 QUESTIONS

1. You are developing a data backup policy and know that there are two areas the policy must address. Which of the following are the key elements of a data backup policy? (Choose two.)

   A. Storage space

   B. Frequency

   C. Type of media

   D. Retention

2. Which of the following is *not* one of the four backup types discussed in this objective?
   A. Differential
   B. Incremental
   C. Synthetic
   D. Full
   E. Selective

3. Which of the following are backup rotation schemes? (Choose two.)
   A. 3-2-1
   B. Oldest-old-younger
   C. Yearly-monthly-daily
   D. Grandfather-father-son

4. What is the attribute of a file or folder that flags it as a candidate for inclusion in a backup?
   A. Permissions
   B. Sharing
   C. Archive
   D. Modification

5. A data retention policy should address, when applicable, which of the following characteristics and actions?
   A. Duration
   B. Retention
   C. Law
   D. Company needs
   E. All of the above
   F. None of the above

4.3 ANSWERS

1. **B D**   A backup policy should be based on frequency and retention.

2. **E**   A selective backup is typically created as merely a copy of certain files or folders.

3. **A D**   Both 3-2-1 and GFS are commonly used rotation schemes.

4. **C**   The archive attribute (bit) flags a file as being a candidate for backup.

5. **E**   The items in answers A through D are all factors that determine a backup policy, thus making answer E the best choice.

Given a scenario, use common safety procedures

S afety is of paramount importance when working as an IT tech. You need to protect yourself and others from the dangers of high-voltage equipment, toxic materials, and workplace hazards. You also need to protect valuable equipment from electrostatic discharge and other environmental risks. Use this objective to learn the basic safety procedures you need to follow to go home safely after a long day in the IT trenches.

Electrostatic Discharge Straps

Electrostatic discharge (ESD) occurs only when two objects that store different amounts (or *potentials*) of static electricity come into contact. *ESD straps,* commonly known as *antistatic wrist and ankle straps,* avoid ESD by keeping you at the same relative electrical ground level as the computer components on which you're working. An ESD strap consists of a wire that connects on one end to an alligator clip and on the other end to a small metal plate that secures to your wrist (or ankle) with an elastic strap. You snap the alligator clip onto any handy metal part of the computer and place the wrist strap directly on either wrist (but not over a shirt sleeve). Figure 4.4-1 shows an antistatic wrist strap grounded to a computer chassis. Other types of ESD straps have a prong that you plug into the ground wire of an electrical wall outlet.

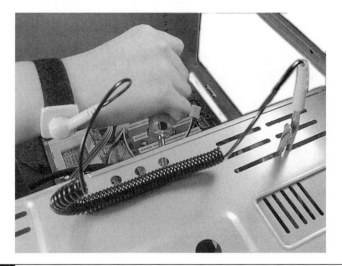

FIGURE 4.4-1   An antistatic wrist strap grounded to a computer

CAUTION   Antistatic wrist (and ankle) straps use a 1-megohm resistor that is suitable for protection against only very low-level static electricity. They are unsuitable as protection against high voltage and can even make high-voltage shocks more dangerous! Make sure you always remove your antistatic strap before you work on or near high-voltage components.

By the way, don't forget to remove your antistatic strap (or at least detach it from the computer) before walking away from your work area!

Electrostatic Discharge Mats

Portable antistatic mats (see Figure 4.4-2) provide a work surface that dissipates ESD. They have a small metal clip that you can attach to an antistatic strap to ground out ESD. In addition to helping prevent ESD, these mats help keep your work area organized by giving you a place to put your tools and components while you work.

Antistatic floor mats are basically the same as portable antistatic mats, except much larger. Instead of placing them on top of your work area, you place them on the floor and stand on them while you work.

Self-Grounding

One of the most important steps you can take to prevent the effects of ESD is to ground yourself before you handle computer components. Self-grounding is accomplished by touching a metal surface, such as the exterior of the power supply, before touching any of your system components.

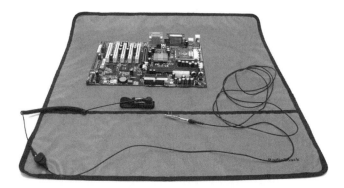

FIGURE 4.4-2   A typical ESD kit contains a mat and an ESD bracelet.

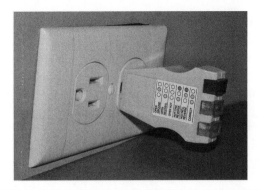

FIGURE 4.4-3   An AC outlet tester indicating the outlet is wired properly

Equipment Grounding

Any AC-powered equipment that uses a three-prong cable (hot, neutral, ground) needs to be properly grounded. Surge suppression depends on having a working ground as a safe place to send power surges.

Unfortunately, some three-wire plugs are improperly wired or have no ground at all. To determine which outlets are working and which have wiring faults, use an outlet tester such as the one shown in Figure 4.4-3. Some surge suppressors also feature wiring fault testing in their circuitry.

Proper Power Handling

Power handling (or *power management,* if you prefer) deals with the uptime for a system and conserving electrical power. A few best practices can be used toward accomplishing both goals, including the following:

- Install quality uninterruptable power supply (UPS) units. A UPS provides electrical power as a battery backup and a stored power source, and some can also block power surges or undervoltage events (brownouts). A rule of thumb is that all servers and internetworking devices should be connected to a UPS.
- Surge protector plug strips aren't adequate for network devices but can provide some protection for a desktop or laptop computer in most cases.
- Take advantage of power-saving apps available from the OS or trusted third-party vendors.

These items must be tailored to the specific systems and power sources they are protecting.

Power-Handling Apps

Power-handling apps (or as they are also known, *power management apps*) provide users with the ability to reduce, increase, or turn on or off power to all or selected hardware on a PC. Many of these apps can also be used to define a power-saving policy that the app uses to automatically handle or manage which devices are powered and at what power level.

Power-saving apps provide the capability to save power when a PC is on and to extend the life of the battery on mobile devices. These apps interact with the OS to apply the different levels of the Advanced Configuration and Power Interface (ACPI), which interfaces with a system's BIOS or UEFI, hardware devices, and the OS hardware and power interactions.

 ADDITIONAL RESOURCES   For more information on ACPI and its modes and codes, read the article "ACPI X64-Based PC Definition & Explanation" at https://computerzilla.com/acpi-x64-based-pc-explained.

Windows Power Options

Windows 10/11 is protected from power issues through the Power & Sleep settings and the Power Options settings, which are used to choose the specific timing of power actions and the power plans in use on a system.

The Power & Sleep settings (see Figure 4.4-4) provide a user with the capability to control when the display and the computer are to be placed in Sleep mode when plugged in (AC power) or on battery power. The Power & Sleep settings are accessed from the Settings app and the System option.

The Choose or Customize a Power Plan settings (aka power plan options), shown in Figure 4.4-5, allow a user to employ a standard power plan (options) or to define a custom plan. Windows 10 has three power plans available by default: Balanced, High Performance, and Power Saver. This option is accessed by going to the Control Panel and choosing Hardware and Sound.

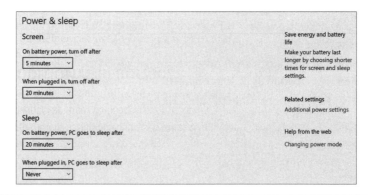

FIGURE 4.4-4   The Power & Sleep settings page

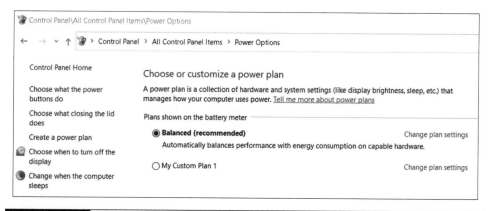

FIGURE 4.4-5   The Choose or Customize a Power Plan page

macOS Power Options

A macOS system provides the Power Manager app for lowing its power consumption and operating costs. The Power Manager enables/disables three basic power plans: Balanced, High Performance, and Power Saver. Although they have the same names as the Windows power plans, they are a bit different. The Power Manager can be used to set when a Mac computer can be turned on and when it is to be powered down.

Proper Component Handling and Storage

Even when your computer is not in use, environmental elements such as heat, moisture, and dust are still hazards. Heat causes plastics to fade and become brittle. Moisture can cause rust, corrosion, and electrical shorts. Dust (and dirt) can build up to clog the cooling system, which can cause overheating and electrical shorts. For these reasons, and several others, computer components and peripheral devices, inside and outside of the computer case, should be stored in a cool, dry location, preferably indoors in a climate-controlled environment.

Beyond environmental hazards, the improper handling of a computer and its electronic components is another threat that can cause some serious damage—damage that is caused by you! You may have protected the computer against heat, rust, and dust, but handling components improperly can cause even greater damage. Understand that the storage and handling of a computer's parts usually is an issue during repair activities. Components are removed and stored for relatively short periods of time. If the removed components (and those that remain installed) aren't properly protected, they could be damaged beyond use, meaning new ones must be obtained for reassembly.

Human-based component failures can be caused by pulling on wires and cables too hard; pulling chips, modules, and expansion cards improperly; not cleaning the chassis inside and out; not being careful inside the case with liquids and static-inducing vacuums; overbending cables and ribbons; and more.

Electrostatic Discharge

Another major hazard to a computer and its components is virtually everywhere: *electro-static discharge (ESD)*. An example of ESD is that slight shock you get when touching a door knob after walking on carpet. Keep in mind that ESD can damage a computer component or circuit with only 10 volts, yet a human won't even feel ESD of less than 3000 volts. The Electrostatic Discharge Association (www.esd.org) states that "ESD is the leading cause of failures in integrated circuits." Therefore, it is something to avoid and protect against when working on or with a computer. Some ESD-protective devices were discussed earlier in this objective, but here are some basic practices you can use to reduce the risk of ESD damage:

- **Don't wear synthetic clothing**   Wear natural fibers, like cotton, bamboo, and linen, but not wool or silk.
- **Protect components**   Keep removed or loose components in protective materials until they are ready for installation.
- **Ground yourself**   Use protective devices, such as ESD straps, mats, and work surfaces. Ground yourself on the metal chassis of the computer case regularly or a grounded metal object in the workspace, such as an iron radiator.
- **Don't touch connectors**   Avoid touching the connector legs and pins on RAM modules, sound and video cards, and especially CPUs. The oil from your fingers can cause connection problems.

The use of antistatic devices is a best practice to protect the system from ESD damage. These devices are discussed in the next section.

Antistatic Bags

Antistatic bags have a special coating or contain small filaments that help dissipate any static charge. Always store expansion cards, storage devices, and any other internal component in antistatic bags when they've been removed or when they're being transported, no matter how far they are moved. Antistatic bags dissipate charge most effectively when they're closed, so it's a good idea to fold the end over and tape it down with an antistatic sticker if possible.

 **EXAM TIP**   The safest way to store any electrical component is in—not on—an antistatic bag.

Do not place loose and unprotected components on top of an antistatic bag. In an antistatic bag, the static charge is directed from the inside of the bag to the outside. Note that regular plastic or paper bags do *not* protect electronic components. In fact, a plastic bag conducts static electricity, so don't use one!

Compliance with Government Regulations

Be sure to follow applicable OSHA (Occupational Safety and Health Administration) and other safety regulations when building, repairing, cleaning, or dismantling equipment. These regulations might address ventilation, protection against dust, cable management, and other issues. Proper compliance with government regulations is essential.

Personal Safety

Whoever told you that IT is a "desk job" didn't know very much about the actual work of an IT technician. In the course of a typical day, you might find yourself under a desk wrestling with stubborn wiring, plunging into the guts of a malfunctioning PC, cleaning out a computer that looks like the inside of a wet-dry vacuum, or fighting an electrical fire! The following sections detail how to stay safe at work.

Disconnect Power Before Repairing a PC

In the old days, the conventional thinking was that you should leave the computer plugged in while working inside it to ensure electrical grounding. The opposite is true for modern computers, because modern motherboards always have a small amount of voltage running any time the system is plugged in, even if it's not running. Therefore, you should completely unplug the system before servicing it or you'll likely toast something!

Unplugging power supplies does not make them safe enough to work on. The capacitors inside can hold a dangerous electrical charge even when the unit is unplugged, making power supplies extremely risky to open. As the label says, "No serviceable components inside." With that in mind, the safest method of repairing power supplies is not to repair them at all. It's better to dispose of them properly and install a brand-new power supply (see Figure 4.4-6).

FIGURE 4.4-6   Typical warning on the label for a computer power supply

CAUTION   As electricians will tell you, it's amperage (the amount of electricity) that's dangerous, not voltage. Power supplies have relatively low voltages but high amperage. It's not worth the risk for you to attempt to service a power supply.

Lifting Techniques

It seems that everything we use—computers, printers, monitors—comes to us in heavy boxes. Remember never to lift with your back; lift with your legs, and always use a hand truck if one's available. If the box says, "team lift," remember you are not a team of one—get some help! You are never paid enough to risk your own health.

Weight limitations also apply to yourself, carts, and other moving equipment. Take a look at the gross weight on a package or look up the weight of an unboxed device. If it's beyond your comfort zone, get help. Pay attention to weight limitations on the devices you use to move anything heavy. Also pay attention to weight limitations when wall-mounting monitors. Even relatively light LCD monitors require a mounting arm strong enough to support them.

Electrical Fire Safety

Thankfully, the risk of fire occurring inside your computer is relatively low. If you do experience a computer fire, however, or any electrical fire for that matter, never try to extinguish it with water. This can cause the electrical current to travel up and straight into you! Instead, use a fire extinguisher certified for fighting electrical fires. These are Class C and Class ABC fire extinguishers (see Figure 4.4-7).

FIGURE 4.4-7   A typical fire extinguisher. Be sure to read the label before using!

EXAM TIP You need to use a Class C or Class ABC fire extinguisher to put out a computer fire.

Safety Goggles

If you need to cut a bit of aluminum to rig up a part for an old PC or use compressed air or a vacuum cleaner to clean out an old PC, put on safety goggles. A bit of dust can be an irritant, but a tiny shard of metal can damage your eyesight.

Air Filtration Mask

You need to protect yourself (and your coworkers) from dust and debris when servicing, storing, or disposing of equipment. Everyone in the work area should wear an air filter mask that is designed to handle appropriate environmental risks.

EXAM TIP Although the CompTIA A+ 220-1102 exam doesn't deal with specific requirements for air filter masks and safety goggles, be aware of the circumstances for which they should be worn.

REVIEW

Objective 4.4: Given a scenario, use common safety procedures Here are the common safety procedures, purposes, and applications you should know for the CompTIA A+ Core 2 exam:

- Electrostatic discharge (ESD) straps
- ESD mats
- Equipment grounding
- Proper power handling
- Proper component handling and storage
- Antistatic bags
- Compliance with government regulations
- Personal safety:
  - Disconnect power before repairing a PC
  - Lifting techniques
  - Electrical fire safety
  - Safety goggles
  - Air filtration mask

4.4 QUESTIONS

1. An electrical fire has broken out in an old laser printer. Which of the following should be used to put out the fire?

    A. Class A fire extinguisher

    B. Water

    C. Class ABC fire extinguisher

    D. Sprinkler system

2. Which of the following is an electric AC device that must be properly grounded so that it has a safe place to send power surges?

    A. A surge suppression device with three-prong AC connections

    B. A non-suppression device with two-prong AC connections

    C. A non-suppression device with three-prong DC connections

    D. A surge suppression device with three-prong DC connections

3. Which of the following is not recommended before working on a PC?

    A. Disconnecting the power supply from the AC outlet

    B. Using an ESD strap

    C. Using an ESD mat

    D. Working inside the computer case with the power on

4. You are walking through a work area where computers and components are being prepared for storage. You notice that a network interface card has been placed on top of an antistatic bag. What should you do?

    A. Connect an ESD strap to the bag.

    B. Move the card to a piece of paper.

    C. Place the card inside the bag after self-grounding.

    D. Nothing; it's okay to use an antistatic bag this way.

5. A coworker has injured his back while carrying new computers still in their "team lift" shipping cartons into the offices where they will be installed. He was observed picking up the boxes by bending at the waist and standing up. What should he have done to try to prevent injury?

    A. Carry the cartons on his back.

    B. Stoop down with bended knees and lift with his legs.

    C. Get help for team-lift cartons.

    D. Use a mechanical lift only.

4.4 ANSWERS

1. **C**   An electrical fire is a Class C fire, so a Class ABC fire extinguisher is the best choice.

2. **A**   A three-prong AC surge suppressor provides "earthing" to protect the electrical connection.

3. **D**   Working inside the computer case with the power on is a recipe for disaster. Always power down the system and unplug the power before working on the system.

4. **C**   The ESD bag can only protect a NIC placed inside it.

5. **C**   Team lift requires two or more persons.

Objective 4.5 **Summarize environmental impacts and local environmental controls**

Environmental impacts are the result of any changes in the environment, such as heat, humidity, and lightning, that can affect computer equipment, or they can be the result of servicing, using, or disposing of technology. This objective covers the details of how to have minimal environmental impact when using technology.

Material Safety Data Sheet/Documentation for Handling and Disposal

All batteries, chemicals, and other hazardous materials should come with a *material safety data sheet (MSDS)* that identifies any safety issues and warnings about the product in general, safe methods of transporting and handling the product, and safe disposal requirements and methods. If you have any doubts or questions about how to handle or dispose of chemicals or compounds, check the applicable MSDS. If the MSDS for a product or substance is missing, you can obtain a copy from the manufacturer or locate it on the Internet.

ADDITIONAL RESOURCES   For more information about MSDSs, go to www.osha.gov and search for "OSHA 3514." To search for a specific MSDS, visit www.msds.com.

NOTE   Although CompTIA continues to reference material safety data sheets, they are now referred to as just safety data sheets (SDSs).

Proper Battery Disposal

Computer batteries vary from small units in many handheld mobile devices and desktops to larger batteries in laptops and notebooks. The primary purposes of computer batteries are to provide a power source to a computer's internal components when the AC power is turned off and/or to be the power source for mobile devices when not connected to AC power. However, a battery can only power a device for a relatively short time before it must be recharged or replaced. The type of battery in use, meaning whether it can be recharged or not, can create a *disposal* problem. Batteries should be disposed of properly because they contain precious metals, which can be recycled or destroyed to extract the rare earth minerals they contain.

The basic types of computer batteries are primary (non-rechargeable) and secondary (rechargeable). A *primary battery* is used once, and after its charge is consumed, it's disposed of, which is the area of concern for the CompTIA A+ Core 2 exam. The most common primary batteries used in computers are alkaline. An alkaline battery is available from nearly all sales outlets in a variety of sizes: AA, AAA, C, D, 9-volt, and coin cell (button) sizes. Since 1997, these batteries can be disposed of as normal trash because they aren't classed as a toxic threat by the Environmental Protection Agency (EPA) in the United States. Some U.S. states have their own disposal regulations, though.

A *secondary battery* can be recharged a certain number of times, which varies by type.

- **Nickel-Cadmium (Ni-Cad)**   This type of battery is available in most of the same sizes as primary batteries. Ni-Cad batteries must be recharged frequently. Ni-Cad batteries require special disposal methods, as they contain toxic materials that are a threat to human health and the environment.

- **Lithium Ion (Li-Ion)/Lithium Ion Polymer**   While not without their dangers (such as fire or explosion), Li-Ion batteries are perhaps the best battery available for computing devices. A Li-Ion battery that can no longer be recharged or is damaged should be taken to a recycle service for disposal.

Proper Toner Disposal

An empty or damaged laser printer or copier *toner cartridge* cannot just be thrown out. Not only do they add more plastic to the environment, but they contain toner, which is mostly super-fine powdered plastic dust. Toner dust can stain or contaminate just about anything it touches, including clothes, carpets, and skin. While stains are annoying, they really aren't a health hazard. However, toner does have some health risks.

In spite of what was believed in the past, toner isn't near the cancer-causing debilitating hazard of legend. Although toner does pose a health risk, that risk is primarily in the form of eye and skin irritations, which are typically temporary and mild.

In addition to plastic, toner also contains polypropylene wax (easily melted and absorbed), carbon black (because the polymer plastics are clear), pigment colors (yellow, red, and blue), fumed silica (glass beads to aid the flow of melted materials), charge control agents (to reduce triboelectrification, aka static cling), and a couple of other materials. These elements, like toner on the whole, are not life-threatening hazards.

The best practice for disposing of toner cartridges, which are never completely empty, is recycling. They can be dropped off at a retailer, placed in special envelopes and mailed to the manufacturer or recycler, or given to a nonprofit agency for recycling.

Proper Disposal of Other Devices and Assets

Many of the components of a mobile device or desktop device, such as the motherboards and display screens, contain toxins and heavy metals. Heavy metals are metallic minerals, such as lead, mercury, arsenic, chromium, silver, and cadmium, all of which are toxic to humans and may cause physical, muscular, and neurological degeneration.

Heavy metals are found in batteries, circuit boards, and plastics. Of course, heavy metals should not be thrown out as everyday trash in a landfill or an incinerator and should be disposed of by an approved waste management or recycling facility.

ADDITIONAL RESOURCES For information on donating or recycling computer electronics, go to the EPA's Electronics Donation and Recycling web page (https://www.epa.gov/recycle/electronics-donation-and-recycling).

EXAM TIP Be sure you understand the purpose and content of an MSDS on the handling and disposal of batteries, toner, and other computer-related devices, especially electronics.

Temperature, Humidity-Level Awareness, and Proper Ventilation

Good techs keep up with weather conditions. The temperature and humidity level outside can dramatically affect the conditions inside. If the weather is cold and dry, the potential for a computer-killing ESD zap is greatly increased. Take extra precautions to prevent ESD when the weather calls for it.

Location/Equipment Placement

Where electronic or computing equipment is located in a facility can make a huge difference in its lifespan and its smooth operations. *Proper environmental controls* can help to secure servers and workstations from environmental impacts, especially those from excessive heat, dust, and humidity. Air conditioning, proper ventilation, air filtration, and heat temperature and humidity monitors, among others, should be properly balanced for the device or its location to prevent issues. An awareness of these conditions allows a CompTIA A+ technician to maintain an awareness of any potential problems caused by environmental levels or settings being out of whack.

Dust and debris aren't good for any electronic components. Equipment closets filled with racks of servers need proper airflow to keep things cool and to eliminate dusty air. Make sure that the room is ventilated and air-conditioned and that the air filters are changed regularly. This provides protection from airborne particles as well as heat and humidity.

Dust Cleanup

A dust-free environment for computing equipment is important because a dusty environment can cause several major issues for electronic devices. Dust can clog up cooling vents, fans, and other components and cause devices to overheat. In addition, dust may contain materials that conduct electricity, such metal or paint. Should conductive dust settle on a motherboard, its circuits could short or perhaps explode if enough accumulates. Dust accumulation is a sure sign of poor ventilation in the room, computer case, or both. Keeping the ventilation and location as dust-free as possible requires constant attention to dust cleanup.

Compressed Air/Vacuums

Two tools for keeping a computer and peripheral equipment as clean as possible are *antistatic vacuums* and *compressed* or *canned air*. Although a household vacuum certainly has the power to remove dust around and inside a computer, it also generates a large electrostatic charge build-up.

A dirty or dusty environment can impede airflow on a computer by blocking its cooling vents, which causes the computer to overheat. Dust can include conductive materials, and the dust particles can stick to circuit boards, such as the motherboard, and cause a short circuit. Removing dust from a computer, keyboard, or any exposed electronic device requires the use of an antistatic vacuum cleaner. Several models are available from computer stores as well as online.

You can use compressed air to loosen dirt and dust from delicate components. Compressed air comes in a couple of forms: the liquid propellant kind and the kind that uses small cartridges of compressed CO_2. You can find both at computer stores, office supply stores, camera shops, and big-box stores that sell electronics.

Follow three rules when using compressed air:

- Never breathe this stuff in. It's not *that* kind of air, and inhaling it can, quite literally, kill you!
- With regard to the liquid propellant type of compressed air, always keep the can upright. Tilting or turning the can upside down causes the liquid inside to come squirting out. This liquid can cause frostbite to the tech and irreparable damage to any computer components that it touches.
- Don't shake compressed air cans. They don't need to be shaken to work, and you run a small but real risk of the can exploding in your hand.

Power Surges, Under-Voltage Events, and Power Failures

Your computer needs power to run properly, but various factors can turn what should be a steady stream of electricity from the wall socket into either a trickle or a fire hose. Power fluctuations can wreak havoc on an unprotected system. Surges and sags can damage power supplies and components and cause file corruption. It's important that you know how to protect your computing environment from electrical power losses. Related issues that CompTIA doesn't specifically list as environmental impacts—but that might appear on the exam—are lightning strikes and electromagnetic interference (EMI).

Power surges, also known as *power spikes,* occur when the voltage on your power line rises suddenly to above-normal levels. Power spikes are extremely dangerous and can destroy computers, monitors, and any other component plugged into the affected power line.

An *under-voltage event* (brownout) occurs when the supply of electricity drops dramatically but does not go out completely. During an under-voltage event, you'll notice lights flickering or growing dim. When the power rises back up to its original level, your computer might not be able to handle the drastic change, and damage may occur.

Power failures (blackouts) occur when power goes out completely. The danger of a power failure is twofold. First, you may have data loss or corruption when the power goes out. Second, the power surge when the electricity comes back on may damage your system's electronics.

The CompTIA A+ Core 2 exam objectives list *battery backups* as something you should know for the exam. In common use, a battery backup is categorized as an uninterruptable power supply (UPS). The purpose of a battery backup or UPS is to provide electrical power to keep a system running in the event of a power interruption. However, backup devices themselves can only supply power for a certain length of time before they, too, run out.

A *surge suppressor* is another power event protection device that can help level out power events, like rises and falls in the AC voltage, to mitigate any damage to the device(s) connected to it. As the name implies, the protection is mostly against surges or sudden rises (spikes) in voltage. The cost of a good UPS or surge suppressor is nothing compared to the cost in time and money caused by lost components or corrupted files that you may have to endure if you don't use either one.

REVIEW

Objective 4.5: Summarize environmental impacts and local environmental controls
To control environmental impacts, understand the following methods:

- Consulting MSDS documentation for proper handling and disposal of chemicals and other substances
- Maintaining temperature and humidity-level awareness and proper ventilation to avoid ESD, equipment overheating, and other issues
- Protecting computer equipment from the dangers of power surges, under-voltage events, and power failures by using battery backups and surge suppressors
- Protecting computer equipment from dust and debris by using compressed air and an antistatic vacuum

4.5 QUESTIONS

1. You are helping to clean out an office that has a chemical you are unfamiliar with stored in a closet. Which of the following is most useful in determining safe disposal and handling procedures?

   A. Government regulations

   B. MSDS

   C. Product labeling

   D. Guesswork

2. As a member of the environmental controls team, you are helping to set up an unfinished building as a hot site for IT use in case of a disaster affecting the primary IT location. Which of the following does not fit into your team's responsibilities?

   A. Networking

   B. Ventilation

   C. Air filtration

   D. Temperature monitoring

3. A client is reporting problems with her computer. Using a multimeter, you determine that the electricity available at the client site is about 87 VAC (the standard for the location is 115 VAC). Which of the following conditions most accurately describes the electrical problem?

   A. Power surge

   B. Complete power failure

   C. Under-voltage

   D. EMI

4. While working on a motherboard with an overheating processor, you decide to clean the fan and heat sink on top of the CPU. Which of the following should you do while using compressed air for this job?

   A. Shake the can before using.

   B. Turn the can to get a better angle.

   C. Sniff the air coming from the can.

   D. Keep the can upright.

5. You have been asked to install an appropriate device to handle a rash of AC power events until the local electrical utility company is able to complete its investigation as to the causes. The company reports that it is experiencing sudden increases in electrical voltage, as high as 150 VAC, that remain for as long as 10 to 15 seconds. What device or solution do you recommend, based on the information available?

   A. Battery backup

   B. Switching the PSU to 220 VAC service

   C. Surge suppressor

   D. Discontinue use of the system

4.5 ANSWERS

1. **B** The material safety data sheet (MSDS) for the chemical has the most information about proper handling and disposal procedures.

2. **A** Networking is not an environmental control issue.

3. **C** Low electrical voltage is considered an under-voltage event.

4. **D** Keeping the can upright is the only recommended procedure of the ones listed.

5. **C** A strong surge suppressor should even out the incoming power.

Objective 4.6 # Explain the importance of prohibited content/activity and privacy, licensing, and policy concepts

Sooner or later, you'll probably come face-to-face with a user who is misusing their computer or network access. Maybe they're storing pornography, running a BitTorrent server, or cranking out posters of their children's favorite bands on the company color printer. In this objective, you learn how to deal with prohibited content or activity. You also learn about privacy, licensing, and policy concepts that can help to keep users and companies out of trouble.

Incident Response

More often than it should, a reported technical problem is actually the evidence of a security incident. There is no one pattern to security incidents, as they can be caused by any number of conditions, attacks, security system failures, and other scenarios. Here are some of the more common causes for an incident:

- Malware and/or virus infection
- A data breach or data exfiltration in which data is viewed or copied without authorization
- An interrupted or failed attempt to break into a system or network through a social engineering, on-path (aka man-in-the-middle), denial of service (DoS), or similar penetration attack
- Unauthorized or unlicensed apps installed on a workstation or network node
- Prohibited material stored on a workstation, such as unauthorized or illegal copies of copyrighted material or confidential documents

In any of these cases, and several more, the next actions of the technician or anyone else that discovers and reports the incident should be defined in an incident response plan that details a series of guidelines that properly deal with the prohibited actions, attacks, content, or activity.

An *incident response plan (IRP)* specifies the procedures and processes that are to be used when responding to a security incident. An IRP in a larger organization or enterprise may form an *incident response team (IRT)* to handle all security incidents to ensure that incidents are reported to the appropriate authorities. The team members should have the authority and skills for the range of decision-making and technology to handle the different types of incidents that can occur. The IRT should be made up of managers and technicians, with the skills to identify and handle minor and major incidents, and senior management, able to authorize the actions necessary to mitigate even the most serious incidents.

 ADDITIONAL RESOURCES A good article titled "What Is an Incident Response Plan and How to Create One" is available on the CompTIA website at https://www.comptia.org/blog/security-awareness-training-incident-response-plans.

Chain of Custody

The *chain of custody* depends, in part, on careful documentation of the computer's location before a violation was detected, who had access to it after the violation was detected, and what steps were taken to isolate it.

Preserving Evidence

A device's data must be preserved in case it becomes evidence, so the device's location and who has touched it need to be recorded to prove the data hasn't been tampered with; you need to establish a chain of custody documenting this history. You should have a legal expert to guide you, but the following are fairly common rules:

- Isolate the system. Shut down the system and store it in a place where no one else can access it.
- Document when you took control of the system and the actions you used: shutting it down, unplugging it, moving it, and so on. Don't worry about too much detail, but you must track its location.
- If another person takes control of the system, document the transfer of custody.

 EXAM TIP A chain of custody is a clear record of the path that evidence takes from purchase/acquisition to disposal.

Tracking of Evidence/Documenting the Process

Record information that indicates the illegal or unauthorized use of the computer or device. Some clues to look for include the following:

- Dates of illegal files
- Event logs
- Dates unauthorized software was installed or updated
- Browser cache
- Recently visited IP addresses
- Dates of and contents of deleted files
- Print server logs
- Proxy server logs

 ADDITIONAL RESOURCES Special forensic software and hardware can be used to examine a computer without changing its contents. This software can make a byte-by-byte copy of the hard drive's contents for analysis. To learn more about forensic software tools, see https://resources.infosecinstitute.com and search for "Computer Forensics."

Inform Management/Law Enforcement as Necessary

Any incident that impacts an organization's operations, assets, or personnel, even indirectly, must be reported to the management of the departments affected and possibly upper management. The incident response plan should identify to whom the incident is to be reported and when this notification is triggered. If the incident violates a local, state, or national ordinance, law, or regulation, it should be reported to the appropriate legal or governing authority, such as law enforcement at local, state, and possibly national levels. Notification may also be triggered based on the type, value, or effect of the incident. For example, an attack that steals proprietary intellectual property (IP) should definitely be reported to the local police. If the IP relates to a government contract, the appropriate agency should be contacted.

Copy of Drive (Data Integrity and Preservation)

Often the best evidence of a security incident is in a device's RAM, but just as often, that evidence is destroyed by well-intended actions of a user or technician. The *integrity and preservation* of all data, including that in RAM, is a key element of an incident response, and all users of an organization must be trained on what to do if an incident is discovered. In the event that all evidence in RAM is removed, the data stored on secondary storage devices such as a hard drive must be protected "as is." Should this also fail, the only fallback is the latest system backups.

The science of collecting and preserving the data evidence on a computer is digital forensics. This process identifies and gathers latent evidence of the incident that can be presented in a court of law. Latent evidence cannot be seen; it must be interpreted by experts or processed by approved and recognized equipment.

The procedure for preserving the integrity of the data related to an incident begins with identifying the incident's scope, including which workstations or servers could be involved and any removable media that could possibly have data evidence. If possible, the workstations and media should be isolated as soon as possible.

 NOTE   There's no such thing as too much evidence. Include any devices with even the slightest chance that they may have been affected by the incident and could even contain evidence. As the investigation proceeds, any unnecessary devices can be eliminated from the evidence collected.

Documentation of the Incident

When an incident is detected or reported, be sure to document the relevant facts, such as the following:

- What account was used?
- What devices were used?
- What software was used?
- What types of content were discovered?
- When did the violation take place?

In addition to isolating the devices and data related to the incident, everything done in the investigation must be documented. The documentation process should also collect physical documentation using steps similar to the following:

1. Investigators must document or record any action taken to identify, collect, and handle possible evidence.

2. Photograph or video the area, devices, audio, and materials in view where the incident is suspected to have occurred.

3. Any and all available evidence on a powered-up system, such as the data in RAM and cache, should be collected using forensic tools.

4. Apply a forensic imaging tool to capture an image of installed data storage devices and use a write blocker to block any attempts to change the data during imaging.

5. Disable encryption, such as BitLocker, or screen locks and, after completing the two preceding steps, power off the devices.

6. Create a separate cryptographic hash value for each storage device included in this process and its image to provide proof that the digital evidence hasn't been modified after its data is collected.

7. Any physical devices that are to be included in the evidence should be placed in tamper-evident bags, and a chain-of-custody form should be attached to each bag.

8. Transport and store all evidence collected in a secure offsite location.

It's also a best practice to create a list of the evidence collected and the documentation created and have a second party review the list for possible missing evidence.

EXAM TIP   Be sure you know each of the elements and their importance to the best practices of incident responses.

Licensing/Digital Rights Management/End-User License Agreement

Software compliance is simple enough if you have an explicit list of allowed software and strict controls on who can install programs, but less restrictive regimes require more effort to stay in compliance with software licenses.

EXAM TIP   Noncompliant systems are also at increased risk of malware infections or other vulnerabilities introduced by unapproved software.

Licensing

Like other creative acts worthy of copyright protection, software developers are granted copyright to software they create, enabling them to decide how or if others can obtain a license to use the software. The *licensing* can be commercial or noncommercial, personal or enterprise. The software can be closed source or open source. You have a legal obligation to use the software in compliance with its license, which typically entails the following:

- Paying money for software released under a *commercial license* and complying with terms that indicate whether the license supports personal or private use.
- Complying with any *end-user license agreement (EULA)* you agree to when you open or install software, which typically specifies how you may use the software and whether you may share it. If the software uses digital rights management (DRM) techniques to protect the application or its files, the EULA typically forbids you from breaking, reverse-engineering, or removing these protections (or helping anyone else do so).
- Observing stipulations in noncommercial software licenses that specify whether the software is free for all uses, free only for personal/educational use, or requires a special commercial license for commercial use.
- Complying with additional stipulations in *open source software* licenses that specify how you may use the source code. These licenses commonly give you the right to modify the source but may require you to release your modifications for free as well.

Valid Licenses and Non-expired Licenses

Only valid licenses should be installed on workstations and network devices. This seems logical to conscientious IT managers, but only software that is enabled through a product key or product ID can be considered as having a valid license.

Licenses are subscribed to for a fixed period of time in most cases. Once a license expires, it must be uninstalled immediately (per the license agreement terms) or the software becomes unusable or its use is limited to a small number of devices. Therefore, for licensed software to remain usable per its terms of use, license dates and terms must be monitored so that only unexpired licenses are in use.

Personal Use License vs. Corporate Use License

Software that is licensed to an individual for a single computer cannot be used on multiple computers: it's a violation of the license agreement. Enterprise licenses may (depending on the specific license agreement) permit individuals to use company-licensed software on their personal systems.

Given the high potential penalties for pirated software, it just makes sense to make sure users understand what the license on a particular program permits and use it per that agreement.

Open Source License

Generally, Windows, iOS, and macOS operating systems and apps are closed source software and require a commercial license. Android and Linux, by contrast, are open source operating systems, even though most Android apps are closed source and require commercial licensing. Linux apps are typically open source and free to use.

 NOTE   *Open source* is not always clear in its meaning. There are "open source" programs that require licensing fees, such as most of the server versions of Linux. Many "for-free" programs, such as demonstration versions of software, are, in contrast, closed source.

Before installing closed source software, review its conditions of use regarding whether the software can be modified or can be included in or distributed in a bundle with the proprietary products of another developer.

Digital Rights Management

Digital rights management (DRM) uses technology, in the form of software, to monitor accesses to copyrighted objects, such as documents, audio and video recordings, and other forms of intellectual property. DRM attempts to protect the rights of a copyright holder and the unauthorized use or modification of the protected materials. DRM has gained importance due to the growth of peer-to-peer object exchanges, torrent sites, and piracy.

 EXAM TIP   Be sure to know the definitions of each of the different licensing types (good and bad) as well as what DRM and EULA are and their purposes.

Regulated Data

Larger organizations, such as government entities, benefit greatly from organizing their data according to its sensitivity and minimizing surprises by keeping computer hardware and software as uniform as possible. This also helps maintain *compliance* with government and internal regulations; common examples are rules regarding approved software and regulations on how you must handle *personally identifiable information (PII)* such as health or academic records.

Data Classifications

A common *data classification* scheme that flags documents as public, internal use only, highly confidential, top secret, and so on helps employees (including techs) know what to do with

TABLE 4.6-1	Types of Regulated Data

Regulated Data Type	Meaning	Notes
PII	Personally identifiable information	PII is the information that specifically identifies an individual. This information includes a person's full name, Social Security number, and so on.
PCI	Payment Card Industry	PCI is an industry association that issues the specific Data Security Standard (PCI DSS) that applies to all organizations that accept payment cards and requirements for the protection of PII and other security measures.
GDPR	General Data Protection Regulation	GDPR is the European Union (EU) standard for data protection that applies to organizations that handle the PII of EU citizens, regardless of the organization's geographic location. It also regulates browser cookie disclosures and other types of personal data use.
PHI	Protected health information	PHI includes data such as patient demographics, test and lab results, insurance information, and so on. PHI is regulated under the Health Insurance Portability and Accountability Act (HIPAA).

documents and hardware containing them (such as using different rules to recycle hard drives that hold top-secret data). Your strategy for recycling a computer system no longer being used, for example, will differ a lot if the data on the drive is classified as internal use only or top secret. Table 4.6-1 identifies different types of regulated data.

ADDITIONAL RESOURCES   To learn more about the protected data types in Table 4.6-1, use these links:
—PII   https://www.cloudflare.com/learning/privacy/what-is-pii/
—PCI DSS   https://www.pcicomplianceguide.org
—GDPR   https://gdpr.eu/what-is-gdpr/
—PHI   https://www.hhs.gov/answers/hipaa/what-is-phi/index.html

EXAM TIP   Be sure you can distinguish between PHI and PII and other types of regulated data.

Data Retention

The retention of regulated data (see the preceding section) on workstations, file servers, database servers, and even in backup files is also defined in the regulations that define each data classification. Here are the elements a regulation must prescribe:

- A minimum period of retention
- A maximum period of retention
- Acceptable storage media
- Retained data security
- Retired data disposal

REVIEW

Objective 4.6: Explain the importance of prohibited content/activity and privacy, licensing, and policy concepts   An incident response plan should include the following items:

- Chain of custody guidelines
- Informing management and law enforcement as necessary
- Drive copy for data integrity and preservation
- Documentation of incident details and evidence

The following are licensing issues:

- Licensing programs
- Digital rights management (DRM)
- End-user license agreements (EULAs)
- Valid vs. non-expired licenses
- Personal use licenses vs. corporate use licenses
- Open source vs. closed source licenses

The following are the types of regulated data:

- Government-regulated personal information
- PII (personally identifiable information)
- PHI (protected health information)
- PCI DSS (Payment Card Industry Data Security Standard)
- GDPR (General Data Protection Regulation for EU citizens)

Protected data also has data retention requirements.

4.6 QUESTIONS

1. You are evaluating a program's source code to see if it can be modified for your company's needs. The program is free for personal use but must be licensed with a fee for company use. Which of the following phrases best describes its company licensing arrangement?

   A. Free open source

   B. Closed source

   C. Commercial open source

   D. Noncommercial

2. Which of the following could be the cause of a security incident? (Choose all that apply.)

   A. Malware and/or virus infection

   B. A data breach

   C. Social engineering

   D. Unauthorized or unlicensed apps

   E. Only B and C

   F. All of the above

   G. None of the above

3. Which of the following is a standard developed by an industry association as a guideline for retailers that accept payment cards and the protection of PII?

   A. GDPR

   B. HIPAA

   C. AUP

   D. PCI DSS

4. Which of the following is an example of PII?

   A. ZIP code

   B. Phone number

   C. Gender

   D. Citizenship

5. A U.S.-based healthcare company has operations in the UK and France. It accepts credit and debit card payments. Which of the following types of regulated data must it protect?

   A. PHI

   B. GDPR

   C. PCI DSS

   D. All of the above

4.6 ANSWERS

1. **C** The software has a licensing fee (making it commercial), but the source code can be modified (open source).
2. **F** The options listed as A through D are all possible security incident causes.
3. **D** The PCI issues the PCI DSS standard to govern credit card processing.
4. **B** A phone number is PII because it can be used to identify a specific individual.
5. **D** The company is involved in healthcare (PHI), has business dealings in the UK and France (GDPR), and handles payment cards (PCI DSS).

Objective 4.7 Given a scenario, use proper communication techniques and professionalism

Professional is a way to describe someone who is in control of an unexpected situation. From traffic jams to customer frustrations, you are likely to encounter less-than-ideal situations. This objective covers some ways to defuse potential trouble spots so you can solve customer problems.

What's more, you will encounter all sorts of people as a tech, and their emotions will range from happy to satisfied, angry, fearful, and frustrated. You'll find bluster, smiles, patience, impatience, and much more. Regardless of their mood, you must always treat the customer with respect. This objective helps you focus on the specifics to make that happen.

EXAM TIP Don't underestimate the importance of this objective! Given a scenario on the exam, be ready to use proper communication and professionalism skills.

Professional Appearance and Attire

The adage "you only have one chance to make a first impression" is true for virtually all customer/client interactions, and in the case of a computer technician, it's especially true. When you enter the client's place of business or work area, how you look can provide everything the client needs to judge your professionalism. If you appear unkempt, the client may assume that your work is sloppy and unskilled. However, if you appear neat, their opinion may be that you are orderly, skilled, and professional.

Your appearance, attire, speech, and attitude are important to the client's perception of you. Your attire should be consistent with the dress policy of the client's location, which could be formal or business casual. In an organization with a *formal* dress policy, such as one in which employees must wear business suits, dress as formally as safety permits (no neckties or jewelry when working inside a computer). A *business casual* dress policy may not require suits and ties, but once again safety should be your guide.

Communication Techniques

Knowing how to communicate with customers is a key "soft skill" for anyone who works with the public. For IT workers in particular, communicating with customers is vital to solving their problems and developing a good long-term professional relationship. Here are some tips to help you achieve these goals.

Use Proper Language and Avoid Jargon, Acronyms, and Slang, When Applicable

We live in a vulgar and informal age, but that's no excuse for sounding like you've overdosed on reality programs when you are speaking with your customers. Slang is out, and proper language is in.

You're the technology expert, but if you don't avoid jargon and acronyms when speaking with your customers, you'll sound like an arrogant jerk, not an expert, and your customers won't understand your tech speak. Make sure you understand technology well enough to translate it into ordinary language—if you don't, you're not as knowledgeable as you think you are. Practice effective communication. The best techs know both technology and how to talk with users.

Maintain a Positive Attitude/Project Confidence

Maintain a positive attitude when dealing with a difficult customer or situation. Project confidence that you can solve the problem efficiently and get the user back to work. Don't argue with the customer or get defensive if they imply that the computer problem is somehow your fault. It happens!

Actively Listen, Take Notes, and Avoid Interrupting the Customer

Effective communication in "computerese" requires active listening to get to the heart of the problem, which in turn calls for the proper use of language. You know and speak tech. Chances are that your customer doesn't. Getting through this language barrier is essential for solving problems.

Actively listening means focusing your attention on the customer's words. They might not make sense at first, so take notes. The customer might say something like, "I was working away, but a clock started ticking inside the CPU, then my screen went blue and I can't get the computer to start at all." Oy! Don't interrupt the customer. Let them tell you the story. Because you wrote it down, you likely can interpret the non-technical language into something that potentially makes sense.

Many users call the case or system unit a CPU. A ticking sound inside a case often points to a dying hard drive. A blue screen is a classic sign of a non-maskable interrupt (NMI), better known in Windows as the *blue screen of death*—a term you don't want to use in front of a customer, by the way! The user's hard drive might have just died. If the user has burned their hand on the case, that could point to an overheating issue that caused the problem—and potentially a lot more than just a dying drive.

Be Culturally Sensitive

With a diverse population needing help from tech experts like you, you need to deal graciously with cultural differences. If a customer's religious holiday conflicts with your work schedule, the customer wins. If the customer wants you to take off your shoes, take them off. If the customer wants you to wear a hat, wear one. If a person's title happens to be in a language you don't speak, figure out how to say it before arriving on the scene. That's what Google Translate is for! Be culturally sensitive. Always use the appropriate title, whether personal or professional. Never assume that using a customer's first name establishes rapport. In fact, you shouldn't use a customer's first name unless the customer requests that you do so.

Be on Time (If Late, Contact the Customer)

Be on time, whether making a scheduled phone call or arriving at a job site. If you are driving, plan ahead to ensure you know the route to the customer's premises and build in extra time for traffic congestion or other unforeseen issues. If you are running late, contact the customer immediately, apologize, and provide an estimated time of arrival. We live in the future: call, text, or alert your dispatcher to notify the customer. This is more than common courtesy; it's an essential skill for the professional tech.

Avoid Distractions

Avoid distractions that take your focus away from the user and addressing their computer problem:

- Don't take a personal call when interacting with a customer.
- Don't text, tweet, or respond to messages on other social media sites.
- Don't chat with coworkers; keep your focus on interacting with the customer.
- Avoid any kind of personal interruption that doesn't deal directly with fixing the computer; it will only irritate the customer.

Dealing with Difficult Customers or Situations

Inevitably, you're going to encounter difficult customers in difficult situations. Computer issues tend to cause stress, and some people become difficult to deal with when they are stressed out. As a professional tech, you need to know how to defuse the tension and get the job done.

Do Not Argue with Customers and/or Be Defensive   You want to fix the customer's problem—and the customer really wants it fixed. You have the same goal. Don't argue or be defensive. Assure the customer that you're here to help—and be helpful!

Avoid Dismissing Customer Problems   What might be an easy, five-minute fix to you might be the potential "end of the world" for the customer. Don't dismiss their problems, no matter how many times you've seen a similar problem before. Remember, this one might be different!

Avoid Being Judgmental   Customers would fix their problems themselves if they knew how. They don't—and that's why they call you. If you discover that a customer caused the problem, don't be judgmental about how the device was damaged or files were deleted. Keep an even, non-accusatory tone. You've probably made a few mistakes in your professional life, too. Fix the problem and be thankful the customer called you—and not somebody else—for help. It's good job security.

Clarify Customer Statements (Ask Open-Ended Questions to Narrow the Scope of the Problem, Restate the Issue, or Question to Verify Your Understanding)   Customers with technology problems are likely to be long on fear and frustration and short on clarity when you first talk to them. Therefore, it's up to you to clarify customer statements. Ask open-ended questions, such as "What other strange or unusual things about the computer have you noticed recently?" A "nothing, really" response from the customer has a wildly different meaning than "I burned my hand on the CPU a couple of days ago." Open-ended questions help narrow the scope of the problem.

Also, *restate the issue or question to verify your understanding,* but use proper, simple language. Avoid jargon and acronyms. Definitely skip the silly computer-guy slang, like calling a Windows PC "the comp" or a motherboard a "mobo." That stuff just makes customers defensive. Once you think you understand both the scope and nature of the problem, go back to your notes, and you might find a good explanation.

Do Not Disclose Experiences via Social Media Outlets   After you finish a job (or even during one in progress), never share any "funny" stories about the customer or the activities around you. Certainly share professional and technical details with coworkers and any personal issues with your supervisor, but definitely *do not disclose experiences via social media outlets* such as Facebook, Instagram, and TikTok. Someone knows someone without fail, and your words will come back to haunt you.

Set and Meet Expectations/Time Line and Communicate Status with the Customer

Expectations management means to give a customer as accurate an estimate as possible regarding how long it will take you to fix the computer problem. Plus, it means providing status updates if you expect to finish more quickly than your initial estimate or if things seem to be taking longer than first predicted. Also, many times with a computer issue, you can fix the problem and avoid a similar problem in the future in several ways. These options boil down to money.

Offer Repair/Replacement Options, as Needed   If applicable, offer different repair/replacement options and let the customer decide which route to take.

Provide Proper Documentation on the Services Provided   At the completion of work, provide proper documentation of the services provided. Describe the problem; include the time and day you started work, completed the work, and the number of hours you worked; provide a list of parts you replaced, if applicable; and describe the solution.

Follow Up with Customer/User at a Later Date to Verify Satisfaction   Follow up with a customer/user at a later date to verify satisfaction. This can be a simple follow-up, usually just a phone call, to confirm that the customer is happy with your work.

Deal Appropriately with Customers' Confidential and Private Materials

You have a lot of power as a tech at someone else's computer. You can readily access files, browsing history, downloads, and more. Don't do it! You need to deal appropriately with customers' confidential and private materials. This includes files on the computer, items on a physical desktop, and even pages sitting in a printer tray. If you are caught violating a customer's privacy, you not only will lose credibility and respect, but you could also lose your job.

REVIEW

Objective 4.7: Given a scenario, use proper communication techniques and professionalism   The following are the keys to effective communication and interactions with customers:

- Make sure you have a professional appearance and attire.
- Use proper language and avoid jargon, acronyms, and slang.
- Maintain a positive attitude and project confidence.
- Actively listen, take notes, and avoid interrupting the customer.
- Be culturally sensitive.
- Be on time (and if you're running late, let the customer know).

You can avoid distractions by following these guidelines:

- Don't make or accept personal calls
- Don't send or read text messages or visit social media sites
- Avoid personal interruptions

When you're dealing with difficult customers or situations, keep these points in mind:

- Don't argue with customers or be defensive.
- Avoid dismissing a customer's problems.
- Don't be judgmental.
- Clarify customer statements by asking open-ended questions to narrow the scope of a problem, restate your understanding of the issue, or ask questions to verify your understanding.
- Don't share your experience with a customer on a social media outlet.

You can set and meet the customer's expectations/timeline and communicate status with the customer by doing the following:

- Offer repair/replacement options as appropriate.
- Record and provide proper documentation on the services provided.
- Follow up with customer/user at a later date to verify their satisfaction.

Finally, you should always deal appropriately with customers' confidential and private materials located on a computer, desktop, printer, and so on.

4.7 QUESTIONS

1. You allowed plenty of time to reach your destination, but a massive traffic jam caused by a couple of accidents has disrupted your schedule. You will be late to your next appointment. What should you do?

   A. Don't worry about it. The customer listens to traffic reports every ten minutes and will know why you're late.

   B. Abandon your vehicle and call a taxi to pick you up from the service drive.

   C. Call your supervisor and ask her to call the customer.

   D. Call the customer yourself and explain the situation, apologizing for being late.

2. You open the customer's computer, a four-year-old system running a Core i3 that is no longer being produced, only to find that smoke is coming from the motherboard. What should you do?

   A. Quote the customer a price for replacing the entire computer.

   B. Offer the customer the option to repair or replace the system.

   C. Find out if a similar motherboard is available and order it.

   D. Try to replace the burnt chip.

3. You are planning a date with your spouse and haven't heard back about what time you are meeting. You get a text message while you are discussing repair options with your client. What should you do?

   A. Check the message while trying to conceal the phone from your client.

   B. Ask your client if you can excuse yourself while you view the message.

   C. Check the message after the meeting with the client is over.

   D. Tell your client you can't stay late because you're going out to dinner that night.

4. You have just heard another technician's phone conversation with a client. It went like this: "Dude, your mobo is shot and your distro is dead! Your burner is burned up. Howzabout I get you a deal on a sweet little laptop! Is that OK, Doc?" Which of the following did you hear? (Choose two.)

   A. Use of slang

   B. Use of jargon

   C. Proper use of titles

   D. Customer being offered options to repair or replace computer

5. You have just completed a diagnostic test on your client's computer, identified a defective memory module, replaced it, and removed three of the most dangerous current malware threats. You now need to provide documentation on the services you provided. Which of the following best describes the work you did?

   A. Fixed your PC.

   B. Broke RAM, replaced with good RAM.

   C. Turned your frown upside down.

   D. Diagnostics, defective memory replaced, malware removed.

4.7 ANSWERS

1. **D**   Always call the customer yourself if you're going to be late. If you don't have the right contact information, get it from your supervisor.

2. **B**   Even if you think it's cheaper to replace the computer, offer a repair option. For example, some older systems must be maintained because of compatibility issues with newer hardware or operating systems.

3. **C**   The message can wait. If necessary, excuse yourself after the meeting and head to the restroom to read it.

4. **A B**   Slang and jargon abounded, not good communication techniques!

5. **D**   This represents a professional, accurate, concise description of the services rendered.

Objective 4.8 Identify the basics of scripting

A *script* is a small program used to help automate computing tasks. Scripts are written in a text editor and executed from a command prompt. Scripting, which is a kind of programming, has the power to make complex or repetitive data manipulation and machine configuration easier. For purposes of the CompTIA A+ 220-1102 exam, you don't need to be a scripting expert, but you do need to be able to identify the basic scripting concepts covered in this objective.

Script File Types

Scripts are stored as text files using the extensions discussed in the following sections. Because they are stored as text files, scripts can be created using a text editor such as Notepad. However, some scripting languages include some type of an integrated development environment (IDE), an integrated development and learning environment (IDLE), or an integrated scripting environment (ISE) that can be used to edit and run scripts.

.bat

The *.bat* file extension is used by the simple scripting language originally developed for MS-DOS and is still used from the command prompt in Windows. In addition to running commands in sequence, a .bat file (also known as a batch file) can also display each command as it runs (using echo) and include remarks that explain the purpose of the file (using REM).

Use Notepad or a word processing program that can save files as plain-text files to edit a .bat file. There are no restrictions on .bat files, so a potentially harmful .bat file can be run without being blocked by Windows. Be sure to view the contents of an unfamiliar .bat file before running it.

The sample batch file shown in Figure 4.8-1 creates a list of subfolders of the C: drive's root directory (folder) after pausing and redirecting its output to a text file.

.ps1

The *.ps1* file extension is used by PowerShell scripts. PowerShell is an object-oriented scripting language built into Windows 10/11. On Windows 10/11 systems, PowerShell can be configured as the go-to command prompt in place of cmd.exe (WIN-R). You can also run PowerShell from within its ISE.

```
@echo off
REM preceding line prevents commands from being echoed to display
REM A statement preceded by REM is a remark statement that can be used to explain a step
REM Create this file in your default Documents folder and change to that folder to run it
echo This batch file will create a sorted list of your system drive's root folder's folders
pause
REM The pause statement makes the batch file wait until you press a key to continue
REM The following 3 lines explain the command that is used to create the list
REM dir C:\ Displays the contents of the root folder (directory) of C: drive
REM /AD Lists folders (directories) only; /ON Sorts folders by name
REM >folders.txt Redirects output that normally goes to the screen to a file called folders.txt
dir C:\/AD /ON>folders.txt
pause
REM Following opens the file in Notepad
notepad folders.txt
```

FIGURE 4.8-1   A sample .bat file

PowerShell includes support for variables, looping, cmdlets (small .NET-based apps), and consistent syntax using a verb-noun command structure. To make the transition easier to PowerShell, it supports aliases. Users can enter commands from cmd.exe or a Linux terminal, and PowerShell will run its matching command.

ADDITIONAL RESOURCES   An open source version called PowerShell Core is available for macOS and for the Ubuntu and CentOS Linux distros. Learn more about PowerShell at https://docs.microsoft.com/en-us/powershell/.

The script shown in Figure 4.8-2 displays the current operating mode of a Windows system, and its output is shown in Figure 4.8-3.

.vbs

The *.vbs* file extension is used for *Visual Basic Script,* also known as VBScript. This is a Microsoft scripting language derived from Visual Basic. The macro functions of Microsoft Excel and other Office apps with macro support refer to it as Visual Basic for Applications (these use the .vba file extension). By default, VBScript is executed by the wscript.exe interpreter, which displays any output produced by the .vbs script in a Desktop window or dialog box. A VBScript file can also be executed using Windows Script Host and supports HTML applications such as Microsoft Edge. Any plain-text editor can be used to create or edit VBScript files.

```
param( [string]$arg = "")
if ( ( $arg -ne "") -or ($HOME[0] -eq "/") ) {
        Write-Host "Notes:   Boot State is returned as string and as return code (`"errorlevel`"):"
        Write-Host"             `"Normal`"               (errorlevel = 0)"
        Write-Host "            `"Safe mode`"             (errorlevel = 1)"
        Write-Host"             `"Safe mode with network`"  (errorlevel = 2)"
        Write-Host "            `"Other`"                (errorlevel = 3)"
        exit -1
}
foreach ( $computer in Get-WmiObject -Class Win32_ComputerSystem) {
        switch ($computer.TestState) {
                "Normal boot" {
                        Write-Host 1'Normal"
                        exit 0
                }
                "Fail-safe boot" {
                        Write-Host "Safe mode"
                        exit 1
                }
                "Fail-safe with network boot" {
                        Write-Host "Safe mode with network"
                        exit 2
                }
                "Other" {
                        Write-Host "Other mode''
                        exit 3
                }
        }
}
exit -1
```

FIGURE 4.8-2   The statements in a PowerShell .ps1 script

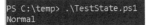

FIGURE 4.8-3   The PowerShell command line and output from the TestState.ps1 script shown in Figure 4.8-2

Here's a simple VBScript that totals the numbers 1 to 34 and displays the answer in a message box. After the first message box is closed, the script then multiplies the result by 2.3 and displays the product in another message box. Figure 4.8-4 shows the two message boxes this script produces.

```
' Comment - DIM declares a variable
Dim N
' Sets value of N to 0
N = 0
' For/Next loop
For i = 1 to 34
   N = N + i
```

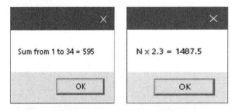

FIGURE 4.8-4   The first (left) and second (right) message boxes displayed by the sample .vbs script

```
Next
' Msgbox displays text and variables in a GUI box.
' Click OK to close the box and continue.
Msgbox "Sum from 1 to 34 = " & N
Msgbox "N x 2.3 = " & N * 2.3
```

.sh

The *.sh* file extension is used for Bash shell files, a type of executable file used originally on UNIX systems and now used on Linux or macOS in Terminal mode.

 NOTE   Linux systems support several text editors, as would be used to create and modify .sh scripts: the legacy vi and ed and the newer nano and Vim.

 EXAM TIP   Bash scripts use echo to print text to the screen and use $ as part of variable names for both text and numeric variables.

Bash files require execute permission to run. The easiest way to gain access to run an .sh file is to use the sudo command (sudo enables the current user to run as root, or superuser) in front of the bash command, as shown in this example:

```
sudo bash script.sh
```

 EXAM TIP   As with any sudo command, the user is prompted to type their password before continuing.

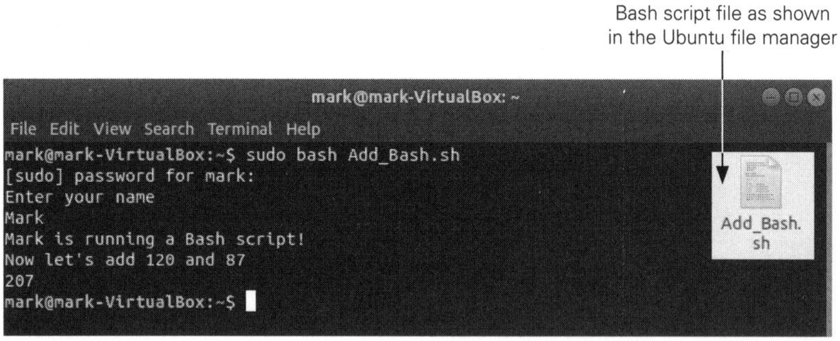

Bash script file as shown
in the Ubuntu file manager

```
mark@mark-VirtualBox: ~
File Edit View Search Terminal Help
mark@mark-VirtualBox:~$ sudo bash Add_Bash.sh
[sudo] password for mark:
Enter your name
Mark
Mark is running a Bash script!
Now let's add 120 and 87
207
mark@mark-VirtualBox:~$
```

Add_Bash.
sh

FIGURE 4.8-5   Terminal window in Ubuntu Linux running Add_Bash.sh

The following is a simple .sh script that includes a statement that displays text using echo, gets the user's name, uses comments (#), and performs math. Figure 4.8-5 illustrates the output from this file as displayed in Ubuntu Linux's Terminal.

```
#!/bin/bash
echo "Enter your name"
read name
echo "$name is running a Bash script!"
echo "Now let's add 120 and 87"
# Addition command
((sum=120+87))
# The next line displays the result
echo $sum
```

CAUTION   Linux, UNIX, and macOS consider uppercase and lowercase filenames and commands to be different. Therefore, if you use the wrong case in a script or when referring to a filename, you will see an error.

.js

A *.js* extension is used for JavaScript scripts. JavaScript is widely used in web development and web applications, web servers and server apps, smartwatch and mobile apps, and more. It is an object-based, interpreted language that, despite its name, has no connection to the Java programming language.

In addition to the free JavaScript IDE available for Windows, macOS, and Linux from Visual Studio Code (https://code.visualstudio.com), several online JavaScript editors are available on the Web (for a list of the more commonly used, see https://codecondo .com/16-online-javascript-editors-for-web-developers/).

EXAM TIP   JavaScript scripts start with <script> and end with </script>.

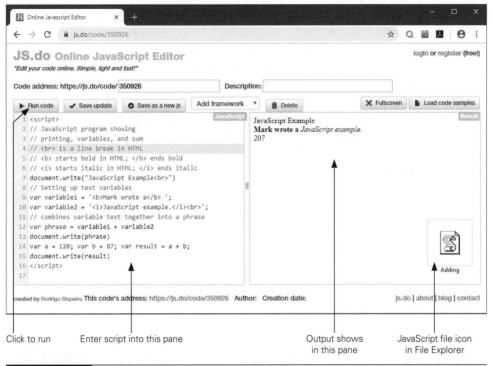

FIGURE 4.8-6   Running Adding.js at the JS.do website

Here's a simple .js script that can be inserted into HTML code. It includes statements that set up variables, print text, and insert comments (//). It also includes some HTML and performs math. Figure 4.8-6 illustrates how this script appears when entered and run at the JS.do website, along with the icon used by File Explorer for JavaScript files.

```
<script>
// JavaScript program showing
// printing, variables, and sum
// <br> is a line break in HTML
// <b> starts bold in HTML; </b> ends bold
// <i> starts italic in HTML; </i> ends italic
document.write("JavaScript Example<br>")
// Setting up text variables
var variable1 = '<b>Mark wrote a</b> ';
var variable2 = '<i>JavaScript example.</i><br>';
// combines variable text together into a phrase
var phrase = variable1 + variable2
document.write(phrase)
var a = 120; var b = 87; var result = a + b;
document.write(result)
</script>
```

.py

A *.py* extension is used for Python scripts. Python is a versatile scripting and programming language that is included in macOS and most Linux distros. The current version is Python 3.10, although Python 2 is still in use. Python versions are available for Windows as well as macOS and Linux from https://www.python.org/downloads/.

The Python IDLE combines a text editor with a Python interpreter, but Python can also be executed in a browser at various websites such as Code Academy (www.codeacademy.com) and Online Python IDE (https://www.online-python.com/), among others.

EXAM TIP   Python scripts include simple variable statements (n = 5) and # at the start of each comment.

Here's a simple .py script that includes a statement that prints text onscreen, gets the user's name, inserts comments (#), and performs math. Compare it to the Bash (.sh) script shown in an earlier section.

```
# Python program showing
# a use of input(), variables, and sum
n = input("Type your name: ")
print (n, "is running a Python script!")
print ("Now let's add 120 and 87")
# Addition command
z = (120,87)
y = sum (z)
# The next line displays the result
print (y)
```

Figure 4.8-7 illustrates the input and output of this script when run on the Online Python IDE website.

EXAM TIP   Be able to identify the scripting file type extensions .bat, .ps1, .vbs, .sh, .js, and .py for the exam!

```
Type your name:
User1
User1 is running a Python script!
Now let's add 120 and 87
207
```

FIGURE 4.8-7   The input and output of the sample Python script

Use Cases for Scripting

Perhaps the most common reason for using scripting is for basic automation, which is performing a series of actions automatically rather than performing them one at a time manually. Scripts, regardless of the OS on which they are executed, allow a series of built-in commands to be used as an algorithm to perform a task, calculate a result, or measure and report system conditions, among a whole host of other reasons.

Scripting languages, such as JavaScript and Python, use the application programming interfaces (APIs) of the host OS, many of which already perform all or some of a function. A script is interpreted, which is usually more efficient and easier to create and use than writing a compile program for the same purpose. Some of the more common uses for scripts are described in the following sections.

Restarting Machines

Unfortunately, OSs do occasionally need to be restarted, most commonly to complete an installation or update. Examples of a PowerShell cmdlet and a Linux command that can be used standalone or in a script to restart Windows and Linux systems are

- The PowerShell cmdlet **Restart-Computer** restarts the OS on local and remote computers. Its parameters can be used to set authentication levels, alternate credentials, or force an immediate restart.

- Linux systems require far fewer restarts than Windows systems and can literally run seemingly forever without restarting. However, should a restart be necessary or desired, the **shutdown -r** command will restart the system.

Remapping Network Drives

On a Windows OS, each data storage device, partition, logical drive, or volume can be assigned an alphabetic drive identifier, such as the "C:" assigned to the primary disk unit and the "D:" through "Z:" assigned to any subsequently added units. These designations are called drive mappings. When a new partition is mapped (mounted) to a system, it is typically assigned the next drive ID in sequence. However, if a drive is removed from the system (unmapped) or a software app requires a particular drive ID, the drives may need to be remapped. This is especially common on larger networks. Mapping a drive provides a connection between a local drive and a shared folder or file on a remote device. A mapped drive gives the appearance that the drive is local to the user.

In a Windows script, the **net use** command or the **New-PSDrive** PowerShell command is used for drive mapping. A sample script is shown here:

```
If (Test-Path L:) {
Get-PSdrive L | Remove-PSDrive
}
New-PSDrive -Name "L" -Persist -PSProvider
FileSystem -Root "\\MS10\LABFILES"
```

In this script, the initial If statement is a provision for error handling, such as would be needed if the drive mapping is attempting to assign a drive ID that is already in use. Drive mapping is a Windows thing. On Linux systems, file systems, which are logical structures, are mounted to the root file system without a specific drive ID assignment other than the directory to which they are mounted.

Installation of Applications

If you need to install multiple apps on several standalone or networked workstations, you should consider using an installation script to do so. Using a script would eliminate the need to individually install each of the apps.

On a Windows system, a script file can be used to install software silently (meaning in background). The script can be created using any text editor or specialized script editor software, such as Notepad++ (https://notepad-plus-plus.org/downloads/), AutoHotKey (www.autohotkey.com/), or SilentInstallBuilder (www.silentinstall.org/).

If you choose to create a text-formatted script file, you should find the silent mode parameter or switch for the setup or installer for each of the applications you wish to install. Remember that the statements in a script file are executed one at a time and serially. A next statement doesn't start before the preceding statement completes or fails.

Installers are typically implemented either as .exe files or as Windows Installer (.MSI) packages. To use an EXE setup in a batch file, just add the path to the installer with the appropriate switches. A command in a Windows script that executes the setup.exe utility for a new app in silent (/S) mode and adds an icon for the app on the Desktop would be something like this example:

```
C:\NewAppFiles\setup.exe /S /desktopicon=yes
```

To use the Windows Installer to add an app from a script in silent (/qn) mode, use the msiexec command:

```
msiexec C:\NewAppFiles\install.msi /qn
```

If you wish to run the installs from a PowerShell script, the **Start-Process** cmdlet has more installation control and error-handling options. In Linux, scripts are often used to compile apps from source code using the apt or yum command.

Automated Backups

At the command prompt, a simple type of backup can be performed by using the ordinary file-copy tools, such as robocopy in Windows. However, if the backup is to include only a specific set of folders and files or call options or functions of a backup utility, perhaps a script would be a better choice. A script, like any executable, can be set to run automatically using the Windows Task Scheduler or a Linux cron setting.

Gathering of Information/Data

Windows PowerShell has literally hundreds of **Get-** cmdlets that can be used to access and return configuration and status information from Windows subsystems. For example, to capture the log file from a single app or the apps in an install script, use the **Get-AppPackageLog** cmdlet, as follows:

```
Get-AppXPackageLog -AllUsers | Out-File -FilePath C:\NewApp\NewAppLog.txt
```

Figure 4.8-8 shows this cmdlet and its output displayed by a cat command.

Initiating Updates

On a Windows 10/11 system command prompt, the Windows Update Standalone Installer (wusa.exe) can be initiated from a script and used to complete routine update tasks. The PowerShell cmdlet **Install-Module** contains a variety of cmdlets that can be applied to manage the module update process. There are also several third-party apps that provide for update checking though an API.

On Linux systems, the **apt-get/apt** or **yum** command can be executed from within a Bash script to install an app as well as update it.

 EXAM TIP   Know the many use cases for scripting covered in this section.

```
Administrator: Windows PowerShell
PS C:\> Get-AppPackageLog -All | Out-File -FilePath C:\NewAppLog.txt
PS C:\> cat newapplog.txt

Time                    ID          Message
----                    --          -------
9/12/2022 10:51:17 PM   325         Microsoft.AAD.BrokerPlugin_cw5n1h2txyewy is registered in good state, skip re-registering it
9/12/2022 10:51:17 PM   325         Microsoft.AAD.BrokerPlugin_cw5n1h2txyewy is registered in good state, skip re-registering it
9/12/2022 10:51:17 PM   325         Microsoft.AAD.BrokerPlugin_cw5n1h2txyewy is registered in good state, skip re-registering it
9/12/2022 10:48:28 PM   325         Microsoft.AAD.BrokerPlugin_cw5n1h2txyewy is registered in good state, skip re-registering it
9/12/2022 10:48:28 PM   325         Microsoft.AAD.BrokerPlugin_cw5n1h2txyewy is registered in good state, skip re-registering it
9/12/2022 10:48:28 PM   325         Microsoft.AAD.BrokerPlugin_cw5n1h2txyewy is registered in good state, skip re-registering it
9/12/2022 10:45:06 PM   325         Microsoft.AAD.BrokerPlugin_cw5n1h2txyewy is registered in good state, skip re-registering it
9/12/2022 10:45:06 PM   325         Microsoft.AAD.BrokerPlugin_cw5n1h2txyewy is registered in good state, skip re-registering it
9/12/2022 10:45:06 PM   325         Microsoft.AAD.BrokerPlugin_cw5n1h2txyewy is registered in good state, skip re-registering it
9/12/2022 10:39:00 PM   325         Microsoft.AAD.BrokerPlugin_cw5n1h2txyewy is registered in good state, skip re-registering it
```

FIGURE 4.8-8   The top portion of the output from a PowerShell Get- command used to extract and store app data

Other Considerations When Using Scripts

While scripting provides many benefits to system administrators, they can also cause some problems for not only the administrators but the managers, employees, and perhaps even customers of an organization. In general, the types of problems that can be caused or initiated by a script are related to scripting languages being open source for the most part, requiring the installation of an interpreter, and, depending on the scope of the script, being slower than a compiled program.

Some of the most damaging problems associated with scripts are described in the following sections.

Unintentionally Introducing Malware

Installing new programs or scripts also adds the risk that new vulnerabilities are also introduced to the system. A customized script can be accessed and altered and, when used, provide a vulnerability that may allow an attacker to install malware or launch a privilege escalation attack.

Here are some of the ways unintentional malware infections can occur:

- If the scripting language interpreter is not a default feature of the OS, a downloaded interpreter can expand the attack surface. Some attackers use PowerShell to create malware that can be inserted into a script.
- A valid script can be modified by an attacker to become effectively a Trojan.

In addition to rigorous testing, new system scripts should be run with the lowest level of privileges necessary. Unintentional malware is primarily poorly written script statements that provide an attacker access to system information or user accounts.

Inadvertently Changing System Settings

Not all scripts are malicious or subject to creating threats inadvertently, but even non-malicious scripts can perform a utility or change system settings that may affect a system. A script may call a system function that was replaced by malware. For example, a script may shut down a software firewall, open port settings, and disable antimalware software.

Browser or System Crashes Due to Mishandling of Resources

A poorly constructed or ill-conceived script, on any OS, can cause inadvertent errors by possibly mishandling a system's resources. A script that contains one or more of any number of cmdlets or commands that perform an action on a system resource, such as memory, registers, or cache, can reconfigure the resource or cause a condition that conflicts with the normal actions of the CPU or perhaps the OS. In these cases, the problem isn't typically with the scripting language or its interpreter, which are generally safe. Instead, script statements or misapplied commands are mishandling resources, as in the following examples:

- Creating files that overwrite sensitive data resources, such as log files and some temp files, while they are in use.
- Creating an endless loop in the statements of a script that runs forever.
- Replacing a default API with a malicious one that affects any coding that calls it.

Scripts must be tested under the most rigorous conditions to identify that these or similar faults don't exist.

REVIEW

Objective 4.8: Identify the basics of scripting   The following are some common script file types:

- **.bat**   Batch files, used by Windows command prompt
- **.ps1**   PowerShell files, used by the Windows PowerShell command environment or by the PowerShell ISE
- **.vbs**   VBScript (Visual Basic Script) files, used by Windows Script host and Microsoft Edge
- **.sh**   Bash shell files, used by Linux (commonly created using the Linux Vim or nano command) and used by macOS in Terminal mode
- **.js**   JavaScript files, used by web apps and browsers and by JavaScript IDEs
- **.py**   Python files, used by Python interpreters

Here are some use cases for scripting:

- Basic automation
- Restarting machines
- Remapping network drives
- Installation of applications
- Automated backups
- Gathering of information/data
- Initiating updates

Here are some considerations to keep in mind when using scripts:

- Unintentionally introducing malware
- Inadvertently changing system settings
- Browser or system crashes due to the mishandling of resources

4.8 QUESTIONS

1. You are using a Windows computer and need to create a list of files stored on a Linux server. Which of the following scripting languages can you use without special setup or installation?

   A. Batch

   B. JavaScript

   C. PowerShell

   D. Shell

2. A new tech is puzzled by the # symbols at the beginning of several lines in a scripting language. Which of the following most accurately describes what they mean?

   A. Comments

   B. Changes in variable values

   C. Placeholders

   D. End of text

3. You've been given the assignment to audit the file systems on your company's Windows network servers to identify any unauthorized or suspicious script files. Your search should be looking for which of the following file extensions? (Choose two.)

   A. .vbs

   B. .ps1

   C. .sys

   D. .sh

4. What are some of the possible disadvantages of a script?

   A. The interpreter is not a default feature.

   B. Attacker could modify script code to make it act as malware.

   C. Misuse or errors in the code statements create vulnerabilities.

   D. All of the above.

5. Which of the following is *not* a possible use for a script on a computer system?

   A. Basic automation

   B. Restarting machines

   C. Remapping network drives

   D. Editing documents

   E. Installation of applications

   F. Automated backups

4.8 ANSWERS

1. **A** Batch files can be created in Notepad and run from the command prompt; no setup is needed.

2. **A** The hashtag (#) symbol is used for comments in Python, Bash, and PowerShell.

3. **A B** Windows scripts are .ps1 (PowerShell) and .vbs (Visual Basic script), as well as .exe and .bat.

4. **D** All of the choices, plus others, are possible disadvantages of using a script.

5. **D** If only this were true. All of the other choices are possible uses for a script.

 **Objective 4.9** # Given a scenario, use remote access technologies

Remote access technologies allow technicians to diagnose and fix many computer problems, including malware removal and data recovery, without going to the client site. Understanding the technologies and the potential security issues these technologies pose is important for technicians and their clients.

Methods and Tools

Remote access utilities, methodologies, and tools allow users to connect with and run a logged-in session on another computer, either locally or remotely. These tools can be desktop apps or command-line commands. However, regardless of their form, because they are able to be used with a remote system, they must be secure. In this objective, the features of different remote access tools and the security considerations of using them are discussed.

Remote Desktop Protocol

Remote Desktop Protocol (RDP) is the protocol that supports Microsoft's remote desktop software. Remote desktop software enables you to use another system's GUI as if you were sitting in front of that computer. Microsoft's *Remote Desktop Connection (RDC)* can connect to and control a Windows system with a fully graphical interface (see Figure 4.9-1).

 EXAM TIP The RDP executable is mstsc.exe, which can be executed from a command prompt or on the Home taskbar's Search box.

FIGURE 4.9-1   Windows Remote Desktop Connection dialog box with Options displayed

Similar programs enable techs to see what a client sees on their screen and use the client's system to resolve the issue. *Windows Remote Assistance,* shown in Figure 4.9-2, enables you to grant or assume control, enabling a user to request support directly from you. Upon receiving the support-request e-mail, you can log on to the user's system and, with permission, take the driver's seat.

In both these methods, the connecting system is a client and the remote system is a server providing access to its Desktop. To configure whether your Windows system can act as a Remote Assistance or Remote Desktop server, go to the System applet and select the Remote Settings link on the left. The Remote tab in System Properties has checkboxes for both Remote Assistance and Remote Desktop, along with some detailed settings.

 EXAM TIP   Windows Home editions are limited to running as an RDP client. The Windows Professional editions are able to run as both an RDP server and an RDP client.

To make RDP more secure, find out the IP address or range of addresses of the remote computer(s) connecting with your computer. Then, use Windows Defender Firewall with Advanced Security to restrict access to the RDP port to that IP address or range—a process known as *scoping.* You can also use a VPN (virtual private network) with RDP connections.

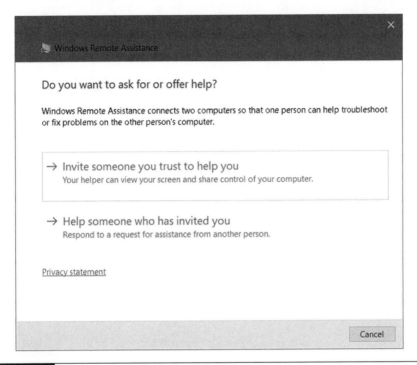

FIGURE 4.9-2   Windows Remote Assistance dialog box

ADDITIONAL RESOURCES   To learn more about protecting an RDP session, go to https://remoteaccess.itarian.com/how-do-i-protect-my-remote-desktop-connection.php and read the article "How to Protect Remote Desktop Connection?"

Virtual Private Network

RDP or SSH (covered a bit later in this objective) is used to set up a peer-to-peer connection between two devices. On the other hand, a *virtual private network (VPN)* does this same action but adds a secured tunnel for the transmissions between a host and a remote network. A *VPN tunnel* is an encrypted WAN connection that routes messages through an intermediary server to maintain their security.

A VPN provides online privacy and security on the public Internet and hides the IP address of the message source to make it virtually untraceable. You can log on to the Internet anywhere Wi-Fi is available using a VPN, such as coffee shops, libraries, hotels, and schools.

ADDITIONAL RESOURCES   Read the article "Connect to a VPN in Windows" located at https://support.microsoft.com/en-us/windows/connect-to-a-vpn-in-windows-3d29aeb1-f497-f6b7-7633-115722c1009c.

FIGURE 4.9-3   The TightVNC Service Configuration dialog box for the TightVNC desktop control

Virtual Network Computing

Virtual Network Computing (VNC) is a remote desktop-sharing protocol that can be used to remotely control another computer. VNC transmits all keyboard input and mouse movements from one client computer to another. VNC is platform-dependent, which means that each end of a VNC communication must be running the same OS. Any security applied is dependent on the OS or VNC desktop control or viewer app, such as RealVNC Viewer (https://realvnc.com) or TightVNC (https://tightvnc.com). Figure 4.9-3 shows the configuration dialog box for the TightVNC desktop control function.

Secure Shell

Secure Shell (SSH) encrypts the entire connection to prevent eavesdropping and has essentially replaced Telnet for that reason. SSH supports tunneling files or any network traffic through its secure connection, which enables SSH to secure even insecure protocols, such as FTP. On Windows 10/11 systems, two apps are available for SSH implementations: OpenSSH client and OpenSSH server.

To install the OpenSSH server using PowerShell, use the following commands:

1. At the PowerShell command prompt, enter the following command string:

   ```
   Get-WindowsCapability -Online | Where-Object Name -like 'OpenSSH*'
   ```

2. The output of this command lists any app with a name like "OpenSSH" and the state of any found. The output may be something like the following, which shows that the OpenSSH client is installed, but not the server:

   ```
   Name  : OpenSSH.Client~~~~0.0.1.0
   State : Installed
   Name  : OpenSSH.Server~~~~0.0.1.0
   State : NotPresent
   ```

3. To install the client or the server, use the following PowerShell command, inserting the client or server version in the extension after "OpenSSH."

   ```
   Add-WindowsCapability -Online -Name OpenSSH.Server~~~~0.0.1.0
   ```

4. To start an OpenSSH server on your system, run the following command:

   ```
   Start-Service sshd
   ```

5. To open an OpenSSH shell on any network-related host (or even your localhost), run the following command:

   ```
   ssh username@hostIP
   ```

   Replace *username* with your user name on the local/remote computer, and replace *hostIP* with that computer's IP address.

6. You will be prompted for your account password on the remote computer.

7. If SSH uses a different TCP port than the default (22), add **-p *portnumber*** to the ssh command, replacing *portnumber* with the actual port number. Here's an example:

   ```
   ssh rgilster@localhost -p 33255
   ```

Another way to install or verify the installation of an OpenSSH client is to access Apps on the Settings app. Then, on the Apps & Features menu, click Manage Optional Features. Then click OpenSSH Client.

 ADDITIONAL RESOURCES The www.ssh.com website provides information about using SSH on Linux or Windows.

Remote Monitoring and Management

Remote Monitoring and Management (RMM) is a process that is used to monitor and scan user workstations, network devices and servers, and remote devices. RMM services are provided for the most part by companies called *managed IT service providers,* and their products and services are officially referred to as *remote IT management* or *network management* services.

The base element of RMM services is an agent installed on each network workstation or node that provides the management system with the information it needs. Any issues encountered between the agent and the service will trigger an alert, much like a home security system triggers an alarm to the monitoring service of an issue. The monitoring and management service then launches its process for resolving the issue many times before the subscriber even knows about it.

Microsoft Remote Assistance

Microsoft Remote Assistance (MSRA) is a Windows system feature available on all Windows 10/11 versions. It gives users the ability to provide or receive help with a system problem over an RDP remote connection. The user provides an issue invitation file protected by a passcode that the technician can open for information. The technician can then activate the chat feature to discuss the issue with the user.

To request or offer help through the MSRA app, open either a Command Prompt (WIN-R) or a PowerShell command prompt and enter the command msra.exe. The dialog box shown in Figure 4.9-2 earlier will display. On the Windows Remote Assistance dialog box, choose either the "Invite someone you trust to help you" option or the "Help someone who has invited you" option.

If you choose the "Invite someone…" option, the dialog box shown in Figure 4.9-4 appears. You now have the following options:

- Save this invitation as a file
- Use e-mail to send an invitation
- Use Easy Connect (if enabled)

Typically, a user selects the e-mail option, which opens a dialog box in which they can create a passcode that the helper can use to connect with that user.

 ADDITIONAL RESOURCES   For more information on using the Easy Connect feature, read the article "Solve PC problems remotely with Remote Assistance and Easy Connect" at https://support.microsoft.com/en-us/windows/solve-pc-problems-remotely-with-remote-assistance-and-easy-connect-cf384ff4-6269-d86e-bcfe-92d72ed55922.

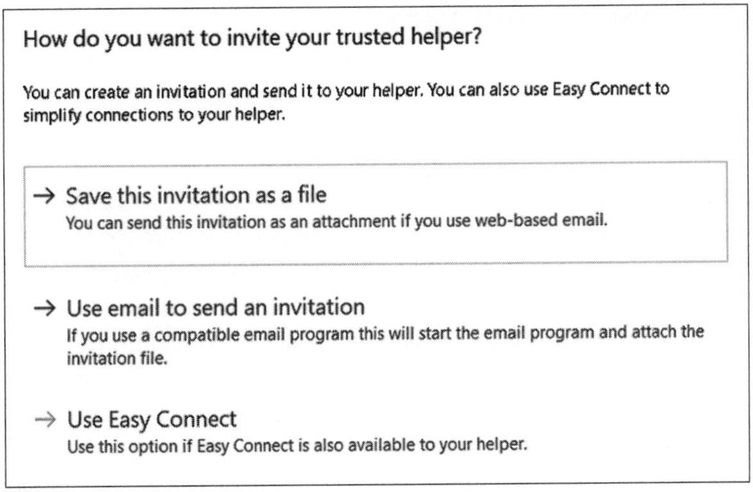

How do you want to invite your trusted helper?

You can create an invitation and send it to your helper. You can also use Easy Connect to simplify connections to your helper.

→ Save this invitation as a file
   You can send this invitation as an attachment if you use web-based email.

→ Use email to send an invitation
   If you use a compatible email program this will start the email program and attach the invitation file.

→ Use Easy Connect
   Use this option if Easy Connect is also available to your helper.

FIGURE 4.9-4   The "How do you want to invite your trusted helper?" dialog box

Third-Party Tools

Third-party remote access tools offer a number of advantages over command-line SSH clients. These tools might include one or more of the following features:

- Support for Windows, macOS, and Linux clients and remote access, using a graphical user interface (GUI) or command-line interface (CLI)
- Screen sharing
- Videoconferencing
- Transferring files and objects
- Managing local or remote desktops

Screen Share Feature

One of the advantages of many GUI-based remote clients is the ability to share screens. Depending on the app, screen sharing can run in either or both directions.

A client who needs help can share their screen with a remote help desk worker so that the worker can diagnose and solve the problem far faster than trying to describe the solution to a user who is unfamiliar with the diagnostic features of their operating system.

Another application of screen sharing is for a trainer to share screens with students so that students can learn by watching as the instructor explains the settings needed for an app, a document, or another use.

Videoconferencing Software

Audio capability and videoconferencing software are essentially just what the name implies—software that sets up an audio and video link between two or more participants, typically over the Internet, to share and collaborate on files.

File Transfer Software

There have been file transfer tools almost from the beginning of the Internet, beginning way back at the release and use of the *File Transfer Protocol (FTP)*, and its many variations, such as *HTTP, BitTorrent,* and others. File transfer protocols and utilities simply move a file or a copy of a file from one host to another, either locally or remotely. File transfers are either push or pull. A *push-based transfer* is launched by the sender, and a *pull-based transfer* is initiated by the receiver.

Desktop Management Software

In spite of the fact that it's called desktop software, *desktop management software* allows an organization to manage and secure some or all of the computing devices it owns, either locally or remotely. This allows the IT department to keep desktop computers up to date in groups or across the board.

Desktop management software is used to install or remove software; initiate backups; troubleshoot workstation or network issues; and access, share, or archive individual files, file systems, or the contents of a storage devices.

 EXAM TIP   Be sure you understand the methods and tools detailed in this section, including RDP, VPN, VNC, SSH, RMM, MSRA, and the third-party tools discussed.

Security Considerations of Each Access Method

The best remote access method is the one that provides the best balance of speed, power, ease of use, and security. Here's how the major methods stack up:

- RDP is relatively secure because it uses encryption, but its default settings make it vulnerable to unwanted connections. Changing the RDP port, using a VPN, and adjusting firewall settings make an RDP setting more secure.
- SSH is very secure, using encryption for the entire connection and supporting VPN (tunneling) connections.
- Third-party remote access apps are typically very secure because they offer advanced encryption and (some) support for one-time passwords. The latter feature generates a list of passwords, each of which can be used just once. Use the list if you need to connect remotely from public network connections to prevent shoulder surfers or keyboard loggers from gaining access to the remote computer. Check the specifications for the specific third-party app to determine its security features and how to improve them.

EXAM TIP   Understand the security considerations of each access method for the exam.

REVIEW

Objective 4.9: Given a scenario, use remote access technologies   The major types of remote access technologies include the following:

- **RDP**   Remote Desktop Protocol
- **VPN**   Virtual Private Network
- **VNC**   Virtual Network Computer
- **SSH**   Secure Shell
- **RMM**   Remote Monitoring and Management
- **MSRA/QA**   Microsoft Remote Assistance and Quick Assist

Third-party tools include the following:

- Screen sharing
- Videoconferencing
- File transfer software
- Desktop management software

4.9 QUESTIONS

1. You are preparing to run Remote Desktop Connection to perform remote troubleshooting. From the command line or Search bar, which of the following commands would you use to start it?

    A. RDC

    B. msvpn

    C. mstsc

    D. WRA

2. What is the TCP port used by the Quick Assist applet?

    A. Ephemeral 65355

    B. TCP 443

    C. UDP 80/81

    D. TCP/UDP 20/21

3. Your organization is looking for a communication service that can be used securely by remote company employees to access the company's internal network. What secure communication service should be used?

   A. MSRA

   B. VPN

   C. Videoconferencing

   D. RMM

4. What protocol is considered to be relatively secure because it uses encryption, even though its settings can make it vulnerable to unwanted connections?

   A. TCP

   B. UDP

   C. RDP

   D. FTP

5. What protocol is very secure, uses encryption to secure an entire connection, and supports VPN tunneling connections?

   A. SSL

   B. SSH

   C. TLS

   D. RMM

4.9 ANSWERS

1. **C** The command to launch Remote Desktop Connection is mstsc.

2. **B** Port 443 opens for the SSL/TLS protocols.

3. **B** VPN provides a secured link between companies and their employees.

4. **C** Access should be scoped to the address or range of the remote site or network.

5. **B** SSH is a very secure protocol for remote access uses.

About the Online Content

This book comes complete with:

- TotalTester Online practice exam software with practice exam questions for exam 220-1102, as well as a pre-assessment test to get you started
- More than an hour of sample video training episodes from Mike Meyers' CompTIA A+ Certification video series
- More than 20 sample simulations from Total Seminars' TotalSims for CompTIA A+
- Links to a collection of Mike Meyers' favorite tools and utilities for PC troubleshooting

System Requirements

The current and previous major versions of the following desktop browsers are recommended and supported: Chrome, Microsoft Edge, Firefox, and Safari. These browsers update frequently, and sometimes an update may cause compatibility issues with the TotalTester Online or other content hosted on the Training Hub. If you run into a problem using one of these browsers, please try using another until the problem is resolved.

Your Total Seminars Training Hub Account

To get access to the online content you will need to create an account on the Total Seminars Training Hub. Registration is free, and you will be able to track all your online content using your account. You may also opt in if you wish to receive marketing information from McGraw Hill or Total Seminars, but this is not required for you to gain access to the online content.

Privacy Notice

McGraw Hill values your privacy. Please be sure to read the Privacy Notice available during registration to see how the information you have provided will be used. You may view our Corporate Customer Privacy Policy by visiting the McGraw Hill Privacy Center. Visit the **mheducation.com** site and click **Privacy** at the bottom of the page.

Single User License Terms and Conditions

Online access to the digital content included with this book is governed by the McGraw Hill License Agreement outlined next. By using this digital content you agree to the terms of that license.

Access   To register and activate your Total Seminars Training Hub account, simply follow these easy steps.

1. Go to this URL: **hub.totalsem.com/mheclaim**
2. To register and create a new Training Hub account, enter your e-mail address, name, and password on the **Register** tab. No further personal information (such as credit card number) is required to create an account.

   If you already have a Total Seminars Training Hub account, enter your e-mail address and password on the **Log in** tab.
3. Enter your Product Key: `5z9p-kwbs-njxk`
4. Click to accept the user license terms.
5. For new users, click the **Register and Claim** button to create your account. For existing users, click the **Log in and Claim** button.

   You will be taken to the Training Hub and have access to the content for this book.

Duration of License   Access to your online content through the Total Seminars Training Hub will expire one year from the date the publisher declares the book out of print.

Your purchase of this McGraw Hill product, including its access code, through a retail store is subject to the refund policy of that store.

The Content is a copyrighted work of McGraw Hill, and McGraw Hill reserves all rights in and to the Content. The Work is © 2023 by McGraw Hill.

Restrictions on Transfer   The user is receiving only a limited right to use the Content for the user's own internal and personal use, dependent on purchase and continued ownership of this book. The user may not reproduce, forward, modify, create derivative works based upon, transmit, distribute, disseminate, sell, publish, or sublicense the Content or in any way commingle the Content with other third-party content without McGraw Hill's consent.

Limited Warranty   The McGraw Hill Content is provided on an "as is" basis. Neither McGraw Hill nor its licensors make any guarantees or warranties of any kind, either express or implied, including, but not limited to, implied warranties of merchantability or fitness for a particular purpose or use as to any McGraw Hill Content or the information therein or any warranties as to the accuracy, completeness, correctness, or results to be obtained from, accessing or using the McGraw Hill Content, or any material referenced in such Content or any information entered into licensee's product by users or other persons and/or any material available on or that can be accessed through the licensee's product (including via any hyperlink or otherwise) or as to non-infringement of third-party rights. Any warranties of any kind, whether express or implied, are disclaimed. Any material or data obtained through use of the McGraw Hill Content is at your own discretion and risk and user understands that it will be solely responsible for any resulting damage to its computer system or loss of data.

Neither McGraw Hill nor its licensors shall be liable to any subscriber or to any user or anyone else for any inaccuracy, delay, interruption in service, error or omission, regardless of cause, or for any damage resulting therefrom.

In no event will McGraw Hill or its licensors be liable for any indirect, special or consequential damages, including but not limited to, lost time, lost money, lost profits or good will, whether in contract, tort, strict liability or otherwise, and whether or not such damages are foreseen or unforeseen with respect to any use of the McGraw Hill Content.

TotalTester Online

TotalTester Online provides you with a simulation of the CompTIA A+ Core 2 exam, 220-1102. The exam can be taken in Practice Mode or Exam Mode. Practice Mode provides an assistance window with hints, explanations of the correct and incorrect answers, and the option to check your answer as you take the test. Exam Mode provides a simulation of the actual exam. The number of questions, the types of questions, and the time allowed are intended to be an accurate representation of the exam environment. The option to customize your quiz allows you to create custom exams from selected domains, and you can further customize the number of questions and time allowed.

To take a test, follow the instructions provided in the previous section to register and activate your Total Seminars Training Hub account. When you register, you will be taken to the Total Seminars Training Hub. From the Training Hub Home page, select your certification from the list of "Your Topics" on the Home page, and then click the TotalTester link to launch the TotalTester. Once you've launched your TotalTester, you can select the option to customize your quiz and begin testing yourself in Practice Mode or Exam Mode. All exams provide an overall grade and a grade broken down by domain.

Pre-Assessment

In addition to the sample exam questions, the TotalTester also includes a CompTIA A+ pre-assessment test to help you assess your understanding of the topics before reading the book. To launch the pre-assessment test, click **Pre-Assessment Test** for the Core 2 exam. The A+ Pre-Assessment test is 50 questions and runs in Exam Mode. When you complete the test, you can review the questions with answers and detailed explanations by clicking **See Detailed Results**.

Mike's CompTIA A+ Video Training Sample

Over an hour of training videos, starring Mike Meyers, are available for free. Select **CompTIA A+ Core 2 Passport (220-1102) Resources** from the list of "Your Topics" on the Home page. Click the TotalVideos tab. Along with access to the videos, you'll find an option to purchase Mike's complete video training series from the Total Seminars website, www .totalsem.com.

TotalSims Sample for CompTIA A+

 From your Total Seminars Training Hub account, select **CompTIA A+ Core 2 Passport (220-1102) Resources** from the list of "Your Topics" on the Home page. Click the TotalSims tab. There are over 20 free simulations available for reviewing topics covered in the book. You can purchase access to the full TotalSims for A+ with over 200 simulations from the Total Seminars website, www.totalsem.com.

Mike's Cool Tools

Mike loves freeware/open source PC troubleshooting and networking tools! Access the utilities mentioned in the text by selecting **CompTIA A+ Core 2 Passport (220-1102) Resources** from the list of "Your Topics" on the Home page. Click the Book Resources tab, and then select **Mike's Cool Tools**.

Technical Support

For questions regarding the TotalTester or operation of the Training Hub, visit **www.totalsem .com** or e-mail **support@totalsem.com**.

For questions regarding book content, visit **www.mheducation.com/customerservice**.

Index

totaltester
Certification Exam Prep

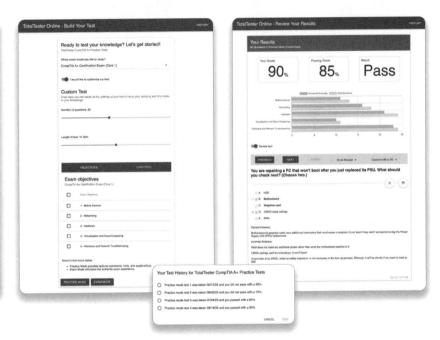